AF771360

Hybridization of Food Governance

Hybridization of Food Governance

Trends, Types and Results

Edited by

Paul Verbruggen

Assistant Professor of Global and Comparative Private Law, Tilburg Institute for Private Law, Tilburg University, the Netherlands

Tetty Havinga

Associate Professor in Sociology of Law, Faculty of Law, Radboud University, the Netherlands

Edward Elgar
PUBLISHING

Cheltenham, UK • Northampton, MA, USA

© The Editors and Contributors Severally 2017

All rights reserved. No part of this publication may be reproduced, stored in a retrieval system or transmitted in any form or by any means, electronic, mechanical or photocopying, recording, or otherwise without the prior permission of the publisher.

Published by
Edward Elgar Publishing Limited
The Lypiatts
15 Lansdown Road
Cheltenham
Glos GL50 2JA
UK

Edward Elgar Publishing, Inc.
William Pratt House
9 Dewey Court
Northampton
Massachusetts 01060
USA

A catalogue record for this book
is available from the British Library

Library of Congress Control Number: 2016957250

This book is available electronically in the **Elgar**online
Law subject collection
DOI 10.4337/9781785361708

MIX
Paper from
responsible sources
FSC
www.fsc.org
FSC® C013604

ISBN 978 1 78536 169 2 (cased)
ISBN 978 1 78536 170 8 (eBook)

Typeset by Servis Filmsetting Ltd, Stockport, Cheshire
Printed and bound by CPI Group (UK) Ltd, Croydon, CR0 4YY

Contents

Figures

Tables

Contributors

Tiffany Andrade Roche is Standards and Assurance Officer for Cocoa and Hazelnut at UTZ. Previously she was advisor to the Market Transformation Initiative of the WWF. She has studied production engineering at the Universidad Simón Bolívar, strategic environmental management at the Università degli Studi di Padova and environment and resource management at the VU University Amsterdam.

Donal Casey is a lecturer at Kent Law School where he teaches European Union law and consumer law. Empirically, his research addresses the policy areas of food safety and gambling. Analytically, Donal's research examines transnational regulation, legitimacy and the role that law, standards and other norms play in shaping regulatory regimes.

Elena Fagotto is Director of Research at Harvard Kennedy School's Transparency Policy Project. Her research focuses on food safety, transparency and transnational governance. She has published on these topics in peer-reviewed journals and has authored several book chapters. She holds an MPA from Harvard Kennedy School and a PhD from Erasmus University Rotterdam.

Michael Faure is Professor of Comparative and International Environmental Law at Maastricht University and Professor of Comparative Private Law and Economics at Erasmus School of Law (Rotterdam), both in the Netherlands.

Andrew Fearne is Professor of Value Chain Management at Norwich Business School, University of East Anglia. His research is focussed on the coordination of value chains, from field to fork. He is the founding editor of the International Journal of Supply Chain Management, author of over 100 articles, the 14th Adelaide Thinker in Residence and son of a Kentish pig farmer.

Marian Garcia Martinez is Professor in Marketing and Innovation at Kent Business School, University of Kent. Her primary research interests relate to New Product Development and Innovation Management, in particular how SMEs use consumer insights to enhance innovation outputs.

Tetty Havinga is Associate Professor in Sociology of Law at the Radboud University, Nijmegen, the Netherlands. She has published on the private regulation of food safety and official controls on the food industry, policy implementation and law enforcement, specialized business courts, equal opportunities law, and migration.

Mohamud Hussein is an independent research economist based in the United Kingdom. Mohamud has previously worked for the Food and Environment Research Agency (Fera) where he conducted extensive research related to the impact of food safety and quality regulation on industry and consumer behaviour.

Agni Kalfagianni is Assistant Professor at the Copernicus Institute for Sustainable Development, Utrecht University. She specializes in the development of rules and standards for sustainability by non-state actors, such as businesses and civil society organizations, and examines the effectiveness, legitimacy, and ethical considerations of private and transnational forms of governance.

Kévine Kindji, PhD is Postdoc researcher at the Maastricht European Institute of Transnational Legal Research (METRO) (the Netherlands).

Klementina Kirezieva worked as a researcher and pursued a doctoral degree in Food Quality Management at Wageningen University, the Netherlands. Her PhD thesis and relevant publications concern the socio-economic factors affecting food safety management on a company and policy level. At present Klementina is working as a Food Safety, Quality and Regulatory manager at Cargill Animal Nutrition.

Kai Kottenstede is a communication consultant and a PhD candidate at the Institute of Political Science, University of Tübingen.

Pieternel Luning is Associate Professor at Wageningen University. Current research projects (on average 8 PhDs) are about quality management systems, risk-based auditing, food safety culture, and food handler behaviour in production (company) and consumption systems (domestic level). The common research focus is on understanding the relation between the socio-technical systems, context characteristics, and food quality.

Timothy D. Lytton is Distinguished University Professor and Professor of Law at Georgia State University. His work on food regulation includes *Kosher: Private Regulation in the Age of Industrial Food* (Harvard University Press 2013), and he is currently writing a book on the US food safety system.

Lesley K. McAllister is Professor of Law at the University of California at Davis. She is a member scholar of the Center for Progressive Reform, and she has served as a consultant to the Administrative Conference of the United States.

Fritz Sager, PhD, is a Professor of Political Science at the KPM Center for Public Management at the University of Bern. He specializes in administrative studies and theory, policy research and evaluation, organizational analysis, and Swiss politics.

Eva Thomann is a post-doctoral researcher at Heidelberg University. She specializes in public policy and public administration, with a focus on multi-level and frontline policy implementation. She studied Political Science at the University of Zurich and completed her PhD in Public Administration at the University of Bern.

Bernd M.J. van der Meulen is Professor of Food Law at Wageningen University; President and co-founder of the Dutch Food Law Association (Nederlandse Vereniging voor Levensmiddelenrecht www.NVLR.nl), member of the editorial board of the European Food and Feed Law Review (www.lexxion.eu/effl) and board member of the Global Harmonization Initiative (www.globalharmonization.net). For his books on food law see: http://www.wageningenacademic.com/eifl.

Paul Verbruggen is Assistant Professor of Global and Comparative Private Law at Tilburg Law School, Tilburg University, the Netherlands. He writes on the design and operation of regulatory regimes (both public and private), focusing on questions of legitimacy, accountability and enforcement. His research interests concern European private law, regulatory policy and risk regulation. He is the author of the monograph *Enforcing Transnational Private Regulation: A Comparative Analysis of Advertising and Food Safety* (Edward Elgar 2014).

Abbreviations

AB	Accreditation Body
ACSC	Auditor Competence Scheme Committee (GFSI)
ADF&G	Alaska Department of Fish and Game
AESAN	Spanish Agency of Food Security and Nutrition
AFDF	Alaska Fisheries Development Foundation
ANSI	American National Standards Institute
APA	At-Sea Processors Association (Alaska)
AQSIQ	Administration of Quality Supervision, Inspection and Quarantine (China)
ASC	Aquaculture Stewardship Council
ASMI	Alaskan Seafood Market Institute
ASOEXPEBLA	Whitefish Exporters Association (Ecuador)
BRC	British Retail Consortium
BSE	Bovine Spongiform Encephalopathy or mad cow disease
CB	Certification Body
CCAI	China Certification & Accreditation Institute
CCFA	China Chain Story & Franchise Association
CDC	Centers for Disease Control and Prevention (China, US)
CFDA	China Food and Drug Administration
CFIA	Canadian Food Inspection Agency
CFSA	China National Center for Food Safety Risk Assessment (former CDC)
CFSI	China Food Safety Initiative
CH	Switzerland
CIFSQC	China International Food Safety and Quality Conference
CIQ	China Inspection and Quarantine
CJD	Creutzfeldt–Jakob disease
CJEU	Court of Justice of the European Union
CNAS	China National Accreditation Service for Conformity Assessment

CNCA	Certification and Accreditation Administration of the People's Republic of China
Codex	Codex Alimentarius Commission
COFRAC	Comité français d'accréditation
COLEACP	Liaison Committee Europe-Africa-Caribbean-Pacific
CREQ	Regional Committee for Quality (UEMOA)
CTF	Consultative Taskforce on Environmental Requirements and Market Access for Developing Countries (UNCTAD)
DFO	Department of Fisheries and Oceans (Canadian federal)
DG SANTE	Directorate General for Health and Food Safety (EU)
EA	European Co-operation for Accreditation
EC	European Community
EFSA	European Food Safety Authority
EPESPO	Eastern Pacific Fisheries School
EU	European Union
EUREP	Euro-Retailer Produce Working Group
FAO	Food and Agricultural Organization of the United Nations
FASFC	Federal Agency for the Safety of the Food Chain (Belgium)
FDA	Food and Drug Administration (US)
FDCA	Food, Drug, and Cosmetics Act (US)
FENACOPEC	National Federation of Fisheries Cooperatives of Ecuador
FIP	Fishery Improvement Project (Ecuador)
FLO	Fairtrade International
FPEAK	Fresh Produce Exporters Association of Kenya
FSA	Food Standards Agency (UK)
FSC	Forest Stewardship Council
FSL	Food Safety Law
FSMA	Food Safety Modernization Act (US)
FSMS	Food safety management system
FSSC 22000	Food Safety System Certification 22000
FTVP	Fachtechnisch verantwortliche Person (responsible veterinarian, Switzerland)
GAO	Government Accountability Office (US)
GAP	Good Agricultural Practices
GBP	British Pound
GFL	General Food Law (EU)
GFSA	Global Food Safety Auditor (Foundation)

GFSI	Global Food Safety Initiative
GlobalGAP	Global Partnership for Good Agricultural Practices
GLP	Good Laboratory Practices
HACCP	Hazard Analysis Critical Control Points
HAS	Hygiene Assessment Scheme (UK)
IAF	International Accreditation Forum
IATTC	Inter-American-Tropical-Tuna-Commission
IEC	International Electrotechnical Commission
IFS	International Featured Standards
IGO	International governmental organization
ISBN	International Standard Book Number
ISEAL	The ISEAL Alliance (International Social and Environmental Accreditation and Labelling Alliance)
ISO	International Standaridization Organization
ISSN	International Standard Serial Number
ISVET	Informationssystem für den öffentlichen Veterinärdienst (Switzerland)
KRAV	Kontrollföreningen för alternativ odling (Swedish Association for Control of Organic Production)
MHS	Meat Hygiene Service (UK)
MoU	Memoranda of Understanding
MSC	Marine Stewardship Council
NGO	Non-governmental organization
NHFPC	National Health and Family Planning Commission (China)
NOAA	National Oceanic and Atmospheric Administration (US)
NORMCERQ	Regional Secretariat of Standardisation, Certification and Quality Promotion (UEMOA)
NPOA	National Plan of Action (Ecuador)
NSB	National standardisation body
NVWA	Netherlands Food and Consumer Product Safety Authority
OECD	Organisation for Economic Co-operation and Development
OFM	On-Farm Manufacture (of veterinary medicine, Switzerland)
OIE	Office International des Epizooties (World Organisation for Animal Health)
OIML	International Organization of Legal Metrology

OVMP	Ordinance on Veterinary Medicinal Products (Switzerland)
PCP	Preventive Control Plan (Canada)
PIA	Plant Inspection Assistant (UK)
PSRSA	Regional Special Program for Food Security (UEMOA)
PwC	PricewaterhouseCoopers
RFM	Responsible Fisheries Management
RFMO	Regional Fisheries Management Organization
RSPO	Roundtable on Sustainable Palm Oil
SMEs	Small and Medium-sized Enterprises
SOAC	West African System of Accreditation
SOAMET	West African System of Metrology
SPS	Sanitary and Phytosanitary Measures
SQF	Safe Quality Food
SRP	Secretary of Fishery Resources (Ecuador)
TBT	Technical Barriers to Trade
TPS	Transnational private standard
TUNAC	Tunisian Accreditation Council
TWG	Technical working groups
UEMOA	Union économique et monétaire ouest-africaine (West African Economic and Monetary Union)
UK	United Kingdom
UN	United Nations
UNCTAD	United Nations Conference on Trade and Development
UNIDO	United Nations Industrial Development Organization
US	United States
USDA	US Department of Agriculture
VMAP	Vice Ministry of Aquaculture and Fisheries (Ecuador)
WHO	World Health Organization of the United Nations
WTO	World Trade Organization
WWF	World Wide Fund for Nature

1 Hybridization of food governance: An analytical framework

Paul Verbruggen and Tetty Havinga

1. INTRODUCTION

The governance of food has changed dramatically since the 1990s. The outbreak of recurrent major food safety crises (including BSE), the globalization of food supply chains, the growing concentration of economic power among food retailers, a general perception of failing public regulation, and new concerns among consumers about animal welfare, dietary habits, the environment and fair trade have been identified in the literature as important drivers of changes in the institutions and practices of food governance.[1] These changes have occurred across two dimensions: (i) *national* systems of food governance have been increasingly subject to *international* influences; and (ii) *public* food governance has been challenged, complemented or at times superseded by *private* governance systems.

As regards the first dimension, it should be noted that national food safety laws and enforcement mechanisms have been amended in the light of demands set by international government organizations or global trade. In the context of the European Union, for example, the Member States have been required to revise national legislation and establish new regulatory agencies or reform existing ones to oversee food businesses after the adoption of new EU legislation on food safety.[2] In addition, the European

---

[1] Tetty Havinga, Donal Casey and Frans Van Waarden, 'Changing Regulatory Arrangements in Food Governance' in Tetty Havinga, Frans Van Waarden, Donal Casey (eds), *The Changing Landscape of Food Governance* (Edward Elgar 2015); Paul Verbruggen and Tetty Havinga, 'Patterns of Interplay between Public and Private Food Regulators: An Introduction' (2015) 6 *European Journal of Risk Regulation* – special issue on Patterns of Interplay between Public and Private Regulation in Food Governance 482.

[2] Ellen Vos and Frank Wendler (eds), *Food Safety Regulation in Europe. A Comparative Institutional Analysis* (Intersentia 2006); Gabriele Abels and Alexander

Union established the European Food Safety Authority and the Food and Veterinary Office,[3] in part to improve government responses to food crises and enhance coordination between national food safety authorities to better control risks in transnational food chains.[4] At the global level, standards, codes of practice and guidelines set by the Codex Alimentarius Commission (Codex) play an important role in shaping national laws and government policies on food safety.[5] National systems of food governance may also be exposed to pressures from importing countries to amend and ratchet up local standards. A prominent example here is China, which after experiencing strict food safety demands from importing countries, has sought to improve its national laws and enforcement mechanisms in order to gain access to international markets.[6]

The second dimension of the transition in food governance concerns the increased importance of standards, procedures and networks developed and governed by private, non-state actors to enhance and coordinate matters of food safety and sustainability. Retailers have been at the forefront of this development and have devised elaborate food standards and accompanying certification schemes with the purpose of controlling and managing food safety risks along their transnational supply chains.[7] The uptake of these standards in the market has been significant[8] and

---

Kobusch, 'Regulation of Food Safety in the EU: Explaining Organizational Diversity among Member States' in Havinga, Van Waarden, Casey (n 1) 39.

[3] In 2016 this office was renamed the Health and Food Audits and Analysis Directorate of the European Commission's Directorate General Health and Food Safety (DG SANTE).

[4] Alberto Alemanno, 'Food Safety and the Single European Market' in Christopher Ansell and David Vogel (eds), *What's the Beef? The Contested Governance of European Food Safety* (MIT Press 2006), 237.

[5] Jessica Vapnek and Melvin Spreij, 'Perspectives and Guidelines on Food Legislation, with a New Model of Food Law' (FAO Legislative Study no. 87) 2005, accessed 24 November 2016 at http://www.fao.org/3/a-a0274e.pdf, 38 and Caoimhín MacMaoláin, *Food Law. European, Domestic and International Frameworks* (Hart Publishing 2015), 45.

[6] Fred Gale and Jean C. Buzby, *Imports from China and Food Safety Issues* (United States Department of Agriculture Report), accessed 24 November 2016 at https://papers.ssrn.com/sol3/papers.cfm?abstract_id=1739127 and Kai Kottenstede, Chapter 10 in this volume. See for experiences of African countries the contribution of Kévine Kindji and Michael Faure, Chapter 12 in this volume.

[7] Tetty Havinga, 'Retail Driven Food Safety Regulation' in Abdelhakim Hammoudi, Christina Grazia, Yves Surry and Jean-Baptiste Traversac (eds), *Food Safety, Market Organization, Trade and Development* (Springer 2015) 59, 72.

[8] As early as 2006, a survey of the world's leading supermarkets found that an estimated 75–99% of food supplies sold by supermarket chains were certified against their private food safety standards. See Linda Fulponi, 'Private Voluntary

the standards are reported to have an impact on market access, production processes and public standard setting activities.[9] Civil society actors (NGOs, consumers, religious organizations and other public interest groups) have also developed private standards and certification schemes that have come to play an important role in specific domains of food governance, such as fair trade, sustainability and religious qualifications.[10] On other occasions, business and civil society have teamed up to devise joint ventures (such as the Marine Stewardship Council) or meta-regulatory organizations (such as the Global Food Safety Initiative – GFSI and the ISEAL Alliance) to improve and coordinate their methods of setting standards and certification of food businesses.[11]

Both transitions challenge – yet do not dismiss – the capacity of nation states to devise effective systems of food governance. Today's food governance is no longer an attribute of national governments alone, but is increasingly hybrid, that is, the result of coordinated public and private regulatory activities that frequently transcend national state boundaries.[12] It is this *hybridization* of food governance, its trends, types and results that this book discusses. In analysing this practice and its consequences, as we explain in further detail below, the contributions in this book adopt an actor-centred perspective as the key to understanding that contemporary food governance lies in the *interplay* between different public and private

---

Standards in the Food System: The Perspective of Major Food Retailers in OECD Countries' (2006) 31 *Food Policy* 1.

[9] Spencer Henson and John Humphrey, *The Impacts of Private Food Safety Standards on the Food Chain and on Public Standard-Setting Processes*, Paper Prepared for FAO/WHO May 2009, accessed 24 November 2016 at http://www.fao.org/docrep/012/i1132e/i1132e00.pdf.

[10] Frans Van Waarden and Robin Van Dalen, 'Halal and the Moral Construction of Quality: How Religious Norms Turn a Mass Product into a Singularity' in Jens Beckert and Christine Musselin (eds), *Constructing Quality: The Classification of Goods in Markets* (Oxford University Press 2013) 197; Timothy D Lytton, *Kosher: Private Regulation in the Age of Industrial Food* (Harvard University Press 2013).

[11] Allison Loconto and Eve Foullieux, 'Politics of Private Regulation: ISEAL and the Shaping of Transnational Sustainability Governance' (2013) 8 *Regulation & Governance* 166; Paul Verbruggen and Tetty Havinga, 'The Rise of Transnational Private Meta-Regulators' (2016) 21 *Tilburg Law Review* 116.

[12] Along the same lines Marsden et al. have suggested that food governance in Europe and beyond has moved towards a 'hybrid model' that reflects a new balance between public and private actors in the regulation and governance of food. Terry Marsden, Robert Lee, Andrew Flynn and Samarthia Thankappan, *The New Regulation and Governance of Food. Beyond the Food Crisis?* (Routledge 2010). See for a US perspective: Alexia Brunet Marks, 'A New Governance Recipe for Food Safety Regulation' (2016) 47 *Loyola University Chicago Law Journal* 907.

actors, including their relative interests and capacities, and their activities at different levels of governance.

2. CONCEPTUALIZING HYBRIDIZATION

What is meant by 'hybridization'? Scholars have observed a trend towards hybridization in regulation and governance. Levi-Faur developed the notion of regulatory capitalism to map and explain the mushrooming of regulation in the last decades in response to the rhetoric of many governments that we are supposed to live in an 'era of deregulation'.[13] More specifically, regulatory capitalism denotes the changes and growth in instruments, scope, sectors and depth of regulation and is suggestive of a concept of regulation that is increasingly hybrid in nature.[14] This hybridization not only covers the 'who' (public v. private actors) of today's regulation, but also the 'how' (command-and-control v. responsive regulation, coercive v. voluntary), the 'where' (global, local or intermediate level), and the 'what' (business v. social regulation). Levi-Faur therefore submits that: 'the study of regulatory governance should proceed beyond states, markets and societies into the identification of hybrid forms of regulation and towards the creation of autonomous regulatory spaces that blur the distinctions between the global and the national'.[15] Elsewhere he writes:

> [T]he major question [. . .] is to determine not which pure mode of governance is more effective or more legitimate but which hybrids are. We need to conceptualize a world order where governance is increasingly a hybrid of different systems of regulatory control (. . .)[16]

The new landscape of food governance offers a playground, as it were, to start exploring these issues.

In the existing literature on (regulatory) governance, the concept of

---

[13] David Levi-Faur 'The Global Diffusion of Regulatory Capitalism' (2005) 598 *The Annals of the American Academy of Political and Social Sciences* 12.

[14] John Braithwaite, *Regulatory Capitalism: How it Works, Ideas for Making it Work Better* (Edward Elgar 2008) and David Levi-Faur, 'Regulation and Regulatory Governance', (2010) *Jerusalem Papers in Regulation & Governance Working* (No 1), accessed 24 November 2016 at http://regulation.huji.ac.il/papers/jp1.pdf, 9–10.

[15] Levi-Faur (n 14), 3.

[16] David Levi-Faur, 'From "Big Government" to "Big Governance"' in David Levi-Faur (ed), *Oxford Handbook on Governance* (Oxford University Press 2012) 3, 14.

'hybridization' or 'hybrid forms of governance' is not clearly demarcated. At least two different components are involved in a hybrid, and together they form a mixture, crossover or intermediate form of governance. Authors differ as regards the components they refer to. For some a hybrid form of governance involves both public (state) and private (non-state) actors.[17] Others include different combinations of actors in the concept of hybridization. Levi-Faur, for example, distinguishes four hybrid forms of regulation, three involving a combination of different regulators and regulatees, the fourth being multilevel regulation.[18] Thus, for Levi-Faur, a hybrid form can consist of only state or only non-state actors as long as they perform different roles or operate on a different level.

Yet others link hybridity to the combination of different regulatory approaches or instruments. For Bartle, for example, a 'hybrid approach' is a combination of command-and-control, market-based, and voluntary approaches involving 'a variety of actors and institutions pursuing different strategies and interacting in complex ways'.[19] Here, hybridity is primarily the combination of various approaches or mechanisms employed by different actors. Halpern introduces yet another perspective, namely that of multi-stakeholder governance. For him, hybridity in regulatory governance not only emerges from regulation that combines public and private components or oversight arrangements with multiple levels (joining centralized and regional or local features), but also from regulatory processes that engage the full range of participants concerned with regulatory regimes, including professionals, divisions of government, public interest advocates, and representatives of groups being regulated.[20]

---

[17] Julia Black 'Decentring Regulation: Understanding the Role of Regulation and Self Regulation in a "Post-regulatory" World' (2001) 54 *Current Legal Problems* 103; Jeroen Van der Heijden, 'Friends, Enemies or Strangers? On Relationships between Public and Private Sector Service Providers in Hybrid Forms of Governance' (2011) 33 *Law & Policy* 367 and Peer Zumbansen, 'Neither "Public" nor "Private", "National" nor "International": Transnational Corporate Governance from a Legal Pluralist Perspective' (2011) 38 *Journal of Law and Society* 50.

[18] David Levi-Faur, 'Regulation and Regulatory Governance' in David Levi-Faur (ed.) *Handbook on the Politics of Regulation* (Edward Elgar 2011) 3, 10–11.

[19] Ian Bartle 'Regulatory Approaches to Climate Change Mitigation' in Levi-Faur (n 18) 635.

[20] Sydney Halpern, 'Hybrid Design, Systemic Rigidity: Institutional Dynamics in Human Subjects Oversight' (2008) 2 *Regulation & Governance* 85, 85.

3. AN ACTOR-CENTRED PERSPECTIVE

Common to these conceptualizations of hybridization in regulation and governance is the involvement of different types of actors in governance arrangements. In discussing the hybridization of contemporary food governance, the contributions in this book focus on arrangements that combine public and private (both business and civil society) actors, and analyse and discuss the interplay between these actors in such arrangements.

Examining the ongoing hybridization of food governance from this actor-centred perspective is particularly interesting for a number of reasons. First of all, food governance arrangements involving both public and private actors are relatively new and have not often been studied.[21] Most food safety rules are developed either by the state or industry, whereas initiatives concerning interests such as fair trade, environment or animal welfare stem largely from civil society. Hybrid arrangements have emerged to overcome problems associated with state, industry or NGO-driven governance, but research on the attributes and added value of hybrids is still scarce.

Furthermore, the mixing and matching of public and private initiatives in hybrid governance arrangements is certain to give rise to specific challenges. Government and business organizations operate through different rationalities (public interest v. market gains). These opposing logics are likely to lead to conflict at the level of the protection offered, the way in which monitoring should be organized or the sanctions that should follow, should the regulated food business fail to comply. This raises the question of how such conflicts might be managed and resolved. At a more fundamental level, the question arises of how responsibilities and risks are allocated between the different actors constituting the hybrid arrangement. Who gets to decide, and how are the interests of those concerned represented in decision-making? To what extent do these practices meet conventions of (democratic) legitimacy and accountability? These questions are explored in the contributions in the first part of this volume.

To be sure, an actor-centred perspective regarding the theme of hybridization of food governance does not discard the important questions concerning governance strategies and the appropriate level of today's food

---

[21] A notable exception is the self-regulatory mechanism developed by the Dutch dairy industry in the late 1800s to reduce adulteration of and fraud with dairy products, which received government support as of 1904. See Frans van Waarden, 'Varieties of Collective Self-Regulation of Business: the Example of the Dutch Dairy Industry' in Wolfgang Streeck and Philip Schmitter (eds), *Private Interest Government. Beyond Market and State* (Sage 1985).

governance. The question of 'who' governs is intimately connected with the question of 'how' one governs, that is, by which strategies the actors concerned seek to influence food production (command-and-control v. responsive regulation, coercive v. voluntary) and at which level of governance the actors choose to operate (global, local or intermediate levels).

4. ORGANIZING HYBRIDIZATION OF FOOD GOVERNANCE

Abbott and Snidal organize the variety of actors involved in transnational regulatory standard setting in their influential 'Governance Triangle'. Their illustration is based on the direct involvement of three groups of actors in standard setting processes, namely states, firms and NGOs. The separate zones in the triangle suggest three forms of single-actor standards (zones 1–3), three forms of dual-actor standards (zones 4–6), and one form of standard involving direct participation of all three groups of actors (zone 7). As noted, most food safety standards can be situated in zone 1 (state regulation) and zone 2 (industry self-regulation), whereas food standards regarding fair trade, environment or animal welfare largely appear in zone 3 (civil society). Figure 1.1 depicts the Governance Triangle for standard setting in the domain of (transnational) food governance and locates in its different zones examples discussed in the contributions to this volume (see Table 1.1).

Organizing food standard setting along the lines of Abbott and Snidal's Governance Triangle appears to suggest that hybridization in this field emerges mostly in zones 4 and 6. An example of food standards that are set in collaboration between states and firms concerns guides to good hygienic practice. These guides offer food businesses in Europe practical guidance on how to comply with the obligation under EU hygiene law to have in place an HACCP-based risk management system (see in detail Bernd van der Meulen, Chapter 6 in this volume). While these guides are drafted by the food industry representatives or specific food sectors, competent authorities of the EU Member States must approve these codes and forward them to the European Commission to register them in a database. Similarly, pan-EU codes might be developed by European industry associations, which then require the approval of the European Commission.

An example of hybrid standard setting that can be situated in zone 5 is ISEAL. This non-profit, membership organization develops codes of good practice for standard-setting organizations. The codes developed by ISEAL offer best practice guidelines for standard setting, compliance verification, and impact assessment. To develop these codes, ISEAL draws on (inter alia) experience by its member organizations, which include standard

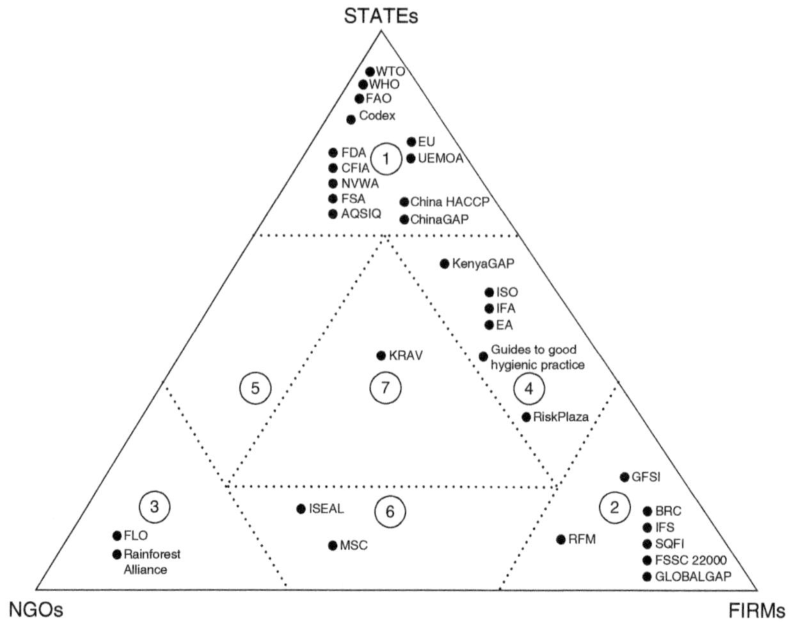

Source: Adapted from: Kenneth W. Abbott and Duncan Snidal 'The Governance Triangle: Regulatory Standards Institutions in the Shadow of the State' in Walter Mattli and Ngaire Woods (eds), *The Politics of Global Regulation* (Princeton University Press 2009) 50.

Figure 1.1 The Governance Triangle of food standard setters

setters from both civil society (for example, Fairtrade International and Rainforest Alliance) and industry (for example, UTZ). ISEAL Members may themselves also constitute hybrid standard setters. For example, the Marine Stewardship Council (MSC), which was established jointly by the World Wide Fund for Nature (WWF) and Unilever, adopts private standards for sustainable wild-captured fish. Another example is the Roundtable on Sustainable Palm Oil (RSPO), which includes members drawn from both industry and civil society to set standards for the sustainable production of palm oil products (including food).

Finally, the governance of organic food in Sweden through the KRAV label can be presented as an example of hybridization of standard setting in zone 7. The label seeks to ensure compliance with the government (European Union) requirements for organically produced food and is as such officially recognized by the Swedish government.[22] KRAV, which

[22] Magnus Boström and Mikael Klintman, 'State-Centered versus Nonstate-

Table 1.1 Standard setters in (hybrid) food governance

Zone	Organization/standard	Discussed in
Zone 1	WTO – World Trade Organization	Chapters 2, 9
	WHO – World Health Organization	Chapter 9
	FAO – Food and Agriculture Organization	Chapters 9, 11
	Codex – Codex Alimentarius Commission	Chapters 1, 9
	EU – European Union	Chapters 6, 7, 8
	UEMOA – *Union économique et monétaire ouest-africaine*	Chapter 12
	FDA – US Food and Drug Administration	Chapters 4, 9
	CFIA – Canadian Food Inspection Agency	Chapter 9
	NVWA – Nederlandse Voedsel- en Warenautoriteit	Chapter 9
	FSA – UK Food Standards Agency	Chapter 7
	AQSIQ – Chinese Administration of Quality Supervision, Inspection and Quarantine	Chapter 10
	China HACCP	Chapters 9, 10
	ChinaGAP	Chapters 10
Zone 2	GFSI – Global Food Safety Initiative	Chapters 3, 4, 9, 10
	BRC – British Retail Consortium	Chapters 9, 10
	IFS – International Featured Standards	Chapter 10
	SQF – Safe Quality Food	Chapter 4
	FSSC 22000 – Food Safety System Certification	Chapters 9, 10
	GLOBALGAP – Global Partnership for Good Agricultural Practices	Chapters 2, 9, 10
	RFM – Responsible Fisheries Management	Chapter 11
Zone 3	FLO – Fairtrade International	Chapter 1
	Rainforest Alliance	Chapter 1
Zone 4	KenyaGAP	Chapters 1, 12
	ISO – International Standardization Organization	Chapter 2
	IAF – International Accreditation Forum	Chapter 2
	EA – European Co-operation for Accreditation	Chapter 2
	Guides to good hygienic practice	Chapter 6
	RiskPlaza	Chapter 9
Zone 5		
Zone 6	ISEAL – The ISEAL Alliance	Chapters 1, 2
	MSC – Marine Stewardship Council	Chapter 11
Zone 7	KRAV – *Kontrollföreningen för alternativ odling*	Chapters 1, 11

sets the standards underpinning the certificate, is a private association with a membership that represents farmers, processors and trade, as well as consumer, environmental and animal welfare interests.

Driven Organic Food Standardization: A Comparison of the US and Sweden' (2006) 23 *Agriculture and Human Values* 163.

The Governance Triangle illustrated in Figure 1.1 draws a very rough picture of the hybridization of food governance. First of all, the threefold categorization of actors involved in standard setting (states, firms and NGOs) appears insufficient to analyse the dynamics of private or hybrid systems of food governance since it fails to capture the interdependence between these actors, as well as the conflicts of interest and power struggles between them.[23] To do so, we need a more sophisticated classification, distinguishing between private actors that are being regulated (*regulatees*), private actors that are part of the production chain but are not themselves regulated by the regulation under consideration but benefit from its application (*beneficiaries*, such as suppliers, retailers and consumers),[24] and private actors providing compliance and intermediary services to the regulated industry (*intermediaries*, such as accreditation, certification and consultancy bodies).[25]

Consider the example of GlobalGAP (see in detail Donal Casey, Chapter 2 in this volume). GlobalGAP is a private, not-for-profit organization setting voluntary private standards for the certification of agricultural products. Its standards are classified as a single-actor standard in the Governance Triangle (zone 2). In reality, however, GlobalGAP's membership is far from homogeneous and represents a wide range of industry actors, all with very different positions and interests. GlobalGAP was originally set up by European supermarket chains to adopt standards for the certification of agricultural products around the globe, but now also involves non-European retailers. Moreover, GlobalGAP's membership is no longer limited to retailers but includes retailers and food service firms, producers and suppliers, and associate members such as certification bodies, consultancy firms and the pest control industry (crop protection). Conflicts of interest exist among these membership categories, that is, between retailers and suppliers, between developed and developing countries, between small farmers and large food wholesalers. But conflicts also arise within membership categories, as the struggles between

[23] Cf Tetty Havinga, 'Conceptualizing Regulatory Arrangements: Complex Networks of Actors and Regulatory Roles' in Havinga, Van Waarden, Casey (n 1) 24–5.

[24] Fabrizio Cafaggi, 'New Foundations of Transnational Private Regulation' (2011) 38 *Journal of Legal Studies* 20, 31–8.

[25] Kenneth W. Abbott, David Levi-Faur and Duncan Snidal, 'Regulatory Intermediaries in the Age of Governance' (2017) 670 *Annals of the American Academy for Political and Social Sciences* – Special Issue (forthcoming) and Tetty Havinga and Paul Verbruggen, 'Understanding Complex Governance Relationships in Food Safety Regulation: The RIT Model as a Theoretical Lens' in this special issue.

multi-national supermarket corporations and small local retailers, or between national aquaculture industries in Norway and Thailand show. Beyond GlobalGAP's membership, other stakeholders (for example, environmental NGOs, scientific experts or government officials) are also involved in the standard-setting activities of GlobalGAP, such as through working groups and technical committees. In countries such as Kenya even national governments are involved in establishing domestic guidelines, adapting the GlobalGAP standard to the local situation to create KenyaGAP.[26]

5. HYBRIDIZATION BEYOND STANDARD SETTING

A second reason why the Governance Triangle illustrated in Figure 1.1 draws an incomplete picture of the hybridization of food governance is that it is focused on standard setting. As the various contributions in this volume show, the trend to hybridization of food governance extends beyond standard setting and involves other dynamics of food regulation. One example offered in this volume concerns the implementation of MSC certification by local fisheries and the support given to this process by state authorities. As Agni Kalfagianni and Tiffany Andrade Roche show in their analysis, states may provide powerful drivers of local MSC adoption and implementation by providing public funding schemes to achieve certification.

Clearly, regulatory governance does not concern activities of standard setting only. Hood, Scott and Baldwin conceptualize regulation as comprising three constitutive elements: standard setting, monitoring compliance, and enforcement.[27] For Abbott and Snidal the regulatory process comprises at least five stages (or tasks), namely agenda-setting (placing an issue on the regulatory agenda), negotiation (bargaining, drafting and promulgating standards), implementation (implementing standards within the operations of targets of regulation such as firms), monitoring

---

[26] Christine Carey, 'Kenya and the KenyaGAP Standard for Good Agricultural Practice. Governmental Use of Voluntary Standards'. ISEAL Case Study No 6 (2008) 11–12, accessed 24 November 2016 at http://www.isealalliance.org/sites/default/files/E051_Kenya_KenyaGAP.pdf.

[27] Christopher Hood, Henry Rothstein, Robert Baldwin (eds), *The Government of Risk* (Oxford University Press 2011) 26–27. See also Colin Scott, 'Regulating Everything: From Mega- to Meta-regulation' (2012) 60 *Administration* 61.

compliance, and enforcement (promoting compliance and responding to non-compliance).[28]

In analysing private and hybrid forms of governance one important stage seems to be missing here. As regards state regulation, the step following the setting of the standards is the implementation of these standards. This can be different for private and indeed hybrid forms of governance, since they do not necessarily entail the automatic application of or the obligation to comply with the set rules. After drafting and promulgating the standards, they first need to be *adopted* by regulatees. Henson and Humphrey stress that the distinction between standard setting and adoption clarifies the issue of compulsion and obligation.[29] Adopting a standard means deciding to accept the rules and to aim at compliance. A private entity may adopt a standard for several reasons: (i) adoption is legally mandatory, either under state law or by private contract; (ii) compliance is *de facto* mandatory as a result of demands by dominant actors in the market (such as retailers); or (iii) because the entity considers adoption beneficial to gain market access, to improve its reputation, to get a better price, or for some other (ethical) reason.

All in all, five principal functions seem to apply to every governance arrangement of food.[30] For a food governance arrangement to be effective, rules have to be laid down and subsequently adopted and implemented, and compliance with the rules has to be monitored and enforced. All regulatory activities can be thought of as part of one of these functions: (a) agenda setting and rule-making; (b) adoption and implementation; (c) monitoring compliance; (d) enforcement; and (e) evaluation and review.

(a) Agenda Setting and Rule-Making

Agenda setting is the phase in the regulatory process in which the issue is framed as a matter of food governance, where an arena for discussion and solution of the issue is chosen, and lobbying and coalition building takes place to succeed in agreeing to the regulatory norms. Rule-making is then

---

[28] Kenneth W. Abbott and Duncan Snidal 'The Governance Triangle: Regulatory Standards Institutions in the Shadow of the State' in Walter Mattli and Ngaire Woods (eds), *The Politics of Global Regulation* (Princeton University Press 2009) 63.

[29] Spencer Henson and John Humphrey, 'Codex Alimentarius and Private Standards' in Bernd Van der Meulen (ed.), *Private Food Law. Governing Food Chains through Contract Law, Self-Regulation, Private Standards, Audits and Certification Schemes* (Wageningen Academic Publishers 2011) 149, 157.

[30] Compare Havinga (n 23), 28–9 and Henson and Humphrey (n 29) 155–6.

the activity through which the negotiations on the regulatory norms are finalized and find their way into written rules and procedures. Through rule-making, new standards are introduced and old standards revised or discarded.

(b) Adoption and Implementation

After the standard is set, the regulated business has to adopt the standard before the standard can take effect. This can take various forms. For example, a firm or group of firms can develop a standard, which they adopt voluntarily for internal purposes. The adoption of food standards may also be required by businesses (either buyers or sellers) in the supply chain. The decision of major food retailers to adopt particular food standards such as GlobalGAP or BRC and require compliance with them in their supply contracts is considered a key driver of the diffusion and influence of private foods standards, making these standards mandatory for farmers and other food producers that supply these retailers.[31] The adoption by firms in the supply chain (market uptake) of standards that are developed by NGOs, such as those on kosher foods, is also crucial to their impact.[32]

For state regulation, the importance of the phase of adoption of the standard seems to be less obvious. From a socio-legal perspective, however, state law also has to be adopted, implemented and internalized – a firm needs to identify the legislation as relevant to its own operations and decide to implement the law. A firm may be unaware of relevant laws or decide to ignore them. Implementation of the standard is all that is done by an organization to abide by the standard in its own operations.

(c) Monitoring

Monitoring involves the procedures and activities used to verify compliance with the standards. Conformity can be assessed in various ways: by internal monitoring, by self-declaration, by inspection by the buyer (second-party audit), by a third party (certification agency), by the standard

---

[31] Fabrizio Cafaggi, 'Transnational Governance by Contract: Private Regulation and Contractual Networks in Food Safety' in Axel Marx, Miet Maertens, Johan Swinnen and Jan Wouters (eds), *Private Standards and Global Governance. Economic, Legal and Political Perspectives* (Edward Elgar 2012).

[32] Timothy Lytton, 'Competitive Third-Party Regulation: How Private Certification Can Overcome Constraints That Frustrate Government Regulation' (2014) 15 *Theoretical Inquiries in Law* 539.

setter, or by a state agency. Consumer complaints or media attention can also play a role in bringing non-compliance to the fore.[33] Monitoring compliance can involve various activities such as checking documents and registrations, taking samples and lab analysis, and inspections of premises. Most private standards require some sort of (third-party) certification.

(d) Enforcement

Enforcement refers to the activities, both formal and informal, that aim to secure compliance by regulated firms with the applicable regulatory standards and the objectives these standards embody.[34] Enforcement action is often taken in response to non-compliance, but in a broader understanding it may also induce compliance before an infringement is formally committed. The actor responsible for monitoring compliance might also enforce compliance. However, often other actors may become involved in case of non-compliance. Public inspectorates may forward cases of non-compliance to public prosecutors or to courts. Compliance reports from private third-party auditors will typically be sent to the certification agency or the standard owner to take further enforcement action. Sanctions can vary from warnings, instructions and advice, to fines, suspension of certification, contract termination, naming and shaming, and even consumer boycotts.

(e) Evaluation and Review

For a food governance arrangement it is crucial to be reflective, that is, the standard setter should be receptive to criticism, to the regulatory outcomes, and to new developments in food processing, food products, trading, scientific knowledge about risks and ways to prevent and detect them. Most standard owners have a procedure in place for the periodic review of their standards. The period for the review of standards is typically three to four years. Increasingly, the procedures for the revision of private standards also include consultation rounds and meetings with stakeholders.

---

[33] See for example Lytton (n 32) 566. This only works, however, if consumers are aware of the certificate (business-to-consumer label) and are able to discover non-compliance. Frequently, certification for food (safety) standards is only allowed in business-to-business relationships and therefore consumers are not affected by any of these certificates when buying food.

[34] See in greater detail: Paul Verbruggen, *Enforcing Transnational Private Regulation: A Comparative Analysis of Advertising and Food Safety* (Edward Elgar 2014) 16–17.

6. EXAMINING HYBRIDIZATION: AN ANALYTICAL FRAMEWORK

To analyse the hybridization of food governance we propose an analytical framework that is based on the framework introduced by Eberlein et al. for the analysis of interactions in regimes of transnational business governance.[35] In the previous sections, we have broken (regulatory) governance down to five different phases or functions: (a) agenda-setting and rule-making; (b) adoption and implementation; (c) monitoring; (d) enforcement; and (e) evaluation and review. Following Eberlein et al., we suggest that a comprehensive and systematic analysis of hybridization of food governance should address these five phases and functions, taking the following six dimensions into account:

(a) Actors

Which actors are involved in the hybrid governance arrangement? Each phase or function can be performed by different actors. One single actor can also perform several functions (or even all of them). Hybridization can occur when both private and public actors are involved in the same activity, for example, state actors and industry are concurrently involved in drafting the rules or in monitoring and enforcing public regulation. To give an example from this volume, the Swiss public ordinance on the use of veterinary drugs for livestock involves both state-employed and for-profit veterinarians to monitor compliance with its rules. As the contribution by Eva Thomann and Fritz Sager (Chapter 5) demonstrates, this hybrid arrangement triggers distinct accountability problems.

Hybridization may also mean that an environmental NGO succeeds in setting an issue related to food governance on the political agenda. Likewise, hybridization can concern the legislative enactment by the state of food standards, compliance with which by the regulated food businesses is overseen by both public (ministries, enforcement agencies) and private actors (industry associations, certification bodies). We have already stressed the importance of differentiating between actors in the 'actor categories' of states, firms and NGOs. In the same way, distinctions can also be drawn regarding the level of governance at which the actors

[35] Burkard Eberlein, Kenneth W. Abott, Julia Black, Errol Meidinger and Stephan Wood 'Transnational Business Governance Interactions: Conceptualization and Framework for Analysis' (2014) 8 *Regulation & Governance* 1, 14.

are operating. Are they active on a global, local or intermediate (European Union, federal) level?

(b) Drivers and Motives

What are the drivers and motives of the various actors to engage in regulatory activities and, as such, to contribute to hybrid food governance? Why do the respective actors involved 'buy into' the arrangement? What are the ambitions of the actors? Insights regarding the drivers and motives for regulation offer important input for qualifying the results and determining the effectiveness that is achieved by the governance arrangement. Both Fagotto and Lytton and McAllister (Chapters 3 and 4 respectively in this volume) argue that economic motives of for-profit auditors have a negative impact on their performance. In this respect it may also be significant to examine whether the inclusion of different public and private actors was intended, or whether the mix was coincidental. Furthermore, one might ask whether the hybridization is *ad hoc*, experimental or whether a broader (public) policy is behind it? Is hybridization voluntary or coerced? As Kirezieva and Luning make clear in their contribution, context factors like the agro-climatic environment, the political arena, and dependence on international markets also play a key role in shaping the governance of the food safety management systems of individual firms and, by extension, the hybridization of food governance.

(c) Mechanisms and Instruments

Actors in hybrid governance arrangements interact through different means and forums. Which mechanisms and instruments are used for that purpose? Are these formal (membership, voting procedures, consultation) or informal (networks, markets and communities)? How do these mechanisms relate to organizational and governance structures, and what is their (legal) basis? A frequently applied mechanism of coordination in food standards is conditional referencing.[36] Standard X then notes 'compliance with this standard can be demonstrated by compliance with Standard Y or Z'. As Havinga and Verbruggen demonstrate in this volume (Chapter 9), several public enforcement agencies employ this mechanism to involve

---

[36] See more generally Eberlein et al. (n 35) 11 and Nina A. Mendelson, 'Private Control over Access to Public Law: The Perplexing Federal Regulatory Use of Private Standards' (2014) 112 *Michigan Law Review* 737.

private assurance schemes in their risk-based policy for food safety controls. Statutory obligations on food businesses to have food safety management systems in place are also common in many jurisdictions (Van der Meulen (Chapter 6) and Hussein, Garcia Martinez and Fearne (Chapter 7) and Kottenstede (Chapter 10)). As the contribution by Kindji and Faure (Chapter 12) shows, however, the uptake of food safety management systems by individual firms in the member countries of the West African Economic and Monetary Union is not mandated by law. Instead, its introduction is the result of requirements imposed by European buyers sourcing from local producers.

(d) Character of Interaction

The interaction between the private and public actors involved in governance arrangements and the institutions of such arrangements can be characterized in many ways.[37] Eberlein et al. distinguish four broad categories of interaction among transnational business governance schemes, and with state-based institutions.[38] A first form is *competition*: different actors and institutions compete with each other to obtain governance capacities, including reputation, legitimacy and 'turf'. Second, actors and institutions may *coordinate* governance activities by devising tasks, collaboration or imitation, either conscious or inadvertent. A third form is *cooptation*, which emerges when actors and their institutions adopt or converge around specific standards and procedures developed by others. In the domain of food safety, norms developed by the Codex and ISO have had a significant impact on the design of hygiene regulation and procedures of food certification and accreditation (Donal Casey, Chapter 2 in this volume). Finally, the interaction may also be *chaotic* in that relationships have not stabilized, remain undirected and are subject to conditional swings.

Of course, while relationships between public and private actors and their institutions evolve, the interactions also evolve. Interaction may also be characterized by several forms at the same time, being, for example, cooperative in one respect and competitive in another. This means that the interaction may change form over time and can display characteristics of multiple forms.[39]

---

[37] See for example Van der Heijden (n 17).
[38] Eberlein et al. (n 35) 11–12.
[39] Eberlein et al. (n 35) 12.

(e) Results and Effects

Next the question arises regarding the (intermediate) results or effects of hybridization. What are the challenges and benefits, and how are these different from previous experiences with governance arrangements? How are concerns of (democratic) legitimacy and accountability addressed, if they are deemed necessary at all? Are hybrid forms of governance more effective or cost-effective than traditional state regulation? As several chapters in this volume indicate, hybrid governance arrangements may not be entirely effective due to incompatible incentives and inadequate oversight mechanisms.[40]

(f) Change Over Time

Finally, what changes occur in the participation of actors, the roles and functions they perform and the interactions among them? Clearly, governance arrangements develop over time.[41] Standards may change ownership,[42] new actors may be incorporated in the governance structure or in separate regulatory activities such as standard setting and monitoring,[43] and actors may withdraw from a standard.[44] Generally, we see that more actors become involved as a standard or governance arrangement matures. For transnational standards this often means that the geographical spread of the actors also increases over time. Understanding why and how these changes take effect is key to predicting the outcomes of food governance.

These six 'dimensions' of hybridization, combined with the five different phases or functions of regulatory governance, make up the analytical framework summarized by Table 1.2.

---

[40] See Fagotto (Chapter 3), Lytton and McAllister (Chapter 4), Thomann and Sager (Chapter 5), and Hussein, Garcia Martinez and Fearne (Chapter 7) in this volume.

[41] This phenomenon is widely observed in the scholarship on (regulatory) governance. See in general: Fabrizio Gilardi and Claudio Radaelli, 'Governance and Learning' in Levi-Faur (n 16) 155.

[42] For example, the Safe Quality Food (SQF) standard was sold by its original developer the Government of Western Australia to the Food Marketing Institute, the trade association for US retailers.

[43] For example, food manufacturers have been integrated in the governance structures of GlobalGAP (Donal Casey, Chapter 2 in this volume) and the Global Food Safety Initiative (Havinga and Verbruggen, Chapter 9 in this volume).

[44] For example, after having formally established the Marine Stewardship Council (MSC) in 1997, the multinational company Unilever and the World Wide Fund for Nature withdrew from its management (see Kalfagianni and Andrade Roche, Chapter 11 in this volume).

*Table 1.2 Analytical framework for hybridization of food governance**

Regulatory functions / Dimensions of hybridization	a. Agenda-setting & rule-making	b. Adoption & implementation	c. Monitoring	d. Enforcement	e. Evaluation & review
i. Actors involved					
ii. Motivations and drivers					
iii. Mechanisms and instruments					
iv. Character of interaction					
v. Results and effects					
vi. Change over time					

Note: * Adopting Eberlein et al. (n 35) 14.

To be sure, the contributions in this volume do not address all dimensions and functions identified in the table. Instead, the contributions focus on one or two particular functions of a food governance arrangement (the columns) and then address the questions triggered by the various dimensions (the rows). It should also be noted that the analytical framework proposed here does not impose a specific theoretical lens through which the contributors of the volume should look. Instead, the purpose of the framework is to provide guidance for systematically analysing the origins, forms and results of hybridization of food governance now and in the future.

7. HYBRIDIZATION OF FOOD GOVERNANCE: TRENDS, TYPES AND RESULTS

This volume brings together 12 contributions that examine the trends, types and results of hybridization of food governance arrangements.

Part I

The first part of the volume deals with the contested legitimacy and integrity of private food governance and asks whether and to what extent hybridization should be seen as a cause or solution to this. The rise of private food standards and its impact on (transnational) food supply chains have triggered fundamental questions about stakeholder participation, transparency, accountability, and effectiveness in standard setting and implementation. Donal Casey first examines how GLOBALGAP, which administers the most widely implemented private food certification scheme worldwide, has sought to meet legitimacy demands from various state, industry and civil society actors in relation to its scheme. As Casey shows in his analysis, the search for legitimacy by GLOBALGAP is a key driver of its interaction with state actors and civil society. More specifically, GLOBALGAP has strategically engaged with non-industry stakeholders to gather support for its standard-setting activities and has tapped into the existing system of third-party certification and accreditation in order to legitimate its own organizational structures, its practices and processes. Several strategies were used for legitimation. First, GLOBALGAP deliberately chose to build its standards on pre-existing international standards of verification and accreditation (ISO) and international standards of standard setting procedures (ISO, ISEAL, WTO). Furthermore, it engaged and communicated with state and civil society actors in order to gain their support. GLOBALGAP also recognized that independent verification of compliance was critical to its legitimacy. It thus relies on accredited third-party certification as the internationally accepted best practice. GLOBALGAP received endorsement from the European Co-operation for Accreditation and responded to criticism relating to inconsistent certification practices with closer cooperation with the international accreditation communities. Casey concludes that state actors, certification and accreditation organizations constitute key legitimacy communities that play a central role in providing legitimacy to non-state regulatory organizations such as GLOBALGAP.

In her contribution, Elena Fagotto addresses a specific problem that has triggered wide discussions about the integrity of private food governance, namely the conflict of interest in third-party certification. Certification plays a central role in many private and hybrid food safety arrangements. Reviewing the literature from the fields of food, accounting, labour and environmental standards, she reveals four limitations in the institutional design of third-party certification that create conflicts of interest: risks to auditor independence, poor auditor competence, inadequate audit design, and limited audit transparency. She then asks whether and to what extent the meta-rules set by the Global Food Safety Initiative (GFSI) address these four weaknesses. Although GFSI acknowledges the identified risks in its benchmarking requirements, as Fagotto acknowledges, certain gaps still remain, the most important of which is that auditors are paid by the firms they audit and that GFSI does not offer a way to avoid the resulting conflicts of interest. Other gaps include the fact that audit visits are announced in advance and that audit reports are not shared. Fagotto thus cautions that public regulators should first understand how private initiatives operate and assess their effectiveness before they devise hybrid forms of food governance. If not, such hybrid governance arrangements are likely to yield sub-optimal results.

Timothy Lytton and Lesley McAllister specifically focus on one of the institutional weaknesses of third-party certification discussed by Fagotto: the conflict between financial interests and professional obligations that arises when auditors are paid by the firms they audit. In their contribution they investigate the various oversight mechanisms that have been developed by both private and public actors in the United States to address this problem. They highlight the strengths and disadvantages of oversight by these mechanisms, which involve tort litigation in the courts, certifier accreditation and licensing, GFSI benchmarking, and government recognition of accreditation bodies. These oversight mechanisms create or increase incentives to counterbalance the incentives that result in poor food safety audits and unreliable third-party certification. The different oversight mechanisms together, as Lytton and McAllister contend, comprise a network of private and public actors that may fill gaps left by individual actors. Separating functions among different actors may reduce vulnerability to conflicts of interest, but networks also have disadvantages as they may result in diffuse responsibilities and increased administrative burdens and costs. Lytton and McAllister conclude that their analysis can be helpful in the design of hybridized or networked regulatory arrangements in food governance in order to reduce conflicts of interest in private auditing and improve regulatory outcomes in the United States and beyond.

In the final contribution in this section, Eva Thomann and Fritz Sager discuss the conflicting roles and accountabilities of street-level professionals in a hybrid governance regime. They use empirical data on the enforcement of the Swiss regulations on the dispensing and use of veterinary drugs for livestock by public and private veterinarians. Thomann and Sager compare the performance of public and private veterinarians and conclude that implementation failures exist both with public and private veterinarians, but are more severe among the latter. They use the concept of accountability regimes to explain how veterinarians do their job. The complex relationships between actors in a hybrid regime create conflicting roles. Private veterinarians are simultaneously implementing agents, policy addressees, professionals, and market actors. Private veterinarians provide for-profit services to farmers and are at the same time supposed to enforce public regulations on the same farmers. The resulting conflicts of interest are very similar to the conflicts of interest faced by auditors in third-party certification schemes, as Lytton and McAllister have shown. The public veterinarians are supposed to monitor their private colleagues. The relationship between public and private veterinarians is complex because private veterinarians are simultaneously professional peers, enforcement agents and target group, and this restricts the possibilities the public veterinarians have to enforce the regulations on their private colleagues. The authors contend that two aspects of hybrid governance regimes are problematic: private actors who are assigned different tasks (addressee and enforcement agent) and the irreconcilable rationalities of the state and the market (each controlling their own customers). Thomann and Sager conclude that hybridity can have concrete, negative effects that should be taken into account to ensure the compliance of regulatees with food safety regulations.

Part II

The second part of the volume focuses on the hybridization of food governance in the European Union. Legislation and public policy have both provided a powerful impetus for this development in Europe. Bernd van der Meulen therefore first examines how the European legislature has contributed to the rise of hybrid food governance. By focusing on EU food hygiene law, he contends that public and private regulation live in close symbiosis to ensure the policy objective of food safety. He distinguishes between three forms of private regulation in which this symbiosis exists: firm-level HACCP systems made mandatory through statutory rules, guides for good hygienic practices adopted by industry associations, and so-called 'external private regulation' set by powerful firms in the food supply chain (that is, large corporate retailers and producers) with a view to ensuring that food safety is effectively ensured in any of the preceding links in the chain. As Van der Meulen shows, both EU legislation and the case law of the European Court of Justice contribute to the trend towards the hybridization of food governance in the European Union. Inevitably, this will entail a more complex regulatory framework for food safety.

While Van der Meulen's contribution is mainly concerned with the interplay between public and private actors in rule-making activities, the other two contributions in this second part provide empirical insights into the adoption, implementation and enforcement of hybrid regulatory arrangements at individual firm level. First, Mohamud Hussein, Marian Garcia Martinez and Andrew Fearne analyse the operation of so-called 'management-based regulation' in the fresh poultry meat sector in the United Kingdom. This hybrid form of food regulation requires individual companies to engage in their own planning, rule-making and enforcement activities to deliver safe food products based on HACCP principles. While management-based regulation is expected to ensure higher levels of food safety at lower cost to the public regulators, it has not met these expectations in the UK poultry sector. Firms in this sector may not only lack the necessary knowledge and financial resources to deliver safe food, but may also have conflicting incentives to comply with the rules. Hussein, Garcia Martinez and Fearne thus caution that without a well-crafted regulatory incentive mechanism capable of committing firms to ensuring a safe meat supply, the regulatory outcomes of hybrid food governance will be sub-optimal.

Subsequently, Klementina Kirezieva and Pieternel Luning discuss the influence of context factors on food safety management systems in the fresh produce sector (leafy greens), the performance and uptake of private standards by individual firms in that sector, in the European Union and beyond. Building on concepts derived from systems theory, they develop an assessment tool to measure the performance of food safety management systems for leafy greens. Climatic conditions for agricultural production, the degree of export to international markets, and government responsiveness to private standards are found to be important factors that contribute to demands for private standards and certification in different countries. Furthermore, where local institutional environments fail to support companies in adopting, implementing and evaluating food safety management systems, as in developing countries, there is a high demand for private standards to help to deliver food safety from individual firms that supply to international markets. Kirezieva and Luning stress the need for further investigation of how individual companies in the fresh produce sector can best design and operate their own food safety management systems while being responsive to the institutional environment in which they operate.

Part III

The third and final part of the volume concerns hybridization in global food governance. The contributions in this part are clustered around the question of how global private food standards interact with public actors and regulation at the domestic level.

Tetty Havinga and Paul Verbruggen first examine the interaction between the leading global private governance organization, the Global Food Safety Initiative (GFSI), and government actors in Canada, China, the Netherlands and the United States. Havinga and Verbruggen set out to assess why and how such public-private interaction unfolds, and with what results. For GFSI the principal reason for engagement with public authorities is to gain broad acceptance of its benchmarking process, recognized food safety schemes and the system of third-party certification. While such engagement might also strengthen their legitimacy claims, the ultimate goal of these activities is that national and international government actors recognize or adopt GFSI third party certification as accepted tools to assist in the prioritization of public food safety inspections. The principal strategy pursued by GFSI has been providing information about its organization, activities and achievements to public officials and responding to public concerns about GFSI. Havinga and Verbruggen contend that government actors have two main arguments to engage with GFSI and related private governance arrangements in the food industry. First, they want to communicate with key actors in the private sector because they are concerned about the spread of private food standards and want to stress the importance and prevalence of public laws and enforcement. Second, they want to explore the potential of private food safety schemes to contribute to public policy goals. The recently adopted food laws in Canada and the United States, for example, have benefited from the experience of GFSI and private food safety schemes, and incorporate (to different degrees) these schemes in the new legal framework for food regulation. Also in China and the Netherlands public food authorities entertain relationships with GFSI and its recognized third party certification schemes, albeit for very different reasons and motivations. Nevertheless, the result is an increasingly hybrid system of food governance.

The contribution by Kai Kottenstede focuses specifically on the reception of transnational private food safety standards in China. As his empirical analysis shows, the interaction between transnational private standards and the Chinese regime of food safety regulation creates a specific type of hybridization, not seen elsewhere. The Chinese government is currently actively engaging with private organizations representing the western food industry to ratchet up the implementation and enforcement of food safety standards locally. It is well known that China has experienced multiple high-impact food safety crises in the last two decades. In response, China has adopted new legislation that meets internationally accepted standards for food safety regulation. Nevertheless, important practical obstacles remain to the effective implementation and enforcement of these laws. One way the Chinese government has sought to address these obstacles has been to adopt the voluntary standards of ChinaGAP and China HACCP, and submit these standards to the benchmarking procedures provided by GLOBALGAP and GFSI to assess their equivalence to internationally accepted food safety standards. This submission of public regulation to private regulatory structures is clearly strategic. As Kottenstede shows, the Chinese government thus aims to harness the content of its own voluntary standards and increase the status and credibility of these standards among western food manufacturers sourcing products from China. At the same time, however, it seeks to limit the influence of major transnational private schemes in China, such as BRC and GLOBALGAP, by presenting to local producers a national standard that is considered technically equivalent to these international standards. While hybridization is thus clearly happening, its form and degree is closely orchestrated by the Chinese government.

Agni Kalfagianni and Tiffany Andrade Roche also engage in an empirical analysis of the reception at the domestic level of transnational private food standards. Their analysis, however, focuses on the world's most widely implemented private certification scheme for sustainable wild-captured fish, namely the Marine Stewardship Council (MSC). Building on extensive documentary analysis and interviews with experts, they highlight the variation of domestic responses to the MSC scheme in Alaska, Australia and Ecuador. To measure that variation they use the indicators of public funds to support local MSC uptake, the co-option of the MSC scheme in domestic public regulation, and the development of rival standards supported by the state. While the reception of MSC in Australia and

Ecuador has been quite smooth, MSC has been widely criticized in Alaska for inconsistencies in certification and the level of protection offered by the scheme itself. These variations, Kalfagianni and Andrade Roche argue, can be explained by the perceived credibility of MSC by domestic actors, MSC's complementarity to public regulation, and the significance of MSC certification for local fisheries to access international markets. In Alaska, MSC scores rather poorly on all of these explanatory factors, whereas the opposite is true in Australia and Ecuador.

Overall, the studies by Kalfagianni and Andrade Roche and Kottenstede draw attention to the importance of domestic and local levels of governance for the legitimacy and effectiveness of transnational private standards in food and other domains. Moreover, the study by Kévine Kindji and Michael Faure also stresses the role of local context factors to the uptake and effectiveness of transnational private food standards, and more generally, food safety regulation. In this contribution, Kindji and Faure explore the role of transnational private standards in harnessing the capacity of the public and private sector in the West African Economic and Monetary Union (*l'Union économique et monétaire ouest-africaine* – UEMOA). The seven Member States of this international organization for cooperation between countries in West Africa (Benin, Burkina Faso, Ivory Coast, Mali, Niger, Senegal and Togo) face great difficulties in meeting modern demands for food safety in international markets. While regulatory reforms have been initiated, partly in dialogue with food manufacturers and producers, states frequently lack the financial means, expertise and organizational capacities (such as competent laboratories) to implement the new laws effectively. Transnational private standards may fill this governance gap, especially for producers in export-oriented supply chains. However, these producers form the top of the market. Small-and-medium sized enterprises lack the financial means to meet the requirements under transnational private standards and have sufficient difficulties meeting the newly implemented public standards.

8. CONCLUSION

The contributions in this book highlight the diversity in the hybridization of today's food governance. The chapters document that across a wide variety of contexts public and private actors are engaging with each other to enhance their individual or combined regulatory capacity. The collection also shows that collaboration – in whatever shape – between public and private actors is not a given, and even if such collaboration is established, the actors meet great difficulties in maintaining the carefully constructed balance of that collaboration because of changing and conflicting interests, rationalities, laws and organizations. It is evident that both public and private actors will only to some extent submit their autonomy to collaborative efforts. Clearly, contemporary food governance, and in particular the development of hybrid governance arrangements, is in a state of flux. It is to be expected that the trend towards hybridization discussed in this book will continue to progress. In analysing this development and the challenges it brings about, we hope the reader of this volume finds guidance in the contributions that it holds and the analytical framework we propose.

PART I

Legitimacy and integrity of private food governance

2 Structuring private food safety governance: GLOBALGAP and the legitimating role of the state and rule intermediaries

Donal Casey

1. INTRODUCTION

In November 1996, quality managers and fresh produce buyers from a number of European retailers met informally in London.[1] The group met once again in Berlin, two months later, on a more formal footing. In July 1997, the representatives from 13 European retailers agreed to name the group the Euro-Retailer Produce Working Group (EUREP).[2] Over the next 15 years, EUREP would become EUREPGAP, and EUREPGAP would eventually be renamed GLOBALGAP. Since its inception, GLOBALGAP has developed into the 'most widely implemented farm certification scheme worldwide'.[3] In this period, we see the transformation of what was an informal grouping of retailers, into a highly elaborate regulatory organization consisting of formal governance structures, standard-setting procedures, and monitoring and enforcement systems.

What can explain this transformation? In order to understand the development of GLOBALGAP, it is helpful to look beyond functional and market-based explanations such as protecting against reputational and legal liability, responding to changing consumer concerns and preferences, and the need to rationalize globalized supply chains.[4] Such rationales are clearly significant drivers for new regulatory systems, and provide

[1] Willem Hofmans, 'EUREP's Accomplishments to Date' in Kristian Möller (ed), *EUREPGAP Verification 2000* (EHI EuroHandelsinstitut Gmbh 1999) 6.

[2] Kristian Möller (ed), *Integrated Production of Fruit and Vegetables* (EHI EuroHandelsinstitut Gmbh 1998) 71; Hofmans (n 1) 6.

[3] Eurofruit Magazine, 'News Focus: GLOBALGAP' [2008] *EUROFRUIT Magazine*.

[4] Tim Bartley, 'Institutional Emergence in an Era of Globalization: The Rise

important context to their goals and objectives. Despite this, examining GLOBALGAP's legitimation dynamics further contributes to our understanding of the organization's transformation, and in particular, why certain organizational forms, structures, practices and processes emerge and develop. As Suchman contends, legitimacy and legitimation have a significant influence on 'how the organization is built, how it is run, and simultaneously, how it is understood and evaluated'.[5]

This chapter outlines how GLOBALGAP's transformation was driven, in part, by a search for legitimacy in which state actors and rule intermediary organizations played a significant role. In so doing, I argue that the emergence of non-state regulatory organizations has not led to the demise of the state, and that states 'still play key roles in creating and negotiating global orders'.[6] The state and its delegated entities play a particularly important role in legitimating non-state regulatory organizations through the power of their support and endorsements, and by providing standards and guidelines that non-state regulatory organizations use as building blocks for their structures, practices and processes. One such group of delegated entities are accreditation bodies. Indeed, the accreditation system within the European Union 'is fully controlled by the State', and accreditation bodies are provided with 'public authority' by virtue of Regulation 765/2008.[7] Accreditation bodies not only blur the traditional distinction between public and private actors, they also bridge the gap between the State and the 'tripartite standards regime of governance . . . that links standard setting, certification, and accreditation'.[8] Flowing from this, I further contend that accreditation bodies and certification bodies play a significant role in legitimating non-state regulatory organizations, and act as carriers of the international norms and standards developed by states and their delegated entities.

The practices of non-state standard-setting organizations, state actors, accreditation bodies and certification bodies contribute to the continued hybridization of contemporary food governance. Furthermore, identifying the state, certification bodies and accreditation bodies as significant

of Transnational Private Regulation of Labour and Environmental Conditions' (2007) 113 *American Journal of Sociology* 297–351, 310.

[5] Mark Suchman, 'Managing Legitimacy: Strategic and Institutional Approaches' (1995) 20 *Academy of Management Review* 571–610, 576.

[6] Bartley (n 4) 310.

[7] Eve Fouilleux and Allison Loconto, 'Voluntary Standards, Certification, and Accreditation in the Global Organic Agriculture Field: a Tripartite Model of Techno-Politics' *Agriculture and Human Values* 1–14 (forthcoming).

[8] ibid; Allison Loconto and Lawrence Busch, 'Standards, Techno-Economic Networks, and Playing Fields: Performing the Global Market Economy' (2010) 17 *Review of International Political Economy* 507–36, 508.

legitimacy communities and the creators and carriers of legitimating models, provides an insight into some of the key questions posed by hybridization. These questions ask: how do public and private actors interact, what are the drivers for these interactions, and what is the character of the relationship between public and private actors? Furthermore, the research provides an answer to the questions of who the particular actors are in hybrid regulatory regimes, and the changes that result from interactions between these actors. In so doing, I seek to contribute to not only existing discussions of the hybridization of food governance, but also our understanding of how non-state regulatory organizations seek to legitimate themselves by providing a detailed and theoretically informed account of GLOBALGAP's management of legitimacy.

The analysis in the chapter draws upon documentary evidence (primary and secondary), archival records and elite interviews with GLOBALGAP representatives, and market, state and NGO actors. The chapter unfolds in three parts. I begin by unpacking the central argument of this chapter and situate it within the context of this collection's central concern of the hybridization of food safety and quality governance. From here, I examine the role that state actors play in the legitimation of non-state regulatory organizations. In particular, I focus on the importance of international standards and state endorsement in the process of GLOBALGAP's legitimation. Finally, I outline how GLOBALGAP sought to enrol in the tripartite standards regime of standard-setting organizations, certification bodies and accreditation bodies in order to legitimate the organization, how accreditation bodies act as carriers of international standards developed by state actors, and the importance of accreditation bodies in ensuring the continued integrity of GLOBALGAP's system of implementation. In so doing, this chapter seeks to bring into sharp focus the important role that states, accreditation bodies and certification bodies play in constructing and maintaining the legitimacy of non-state standard-setting organizations in the policy sphere of food safety and quality.

2. LEGITIMATION AND HYBRIDIZATION

Verbruggen and Havinga propose an actor-centred approach to the hybridization of food governance that seeks to examine hybridization beyond the regulatory process of standard setting.[9] Building upon the

[9] Paul Verbruggen and Tetty Havinga, 'Hybridisation of Food Governance: An Analytical Framework', Chapter 1 in this volume.

work of Eberlein et al., the analysis includes not only the actors, drivers and forms of interaction in hybrid food governance regimes, but also the mechanisms through which interactions occur and the effects of hybridization.[10] Examining the legitimation dynamics of GLOBALGAP sheds light upon the role the state, accreditation bodies and certification bodies play in structuring non-state regulatory organizations, and the central questions posed by the contributions in this volume in relation to the hybridization of food governance. Furthermore, focusing upon how and why GLOBALGAP has managed legitimacy allows us to see how its interactions with state actors, accreditation bodies and certification bodies impacts upon the key governance activities of agenda setting and rule making, adoption and implementation, monitoring, enforcement, and evaluation and review.

2.1 Conceptualizing Legitimacy and Legitimation

I conceptualize legitimacy as an empirical phenomenon rather than a normative abstraction. Here, we can conceive legitimacy as an objective constituent that may or may not be present in a particular regulatory organization. In line with a sociological approach, organizations are viewed as 'subjects of legitimation' in the sense that their legitimacy is assessed and bestowed by internal/external audiences, and their environment – the sources of legitimacy or legitimacy communities.[11] Drawing upon the work of Suchman, I define legitimacy as 'a generalized perception or assumption that the actions of an entity are desirable, proper, or appropriate within some socially constructed system of norms, values, beliefs, and definitions'.[12] Thus, from a regulatory perspective, I conceptualize legitimacy as congruence between the regulatory structures and activities of an organization and broadly accepted models, norms and/or beliefs that permeate a society or which are held by an organization's legitimacy communities.

Legitimation as a process denotes the practices that organizations

---

[10] Burkard Eberlein and others, 'Transnational Business Governance Interactions: Conceptualization and Framework for Analysis' (2014) 8 *Regulation & Governance* 1–21, 14; Verbruggen and Havinga (n 9).

[11] David L. Deephouse and Mark Suchman, 'Legitimacy in Organizational Institutionalism' in Royston Greenwood and others (eds), *The Sage Handbook of Organizational Institutionalism* (Sage 2008), 54; Julia Black, *Legitimacy and the Competition for Regulatory Share* (LSE Law, Society and Economy Working Papers, 2009) 10.

[12] Suchman (n 5) 574.

engage in to gain, maintain and repair their legitimacy.[13] 'Legitimation is a process that brings the unacceptable into accord with acceptable norms, values, beliefs, practices and procedures.'[14] I argue that in order to comprehend the legitimating dynamics of GLOBALGAP we must take seriously three interrelated propositions. First, GLOBALGAP is embedded within an environment occupied by a diversity of legitimacy communities and structured by institutional forces or social structure norms. Embeddedness rests the recognition of organizations as open systems.[15] In this sense, non-state regulators such as GLOBALGAP are not sealed off from their environments, but rather, organizations interact with and are interdependent on their environment for important resources such as legitimacy. Second, through the imposition of legitimacy demands, communities and norms both constrain and empower the emergence and development of GLOBALGAP's structures, practices and processes.[16] Third, agency remains.[17] Non-state regulators are not passive in relation to legitimacy demands. Although 'their scope for strategic action may be bounded, and in any event structured by their institutional environment', non-state regulatory organizations possess autonomy and agency in respect to how they manage their legitimacy.[18]

---

[13] ibid.

[14] Morris Zelditch, 'Processes of Legitimation: Recent Developments and New Directions' (2001) 64 *Social Psychology Quarterly* 4–17, 9.

[15] John W. Meyer, 'Reflections on Institutional Theories of Organizations' in Royston Greenwood and others (eds), *The Sage Handbook of Organizational Institutionalism* (Sage 2008) 453.

[16] Steven Bernstein, 'Legitimacy in Intergovernmental and Non-State Global Governance' (2011) 18 *Review of International Political Economy* 17–51, 19.

[17] John Child, 'Organizational Structure, Environment and Performance: The Role of Strategic Choice' (1972) 6 *Sociology* 1–22, 4; Suchman (n 5) 585–6.

[18] John Dowling and Jeffrey Pfeffer, 'Organizational Legitimacy: Social Values and Organizational Behavior' (1975) 18 *Pacific Sociology Review* 122–36, 127; Blake E. Ashforth and Barrie W. Gibbs, 'The Double Edge Sword of Organizational Legitimation' (1990) 1 *Organizational Science* 177–94, 180; Christine Oliver, 'Strategic Responses to Institutional Processes' (1991) 16 *Academy of Management Review* 145–79, 153; Benjamin Cashore, 'Legitimacy and the Privatization of Environmental Governance: How Non-State Market-Driven (NSMD) Governance Systems Gain Rule-Making Authority' (2002) 15 *Governance: An International Journal of Policy, Administration and Institutions* 503–29; Benjamin Cashore, Graeme Auld and Deanna Newsom, *Governing Through Markets: Forest Certification and the Emergence of Non-State Authority* (Yale University Press 2004); Julia Black, 'Constructing and Contesting Legitimacy and Accountability in Polycentric Regulatory Regimes' (2008) 2 *Regulation and Governance* 137–64, 139; Anne-Claire Pache and Filipe Santos, 'When Worlds Collide: The Internal Dynamics of Organizational Responses to Conflicting Institutional Demands'

2.2 The Importance of Legitimacy for Non-State Regulatory Organizations

The search for legitimacy is a key driver for interactions between public and private actors in the policy sphere of food safety and quality. Simply put, legitimacy is an important resource for organizations, including regulators.[19] Legitimacy creates a sense of obligation to act in accordance with particular norms. As such, the legitimation of a regulator may obviate the need for extensive and inefficient monitoring and enforcement mechanisms within a regulatory system.[20] A legitimate regulator will be able to foster not just passive support for its regulatory activities, but it will also be able to garner active support from those actors that it seeks to regulate and enrol.[21] This is of particular importance in relation to regulators as active support is a 'critical element in motivating behavioural responses'.[22] Furthermore, by providing a 'reservoir of support',[23] legitimacy can lead to the stability and persistence of a non-state regulatory organization, even when the regulator attempts to shape behaviour in ways that are immediately undesirable.[24]

While legitimacy is an important resource of all regulators, legitimation

---

(2010) 35 *Academy of Management Review* 455–76, 160–1; Royston Greenwood and others, 'Institutional Complexity and Organizational Responses' (2011) 5 *The Academy of Management Annals* 317–71, 344; Luc Fransen, 'Multi-Stakeholder Governance and Voluntary Programme Interactions: Legitimation Politics in the Institutional Design of Corporate Social Responsibility' (2012) 10 *Socio-Economic Review* 163–92.

19 See Talcott Parsons, 'Suggestions for a Sociological Approach to the Theory of Organizations – I'; Talcott Parsons, 'Suggestions for a Sociological Approach to the Theory of Organizations – II' (1956) 1 *Administrative Science Quarterly* 225–39; Alan J. Richardson and Burkard Eberlein, 'Legitimating Transnational Standard Setting: The Case of the International Accounting Standards Board' (2011) 98 *Journal of Business Ethics* 217–45, 221; Tom R. Tyler, 'The Psychology of Legitimacy: A Relational Perspective on Voluntary Deference to Authorities' (1997) 1 *Personality and Social Psychology Review* 323–45, 335; Tom R. Tyler, 'Psychological Perspectives on Legitimacy and Legitimation' (2006) 57 *Annual Review of Psychology* 375–400, 381; Rainer Hülsse, 'Even Clubs Can't do Without Legitimacy: Why the Anti-Money Laundering Blacklist was Suspended' (2008) 2 *Regulation and Governance* 459–79; Christian Reus-Smith, 'International Crises of Legitimacy' (2007) 44 *International Politics* 157–74, 163; Suchman (n 5) 575; Black (n 18) 148.

20 Tyler (n 19) 335.

21 Hülsse (n 19); Reus-Smith (n 19); Suchman (n 5) 575.

22 Black (n 18) 148.

23 Tyler (n 19) 381.

24 Suchman (n 5) 574–75; Tyler (n 19) 381; Tyler (n 19).

can be particularly problematic for non-state regulators for a number of reasons. The first is the 'liability of newness'.[25] New forms of regulatory organizations face challenges in terms of being able to justify their existence and their organizational structures and activities. Furthermore, legitimacy is linked to the particular role played by an actor and 'not all organizations will be perceived as legitimate in performing regulatory roles'.[26] This is especially so when organizations are seen as new entrants into regulatory space. Importantly, legitimacy is a great panacea for the ills of newness.[27] Second, non-state regulatory organizations are detached from the existing legitimating structures assembled by nation-states. Indeed, 'many of the chief sources of legitimacy at the domestic level, such as constitutional mandates, electoral processes, legality, and tradition are not available to transnational corporations'.[28] As such, non-state regulators must learn how, and seek legitimacy from other sources in the form of legitimacy claims. Thus, rather than being buttressed by existing legitimating architecture, non-state regulators must build legitimacy from the ground up.[29]

2.3 Legitimation and Hybridization

The practices of non-state standard-setting organizations, state actors, accreditation bodies and certification bodies contribute to the continued hybridization of contemporary food governance. As Verbruggen and Havinga note in this volume, 'the key to understanding contemporary food governance lies in the *interplay* between different public and private actors'.[30] When we speak of the legitimacy of non-state regulatory organizations we must remember that, like all organizations, regulators are the subjects of legitimation.[31] Non-state regulators' legitimacy is rooted in the evaluations and assessment of their sources of legitimacy – legitimacy communities.[32] For many non-state standard-setting organizations, states,

[25] Arthur J. Stinchcombe, 'Social Structure and Organizations' in James G. March (ed.), *Handbook on Organizations* (Rand McNally 1965) 148–50.
[26] Black (n 18) 145.
[27] Monica A. Zimmerman and Gerald J. Zeitz, 'Beyond Survival: Achieving New Venture Growth by Building Legitimacy' (2002) 27 *Academy of Management Review* 414–31, 414; Stinchcombe (n 25) 148–50.
[28] Ruth W. Grant and Robert O. Keohane, 'Accountability and Abuses of Power in World Politics' (2005) 99 *American Political Science Review* 29–43, 35.
[29] Black (n 18) 149; Bartley (n 4).
[30] Verbruggen and Havinga (n 9).
[31] Deephouse and Suchman (n 11) 54; Suchman (n 5).
[32] Black (n 18) 144.

accreditation bodies and certification bodies play a significant role in this process of legitimation. As we see below, the practices and process of legitimation involve different forms of interactions between GLOBALGAP and states, accreditation bodies and certification bodies such as enrolment, endorsement, collaboration, co-option and imitation. Furthermore, these interactions occur through informal mechanisms such as networks and markets, and also through formal mechanisms such as membership, legal contracts, referencing of normative output and memoranda of understanding (MOUs). In what follows I develop upon this discussion and examine the development and legitimation of GLOBALGAP. In so doing, I shed light on how interactions with states, accreditation bodies and certification bodies shaped the organization's governance activities of agenda setting and rule making, adoption and implementation, monitoring, enforcement, and evaluation and review.

3. THE STATE

The emergence of non-state regulatory organizations has not led to the demise of the state.[33] As Bernstein notes: 'the deep structure of the system remains the norms that have legitimated the sovereign authority of states. Governance rooted in sovereign state authority remains the privileged form of legitimate global governance.'[34] The important point here is not that non-state regulatory organizations cannot achieve legitimacy in the absence of delegated state authority, but rather that state authority has a privileged position in the regulation of food safety and quality. As we will see below, the legitimacy afforded to states can also empower non-state regulatory organizations that enrol states and draw upon states' principles and procedures developed to build and legitimate their structures, practices and processes. This section outlines how GLOBALGAP has drawn upon international standards developed by state actors to legitimate its standard-setting and implementation procedures, and also sought the support and endorsement of state actors in order to build its legitimacy.

---

[33] Bartley (n 4) 310; Marie-Laure Djelic and Kerstin Sahlin-Anderson, 'Introduction: A World of Governance: The Rise of Transnational Regulation' in Marie-Laure Djelic and Kerstin Sahlin-Anderson (eds), *Transnational Governance: Institutional Dynamics of Regulation* (Cambridge University Press 2006) 388.

[34] Bernstein (n 16) 25.

3.1 Drawing on International Standards of Implementation

In an evaluation of the history of GLOBALGAP, Nigel Garbutt (the then GLOBALGAP Chairman) noted that after GLOBALGAP was launched in 1997, one challenge that arose was how to 'operate a robust certification system on a global level' as '[t]here wasn't a model you could take off the shelf for this and we had to learn as we went along'.[35] However, international standards for verification, developed by state actors, provided the building blocks with which GLOBALGAP sought to develop and legitimate its system of implementation. Indeed, as Meyer and Rowan have observed, the 'building blocks for organizations come to be littered around the societal landscape; it only takes a little entrepreneurial energy to assemble them into a structure'.[36]

GLOBALGAP drew upon internationally recognized models of verification already in existence to build and legitimate its system of implementation. The then newly published ISO Guide 65: *General Requirements for Bodies Operating Certification Systems* provided an important international normative document on which to base the foundations of the verification system. Following GLOBALGAP's decision to base its implementation on third-party certification, a GLOBALGAP representative noted that conformance with internationally recognized norms of verification would ensure the integrity and robustness of the system of implementation.[37] Furthermore, GLOBALGAP representatives stressed that meeting 'the exacting requirements of International Accreditation Norms' was a significant development to ensure the 'integrity and credibility' of the regulatory system and that '[t]he key to all stakeholder and government recognition of . . . schemes is an ISO accreditation'.[38]

---

[35] EUREPGAP, 'EUREPGAP Global Report 2005' (FoodPLUS GmbH, 2005), accessed 25 November 2016 at www2.globalgap.org/documents/webdocs/E-book-Globalreport.pdf.

[36] John Meyer and Brian Rowan, 'Institutionalized Organizations: Formal Structure as Myth and Ceremony' (1977) 83 *American Journal of Sociology* 340–63, 345.

[37] Nigel Garbutt, 'Integrity and Transparency' in Kristian Möller (ed.), *EUREPGAP Implementation 2000 Plus* (EHI EuroHandelsinstitut Gmbh 2000) 5.

[38] EUREPGAP, 'Press Release: EUREPGAP Implementation 2000 Plus' Internet Archive 6 December 2000, accessed 25 November 2016 at http://web.archive.org/web/20010714220158/http://www.eurep.org/arbeitskreise/seiten/eurep-ak-eurep-pressconference2000.htm; Willem Hofmans and Nigel Garbutt (eds), *EUREPGAP: The Global Partnership for Safe and Sustainable Agriculture – Partnership 2001 Plus* (EUREPGAP c/o FoodPLUS GmbH 2001) 16.

Implementation of standards is one of the core activities of non-state regulatory organizations, and is a significant focus in terms of the legitimation of such organizations. Indeed, an interviewee who was a retailer representative on the GLOBALGAP board stressed the importance of having a robust and credible implementation system.[39] The interviewee noted that it was more important to have a weak standard and a robust enforcement regime, than a strong standard and a weak enforcement regime.[40] The discussion above showed how GLOBALGAP drew upon standards developed by state actors in order to legitimate its system of implementation, and indeed, respond to anticipated legitimacy demands made by state actors. As a consequence, we see the way in which state actors play a role in structuring the implementation systems of non-state regulatory organizations, and as such, the importance that the state plays in legitimating organizations such as GLOBALGAP.

3.2 Drawing on International Standards of Standard Setting

GLOBALGAP's standard setting has developed significantly since the inception of the organization in response to challenges to the legitimacy of the manner in which the organization developed its standards. Both civil society and state actors raised particular concerns relating to lack of transparency and participation in GLOBALGAP's standard-setting procedure. In addition, pressure also came from inside the organization by way of the concerns of retailers in relation to their engagement with an organization that was not participatory or transparent given Corporate Social Responsibility policies and commitments.[41] These pressures increased as GLOBALGAP expanded, with the result that the informal and opaque procedures that were suitable for the organization in its early years were no longer appropriate as the organization grew. In seeking to repair the legitimacy of its standard setting, GLOBALGAP sought to tap into the legitimacy afforded to states by drawing upon principles and practices of standard setting developed by state actors.

In 2008, GLOBALGAP published its Procedures for the Setting and Revision of GLOBALGAP Standards, which builds upon the 2007 revision process.[42] The new formalized standard-setting procedure sought

[39] Interview, *Informant 8*.

[40] ibid.

[41] Interview, *Informant 4*.

[42] GLOBALGAP, 'Procedures for the Setting and Revision of GLOBALGAP Standards', on file with author.

to address the criticisms noted above.[43] The procedure not only brims with principles and practices drawn from international guidelines and standards, but also explicitly aligns itself with the most widely diffused international standard-setting procedures. A GLOBALGAP representative highlighted that, in developing the new standard-setting procedure, 'a big concern was to make things transparent'.[44] In developing a formalized, documented and transparent standard-setting process, GLOBALGAP stressed that, '[t]his formal procedure will provide external and internal guidance and a level of openness and transparency to our standard development process, which is needed when operating on a global scale'.[45] The fourth revision process that began in February 2007 applied this new formalized standard-setting and revision procedure for the first time.[46]

In order to develop its new standard-setting procedure, GLOBALGAP surveyed model standard-setting procedures, and chose what were seen as the established procedures for setting standards in the area which represented what GLOBALGAP perceived as 'best practice'.[47] When formulating the standard-setting process, GLOBALGAP explicitly aligned the procedure with those standard-setting procedures found in international standards and guidelines, namely ISO Guide 59, the ISEAL *Code of Good Practice for Setting Social and Environmental Standards*, and the WTO TBT Agreement's *Code of Good Practice for the Preparation, Adoption and Application of Standards*.[48] Upon publication of the new standard-setting procedure, GLOBALGAP emphasized that the organization could now show that the process used to develop and revise GLOBALGAP's standards was 'based on' the standard-setting procedures developed by ISO, ISEAL and the WTO.[49]

It is clear that GLOBALGAP sought to legitimate its standard-setting procedure by borrowing from principles of standard setting contained in international guidelines and standards, and through communicating conformance with these guidelines and standards to stakeholders. An

---

43 Interview, *Informant 4*.

44 Interview, *Informant 2*.

45 GLOBALGAP (n 42).

46 GLOBALGAP also revised its revision period from every three years to every four years during Phase 3. GLOBALGAP, 'GLOBALGAP Revision – V4.0-Effective 2011: Press Release 30 May 2008' Internet Archive 20 December 2008, accessed 25 November 2016 at http://web.archive.org/web/20120813035528/http://www.globalgap.org/cms/upload/Documents/Press_releases/Press_releases_2008/GLOBALGAP_Revision_V4.0_2011_eng.pdf.

47 Interview, *Informant 6*; Interview, *Informant 2*.

48 GLOBALGAP (n 42).

49 GLOBALGAP (n 42).

interviewee highlighted that the TBT Code of Good Practice and ISO Guide 59 'are now almost given' and that GLOBALGAP 'recognised that these should be the procedures'.[50] The perceived taken-for-granted nature of these international guidelines and standards indicates the legitimacy and authority conferred upon procedures developed by states and their delegated entities. GLOBALGAP's normative borrowing from, and reliance placed upon, principles of standard setting and implementation developed by states and their delegated entities once again shines a light on the role played by state actors in structuring and legitimating non-state regulatory organizations.

3.3 Informing, Converting and Endorsement by State Actors

A key aspect of the governance of non-state regulatory organizations is how such organizations interact with their environment. Once established, GLOBALGAP began to engage and communicate with civil society and state actors in order to gain broader support for the organization. In order to gain such support, GLOBALGAP engaged in strategies of seeking to convert and inform actors. Initially, GLOBALGAP targeted these strategies at supply-chain actors and rule intermediary organizations such as certification bodies and accreditation bodies.[51] From 2001 onwards, GLOBALGAP escalated its strategies of converting and informing state actors through communication and the creation of organizational linkages.

Some scholars have argued that 'systematic cooperation and consultation with other relevant governing entities in order to mitigate negative interferences is not something that GLOBALGAP is endeavouring in a systematic fashion'.[52] However, an interviewee stated that GLOBALGAP has a distinct strategy to 'find interfaces' with international organizations.[53] GLOBALGAP's annual conference was one of the key mechanisms by which the organization sought to create linkages with state actors and from 2001 onwards, GLOBALGAP invited and sought endorsement from significant state actors. For example, David Byrne,

---

[50] Interview, *Informant 3*.

[51] EUREP, 'EUREPGAP Verification 2000 Official Launch Conference: List of Represented Countries and Companies' Internet Archive 12 February 2001, accessed 25 November 2016 at http://web.archive.org/web/20010212101438/http://www.eurep.org/arbeitskreise/seiten/eurep-ak-eurep-Part_Org.htm.

[52] Nicolas Hachez and Jan Wouters, 'A Glimpse at the Democratic Legitimacy of Private Standards – Democratic Legitimacy as Public Accountability: The Case of GLOBALG.A.P.' (2011) 17 *Journal of International Economic Law* 677–710, 705.

[53] Interview, *Informant 2*.

the then European Commissioner for Health and Consumer Protection, gave a video address at the 2003 GLOBALGAP conference held in Madrid.[54] GLOBALGAP placed a huge amount of significance on the apparent endorsement from the European Commission.[55] Furthermore, from 2004 to 2006, GLOBALGAP engaged in UNCTAD's Consultative Taskforce on Environmental Requirements and Market Access for Developing Countries (CTF).[56] Following the creation of such linkages with UNCTAD, GLOBALGAP attended a workshop at the fringes of the WTO SPS Committee meeting held in October 2006 to address the concerns of states, to 'raise awareness of GLOBALGAP' and to explain 'to the international organisations what the benefits of GLOBALGAP were'.[57] The ability to inform organizations about GLOBALGAP was a critical tool to build awareness of the organization and respond to concerns raised in outside forums. The importance of these types of legitimation strategies for building support was highlighted by a European Commission representative who noted that GLOBALGAP could have ignored the concerns raised at the SPS Committee, but 'for their own reasons they have been open, transparent and cooperative and you must give them credit for this'.[58]

The question remains as to why GLOBALGAP engaged in such informing and converting strategies. It has been observed that non-state regulatory organizations must seek to engage with 'stakeholders in the environment, including a number of strong, high profile actors that grant *moral* legitimacy, *market* legitimacy, *democratic* legitimacy, or *cognitive* legitimacy and authority to the standard setting'.[59] It is clear

---

[54] Nicolien van der Grijp, Terry Marsden and Josefa Salete Barbosa Cavalvanti, 'European Retailers as Agents of Change Towards Sustainability: The Case of Fruit Production in Brazil' (2005) 2 *Environmental Sciences* 31–46, 43.

[55] EUREPGAP, 'EurepGAP Protocols Wins Support from EU Commissioner: Press Statement 28 October 2003' Internet Archive 6 November 2003, accessed 25 November 2016 at http://web.archive.org/web/20040215131700/http://www.eurep.org/sites/index_e.html; EUREPGAP, 'Madrid Conference Integrated Farm Assurance Report November 2003', accessed 25 November 2016 at http://www2.globalgap.org/documents/webdocs/Newsletter_IFA_November_2003.pdf.

[56] For a list of meetings, and documents relating to these meetings see: UNCTAD, 'Consultative Task Force on Environmental Requirements and Market Access for Developing Countries', accessed 25 November 2016 at http://unctad.org/en/Pages/DITC/Trade-and-Environment.aspx.

[57] Interview, *Informant 2*.

[58] Interview, *Informant 7*.

[59] Kristina Tamm Hallström and Magnus Boström, *Transnational Multi-Stakeholder Standardization: Organizing Fragile Non-State Authority* (Edward Elgar 2010) 146–7.

that GLOBALGAP recognized the importance of engaging in informing strategies that seek to target actors that might grant support for the organization if they were aware of GLOBALGAP's activities, objectives and accomplishments.[60] In building organizational linkages like those with state actors such as the European Commission and UNCTAD, GLOBALGAP sought to not only build support from these actors, but also to gain endorsement for the activities of the organization. An interviewee highlighted that endorsements from state actors and the creation of linkages with state actors was particularly important for GLOBALGAP's acceptance from the retail, producer and suppliers members of GLOBALGAP.[61] The interviewee noted that the willingness of organizations such as the FDA and the European Commission to endorse the activities of GLOBALGAP conferred credibility upon the organization.[62] Furthermore, a GLOBALGAP representative noted that these apparent endorsements had led to greater acceptance of GLOBALGAP in the past, and that the organization would continue to seek to strengthen these relationships in the future.[63] Once again, we begin to see the importance of the state in legitimating non-state regulatory organizations. As a representative from the European Commission noted, GLOBALGAP 'do not need us to be attacking them, or calling into question the quality of their work because, obviously, that is going to have a knock on effect on their credibility and the value of what they do'.[64] Indeed, the above examination spotlights the importance of states as 'sponsors of institutional projects and key sources of institutional endorsement' for non-state regulatory organizations such as GLOBALGAP.[65]

The discussion above has highlighted how state actors play a particularly important role in legitimating non-state regulatory organizations. State actors are significant for the legitimation of non-state regulatory organizations such as GLOBALGAP due to the power of their support and endorsements, and by providing standards and guidelines with which non-state regulatory organizations use as building blocks for their structures, practices and processes. The authority conferred upon state norms and endorsements ensures that the state, at different levels, remains a powerful actor that possesses at least the potential to

[60] Tommy Leighton, 'EurepGAP Makes its Voice Heard' [2003] *Fresh Produce Journal*; Cashore, Auld and Newsom (n 18) 34.
[61] Interview, *Informant 6*.
[62] Interview, *Informant 6*.
[63] Interview, *Informant 6*.
[64] Interview, *Informant 7*.
[65] Bartley (n 4) 310.

dictate the structures, practices and processes of non-state regulatory organizations.[66]

4. THE TRIPARTITE STANDARDS REGIME

While the role of the state has received much attention by regulatory governance scholarship, most literature related to private standard setting does 'not pay acute attention to the interdependent dynamics of certification and accreditation actors and activities'.[67] The legitimacy afforded to accreditation and certification bodies springs in part from the legitimacy that is increasingly afforded to science and expert knowledge and practice as certification and accreditation are carried out by trained professional experts and 'consist of clearly defined rules and procedures that are based on scientific practices and norms' that seek to remove value or political judgements from their operation.[68] As Drori and Meyer observe, one of the most 'striking feature[s] of contemporary society is that science speaks with highly legitimate authority on the widest range of questions'.[69] The expanded authority of science and expertise provides the opportunity for the emergence of various forms of regulatory organizations to base their legitimacy by reference to science and expertise.[70] Accreditation and certification also have a perceived 'character as independent and objective' that is necessary for a credible system of implementation.[71] These factors

---

66 Djelic and Sahlin-Anderson (n 33) 388.

67 Fouilleux and Loconto (n 7).

68 Maki Hatanaka, 'Assessing Rule-Based Governance Mechanisms in an Era of Scientism' (141) 25 *Journal of Rural Social Sciences* 141–59, 154. Maki Hatanaka, Carmen Bain and Lawrence Busch, 'Third Party Certification in the Global Agrifood System' (2005) 30 *Food Policy* 354–69. Bob Tanner, 'Independent Assessment by Third-Party Certification Bodies' (2000) 11 *Food Control* 415–17; Carmen Bain, James B. Deaton and Lawrence Busch, 'Reshaping the Agri-Food System: The Role of Standards, Standard Makers and Third Party Certifiers' in Vaughan Higgins and Geoffrey Lawrence (eds), *Agricultural Governance: Globalization and the New Politics of Regulation* (Routledge 2005). Maki Hatanaka and Lawrence Busch, 'Third-Party Certification in the Global Agrifood System: An Objective or Socially Mediated Governance Mechanism?' (2008) 48 *Sociologia Ruralis* 73–91.

69 Gili Drori and John Meyer, 'Scientization: Making the World Safe for Organization' in Marie-Laure Djelic and Kerstin Sahlin-Anderson (eds), *Transnational Governance: Institutional Dynamics of Regulation* (Cambridge University Press 2006) 40.

70 Djelic and Sahlin-Anderson (n 33) 24.

71 Hatanaka, Bain and Busch (n 68); See ISEAL Alliance, 'Factors

drive non-state standard-setting organizations to enrol in what has been conceptualized as the 'tripartite standards regime' comprising standard-setting organizations, certification bodies and accreditation bodies in their search for legitimacy.[72] As a result, accreditation and certification bodies become significant legitimacy communities for non-state standard-setting organizations such as GLOBALGAP. Furthermore, accreditation and certification bodies act as carriers for international standards that non-state regulatory organizations rely on to legitimate both their processes of implementation and standard setting, while accreditation bodies also ensure the continued integrity of non-state regulators systems of implementation.

4.1 Endorsement and Enrolment in the Tripartite Standards Regime

From its inception, GLOBALGAP recognized that third-party verification was critical to the legitimacy of the organization. In early field trials, it became evident that independent verification was the most effective way to implement the GLOBALGAP protocol.[73] More importantly, however, GLOBALGAP's founding members' experience in the United Kingdom's 'Assured Produced' scheme led to an understanding that 'an independent verification system is an essential part of any credible and transparent assurance scheme. Experience shows that consumers and opinion formers place little reliance on self-regulation.'[74] Although GLOBALGAP initially proposed to implement its standards through either inspection or certification, demands from accreditation bodies moved GLOBALGAP to rely upon accredited third-party certification based upon international norms.[75] At a meeting in Stockholm on 28–29

Contributing to the Credibility of Social and Environmental Standards: ISEAL Survey Results Summary' (ISEAL Alliance, 2007), accessed 25 November 2016 at http://www.isealalliance.org/sites/default/files/R084_ISEAL_Standards_Survey_SummaryReportFINAL.pdf. The survey found that the need for verification of standards to be carried out by an actor independent from the standard setter as the eighth most important criteria in whether or not a standard was evaluated as credible.

[72] Loconto and Busch (n 8) 508.

[73] Nigel Garbutt and Kristian Möller, 'Pathway to Independent Verification' in Kristian Möller (ed.), *EUREPGAP Verification 2000* (EHI EuroHandelsinstitut Gmbh 1999) 32.

[74] Christopher Wise, 'The NFU-Retailer Partnership's "Assured Produce" Scheme' in Kristian Möller (ed.), *Integrated Production of Fruit and Vegetables* (EHI EuroHandelsinstitut Gmbh 1998) 96; Garbutt and Möller (n 73) 32.

[75] Garbutt and Möller (n 73) 33.

June 2000, following recommendations from accreditation bodies, the retail membership of GLOBALGAP took the decision that accredited third-party certification would be required for all grower options.[76] With this, we see GLOBALGAP seeking to enrol in the tripartite regulatory standards regime, in which both certification bodies and accreditation bodies are significant legitimacy communities.

In seeking to enrol in the tripartite standards regimes, GLOBALGAP representatives recognized the importance of accreditation bodies' acceptance and endorsement of its system of implementation. A GLOBALGAP representative noted that '[t]he retailers put a high preference on having a good start of the implementation rather than one that has no backing from *official sides like accreditation bodies*'.[77] This statement shines a light on why GLOBALGAP perceived accreditation body support and endorsement as critical for the legitimacy of the organization. Representatives clearly thought that accredited third-party certification was necessary for a robust system of implementation, the integrity of which stakeholders would more readily accept. Interestingly, however, reference to accreditation bodies as 'official' hints at the public nature of accreditation in many countries within the European Union.[78] Furthermore, in the context of standard setting, it was also vital that GLOBALGAP received endorsement of its standard from the European Co-operation for Accreditation (EA). EA's endorsement was necessary to allow its members to accredit certification bodies to EN45011/ISO Guide 65 and the GLOBALGAP normative document. Two weeks after the GLOBALGAP's first Technical and Standards Committee meeting in March 2001, GLOBALGAP announced that the members of the EA, the then newly formed representative and governing body of EU accreditation bodies, had accepted the first GLOBALGAP standard for accreditation.

The demand for GLOBALGAP to base its system of implementation on internationally accepted norms and practices discussed above also explicitly came from national accreditation bodies' oversight organizations.[79] In

---

[76] Kristian Möller, 'EUREP Info E-Mail 02/2000' Internet Archive, 24 April 2001, accessed 25 November 2016 at http://web.archive.org/web/20010424175559/http://www.eurep.org/arbeitskreise/seiten/eurep-info-email-2-2000.htm.

[77] ibid.

[78] Loconto and Busch (n 8); See Regulation (EC) 765/2008 of the European Parliament and of the Council of 9 July 2008 setting out the requirements for accreditation and market surveillance relating to the marketing of products and repealing Regulation (EEC) 339/93 [2008] OJ L218 Article 4.5 and Article 14.

[79] European Co-operation for Accreditation, 'EA Annual Report 2000' EA-01/03E, 4, accessed 25 November 2016 at http://web.archive.org/web/20041111023240/http://www.european-accreditation.org/pdf/EA-01-03erev00.pdf.

2000, the EA noted that it had received a request from GLOBALGAP for endorsement of its system of implementation, and that in order to provide such an endorsement GLOBALGAP would have to develop an implementation system accredited to international standards.[80] Consequently, we see the important role played by accreditation bodies as carriers of international norms and models for the implementation of standards. As we will see below, GLOBALGAP's conformance to the accreditation bodies' demands highlights the ability of accreditation bodies not only to determine the scope of the GLOBALGAP method of implementation, but also the organization's standard.

Prior to endorsement, GLOBALGAP had to conform to demands made by certification bodies and the EA that the content and the structure of the standard complied with ISO Guide 7, and was certifiable to ISO Guide 65. At a meeting held in May 2000 in Cologne, associate members of GLOBALGAP created the first draft of the compliance criteria taking into account changes that accreditations bodies had demanded prior to them endorsing the GLOBALGAP standard.[81] At the second GLOBALGAP conference held in Barcelona in October 2000, GLOBALGAP presented the draft GLOBALGAP standard, which comprised the normative documents that conformed to ISO/IEC Guide 7:1994 *Guidelines for drafting of standards suitable for use for conformity assessment*.[82] In light of the requirements from certification bodies and accreditation bodies, the GLOBALGAP normative documents evolved from the initial protocol and checklist, to a document that also contained Control Points and Compliance Criteria as a reference for interpretation, and General Regulations that set out the rules for certification bodies.[83]

The above discussion highlighted the importance of GLOBALGAP gaining endorsement of its system of implementation and standard from certification bodies and accreditation bodies for the legitimacy of its regulatory system. In so doing, the emergence of the 'tripartite standards regime' comprising standard-setting organizations, certification bodies and accreditation bodies comes into focus. More importantly for the

---

80 ibid.

81 Möller (n 76).

82 Kristian Möller (ed.) *EUREPGAP Implementation 2000 Plus* (EHI EuroHandelsinstitut Gmbh 2000); Kristian Möller, 'EUREP Info E-Mail 3/2000' Internet Archive, 29 April 2001, accessed 25 November 2016 at http://web.archive.org/web/20010129112100/http://www.eurep.org/arbeitskreise/seiten/eurep-ak-eurep-newsletter.htm; ISO, ISO/IEC Guide 7: Guidelines for Drafting of Standards Suitable for use for Conformity Assessment (ISO 1994).

83 Möller (n 82).

purpose of this study, however, is the extent to which non-state regulatory organizations such as GLOBALGAP seek to rely on these organizations to legitimate their standard-setting and implementation activities. In seeking endorsement from certification bodies and accreditation bodies, GLOBALGAP conformed to demands from these organizations to structure its system of implementation and standards document in conformance with international standards developed by state actors. With this, we begin to see the important role that accreditation bodies, and international standards transmitted through rule intermediaries, play in the process of standard development and implementation.

4.2 Ensuring Continued Integrity

Market credibility provides much of GLOBALGAP's legitimacy, which in turn is reliant upon the integrity and robustness of its system of implementation. As I discussed above, during the initial development of GLOBALGAP retailers recognized that some form of accredited third-party verification was essential for the credibility of its system of implementation.[84] However, as GLOBALGAP expanded both geographically and in size, accredited third-party verification proved insufficient to ensure acceptance of the monitoring and enforcement of the GLOBALGAP standard by key stakeholders, in particular retailers.[85] An interviewee noted that GLOBALGAP had moved 'into different regions where accreditation had different levels, and where accreditation bodies were not working on the same level'.[86] A producer representative highlighted that there were many concerns expressed within GLOBALGAP in relation to the auditing practices of many certifiers, particularly in Asia.[87] Indeed, GLOBALGAP could not rely upon the initial system of implementation to ensure the integrity of the system, and thus the support of market actors.[88] Challenges to the system of implementation had an effect on the credibility of the entire regulatory process.[89]

One of GLOBALGAP's key responses to criticisms relating to inconsistencies in certification bodies' practices was closer cooperation with the EA and the International Accreditation Forum (IAF). In developing

---

84 Garbutt and Möller (n 73) 32.
85 Interview, *Informant 1*; ISO, ISO/IEC Guide 65: General Requirements for Bodies Operating Product Certification Systems (ISO 1996).
86 Interview, *Informant 3*.
87 Interview, *Informant 1*.
88 Interview, *Informant 2*.
89 Interview, *Informant 1*.

cooperation agreements with the EA and the IAF through Memoranda of Understanding (MoU), GLOBALGAP began a process of addressing threats to the integrity of its implementation system brought about by inconsistencies in the accreditation of certification bodies. In 2005, the EA confirmed that a 'draft MoU with EUREPGAP was presented to the General Assembly. It is a response to EUREPGAP concern that accreditation practices within their scheme need harmonization.'[90] Following the letter of application in 2005, GLOBALGAP signed a MoU with the IAF in 2006. The MoU between GLOBALGAP and the IAF noted that GLOBALGAP had detected inconsistencies in the interpretation of its rules by accreditation bodies, and 'that this could be solved by better communication between EurepGAP and the Abs'.[91] With these two MoUs, GLOBALGAP began to take a more active role in managing relations within the 'tripartite standards regime' in order to ensure the integrity of its regulatory system.[92]

GLOBALGAP's response to the challenges to the integrity of the system of implementation highlights the iterative nature of legitimacy management. While GLOBALGAP was assured that accredited third-party certification was the key to the integrity of its regulatory system, and therefore to broad acceptance of the organization, it was required to develop not just centralized oversight mechanisms for certification bodies, but also closer cooperation with those organizations that provide the oversight of accreditation bodies.[93] As Gustafsson and Tamm Hallström note, certification 'is, however, in itself a business area and as such, it is also organized according to a market logic. This logic may result in the type of perversions and trust issues that the certification operations are thought to prevent.'[94] In guarding against the 'perversions' of the 'certification market', we once again observe the significant role that accreditation bodies and their oversight organizations (the EA and the IAF) play

[90] European Co-operation for Accreditation, 'EA Update, June 2005' Internet Archive 4 September 2012, accessed 25 November 2016 at http://web.archive.org/web/20111110051107/http://www.european-accreditation.org/content/communication/EA_Updates/update_June_2005.pdf; EUREPGAP (n 35).

[91] EUREPGAP/IAF, 'Memorandum of Understanding between FoodPLUS GmbH and the International Accreditation Forum' 2 June 2006, on file with the author.

[92] Loconto and Busch (n 8) 508.

[93] See Hofmans and Garbutt (n 38) 16.

[94] Ingrid Gustafsson and Kristina Tamm Hallström, 'The Certification Paradox: Monitoring as a Solution and a Problem' in Marta Reuter, Filip Wijkström and Bengt Kristensson Uggla (eds), *Trust and Organizations Confidence Across Borders* (Palgrave 2013) 99.

in ensuring the integrity of non-state regulatory organizations that seek to legitimate their systems of implementation through the 'tripartite standards regime'.[95]

While the role of accreditation and certification bodies has received relatively little attention in terms of the role they play in legitimating non-state regulatory organizations, the examination above highlighted the significance of such organizations for the creation and maintenance of the legitimacy of non-state standard-setting organizations. GLOBALGAP sought to enrol in the tripartite standards regime of standard-setting organizations, certification bodies and accreditation bodies in order to legitimate the organization in its early years and continued to rely on these actors for its continued legitimacy. Further, accreditation bodies also act as carriers of international standards developed by state actors which non-state standard-setting organizations draw upon in order to legitimate their systems of implementation and standard setting.

5. CONCLUSION

This chapter has sought to link the concepts and practice of legitimacy and legitimation with the central focus of this collection, hybridization. As such, this chapter contributes to not only existing discussions of the hybridization of food governance, but also our understanding of how non-state regulatory organizations seek to legitimate their structures, practices and processes. The practices of non-state standard-setting organizations, state actors, accreditation bodies and certification bodies contribute to the continued hybridization of contemporary food governance. Legitimacy is a key driver for the interaction between these key actors in hybrid food governance regimes. The legitimation dynamics of GLOBALGAP shed light upon the role that the state, accreditation bodies and certification bodies play in structuring non-state regulatory organizations and the central questions posed by this collection in relation to the hybridization of food governance.

The emergence of non-state regulatory organizations challenges the role that the state plays in governance at the national, international and transnational level. This chapter provides strong evidence that despite suggestions to the contrary, states and their delegated entities are a significant

---

95 Loconto and Busch (n 8) 508.

legitimacy community to non-state regulatory organizations.[96] In the discussions above, I have outlined that throughout GLOBALGAP's existence, the organization has recognized the importance and positive impact of state endorsement of their activities, and actively sought out state support. In seeking endorsements from state actors, GLOBALGAP has attempted to draw upon the legitimacy and authority conferred up states and their delegated entities in the policy sphere of food safety and quality.[97] As Djelic and Sahlin-Anderson remind us, 'endorsement by states and/or administrative units gives much greater clout and strength to a set of rules'.[98]

This chapter has also highlighted the important role played by certification bodies and accreditation bodies in GLOBALGAP's process of legitimation. For non-state regulatory organizations that seek to legitimate their system of implementation based upon third-party certification, accreditation bodies provide a key source of legitimacy through enhancing an organization's credibility. Furthermore, one of the key roles of accreditation bodies 'is to legitimate standards and certification'.[99] Through enrolling in the tripartite standards regime, certification bodies and accreditation bodies became significant legitimacy communities for GLOBALGAP. While these organizations are largely invisible in terms of the role they play in the legitimation of non-state regulatory organizations, they are significant in conferring credibility upon non-state standard-setting organizations.

I suggest that importance of states, their delegated entities and accreditation bodies lies in the complimentary role these actors play as creators and carriers of the building blocks upon which non-state regulatory organizations seek to construct legitimate regulatory systems. States and their delegated entities have created international guidelines and standards that seek to provide blueprints to build the governance, standard-setting and implementation systems of regulatory organizations. The legitimacy afforded to state actors carries over to the norms they produce. As

---

[96] See Stefano Ponte, Peter Gibbon and Jakob Vestergaard, 'Governing Through Standards: Introduction' in Stefano Ponte, Peter Gibbon and Jakob Vestergaard (eds), *Governing Through Standards: Origins, Drivers and Limitations* (Palgrave 2011) 6–7.

[97] See Marie-Laure Djelic and Kerstin Sahlin-Anderson, 'Institutional Dynamics in a Re-Ordering World' in Djelic and Sahlin-Anderson (eds), *Transnational Governance: Institutional Dynamics of Regulation* (Cambridge University Press 2006) 388; Bartley (n 4) 310.

[98] Djelic and Sahlin-Anderson (n 97) 388.

[99] Fouilleux and Loconto (n 7).

GLOBALGAP sought to legitimate its standard-setting procedures and its system of implementation, it turned to the international standards and guidelines developed by states and their delegated entities as a means to gain acceptance from market, state and civil society actors. In addition, this chapter has offered clear evidence that accreditation bodies acted as carriers for these international guidelines and standards, and sought to embed these models within GLOBALGAP during its establishment.

3 Resolving gaps in third-party certification for food safety hybridization

Elena Fagotto

1. INTRODUCTION

Delivering safe foods to consumers is a shared responsibility of the public and private sectors. Governments and food safety authorities design and implement safety regulations applying to the foods produced and commercialized in each country. But in recent decades, the private sector has expanded its regulatory function by introducing a variety of food safety standards imposing hygiene and management requirements on the industry. These private standards apply to supply chains that transcend national boundaries and are a quasi-mandatory requirement that buyers impose on their suppliers, constituting an example of transnational private regulation.[1] Buyers' demand has been the most significant driver for the adoption of private standards.[2] As a matter of fact, proof of certification is a strict contractual requirement for most large retailers and manufacturers who strive to control product safety and quality across complex and global supply chains.[3] Private food safety schemes are monitored and enforced by third-party certification bodies that conduct periodic audits on facilities and issue certificates signaling compliance with private regulation.

Public regulators are looking with interest at private regulation to avoid

---

[1] Cafaggi, F. (2011). 'New Foundations of Transnational Private Regulation' *Journal of Law and Society* **38**(1): 20–49, Curtin, D. and L. Senden (2011). 'Public Accountability of Transnational Private Regulation: Chimera or Reality?' *Journal of Law and Society* **38**(1): 163–88, Verbruggen, P. (2014). *Enforcing Transnational Private Regulation. A Comparative Analysis of Advertising and Food Safety* (Edward Elgar).

[2] Accessed 25 November 2016 at http://www.mygfsi.com/files/Information_Kit/Diversey_GFSI_Efficacy_Study_Results.pdf.

[3] Cafaggi, F. (2013). 'The Regulatory Functions of Transnational Commercial Contracts: New Architectures.' *Fordham International Law Journal* **36**: 1557.

duplication and to deliver safety in arenas where government regulation is still lagging behind. Indeed, multiple hybrid forms of governance are emerging where public functions are carried out by private actors or where governments validate private initiatives.[4] In some countries, including Canada and the United States, regulators have delegated some enforcement functions to third-party certifiers and more regulators are exploring ways to incorporate third-party certification into their toolkit.[5] Whereas private schemes may fill the gaps left by government, especially in the sphere of international food safety regulation, they also raise concerns when it comes to their monitoring and enforcement.[6] In light of this, can we really trust third-party certification to deliver a public good such as safe foods? The answer to this question is complex and critical given a growing trend of hybridization in food safety. This chapter builds on the analytic framework elaborated by Verbruggen and Havinga in the introduction to this edited volume and focuses on the actors (third-party certification bodies) that carry out the monitoring and enforcement of private standards. In doing so it delves on several dimensions of hybridization to understand how they may impact the ultimate objective of delivering safe foods to consumers. This chapter examines the motivations and drivers (also referred to as incentives) of third-party certification bodies and advances several theoretical hypotheses on how these motivations may result in reduced food safety. The chapter also examines whether the meta-rules that the Global Food Safety Initiative (GFSI), the meta-regulator of private food safety schemes, imposes on its recognized schemes can rectify incentives and ensure reliable certification. This chapter identifies shortcomings and suggests ways to change the motivations and drivers of third-party certifiers to better align them with the goal of increased food safety. Its findings should interest not only the industry, who pays for and implements such sophisticated safety and quality controls, but also the public sector, who is increasingly looking at ways to leverage private food

---

4 See Chapter 9 by Havinga and Verbruggen in this edited volume.

5 Accessed 25 November 2016 at http://www.inspection.gc.ca/about-the-cfia/accountability/consultations/regulatory-risk-based-oversight/private-certification-policy/eng/1452808755126/1452808821799?chap=0; http://www.fda.gov/Food/GuidanceRegulation/FSMA/ucm361903.htm.

6 Albersmeier, F., H. Schulze, et al. (2009). 'The Reliability of Third-party Certification in the Food Chain: From Checklist to Risk Oriented Auditing.' *Food Control* **20**: 927–35, Fagotto, E. (2014). 'Private Roles in Food Safety Provision: The Law and Economics of Private Food Safety.' *European Journal of Law and Economics* **37**(1): 83–109, Lytton, T.D. and L.K. McAllister (2014). 'Oversight in Private Food Safety Auditing: Addressing Auditor Conflict of Interest.' *Wisconsin Law Review* **2014**(2): 289.

safety controls to target resources and avoid duplication. The chapter will unfold as follows. Section 2 will describe briefly private food safety standards and the role of third-party certification bodies. Section 3 will propose a theoretical framework to examine whether the motivations and drivers provided by the present institutional design of third-party certification result in adequate monitoring and enforcement, and ultimately food safety. Section 4 discusses the rules introduced by the GFSI to regulate the behavior of certification bodies and whether these rules correct some of the shortcomings identified in the theoretical framework. Section 5 will reflect on whether the GFSI framework addresses gaps in third-party enforcement. Section 6 will offer conclusive remarks.

2. PRIVATE STANDARDS AND THIRD-PARTY CERTIFICATION

Private food safety standards define the requirements that suppliers have to comply with in order to satisfy their buyers' demands for safety and quality. They are imposed by actors operating at the end of the chain (from manufacturers to retailers) on suppliers operating at previous steps of the chain.[7] Given the considerable power exercised by buyers at the end of the supply chain, the adoption of standards has been growing exponentially, with thousands of certified facilities spanning all continents.[8] Examples of private food safety standards include GLOBALG.A.P., FSSC22000, and the BRC Global Standard for Food Safety.[9]

Compliance is verified externally by third-party certification bodies (CBs) that conduct audits of facilities seeking certification. When a firm is found in compliance, the CB issues a certificate stating that a facility meets the requirements of a given standard. Not all certification bodies can certify against a standard. Each scheme-owner (the organization maintaining the standard) selects a list of certification bodies that are

[7] It should be noted that the scope of many standards is expanding to cover all steps in the supply chain, not only primary production and manufacturing, but also phases such as packaging, storage and distribution, with the objective of ensuring food safety 'from farm to fork'. accessed 30 November 2016 at http://www.mygfsi.com/files/Information_Kit/GFSI_GeneralPresentation_201611.pdf.

[8] For example, a list of over 10,000 facilities certified against the FSSC22000 standard can be obtained at https://viasyst.net/fssc accessed 25 November 2016.

[9] For a list of private food safety standards recognized by the GFSI, see http://www.mygfsi.com/schemes-certification/recognised-schemes.html accessed 25 November 2016.

approved to conduct audits and issue certificates against a specific standard.[10] Facilities enter a contract with the certification body they select and bear the financial costs of audits. Audit costs may vary, ranging from $1,000 to $10,000, according to a government report.[11] In the course of an audit, auditors evaluate production facilities, processes, and documentation and issue an audit report describing the results of the audit. Based on the audit report, the CB decides whether to warrant or not certification.

If the industry self-regulates to deliver safe foods to consumers, the government apparatus needed to ensure food safety (administrators, inspectors, research laboratories) could be significantly reduced to the benefit of taxpayers. As promising as this sounds, a more critical analysis of third-party certification shows evidence of limitations and invites a more cautious approach. There have been numerous cases where certified products were involved in major foodborne outbreaks. From Salmonella in peanuts produced by Peanut Corporation of America, a firm that had been found in compliance by private auditors, to certified cantaloupes spreading listeria, and organic certified fenugreek seeds from Egypt causing a major E. coli outbreak in northern Europe in the summer of 2011, the examples abound.[12] Increasingly, certification bodies are held accountable for failures in certification. In the cantaloupe listeria case, for example, auditors were sued for providing misleading advice and for certifying a facility that had several violations.[13] Private certification bodies have also been criticized for certifying the safety of unsound facilities that were soon after involved in the death of over a thousand workers manufacturing goods for major global retail chains.[14] This is not to imply that certification bodies should solely take the blame for these outbreaks and incidents. Surely, government inspections are not perfect either. Yet this evidence suggests that certifiers missed significant violations and passed

---

[10] For example, a list of approved certification bodies for the BRC Food Safety Standard can be found at https://www.brcdirectory.co.uk. Facilities seeking certification against the BRC standard can only hire a CB from that list; accessed 30 November 2016.

[11] Accessed 25 November 2016 at www.gao.gov/assets/650/649010.pdf at p. 23.

[12] http://www.cdc.gov/salmonella/2009/peanut-butter-2008-2009.html; http://www.fda.gov/Food/RecallsOutbreaksEmergencies/Outbreaks/ucm272372.htm accessed 25 November 2016. EFSA and ECDC (2011). 'European Union Summary Report on Trends and Sources of Zoonoses, Zoonotic Agents and Food-borne Outbreaks in 2009.' *EFSA Journal* **9**(3).

[13] http://www.foodsafetynews.com/2014/06/kroger-says-primus-has-primary-liability-for-deadly-outbreak/#.VtS-0ihgPzI accessed 25 November 2016.

[14] Short, J.L., M.W. Toffel, et al. (2015). 'Monitoring Global Supply Chains.' Working Paper. Harvard Business School.

deficient facilities. This evidence also compromises the credibility of certificates and suggests gaps in third-party monitoring and enforcement that deserve further attention. Let us now turn to the literature on third-party certification to identify possible inadequacies in the institutional design of such enforcement mechanism.

3. A THEORY OF THIRD-PARTY CERTIFICATION

Research on the role of private certification bodies in the food sector remains very limited and often lacks empirical evidence. Hatanaka et al. provide an overview of third-party certification and discuss the impact on producers in the developing world.[15] Since producers upstream hold more information on production practices and food safety than downstream buyers, food safety ends up being a credence attribute. This information asymmetry creates incentives for opportunistic behavior from those who operate upstream in the value chain. Third-party certification bodies can reduce the information gap between buyers and sellers by providing market signals of food quality and safety.[16] Others analyze certification mechanisms in the pork industry in Germany and find significant inconsistencies and variations across certification bodies, questioning the reliability of audits as an enforcement tool.[17] Third-party certification bodies appear to respond to multiple, at times conflicting, incentives: on the one hand they have to promote integrity and compliance with a certain standard to protect buyers and consumers, on the other they want to please the clients (the audited firms) that pay their fees and to which they are contractually bound.[18] Acquiring accounts and keeping their customer base is an important priority for food safety auditors.[19]

In order to construct a theoretical framework to analyze third-party certification, it is useful to incorporate more developed literatures in the fields

[15] Hatanaka, M., C. Bain, et al. (2005). 'Third-party Certification in the Global Agrifood System.' *Food Policy* **30**: 354–69.

[16] Deaton, B.J. (2004). 'A Theoretical Framework for Examining the Role of Third-party Certifiers.' *Food Control* **15**: 615–19.

[17] Albersmeier, F., H. Schulze, et al. (2009). 'The Reliability of Third-party Certification in the Food Chain: From Checklist to Risk Oriented Auditing.' *Food Control*. **20**: 927–35.

[18] Havinga, T. (2006). 'Private Regulation of Food Safety by Supermarkets.' *Law & Policy* **28**(4): 515–33.

[19] Lytton, T.D. and L.K. McAllister (2014). 'Oversight in Private Food Safety Auditing: Addressing Auditor Conflict of Interest.' *Wisconsin Law Review* **2014**(2): 289.

of financial auditing, as well as labor and environmental certification. This allows identifying four limitations in the institutional design of third-party auditing systems. Consider these in order.

3.1 Auditor Independence

When facilities seeking certification select and pay for their certification bodies, the auditor's impartiality and independence from the certified firm is at risk. In a comprehensive review of third-party certification, McAllister suggests that, because the company that is evaluated chooses the third-party certifier and pays for his service, verifiers are under pressure to please their client by issuing favorable audit results, putting auditors' independence at risk.[20] The fact that companies can shop around to select a favorable verifier only increases the pressure on auditors to provide positive audit results.[21] Empirical research shows that who pays for an audit does impact audit outcomes, and when audited facilities cover audit costs, audits yielded on average 8% fewer violations.[22] The same authors also found that repeat auditors (auditors who have audited the same facility multiple times) tend to be more lenient, suggesting that building a relationship between clients and auditors may be detrimental for auditors' independence and reflect negatively on audit results.[23] Kraakman suggests that wrongdoers can evade the controls of third-party monitors by trying to corrupt a certifier with whom they have close ties and by shopping for a lenient CB.[24] There may be limitations to third-party enforcement because firms tend to withhold information from outsiders and have incentives to renegotiate their contracts with third-parties who do not treat them favorably.[25] Recent research on third-party certification suggests that firms do shop around for certifiers according to their compliance preferences, with slackers opting for more lenient certifiers.[26] Other authors found that opportunistic manufacturers may opt for certification bodies

---

20 McAllister, L.K. (2012). 'Regulation by Third-Party Verification.' *Boston College Law Review* **53**(1): 1–64.

21 Ibid.

22 Short, J.L., M.W. Toffel, et al. (2015). 'Monitoring Global Supply Chains.' *Working Paper*. Harvard Business School.

23 Ibid.

24 Kraakman, R.H. (1986). 'Gatekeepers: The Anatomy of a Third-Party Enforcement Strategy.' *The Journal of Law, Economics & Organization* **2**(1): 53–104.

25 Arlen, J. and R.H. Kraakman (1997). 'Controlling Corporate Misconduct: An Analysis of Corporate Liability Regimes.' *NYU Law Review* **72**(1): 687–779.

26 Castka, P., D. Prajogo, et al. (2015). 'Understanding firms' selection of their

that assign more lenient grades.[27] A study on third-party auditors in India shows that when auditors are chosen and paid by audited firms, they are more likely to issue lenient reports about their clients.[28] Inevitably, the fact that business volume may depend on leniency is detrimental to auditor independence. Additionally, when auditing firms also provide consulting services, auditors may be under pressure to deliver favorable audit results for fear of losing clients not only for their audit business, but also for the consulting one.[29] In his research on forestry certification, Meidinger notes that certifiers are "placed in an inherently difficult position, since they are in effect public fiduciaries employed by the very private actors whose activities they are supposed to assess and monitor."[30]

The literature on financial auditors corroborates the doubts on auditor independence. Bazerman and co-authors describe several biases that get in the way of impartial financial audits.[31] First, auditors develop an *attachment bias* because they strive to remain in their client's good graces since "auditors are hired and fired by the companies they audit, and it is well known that client companies fire accounting firms that deliver unfavorable audits".[32] Second, a *familiarity bias* makes auditors more inclined to harm strangers than the clients with which they have ongoing ties (and who pay for the audit).[33] Finally, because of a *discounting bias*, individuals are much more responsive to immediate consequences than to delayed ones. This may lead auditors to discount the future negative consequences of a lenient audit (for example the harm to investors) and focus rather on the more immediate outcome of maintaining a good relationship with their client.[34] Prentice notes that auditors tend to behave in ways that best serve

---

ISO 9000 third-party certifiers.' *International Journal of Production Economics* **162**: 125–33.

27 Bar, T. and Y. Zheng (2015). 'Strategic Selection of Certifiers: Evidence from the BRC Food Safety Standard.' *Paper for the 2015 Agricultural & Applied Economics Association and Western Agricultural Economics Association Annual Meeting*. San Francisco, CA.

28 Duflo, E., M. Greenstone, et al. (2013). 'Truth-telling by third-party auditors and the response of polluting firms: experimental evidence from India.' *Quarterly Journal of Economics* **128**(4): 1499–545.

29 McAllister, L.K. (2012). 'Regulation by Third-Party Verification.' *Boston College Law Review* **53**(1): 1–64.

30 Meidinger, E.E. (2002). 'The New Environmental Law: Forest Certification.' Buff. Envt'l. L.J. **10**: 211, 283.

31 Bazerman, M.H., G. Loewenstein, et al. (2002). 'Why Good Accountants Do Bad Audits.' *Harvard Business Review* **November**: 97–102.

32 Ibid, 99.

33 Ibid.

34 Ibid.

their interests, a behavior known as "*self-serving bias*" and that objectivity and independence are hard to achieve when the auditor is compensated by the very firm that is being audited.[35] Shapiro highlights how financial auditors have a *conflicting mandate*: on the one hand they should candidly assess the financial statements of a corporation, which benefits the shareholders, on the other they are called to certify the information submitted by the corporation, which benefits the corporation.[36] This misalignment of incentives corrodes the authenticity of audits.[37]

3.2 Auditor Competence

An auditor may not be competent in all the areas covered by an audit and there have been instances where auditors who did not have specific knowledge of the product they were auditing issued inaccurate reports. Competence is crucial for audit reliability as well as to increase the comparability of audits and improve product information for buyers.[38] Research suggests that auditors may lack the competence necessary to carry out reliable audits, or may have knowledge in several areas of the audit, but not in all the domains that are being verified.[39] Audit quality and reliability depend on the skills of the auditor. Some auditors tend to focus on the "book-keeping" component of the audit, and may neglect more revealing information on food safety during their assessment of facilities.[40] In the egregious Salmonella outbreak involving peanuts, auditors were not even aware that peanuts were particularly susceptible to this type of contamination.[41] The food industry recognizes that limits in auditor competence can seriously undermine the reliability of the audit process and cast a negative

---

[35] Prentice, R.A. (2000). 'The SEC and MDP: Implications of the Self-Serving Bias for Independent Auditing.' *Ohio St. L.J.* **61**: 1597–664.

[36] Shapiro, A. (2005). 'Who Pays the Auditor Calls the Tune?: Auditing Regulation and Clients' Incentives.' *Seton Hall L. Rev* **35**: 1029–95.

[37] Ibid.

[38] Fagotto, E. (2014). 'Private Roles in Food Safety Provision: The Law and Economics of Private Food Safety.' *European Journal of Law and Economics* **37**(1): 83–109.

[39] McAllister, L.K. (2012). 'Regulation by Third-Party Verification.' *Boston College Law Review* **53**(1): 1–64.

[40] Albersmeier, F., H. Schulze, et al. (2009). 'The Reliability of Third-party Certification in the Food Chain: From Checklist to Risk Oriented Auditing.' *Food Control* **20**: 927–35, Albersmeier, F., H. Schulze, et al. (2010). 'System Dynamics in Food Quality Certifications: Development of an Audit Integrity System.' *Int. J. Food System Dynamics* 69–81.

[41] Powell, D., M.S. Erdozain, et al. (2013). 'Audits and Inspections Are Never Enough: A Critique to Enhance Food Safety.' *Food Control* **30**(2): 686–91.

shadow also on thorough and skilled auditors.[42] Research in the area of audits for labor and environmental standards seem to point to similar limitations. A report evaluating PricewaterhouseCoopers (PwC) auditing for labor standards compliance found significant competence flaws.[43] The author shadowed PwC auditors during their work in China and South Korea and observed that they failed to report major violations in labor law, such as overtime and wage laws, as well as violations in health and safety laws.[44] Prominent scholars of labor standards are doubtful that auditors are sophisticated enough to monitor compliance and provide valuable information in environments that are subject to constant change.[45] A recent study by Short and co-authors suggests that the level of education achieved by the auditor may not matter as much as the professional training received, and that audits conducted by better-trained auditors yielded a higher number of violations.[46]

3.3 Audit Design

Several characteristics in the way audits are designed may get in the way of delivering safe foods to consumers. First, audits are generally announced and scheduled in advance. This may represent an obstacle to their effectiveness. Announced audits may not paint a veridical picture of the routine conditions in a facility because facilities have the opportunity to prepare for the audit and modulate compliance according to the time of the audit.[47] Evidence suggests that auditees tend to clean up, fix operations, doctor their documentation and prepare workers in view of the scheduled audit, but after the audit conditions revert to normal.[48] Only the most

---

[42] www.mygfsi.com/news-resources/news/282-spotlight-on-auditor-competence.html accessed 25 November 2016.

[43] O'Rourke, D. (2000). 'Monitoring the Monitors: A Critique of PricewaterhouseCooper's Labor Monitoring.' White Paper, MIT.

[44] Ibid.

[45] Locke, R.M., M. Amengual, et al. (2009). 'Virtue out of Necessity? Compliance, Commitment, and the Improvement of Labor Conditions in Global Supply Chains.' *Politics Society* **37**: 319.

[46] Short, J.L., M.W. Toffel, et al. (2015). 'Monitoring Global Supply Chains.' Working Paper. Harvard Business School.

[47] Fagotto, E. (2014). 'Private Roles in Food Safety Provision: The Law and Economics of Private Food Safety.' *European Journal of Law and Economics* **37**(1): 83–109.

[48] Albersmeier, F., H. Schulze, et al. (2009). 'The Reliability of Third-party Certification in the Food Chain: From Checklist to Risk Oriented Auditing.' *Food Control* **20**: 927–35.

skilled and inquisitive auditors are able to detect whether a problem was fixed right before the audit, and if documents veridically reflect day-to-day operations of a firm, but most auditors tend to accept the information that is provided to them on the day of the audit.[49] The FDA recently incorporated third-party audits to improve the safety of imported foods, asking that audits be unannounced, which signals that announced audits are not deemed rigorous enough to verify compliance.[50] Research in the field of labor standards suggests that several standards have switched to unannounced audits, or a mix of announced and unannounced audits, to promote audit integrity.[51] Some research concludes that unannounced audits play a key role in ensuring the accountability of global labor standards.[52] It should also be noted, however, that recent empirical research on certification outside the food industry found that unannounced audits resulted in a higher number of violations, but that the difference with announced audits' results was not statistically significant.[53]

Second, audits may promote a "checklist mentality," creating incentives for auditors to tick all the boxes in their verification list, while missing more serious risk factors.[54] Research suggests that auditors may indeed *focus more on the management based component* of the audit, for example on document verification, than on the broader topic of compliance performance overall.[55] According to some, there is a disconnect between what audits actually provide, a snapshot in time, and what buyers think they provide, a full verification of products and processes.[56]

Third, during an audit, auditors interact mostly with higher-ranking

---

[49] Powell, D., M.S. Erdozain, et al. (2013). 'Audits and Inspections Are Never Enough: A Critique to Enhance Food Safety.' *Food Control*. **30**(2): 686–91.

[50] www.fda.gov/Food/GuidanceRegulation/FSMA/ucm361903.htm accessed 25 November 2016.

[51] O'Rourke, D. (2003). 'Outsourcing Regulation: Analyzing Nongovernmental Systems of Labor Standards and Monitoring.' *The Policy Studies Journal* **31**(1): 1–29.

[52] Calvo-Friedman, J. (2014). 'Increasing Quality and Accountability in Global Labor Monitoring.' *Georgetown Journal on Poverty Law and Policy* **21**(2): 289–315.

[53] Short, J.L., M.W. Toffel, et al. (2015). 'Monitoring Global Supply Chains.' Working Paper. Harvard Business School.

[54] Albersmeier, F., H. Schulze, et al. (2009). 'The Reliability of Third-party Certification in the Food Chain: From Checklist to Risk Oriented Auditing.' *Food Control* **20**: 927–35.

[55] McAllister, L.K. (2012). 'Regulation by Third-Party Verification.' *Boston College Law Review* **53**(1): 1–64.

[56] Powell, D., M.S. Erdozain, et al. (2013). 'Audits and Inspections Are Never Enough: A Critique to Enhance Food Safety.' *Food Control* **30**(2): 686–91.

employees, such as safety and quality managers, and rely on management to access and verify information. There is limited reliance on workers and other lower-ranking employees even though these are involved in day-to-day operations and may provide valuable information for the audit report.[57]

This passage by labor scholars sums up some of the limitations in audit design and stigmatizes how audits may merely increase bureaucracy rather than improve conditions:

> Auditors arrive with lengthy, detailed checklists aimed at exposing record-keeping lapses and easy-to-detect code violations rather than discovering the sources or root causes of these various workplace problems. Managers, in turn, learn to be inspected by better preparing (sometimes doctoring) their records and do the absolute minimum to remain within compliance of the buyers' codes of conduct. Rather than dedicating the time and resources to redress serious problems, these factory managers engage in a ritual of compliance while growing cynical and resentful, sometimes outright resistant to the audit process as a whole.[58]

3.4 Audit Transparency

Limited audit transparency may reduce the effectiveness of this instrument in achieving food safety. Audit results (generally collected in lengthy audit reports) belong to the audited facility, which in turn discloses them to an existing or prospective buyer. However audit information is not disclosed to regulators or to the general public. This lack of transparency on audit results perpetuates information asymmetries, because producers and auditors hold more information on product quality than regulators and consumers.[59] Given that food safety is a credence characteristic for consumers, having access to additional information on the foods they purchase could help them make more informed buying decisions.[60] In areas ranging from hospital quality

---

[57] O'Rourke, D. (2000). 'Monitoring the Monitors: A Critique of PricewaterhouseCooper's Labor Monitoring.' White Paper, MIT.

[58] Locke, R.M., M. Amengual, et al. (2009). 'Virtue out of Necessity? Compliance, Commitment, and the Improvement of Labor Conditions in Global Supply Chains.' *Politics Society* **37**: 319, 328.

[59] Deaton, B.J. (2004). 'A Theoretical Framework for Examining the Role of Third-party Certifiers.' *Food Control* **15**: 615–19.

[60] Fagotto, E. (2014). 'Private Roles in Food Safety Provision: The Law and Economics of Private Food Safety.' *European Journal of Law and Economics* **37**(1): 83–109.

disclosure to reporting of pollutant emissions, firms forced to become more transparent gained important information about their own performance, and that of their peers, and put in place improvement measures in response.[61] Lack of transparency over audit results undermines the food industry's ability to identify high-risk areas, or areas where compliance is low, and introduce corrective measures. This lack of information limits the government's ability to target enforcement efforts to high-risk industry areas. Lack of transparency over audit results is not limited to the food industry. Also private audits for labor standards are criticized for their lack of transparency and the resulting limited public scrutiny on audit results.[62] The literature points to private standards' lack of transparency to highlight the potential for capture in standard enforcement.[63] The more opaque the industry, the larger the information asymmetry between industry and consumers, and consequently the higher the risk that the private sector will act on its own interest when enforcing private rules.[64]

To conclude, a theoretical analysis of third-party certification in the food industry as well as in the fields of accounting, labor and environmental standards suggests that there are four limitations, which, if left unattended, may compromise the integrity and reliability of audits. These are: auditor independence (when auditors are selected and paid by auditees, auditors have higher incentives to please their clients), auditor competence (auditors sometimes lack the skills necessary to verify compliance), audit design (audits are scheduled in advance, which may increase the incentives to prepare for the audit, and they may also

---

[61] Weil, D., A. Fung, et al. (2006). 'The Effectiveness of Regulatory Disclosure Policies.' *Journal of Policy Analysis and Management* **25**(1): 155–81; Fung, A., M. Graham, et al. (2007). *Full Disclosure: The Perils and Promise of Transparency*. Cambridge University Press.

[62] Fung, A., D. O'Rourke, et al. (2001). *Can We Put an End to Sweatshops?* Beacon Press; O'Rourke, D. (2003). 'Outsourcing Regulation: Analyzing Nongovernmental Systems of Labor Standards and Monitoring.' *The Policy Studies Journal* **31**(1): 1–29.

[63] Konefal, J., M. Mascarenhas, et al. (2005). 'Governance in the Global Agro-food System: Backlighting the Role of Transnational Supermarket Chains.' *Agriculture and Human Values* **22**: 291–302; Fuchs, D., A. Kalfagianni, et al. (2009). 'Actors in Private Food Governance: The Legitimacy of Retail Standards and Multistakeholder Initiatives with Civil Society Participation.' *Agriculture and Human Values* DOI 10.1007/s10460-009-9236-3, Curtin, D. and L. Senden (2011). 'Public Accountability of Transnational Private Regulation: Chimera or Reality?' *Journal of Law and Society* **38**(1): 163–88.

[64] Mattli, W. and N. Woods (2009). *The Politics of Global Regulation*. Princeton University Press.

promote a checklist mentality), and audit transparency (audit results are confidential and are not disclosed with regulators or the general public). After having identified four limitations in the institutional design of third-party certification for food safety, let us now turn to the GFSI to understand whether its meta-regulatory framework mitigates such vulnerabilities in the food safety standards it recognizes and in what way.

4. GFSI AND THIRD-PARTY CERTIFICATION

Launched in 2001, the Global Food Safety Initiative is an effort by food industry leaders within the Consumer Goods Forum association to benchmark and harmonize *existing* private food safety standards. Private standards can be benchmarked and recognized by the GFSI when they meet the requirements set by the GFSI Guidance Document, an extensive set of *scheme management* and *food safety management* requisites developed by a coalition of retailers, manufacturers, safety schemes and third-party certifiers.[65] By following the same set of food safety as well as accreditation and management criteria, recognized standards are based on a common foundation which should deliver equivalent food safety results.[66] Through equivalence and convergence among food safety systems, the GFSI also aims to reduce redundancy and improve efficiency. Before the GFSI, producers had to comply with different standards for each of their buyers and undergo multiple audits every year, which increased compliance costs and caused "audit fatigue." Now they can choose any of the GFSI-recognized schemes and their product can be sold to buyers who accept GFSI, which should reduce the number of audits and compliance costs significantly and expand market access.[67] The GFSI recognizes over ten among the most widespread food safety standards.[68]

---

[65] The Guidance Document has been amended numerous times, the newest 7th edition was announced on 29 February 2016; accessed 25 November 2016 at http://www.mygfsi.com/news-resources/news/472-landmark-guidance-document-edition-7.html.

[66] GFSI Guidance Document. Sixth Edition, Issue 3, October 2013, 11.

[67] The GFSI also introduced new fixed costs, such as developing and maintaining the GFSI Guidance Document, conducting benchmarking activities, and maintaining the necessary organizational infrastructure.

[68] For an updated list of recognized standards, see http://www.mygfsi.com/schemes-certification/recognised-schemes.html accessed 25 November 2016.

Since the GFSI does not directly regulate food production, but rather sets a framework of rules for *existing* private standards, it can be considered an example of a private meta-regulatory system that "regulates the regulators."[69] An analysis of the GFSI is highly relevant because of how widespread and influential the rules designed by the GFSI are and because the requisites designed by the GFSI trickle down to all the standards that adhere to the initiative, shaping their delivery of food safety. To understand the breadth of the GFSI's reach, consider that its meta-rules trickle down to 77,000 factories and 150,000 farms worldwide.[70] Membership and sales volume of the Consumer Goods Forum, of which the GFSI is a pillar, may also be used as a proxy to understand the reach of GFSI. The Consumer Goods Forum is formed by circa 650 retailers, producers and food service providers across 70 countries and its aggregate annual sales total EUR 2.1 trillion.[71] Figure 3.1 illustrates how GFSI's meta-rules govern the schemes it recognizes and how the same rules influence certification bodies and certified sites.

Standards that wish to be GFSI-recognized submit a detailed application to the GFSI Benchmark Committee and must demonstrate that they abide by the GFSI benchmarking criteria. Standards need to show conformity with the GFSI Guidance Document Part II "Requirements for the Management of Schemes" and the relevant sections of GFSI Guidance Document Part III "Scheme Scope and Key Elements." The criteria contained in Part II pertain to scheme management and governance, as well as rules on accreditation and certification bodies. Those in Part III concern food safety good practices according to the scheme's scope as well as HACCP. In order to prove conformity, in their application scheme owners are required to submit a *clause-by-clause cross reference* illustrating how the scheme clauses comply with the clauses of the GFSI Guidance Document Parts II and III. Additionally, they need to submit documentation summarizing the scheme's objectives, food safety procedures as well as certification requirements.[72] Consider now how the GFSI addresses the four limitations identified in the previous section.

---

69 Verbruggen, P. and T. Havinga (2014). 'The Rise of Transnational Private Meta-Regulators.' Osgoode Hall Law School Working Paper Series.

70 http://www.mygfsi.com/files/Information_Kit/GFSI_Infographic_2016.pdf accessed 30 November 2016.

71 GFSI Guidance Document. Sixth Edition, Issue 3, October 2013, 79.

72 GFSI Guidance Document. Sixth Edition, Issue 3, June 2012. 20.

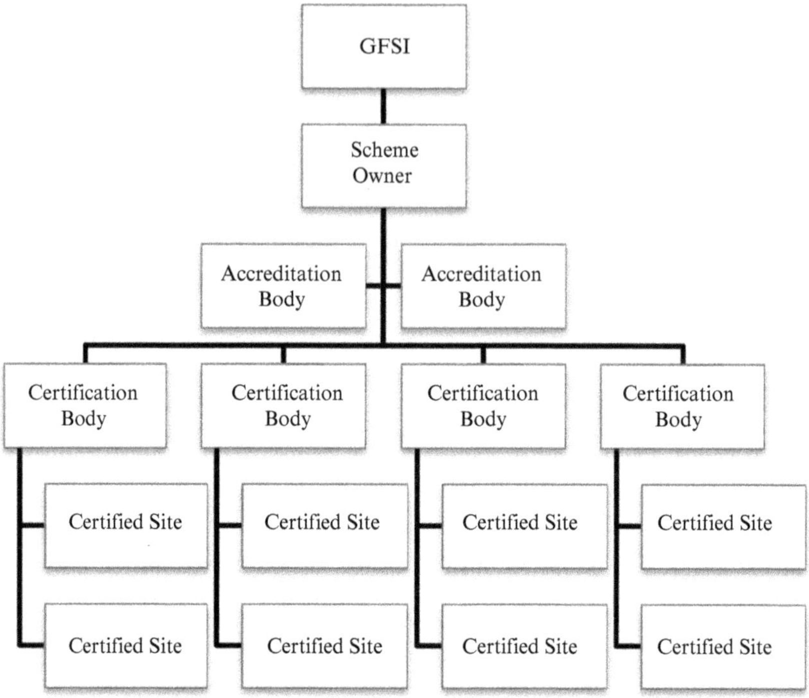

Figure 3.1 Trickle down effect of GFSI Rules

4.1 GFSI Rules on Auditor Independence

Accreditation bodies, the meta-regulators of third-party certification bodies, play a key role in verifying the continued integrity and competence of auditors. Certifiers of GFSI-recognized schemes must be accredited by independent accreditation bodies against ISO/IEC 17065 or ISO/IEC 17021. The accreditation bodies (ABs) must be members of the International Accreditation Forum (IAF) and signatories of the Multilateral Recognition Arrangement.[73] When accrediting CBs, accreditation bodies must follow ISO/IEC 17011:2006 and comply with

[73] Under this Arrangement, accreditation bodies mutually recognize accreditations to facilitate trade and global acceptance of accredited bodies. This means that if a certification body is recognized by an accreditation body that is a signatory of the Arrangement, the accreditation of the CB is valid also in other countries whose accreditation bodies are signatories. http://www.iaf.nu/upFiles/IAF_MLA_0112.pdf accessed 25 November 2016.

additional requirements designed by the GFSI and available in the Guidance Document.[74] Accreditation involves a several day visit to the head office of a certification body, a review of its documents and procedures and interviews with personnel. The accreditation process also involves witnessed audits of auditors, an assessment where auditors are shadowed by another auditor sent by the AB. Through a witnessed audit, it is possible to verify the competences of an auditor, how these are used during the audit, the auditor's behavior and how she conducts the audit. The AB should conduct at least one witnessed audit and for CBs that have more than 20 auditors the witness assessment should be at a rate of 1 per 20 auditors per year. After the initial accreditation, ABs conduct annual surveillance audits on certified bodies to ensure that they continue to meet accreditation requirements.[75] Certification bodies need to be re-accredited periodically.

Besides the pivotal role entrusted on accreditation services, the GFSI also includes other measures intended to avoid conflict of interest. It establishes that a standard cannot be developed, managed or owned by a certification body so that the rule-making and enforcement functions are kept separate.[76] The provision of advisory and certification services, another obstacle to independence, is controlled by compliance with an ISO/IEC 17065, which mandates a complete separation under two distinct legal entities of consulting and auditing services as of September 2015.

The GFSI also prescribes that when the scheme owner is aware of conflicts or problems that may damage the reputation of the scheme or the GFSI, it should agree on specific actions to tackle the problem with the CB.[77] Also CBs control the impartiality of their personnel by asking them to sign a commitment to independence from commercial or personal interests, and to declare any issues that could count as conflicts of interest.[78]

4.2 GFSI Rules on Auditor Competence

The GFSI requires a degree or higher education course in food or related discipline and five years experience in the food industry. The GFSI offers

---

[74] GFSI Guidance Document. Sixth Edition, Issue 3, October 2013, 77.

[75] Most accreditation bodies operate on a two or more year cycle, where they conduct an initial accreditation audit, followed by annual surveillance audits, and eventually a re-accreditation audit. Both accreditation and surveillance audits are announced; generally accreditation audits are more extensive.

[76] GFSI Guidance Document. Sixth Edition, Issue 3, October 2013, 62.

[77] Ibid, 67.

[78] Ibid, 68.

the option to reduce the experience requirement to only two years in case the competence can be verified by an exam administered by the certification body. The competencies and training needs of the auditors should be assessed following the guidelines issued by the scheme owners, who should also maintain records of the qualifications and experience of all personnel involved in certification in specific registers.[79] As discussed above, also accreditation bodies play a key role in assessing the competencies of auditors during the accreditation process and witnessed audits.[80] Training requirements include topics such as auditing techniques based on quality management systems or food safety management systems, HACCP, and training in the standard against which the certification is issued.[81] According to the GFSI, auditor skills shall be assessed on their performance in a combination of 10 audit days and 5 audits. Certification bodies are responsible for employing competent personnel and to verify that they have the qualifications necessary to carry out the auditing and certification functions. The capabilities required are listed in ISO rules and in GFSI addenda.[82]

As regards auditor competence, a discussion of the technical knowledge that auditors should have exceeds the area of expertise of this author, who shall focus on ways to verify competencies instead. Auditor competence is a critical priority of members of the GFSI, which established in 2010 a Technical Working Group on this matter, later transformed into the Auditor Competence Scheme Committee (ACSC) to work on auditor competence and credentialing. In 2013, the GFSI issued a report titled "Food Safety Auditor Competencies" where it clarified the technical, auditing and behavioral skills appropriate for an auditor.[83] The GFSI

---

79 Ibid, 67.

80 Furthermore, the GFSI addenda require that the accreditation steps include assessors with specific food safety experience. For example, the team should include personnel who received training in the relevant GFSI scheme and completed a HACCP course, and the team should have a member with at least two years experience in the food industry.

81 Training requirements are particularly critical in light of recent research that found training to be more critical for audit quality than the education level of auditors. Short, J.L., M.W. Toffel, et al. (2015). 'Monitoring Global Supply Chains.' Working Paper. Harvard Business School.

82 Specifically, ISO 19011, ISO 17021, ISO/IEC Guide 65, ISO 22003 and Part II, Sec. 3.4.2 to 3.4.10 of the GFSI Guidance Document. GFSI Guidance Document. Sixth Edition, Issue 3, October 2013, 69.

83 http://www.mygfsi.com/images/mygfsi/gfsifiles/information-kit/GFSI_Food_Safety_Auditor_Competencies_-_Edition_1_October_2013.pdf accessed 25 November 2016.

later worked on assessing and credentialing auditors' competencies overtime.[84] The result of this long process to sharpen and verify auditor competence is a new Auditor Competence Scheme, published in 2014 and due to be applied to new and existing auditors of schemes benchmarked against the 7th edition of the Guidance Document, introduced in February 2016.[85] The Auditor Competence Scheme introduced, among other things, an online auditor examination process to be taken every four years, verification of auditor skills through witness audits, to be conducted by skilled assessors every four years, and the creation of the Global Food Safety Auditor Foundation (GFSA Foundation), an independent entity to manage assessment activities.[86] Although it is too early to tell, by testing all auditors using the same set of parameters and by putting the administration of auditor competence verification in the hands of independent institutions (rather than CBs), these changes should contribute to making auditor competences and skills more uniform and rigorous across GFSI-recognized standards.

4.3 GFSI Rules on Audit Design

Audits are used to assess that the food safety system in place at a facility adequately controls risks and responds to the guidelines set out in a private standard. The GFSI establishes guidelines on the frequency and duration of audits. At a minimum standards should require annual audits of facilities, but the frequency should be adjusted to reflect past compliance history, risk profile and the seasonality of the production. The duration of an audit should be of at least two days for manufacturing and one day for primary production.[87] Certification bodies that have evidence or suspicion of non-conformity should carry out additional surveillance audits.

In the past, the GFSI did not specify whether audits should be scheduled in advance or unannounced. The norm in the food industry is that audits are announced and scheduled in advance, therefore the CB and the auditee agree on a specific date and time when the audit will take place. The rationale behind announced audits is that personnel dedicated to food safety should be available on the day of the audit to assist the auditor and

---

[84] http://www.mygfsi.com/images/mygfsi/gfsifiles/information-kit/GFSI_Auditor_Competence_Workstream_Information_Package_ed1_August_2014.pdf accessed 25 November 2016.

[85] Ibid. It should be noted that existing auditors of GFSI-recognized standards have three years to transition to the new GFSI Auditor Competence Scheme.

[86] Ibid.

[87] GFSI Guidance Document. Sixth Edition, Issue 3, October 2013, 71.

provide documents and other relevant information by answering questions. Another reason is that not all facilities produce the same product all the time, some productions may be seasonal, so a scheduled audit is necessary to make sure the facility is working within the scope of its certification on the day the audit is conducted. The counterargument is that scheduled audits give facilities a chance to adjust compliance to the time of the audit. Whereas most audits continue to be announced, the GFSI has recently asked its recognized schemes to contemplate the option of unannounced audits for clients that should require them, signaling that there is a change within the industry in favor of unannounced audits as a market signal of superior food safety to clients.[88]

4.4 GFSI Rules on Audit Transparency

The GFSI establishes requirements on audit reporting. It is the responsibility of scheme owners to design a clear system for the generation of audit reports and for possible ranking or scoring of facilities. The audit report is released at the discretion of the certified client, who owns and controls access to the information. As clarified by the GFSI: "Ownership of the audit report, determination of details made available and authorization for access shall remain with the contracted client."[89] Only certified sites, certification bodies, scheme owners and buyers selected by the certified sites have access to audit reports. These reports are not available to competitors in the industry, regulators or the general public. Whereas the content of the audit is private and not disclosed, scheme owners maintain a database of certified sites on their Web page. Anyone can look up the name, address of a facility (sometimes the name of a contact person within the facility is provided as well), the type of product (canned corn) and/or scope of the certification (processing of perishable vegetable products), and information on the validity of the certification and its expiration date. The site should also list whether a certification was granted, suspended or withdrawn. Generally the schemes' web sites post information on whether a site is certified or not (or whether certification was suspended for non-compliance), hence even if an audit found several non-conformances but these were later addressed through a correction plan, this would not be reflected online, the site would be listed as certified.

---

[88] http://www.mygfsi.com/images/mygfsi/gfsifiles/technical-documents/Design_Guidance_Document_Intro.pdf accessed 25 November 2016.

[89] GFSI Guidance Document. Sixth Edition, Issue 3, October 2013, 72.

5. GAPS IN GFSI RULES

If we compare the set of limitations of third-party certification identified in the general literature with the rules that the GFSI imposes on its recognized schemes we can conclude that certain gaps remain. Let us discuss these in order of importance for the topic of hybridization.

First, the area of auditor integrity presents weaknesses. The fact that auditors are hired and compensated by the firms they audit is the "elephant in the room" and remains an unresolved problem even under GFSI's rules. The GFSI framework mandates, rather generically, that conflicts of interest should be declared and that scheme owners and CBs are responsible for the impartiality of their auditors. The GFSI leaves it to certification bodies to have in place procedures to avoid conflicts of interest, yet it does not offer very prescriptive guidance on how to design and implement such principles. Given that the GFSI is a benchmarking initiative and that auditor independence is such a critical area, it is surprising that the meta-regulator has not designed a clear and coherent set of rules applicable to all standards to limit conflict of interest. It seems that leaving recognized standards too ample a margin of flexibility in this area may lead to a patchwork of approaches, some of which may be conducive to opportunistic behaviors. Possible solutions could be a mandatory rotation of auditors, to avoid a close relationship between auditor and auditee, and establishing diverse teams of auditors, for cross checking and peer review, as suggested by empirical research.[90] Additionally, buyers (for example retailers) could be given more say in the choice of certification bodies by making CBs' quality more evident for firms seeking certification and prospective buyers. The BRC standard's star rating of CB performance is a good example of how CB quality could become more explicit and facilitate the selection of better auditors.[91]

Second, the fact that audits (from certification audits to accreditation ones) are scheduled in advance remains an obstacle to the reliability of the system. Announced audits are not a very reliable instrument to capture compliance because audited firms are likely to be on their best behavior in preparation for the audit. Firms are going to improve compliance for the audit because the incentives for passing the audit are very high, given that a serious non-compliance could cost a firm its certification and ultimately

---

[90] Short, J.L., M.W. Toffel, et al. (2015). 'Monitoring Global Supply Chains.' Working Paper. Harvard Business School.

[91] http://www.brcglobalstandards.com/Certificationbodies/Performancereviews.aspx#.WD7pPzYTWUU accessed 30 November 2016.

its buyers. Firms that embrace a food safety culture and have the resources to invest in food safety are likely to display good food safety compliance irrespective of the time of the audit. But it is unclear why less scrupulous firms, for whom audits are a mere nuisance, should maintain high safety levels when they know they are not being watched.[92] Also the witnessed audits carried out by accreditation bodies (both the ones carried out for accreditation as well as the ones carried out during annual surveillance visits) are announced and scheduled in advance. Similarly to certified sites, certification bodies and their auditors have strong incentives to be found in compliance by accreditation bodies because their contracts with scheme owners and their certification business are conditional upon accreditation. Therefore they are likely to display high levels of compliance on the day of the witnessed audits and may switch to lower compliance after achieving accreditation. A system of surveillance audits, unscheduled audits to verify compliance beyond the annual certification audit, should complement scheduled audits. Alternatively, promoting voluntary unannounced audits, as recently introduced by the GFSI, could be a way to gradually improve food safety and ratchet up compliance in the industry.

Third, the lack of transparency of audit reports is detrimental to the industry, to consumers and to the movement toward hybrid forms of food safety governance. By not sharing the rich audit data, the industry as a whole is unable to learn about gaps in specific sectors, or high-risk industries that present more serious non-conformances. Consumers are unable to detect the hidden risks in the foods they consume. Unless a food is patently contaminated, the presence of pathogens in foods does not become manifest until one becomes sick, and even then it may be hard to trace the illness to the contaminated food. Private food safety standards do not curb this information asymmetry because they are business-to-business standards and, unlike environmental or fair labor standards, they are not disclosed to consumers on labels on product packets, so consumers cannot discriminate which producers have the highest compliance levels, and which instead merely pass their certification requirements. Public regulators are harmed by the information asymmetry because it limits their ability to carry out their functions and protect consumers. Because auditors are bound by confidentiality, they may fail to inform regulators if they find food safety breaches that could harm consumers.[93] Given that

---

[92] See also Havinga and Verbruggen's analysis of the GFSI, Chapter 9 in this volume, for concerns expressed by some interviewees that the goal of some facilities is to obtain their certification, rather than achieving high food safety levels.

[93] A recent reform of the food legislation in the US has altered confidentiality for food imports. The 2011 Food Safety Modernization Act has introduced food

government inspections of facilities in most categories remain very limited and that there are gaps of several years between inspections, accessing the information gathered in audit reports would be particularly useful for regulatory agencies.[94] Armed with this information, they could target their inspections to high-risk facilities, or to the ones that present higher non-compliance and reduce controls on more virtuous ones. Experiments of information sharing, where facilities disclose data about their compliance with private standards in exchange for less stringent controls by government regulators, would reduce redundancy and costs and constitute a right step in the direction of hybridization.[95]

The GFSI should be commended for its important benchmarking work, and for promoting food safety within the industry. The GFSI has also taken the issue of auditor competence seriously and has devised a complex new system to periodically assess auditor skills, putting an independent organization in charge of the task. These are important actions to promote rigor, consistency and comparability of certificates, which should translate into higher food safety levels. Yet some of the gaps listed above should still be a concern for the industry, because they could result in low food safety levels. Some schemes, like the BRC and SQF, have started addressing the problem by introducing mandatory and voluntary unannounced audits.[96] Some buyers, like the British retailer ASDA, decided that brand suppliers should undergo unannounced audits with the BRC.[97] Also the horse meat scandal prompted a tightening of controls and a shift toward unannounced

---

safety audits to assess import safety in some circumstances. Section 307 of the law requires third-party auditors in charge of auditing imports to report conditions that could pose a serious risk to public health. Under the same law, the content of audits that verify import safety is available to regulators. In the EU, best practice guidelines ([2010] OJ C341/04) indicate that 'Cases of non-compliance with adverse implications for health protection should be notified to the relevant authorities in accordance with regulatory requirements.' In spite of these requirements, evidence from the interviews conducted for this research suggest that the culture among auditors and CBs is to oblige to their confidentiality duty with their clients.

[94] Fagotto, E. (2011). 'Governing a Global Food Supply: How the 2010 FDA Food Safety Modernization Act Promises to Strengthen Import Safety in the US.' *Erasmus Law Review* **3**(4): 257–73.

[95] For some concrete examples, see Havinga and Verbruggen, Chapter 9 in this volume.

[96] www.brcglobalstandards.com/Portals/0/library/files/knowledgecentre/Study%20of%20BRC%20Unannounced%20Audits.pdf and www.sqfi.com/2014/01/06/sqf-becomes-first-internationally-accredited-third-party-assessment-program-to-require-unannounced-audits/ accessed 25 November 2016.

[97] www.gov.uk/government/uploads/system/uploads/attachment_data/file/262372/fsn-asda-20131112.pdf accessed 25 November 2016.

audits.[98] The fact that the GFSI has recently introduced voluntary unannounced audits in its latest version of the Guidance Document may indicate that there is an industry-wide shift toward unscheduled audits, a desirable change. However, important measures like auditor rotation and diverse auditor teams are not yet common.

6. CONCLUSION

How does exploring the gaps in third-party enforcement of food safety advance the understanding of hybridization? Assessing the vulnerabilities in private regulation is a useful first step for regulators. This way they can learn to what extent they can rely on private certification in its current form and work with the industry to effect improvement. Scholarship is ambivalent on the relationship between public and private food safety regulation. Some researchers view it as a collaborative one, where government and industry strive to achieve the same goals, and even identify a trend of co-regulation.[99] Others fear that private standards might have been strategically introduced by the industry to prevent or displace domestic and international food safety regulation, suggesting a competitive relationship.[100] The evidence presented in this chapter calls for a more prudent approach. Defining the relationship between public and private regulation as *collaborative* might be too optimistic because, even though the GFSI has improved its efforts to reach out to governments and international governmental organizations like Codex, a true collaboration, intended as working in a concerted way with the public sector to achieve the shared goal of food safety, is still distant. Similarly, the view that private standards might have been put in place by the industry to *compete* with government regulation appears implausible. Private standards build on international

---

[98] More than 50% of the audits conducted by the chain Tesco have become unannounced, signaling the industry's anxiety brought about by the scandal. www.foodmanufacture.co.uk/Supply-Chain/Retailers-to-fight-food-fraud-with-unannounced-audits accessed 25 November 2016.

[99] Henson, S. and J. Caswell (1999). 'Food Safety Regulation: An Overview of Contemporary Issues.' *Food Policy* **24**: 589–603; Garcia Martinez, M., A. Fearne, et al. (2007). 'Co-regulation as a Possible Model for Food Safety Governance: Opportunities for Public-Private Partnerships.' *Food Policy* **32**: 299–314.

[100] McCluskey, J.J. (2007). 'Public and Private Food Quality Standards: Recent Trends and Strategic Incentives' in J.F.M. Swinnen (ed.) *Global Supply Chains, Standards, and the Poor*. CABI; McCluskey, J.J. and J.A. Winfree (2009). 'Pre-Empting Public Regulation with Private Food Quality Standards.' *European Review of Agricultural Economics* **36**(4): 525–39.

public food safety regulation and best practices. Furthermore, private actors, especially buyers active at the end of the food supply chain, have a strong interest in providing safe foods to consumers and in protecting themselves from outbreaks. Their interest in food safety is compatible with the government's objectives. The emergence of hybrid forms of food safety governance points to a future where the public and private sector will likely come closer to achieve their shared objectives. In this volume, Havinga and Verbruggen highlight some of the forms that hybrid efforts can take, with good examples from the Netherlands and Canada, and point to the promises and complexities of hybridization.[101] Before considering hybrid forms of food safety regulation, however, regulators and scholars should take a step back and gain a better understanding of how private initiatives operate and whether or not they are effective. This chapter is a modest contribution to clarify these issues. Only this way will public regulators be able to devise hybridization models capable to reap the full benefits of private controls for food safety.

---

[101] See Havinga and Verbruggen, Chapter 9 in this volume.

4 Oversight of private food safety auditing in the United States: A hybrid approach to auditor conflict of interest

Timothy D. Lytton and Lesley K. McAllister

INTRODUCTION

Private food safety auditing is a large and rapidly growing global industry. Although no one has comprehensive data on the size of the industry, there are indications that it operates on a scale comparable to that of government food safety regulation. This chapter focuses on one particular problem that undermines public confidence in private food safety auditing: the conflict of interest that arises when auditors are paid by the entities that they audit. Industry insiders and outside observers believe this conflict of interest to be a significant concern that merits attention, and various institutional actors have developed oversight mechanisms to address it. Our focus is on the institutional design of oversight – organizational structures, administrative routines and professional norms.

Oversight of food safety auditing exemplifies the concept of hybridization analysed in the introduction to this volume. The system of oversight we survey is characterized by the interplay of public and private actors applying a variety of regulatory instruments developed within national, international and transnational institutions. We present an inventory of regulatory instruments that identifies the actors involved, their motivations and the character of their interactions. Although much of what we describe applies globally, our examples of tort litigation and government recognition focus on particular features of US law, so we have limited the scope of our claims to food safety auditing in the United States.

Oversight of private auditing can be provided by a variety of sources, and it can take different forms. We use the term 'oversight' in a very broad sense to cover any ongoing effort to ensure or improve quality. This includes promulgating norms and encouraging administrative routines as well as monitoring performance and imposing sanctions. These forms of oversight can come from personnel within organizations (such as trainers and managers), from external private sources (such as audit firms and trade associations) or from the government (such as agencies and courts). Oversight mechanisms thus involve different combinations of institutional actors and regulatory techniques, each of which has comparative strengths and weaknesses. They may provide alternatives to each other or coexist; they may be redundant or complementary. The effectiveness of oversight may depend upon an ultimate overseer, or it may depend upon a network of overseers and oversight mechanisms.

Before proceeding, we wish to emphasize three caveats regarding the nature and limits of our claims. First, although our analysis is relevant to evaluating the performance of private food safety audits, *we offer no judgment concerning the overall performance of either government regulation or private auditing in the area of food safety.* Such judgments would require analysis of the optimal level of risk reduction, the amount of risk reduction achieved, and the costs of this risk reduction – all of which are beyond the scope of this chapter. Instead, we begin with the premise that government regulation alone cannot satisfy the demand for food safety and that private auditing plays a significant and growing role in the current food safety system, and we analyse different oversight mechanisms designed to improve the quality of private food safety audits. This chapter analyses the integrity of private audits, not their efficacy. Our focus on institutional design illuminates how private food safety auditing works, but it does not assess how well it works. For similar reasons, we analyse the structure and dynamics of various oversight mechanisms, but we offer no recommendation concerning which mechanism or combination of mechanisms offers the optimal mix of incentives to limit conflict of interest.

Second, *our analysis does not endorse private over public regulatory instruments or vice versa.* We claim only that, in the area of food safety, there is demand for both, and they are likely to coexist in the future. Nor do we believe that private and public regulatory instruments are mutually exclusive. Scholars have long recognized that many areas of regulation are characterized by a diverse mix of overlapping – and frequently complementary – public and private regulatory instruments.[1]

Finally, in the interest of brevity, we offer only a sample of the different

[1] Ian Ayres and John Braithwaite, *Responsive Regulation: Transcending the Deregulation Debate* (Oxford University Press 1992); Neil Gunningham, Peter Grabosky and Darren Sinclair, *Smart Regulation: Designing Environmental Policy* (Oxford University Press 1998); Lester Salamon (ed.), *The Tools of Government: A Guide to the New Governance* (Oxford University Press 2002).

oversight mechanisms that address auditor conflict of interest. This sample will serve to illustrate our method of analysing regulatory complexity in food safety auditing and evaluating different regulatory approaches. Readers seeking a more comprehensive and more thoroughly documented account should consult our previously published article, 'Oversight in Private Food Safety Auditing: Addressing Auditor Conflict of Interest', upon which this chapter is based.[2]

OVERSIGHT MECHANISMS

In private third-party food safety audits that buyers frequently require of their suppliers, the supplier typically pays the auditor. This fee arrangement creates a conflict of interest for the auditor. Auditors competing for accounts have incentive to reduce the cost and burden of audits by spending less time, downplaying safety risks and inflating audit scores. Thus, there is a conflict between the auditor's financial interest and his professional obligation to protect the public from food safety risks.[3]

Multiple oversight mechanisms create incentives that counteract auditors' private financial incentive to reduce the rigor of audits. This oversight may be aimed at auditors or at others with direct or indirect influence over auditors. The system of oversight is extensive and complex, and there are significant variations in different sectors of the industry. We do not purport to offer a detailed or comprehensive account. Instead, our analysis in this chapter is schematic, sampling several oversight mechanisms that involve particular institutional actors and regulatory instruments and highlighting their comparative strengths and weaknesses.

Tort Litigation

Motivated by injury compensation and contingency fees, tort plaintiffs and their attorneys can impose costly liability on buyers, suppliers and auditors for their food safety failures. For example, plaintiffs' attorney Bill Marler has won more than $600 million in settlements and verdicts for thousands of victims of foodborne illness in lawsuits against food companies since 1998. In the United States, suppliers and buyers are

---

[2] Timothy D. Lytton and Lesley K. McAllister, 'Oversight in Private Food Safety Auditing: Addressing Auditor Conflict of Interest' [2014] *Wisconsin Law Review* 289.

[3] For a fuller analysis of this conflict of interest, see ibid, 297–304.

strictly liable for injuries caused by unsafe products that they sell, and this liability exposure gives them an incentive to promote rigorous auditing. Liability exposure is a significant driver of investments in food safety among growers, processors and manufacturers. Brad Sullivan, an attorney who represents produce suppliers, asserts that 'liability exposure is a major driver of risk management among growers'. The impact of liability exposure is magnified by the protracted media coverage that typically accompanies litigation, which can cause significant damage to a company's brand. Plaintiffs have also recently begun to file claims against food safety auditors for negligence. Tort doctrine defines negligence as the failure to exercise the care of an ordinary, prudent person acting in similar circumstances, which is often further defined in cases of professional negligence as the failure to exercise a level of care that is cost-effective or the level of care customarily exercised by other professionals in the same field. Plaintiffs and their attorneys have a financial incentive to identify the optimal level of rigor in food safety auditing and to bring claims against those who fall short of it.[4]

As an oversight mechanism, tort law has a number of comparative advantages. Liability exposure creates a powerful incentive for buyers, suppliers and auditors to assure an optimal level of rigor in food safety audits. The litigation process itself offers additional regulatory benefits.

---

[4] Marler Clark, 'Food Attorneys: Law Firm Profile', accessed 25 November 2016 at http://www.marlerclark.com/firm_profile. Interview with Brad Sullivan, an attorney who represents produce suppliers (15 August 2013). See Marler Clark, 'Marler Clark Sues Cantaloupe Distributor & Farm Auditor in Louisiana' (24 September 2012) (announcing the filing of a lawsuit against a leading food safety auditor), accessed 25 November 2016 at www.marlerclark.com/press_releases/view/marler-clark-sues-cantaloupe-distributor-farm-auditor-in-louisiana. cf Jean C. Buzby and Paul D. Frenzen, 'Food Safety and Product Liability,' (1999) 24 *Food Policy* 637–51. Buzby and Frenzen claim that 'current legal incentives to produce safer food are weak'. This claim is based on jury verdicts and settlements reported in the Westlaw and LEXIS-NEXIS data bases from 1988 to 1997. These data exclude non-reported verdicts, which represents a significant omission since large settlements with the producers of branded products are typically conditioned on keeping the amount of settlement confidential. Moreover, claims against food companies for foodborne illness – along with media coverage of the resulting litigation – have increased since 1997 with improved techniques for tracing outbreaks back to particular food safety failures and the emergence of law firms, such as Marler Clark, that specialize in litigating and publicizing such claims. For an extended discussion of the impact of tort litigation on increasing investments in food safety in the beef industry following the Jack in the Box *E. coli* O157:H7 outbreak in 1993, see Timothy D. Lytton, *Outbreak: The Evolution of the U.S. Food Safety System* (University of Chicago Press, forthcoming).

In filing claims, tort plaintiffs may frame foodborne illness outbreaks in ways that highlight particular failures in the private food safety auditing system – for example, carelessness in the selection or supervision of auditors or in the execution of audits. The discovery process generates valuable performance feedback. During discovery, plaintiffs can compel suppliers, auditors and buyers to disclose information about audit quality that might not otherwise come to light. Discovery can also uncover information linking a foodborne illness outbreak to a particular buyer, supplier and auditor. Each stage of the litigation, from filing to final outcome, can generate media coverage that magnifies the reputational effects of food safety failures and places and maintains food safety improvement at the top of corporate, government and public agendas.[5]

Tort litigation also has shortcomings as a regulatory tool. The generation of precise feedback is limited in practice because tort claims against multiple strictly liable defendants are frequently settled without identification of the precise cause of a plaintiff's illness within the supply chain. Supply contracts typically require suppliers to indemnify buyers for any liability arising out of foodborne illness, simply pushing liability up the supply chain. Moreover, critics assert that tort litigation is inefficient. They argue that attorneys' fees on both sides, court costs, and the extensive time and energy expended by parties in litigation are a high price for a modest regulatory benefit.[6]

To be sure, these costs appear very high in comparison to those of supplier self-regulation, auditor quality control and buyer oversight. A complete appraisal, however, would have to weigh these costs against the regulatory benefits, which are difficult to quantify. Similarly, in comparing the efficiency of tort litigation to government regulation, a fair comparison would have to take into account the full cost of the legislative process, the notice-and-comment rule making process and enforcement. One would also need to compare their effectiveness.

Critics have also questioned the legitimacy of tort litigation as a regulatory tool. Participation is limited to a very narrow range of stakeholders, private negotiations and settlements are generally not transparent, and

---

[5] See Timothy D. Lytton, *Holding Bishops Accountable: How Lawsuits Helped the Catholic Church Confront Clergy Sexual Abuse* (Harvard University Press 2008) 81–162 (analysing the framing, information disclosure, and agenda-setting effects of the tort litigation process).

[6] See e.g. Walter Olsen, *The Rule of Lawyers: How the New Litigation Elite Threatens America's Rule of Law* (Truman Talley Books/St. Martin's 2003) 1–24; W. Kip Viscusi, 'Overview' in W. Kip Viscusi (ed.) *Regulation through Litigation* (Brookings Institution Press 2002) 1–21.

plaintiffs' attorneys are not democratically accountable to either the electorate or consumers (nor, in many states, are judges).[7] At the same time, tort litigation allows important stakeholders – victims of foodborne illness – to participate directly in investigating misconduct and enforcing standards in food safety auditing, and much of the process is a matter of public record.

Accreditation

Accreditation bodies, which may be public or private entities, assess the reliability of private food safety auditors through a process of inspection, auditing and ongoing surveillance, using widely accepted standards jointly developed by the International Organization for Standardization (ISO) and the International Electrotechnical Commission (IEC).[8] Many buyers only accept supplier audits conducted by accredited auditors. A peer-review system coordinated by the International Accreditation Forum (IAF) seeks to ensure the reliability of accreditation bodies using ISO/IEC standards that apply to accreditation bodies themselves.[9] Figure 4.1 illustrates the organizational structure of accreditation.

ISO/IEC standards use the concept of impartiality to define ethical norms, institutional structures and administrative practices aimed at counteracting auditor conflict of interest. According to ISO/IEC standards, impartiality means that an auditor's judgment is unbiased, free from prejudice, neutral, fair, open-minded, even-handed, detached and balanced. Under the standards, the upper management of an audit firm must commit itself to impartiality, and it must formalize this commitment in written principles and policies. It must also have in place an oversight committee to advise it on the development of these principles and policies and to monitor its adherence to them. The committee must include 'a balanced representation of significantly interested parties' drawn from suppliers, buyers, trade associations, consumer organizations, auditing experts and government agencies. Personnel from the auditing firm on the committee 'shall not predominate'.[10]

---

[7] Viscusi (n 6) 1.

[8] ISO/IEC standards generally use the term 'certification bodies'. We use the terms 'auditor' and 'auditing firm' for stylistic consistency with the rest of our analysis.

[9] See ISO and UNIDO, *Building Trust: The Conformity Assessment Toolbox*, 6–90, 175–84, accessed 25 November 2016 at www.iso.org/iso/casco_building-trust.pdf.

[10] ISO/IEC accreditation standards address the problem of auditor conflict

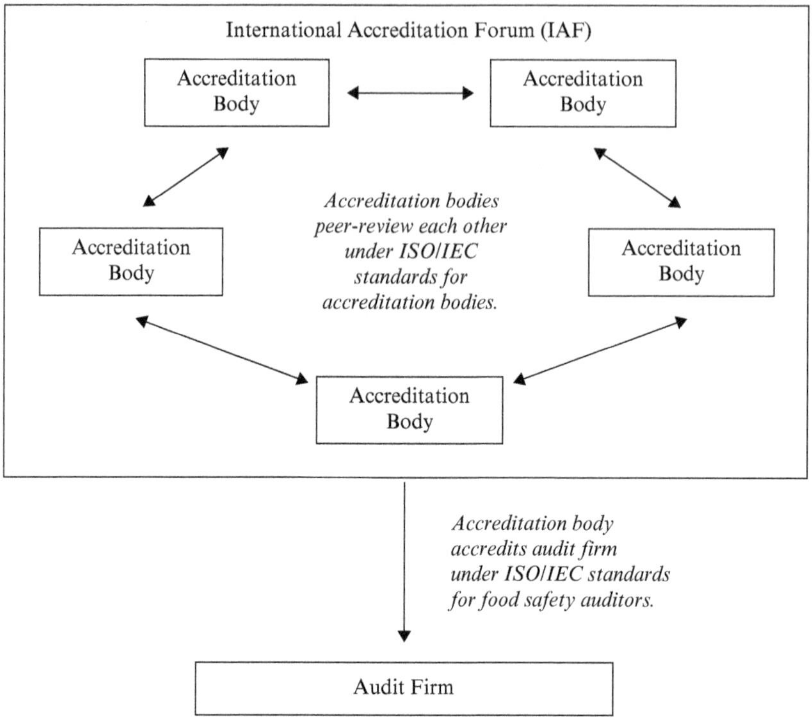

Figure 4.1 Accreditation

Under ISO/IEC standards, an audit firm must 'identify risks to its impartiality on an ongoing basis', report those risks to the committee and demonstrate how the risks have been eliminated or minimized. The committee must have the power to investigate any tendency by the audit firm 'to allow commercial or other considerations to prevent the consistent impartial provision of certification activities', and 'if the top management of the certification body [audit firm] does not follow the input' of the committee, it 'shall have the right to take independent action', such as 'informing authorities, accreditation bodies, [or other] stakeholders'. Audit firms are prohibited from providing consultancy services to clients

of interest in a constellation of standards relevant to conformity assessment in general (ISO/IEC series 17000 standards) and food safety auditing in particular (ISO/IEC 22000 series). Our discussion focuses on standards in ISO/IEC 17065 Conformity Assessment – Requirements for Bodies Certifying Products, Processes and Services (2012) ss 3.13, 4.2.5, 4.2.7 and 5.2.2.

that they certify. Additionally, an audit firm must require auditors to sign a written agreement pledging that they will disclose any current or potential conflicts of interest and comply with rules governing conflicts of interest. An audit firm must conduct an annual internal review of its compliance with applicable ISO/IEC standards, and it must submit itself to ongoing surveillance and periodic reassessment by an accreditation body to maintain its accreditation.[11]

As an oversight mechanism to address auditor conflict of interest, accreditation has several comparative strengths. It offers auditors a valuable credential that increases the marketability of their services. This creates a financial incentive to be impartial that counteracts the financial incentive to reduce the rigor of audits to please a client. The IAF peer-review system provides a similar incentive to accreditation bodies to be impartial in accrediting auditors, thereby counteracting the conflict of interest at the accreditation level. Oversight committees that include stakeholder representatives from industry, government and public interest advocacy groups with the power to report wrongdoing to public authorities increase participation, transparency and accountability in both the certification and accreditation processes. Internal management reviews within auditing firms and ongoing surveillance by accreditation bodies provide auditors with opportunities for feedback and learning.

Accreditation also has comparative weaknesses. Accreditation bodies lack the coercive power of civil discovery to uncover information that auditors wish to conceal. Moreover, accreditation constitutes another level of administration with its own independent institutions and personnel, which imposes additional administrative costs on the auditing process. Access restrictions to standards and confidentiality reduce transparency, participation and public accountability in the accreditation process. ISO/IEC standards are not publicly available – they must be purchased, and fees for a single standard can reach into the hundreds of dollars – and the results of audits and ongoing surveillance of auditors by accreditation bodies are confidential.

Food Safety Scheme Licensing

Industry groups and non-governmental organizations have developed a number of schemes – consisting of principles, policies and

---

[11] ISO/IEC 17065 (n 10) ss 4.2.3, 4.2.6, 5.2, 6.1, 7.11 and 8.5; see also ISO/IEC 17011 Conformity Assessment – General Requirements for Accreditation Bodies Accrediting Conformity Assessment Bodies (2004).

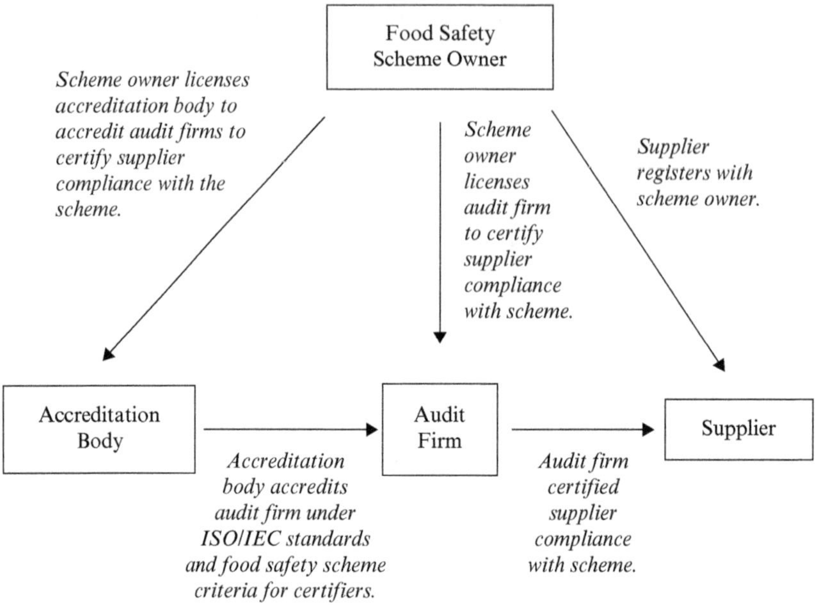

Figure 4.2 Food safety scheme licensing

practices – designed to improve and standardize food safety. Major buyers increasingly demand that their suppliers implement one of these schemes and obtain independent certification that they have done so. Scheme owners license private food safety auditors to certify that suppliers are properly implementing the requirements of their schemes. The schemes require suppliers to adopt ethical norms, institutional structures and administrative practices to reduce conflicts of interest, and they contain similar provisions for audit firms as a condition of obtaining a license to certify compliance with the scheme. Schemes also require audit firms to be accredited under ISO/IEC standards. Figure 4.2 illustrates the structure of food safety scheme licensing.

For example, the Safe Quality Foods Institute (SQFI) – which is a division of the Food Marketing Institute, a leading industry association for food retailers and wholesalers – administers the Safe Quality Food (SQF) scheme. The scheme requires suppliers to register with SQFI and commit themselves to ongoing improvement of their food safety systems. Suppliers must establish detailed written food safety policies in accordance with SQF product-specific standards, train staff in the implementation of these policies, and regularly review the policies and their implementation through internal inspections and self-audits. They must maintain written records of all reviews and violations and submit to third-party certification audits.[12]

Auditing firms must obtain a license from SQFI to certify suppliers as SQF compliant. To obtain a license, an auditing firm must be accredited under applicable ISO/IEC standards and additional SQF criteria. Accreditation bodies must be IAF-approved under ISO/IEC standards for accreditation bodies and licensed by SQF to accredit auditors to provide SQF certification.[13]

SQF licensing criteria require auditing firms to ensure that anyone involved in conducting audits, making certification decisions, or supervising auditors is 'free from any commercial, financial or other pressure that might influence the results of Certification'. Specifically, audit firms must have policies that require individual auditors to disclose any relationship to suppliers that might constitute a conflict of interest. Audit firms must establish a quality-control system in which managers review all SQF certification audit reports and conduct annual internal audits of the quality-control system. Firms must also maintain written records of these reviews and internal audits and make them available to SQFI or accreditors. Certification decisions must be made by a person or persons other than the person who performed the audit. Audit firms may not offer both consulting services related to helping suppliers implement the SQF scheme and audit services designed to evaluate compliance. Audit firms must appoint an independent committee – consisting of representatives from the primary production, processing, food service and retail sectors of the food industry – to oversee the development of these requirements. SQFI also surveys suppliers and buyers about the quality of certification audits.[14]

Food safety scheme licensing has a number of comparative strengths. A license to certify compliance with a popular scheme enables auditors to offer a valuable service to suppliers. The license creates a significant

---

12 SQF Institute (SQFI), SQF Code (7.2 ed July 2014) 30–32, 45–64, accessed 25 November 2016 at http://www.sqfi.com/wp-content/uploads/SQF-Code_Ed-7.2-July.pdf.

13 SQFI (n 12) 31–2.

14 SQFI, 'Criteria for SQF Certification Bodies: SQF Requirements on the Application of ISO/IEC 17065:2012' (January 2015) 6-11, accessed 25 November 2016 at http://www.sqfi.com/wp-content/uploads/Criteria-for-Certification-Bodies-1.16.15.pdf; *SQF Certified Supplier Survey*, SurveyMonkey, accessed 25 November 2016 at http://www.surveymonkey.com/r/supplierfeedback_survey?sm=Ca0NDXDnH6uePCc6S4VwKTbG7EzFmfi9UFHcD3g29pQ%3d; *SQF Buyer Survey*, accessed 25 November 2016 at www.surveymonkey.com/r/sqfbuyersurvey?sm=nntzQf9u%2bS8jqv1FeRMe9lbR2flbyB1dMZoLrlTR32Y%3d.

financial incentive for auditors to conduct audits that meet the conflict-of-interest standards of scheme owners. Moreover, schemes require initial and ongoing training, which gives scheme owners opportunities to influence the food safety culture within supplier operations, audit firms and consulting services, all of which are likely to be mutually reinforcing. In addition, the various oversight mechanisms that schemes require auditors to establish and scheme owners' surveys of suppliers and buyers generate feedback concerning the quality of audits. Scheme owners share this feedback with auditors, and they take it into account in their periodic renewals of licenses and in their frequent revisions of scheme requirements.[15]

Whether food safety scheme licensing has comparative advantages in terms of access to information regarding the rigor of audits and schemes' own susceptibility to conflict of interest is less clear. Oversight mechanisms and surveys provide scheme owners with access to information about the rigor of audits. This access is dependent, however, upon the thoroughness of surveillance by accreditation bodies and oversight committees, the willingness of suppliers and auditors to share information, and the quality of information that buyers have. Presumably, scheme owners have a financial interest in providing rigorous and verifiable food safety standards that buyers can rely upon and have a mission to reduce the risk of foodborne illness. However, scheme owners might be tempted to relax their standards if they feel competitive pressure to reduce the burdens on suppliers using the scheme or on auditors seeking a license.

Food safety scheme licensing also has a number of clear disadvantages. Schemes generate additional administrative costs for suppliers and auditors. Moreover, not all schemes make their standards available free of charge, and none make information concerning individual auditors and certifiers publicly available. Consequently, audit-scheme licensing is relatively deficient in terms of broad stakeholder participation, transparency and public accountability.

Benchmarking

In 2000, the Consumer Goods Forum, a global trade association of over 400 leading manufacturers, retailers and service providers, founded the Global Food Safety Initiative (GFSI) to establish benchmarks that would set minimum standards for food safety schemes and encourage

---

[15] See e.g. SQFI, 'The SQF Technical Advisory Council', accessed 25 November 2016 at www.sqfi.com/about-sqf/technical-committees/ (describing the process of routine updates of SQF standards).

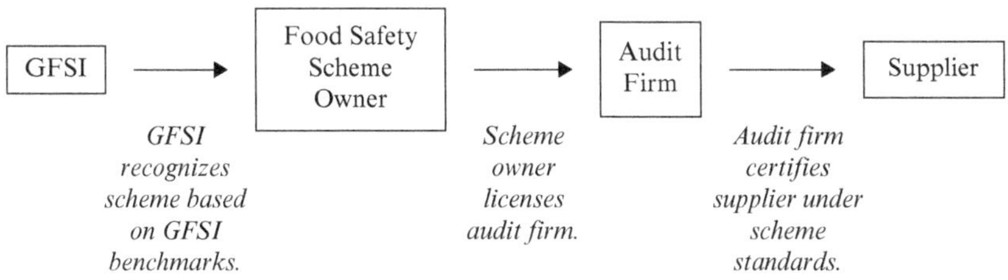

Figure 4.3 GFSI benchmarking

buyers to accept certification under different schemes as equivalent.[16] Suppliers must frequently maintain multiple food safety certifications to sell their products to different buyers, each with its own preferred audit criteria. GFSI recognizes a number of food safety schemes that meet its benchmarks – published in a guidance document – with the aim that buyers will accept certification under any of them and thereby reduce the inefficiency of suppliers needing to obtain multiple audits to satisfy different buyers. This goal is summed up in the GFSI slogan: 'once certified, accepted everywhere'. Dozens of leading food manufacturers, retailers and service providers – including Walmart, Coca-Cola, McDonald's, Delhaize and Sodexo – have agreed to accept certification based on any GFSI-recognized food safety scheme. Figure 4.3 illustrates the relationship between GFSI, scheme owners, auditors and suppliers.

GFSI benchmarking addresses the problem of auditor conflict of interest by prescribing several different types of standards. First, GFSI prescribes standards for food safety schemes' relationship with individual auditors. For example, according to GFSI benchmarks, schemes must require auditors to possess specific minimum qualifications in terms of training, experience and ongoing professional development, and scheme owners must enforce these requirements through an auditor registration system.[17]

---

[16] On the rationales for GFSI, see also Elena Fagotto, 'Resolving Gaps in Third-party Certification for Food Safety Hybridization', Chapter 3 in this volume; Tetty Havinga and Paul Verbruggen, 'The Global Food Safety Initiative and State Actors: Paving the Way for Hybrid Food Safety Governance', Chapter 9 in this volume; Paul Verbruggen and Tetty Havinga, 'The Rise of Transnational Private Meta-Regulators' (2014) 10 Osgoode Hall Law School Working Paper Series, no 71, accessed 25 November 2016 at http://ssrn.com/abstract=2512843.

[17] Global Food Safety Initiative, 'Enhancing Food Safety Through Third Party Certification' (2011) 2–6, 10–12, 14–17, 22–3, accessed 25 November 2016 at www.mygfsi.com/gfsifiles/GFSI_White_Paper_-_Enhancing_Food_Safety_

Second, GFSI prescribes standards for food safety schemes' relationship with auditing firms. For example, GFSI benchmarks prescribe that schemes require audit firms to have written policies regarding conflicts of interest and to make all staff involved in the certification process sign an agreement that commits them to disclosing any actual or potential conflict and to performing their jobs unbiased by commercial or personal interests. In addition, schemes seeking GFSI recognition must define criteria for audit firms – specified in detailed GFSI benchmarks – concerning the frequency and duration of audits, the contents of audit reports, management review of audit reports and auditor performance, documentation of these reviews and quality improvement based on the reviews. GFSI benchmarks further prescribe that schemes require auditing firms to be accredited to ISO/IEC standards and that they have a well-developed performance system that includes methods for obtaining feedback and for addressing complaints.[18]

Third, GFSI prescribes standards for food safety schemes' structure and governance. For example, GFSI benchmarks require that schemes not be developed, managed, or owned by audit firms and that schemes ensure that none of their employees or committee members has a conflict of interest that might influence decisions related to granting certification under the scheme. Additionally, GFSI benchmarks require scheme operation and governance to be open and transparent and standards to be publicly available.[19]

Fourth, GFSI prescribes standards for food safety schemes' relationship with GFSI. For example, following recognition, GFSI requires schemes to submit annual self-assessments of compliance with GFSI benchmarks carried out by a committee of scheme stakeholders and accompanied by supporting documentation. Schemes must reapply for GFSI recognition every four years. The GFSI guidance document also contains detailed qualifications for members of GFSI committees that review scheme applications for recognition as well as detailed procedures for application, evaluation and appeals.[20]

Through_Third_Party_Certification.pdf; Global Food Safety Initiative, 'GFSI Guidance Document' (6th edn 2013) 19–26, 91–6, accessed 25 November 2016 at www.mccain.com/InformationHub/PoliciesAndPledges/GFSI%20Guidance%20Document.pdf. See also The Consumer Goods Forum and GFSI, 'Explaining the Auditor Competence Scheme' (Edition 1, July 2014), accessed 25 November 2016 at www.mygfsi.com/images/mygfsi/gfsifiles/information-kit/GFSI_Auditor_Competence_Workstream_Information_Package_ed1_August_2014.pdf.

18 GFSI Guidance Document (n 17). 62–9, 85–8.

19 Ibid, 62–4.

20 Ibid 19–26, 42, 46–9, 62–5.

GFSI benchmarking is an attempt to strengthen the regulatory capacity of audit schemes to counteract auditor conflicts of interest. GFSI recognition increases the attractiveness of schemes to buyers and suppliers, which creates demand among audit firms for licenses to certify compliance with those schemes. In this way, GFSI recognition creates a financial incentive for scheme owners to set rigorous standards for audits and audit oversight, to verify compliance and to discipline audit firms that fall short. In addition, GFSI benchmarks that prescribe quality assurance oversight at many levels – for example: audit firm review of audits, scheme owner surveillance of audit firms and GFSI assessments of schemes – increase performance feedback and opportunities for learning.

GFSI has also aimed to increase participation, transparency and public accountability by establishing an Advisory Council of representatives from academia and non-governmental organizations and sponsoring an annual conference which attracts retailers, manufacturers, audit firms, accreditation bodies, scheme owners, food safety experts and consultants that is open to anyone interested in participating. GFSI makes its guidance document and related materials publicly available for free on its website. GFSI's mission to encourage widespread acceptance of uniformly high standards of food safety among buyers and suppliers is aligned with the public interest in optimal food safety.[21]

There are also comparative disadvantages to GFSI benchmarking. Except for its annual conference, GFSI has no direct relationship with auditors, so it has no first-hand access to information about the rigor of audits. This distance also limits GFSI's influence on audit firms' sense of mission and commitment to food safety. Moreover, all of the additional oversight prescribed by GFSI, as well as its own operations, generate additional administrative costs in the food safety system. To be fair, however, these costs must be weighed against the efficiency gains from reducing the need for multiple audits and reductions in the number of product recalls due to food safety concerns.[22]

Government Recognition of Accreditation Bodies

The FDA has developed regulations under the Food Safety Modernization Act (FSMA), which require the agency to establish a 'system for the

---

[21] Enhancing Food Safety (n 17) 3; GFSI Guidance Document (n 18).

[22] See Global Food Safety Initiative, 'GFSI General Presentation' (citing food safety gains and cost reductions as a result of GFSI benchmarking), accessed 29 November 2016 at www.mygfsi.com/files/Information_Kit/GFSI_GeneralPresentation_201611.pdf.

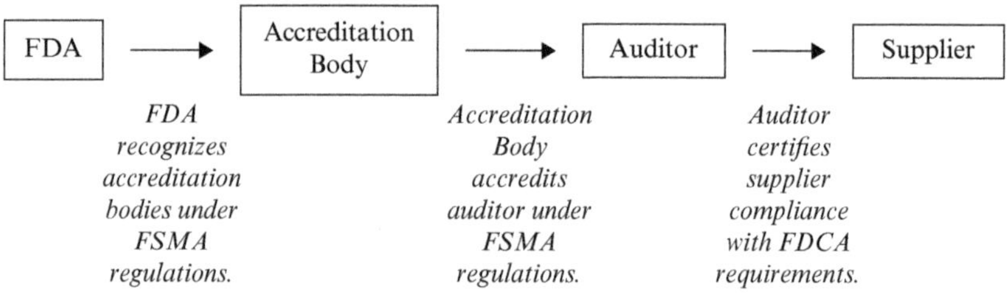

Figure 4.4 FDA recognition of accreditation bodies

recognition of accreditation bodies'. According to the FDA's regulations, the agency will recognize accreditation bodies to accredit auditors that provide regulatory compliance certification to food production facilities.[23] Figure 4.4 illustrates the structure of this regulatory approach.

The FDA's recognition program under FSMA applies only to certification of imported foods for compliance with federal food safety regulations under the Food, Drug, and Cosmetics Act (FDCA). It aims to 'ensure the competence and independence of third-party auditors/certification bodies who conduct foreign food safety audits' and to expedite approval of foods for importation. All imported food under the FDA's jurisdiction is subject to inspection at the point of entry, and importers who voluntarily obtain certification of their facilities under the program are eligible for expedited review. Additionally, under FSMA, the FDA may require importers of high-risk foods to provide certification by a foreign government agency or an accredited auditor that the food complies with federal food safety standards as a condition of permitting its importation.[24]

The regulations prescribe standards for FDA recognition of accreditation bodies and standards for these bodies' accreditation of auditors. Both sets of standards cover personnel training, qualifications and ongoing professional development; auditing, documentation and quality assurance;

[23] Food Safety Modernization Act (FSMA) (2012) 21 U.S.C. s 384d(b)(1)(A); Accreditation of Third-party Auditors/Certification Bodies to Conduct Food Safety Audits and to Issue Certifications, 80 Federal Register (25 November 2015) 74,570, 74,653–8, accessed 25 November 2016 at www.gpo.gov/fdsys/pkg/FR-2015-11-27/pdf/2015-28160.pdf. On how FSMA embraces public-private governance, see Michaela Tarr Oldfield, 'Enactment of the Food Safety Modernization Act' (2015) 6 *European Journal of Risk Regulation* 488.

[24] US FDA, 'Imports', accessed 25 November 2016 at www.fda.gov/Food/GuidanceRegulation/FSMA/ucm257980.htm; US FDA, 'Importing Food Products into the United States', accessed 25 November 2016 at www.fda.gov/Food/GuidanceRegulation/ImportsExports/Importing/.

firm governance, conflict of interest and periodic self-assessment; and evaluation procedures, monitoring and sanctions for non-compliance. The regulations cover much the same ground as, and refer frequently to, ISO/IEC standards for accreditation bodies and food safety auditors.[25]

Government recognition of accreditation bodies has a number of comparative advantages. Under the FDA's recognition program, the agency will provide expedited review for imports certified by auditors accredited by accreditation bodies recognized by the FDA. For high-risk foods, such certification (or certification by a foreign government) will be a condition of entry. The program thus provides financial incentives to suppliers to obtain audits that conform to the FDA's standards. The regulations also provide incentives to auditors to conduct rigorous audits, since the FDA may withdraw an auditor's accreditation if a supplier that it certifies is linked to a serious outbreak of foodborne illness, if it refuses to grant the FDA access to its records, if it demonstrates 'bias or lack of objectivity', or if its 'performance . . . [calls] into question the validity or reliability of its food safety audits'.[26]

The regulations additionally create incentives for accreditation bodies to ensure the rigor of audits performed by auditors that they accredit. The FDA can revoke recognition of an accreditation body that fails to conduct an adequate self-assessment and take necessary corrective action following FDA withdrawal of accreditation from an auditor accredited by the accreditation body. The FDA can also revoke recognition if an accreditation body refuses to grant the FDA access to its records, misleads the agency, demonstrates bias or lack of objectivity, or fails to adequately support a decision to grant accreditation. In addition, accreditation bodies must maintain records on any denial, withdrawal, suspension or limitation in the scope of auditor accreditation so that the agency can detect attempts by poorly performing auditors to shop for favorable accreditation decisions.[27] These record-keeping and disclosure requirements give the FDA access to information about the rigor of audits. Moreover,

---

[25] See Accreditation of Third-party Auditors/Certification Bodies (n 23) 74,656–8 (rules governing the FDA's recognition of accreditation bodies); ibid, 74,658 (rules governing accreditation bodies' accreditation of food safety auditors). The FDA has also issued draft guidance setting forth 'Model Accreditation Standards' (July 2015), accessed 25 November 2016 at www.fda.gov/downloads/Food/GuidanceRegulation/GuidanceDocumentsRegulatoryInformation/UCM455331.pdf.

[26] Accreditation of Third-party Auditors/Certification Bodies (n 23) 74,574, 74,625 and 74,664.

[27] Ibid 74,654, 74,657. The regulations also allow for reinstatement, ibid 74,658.

FDA oversight and self-assessments by auditors and accreditation bodies generate valuable feedback, and the threat of exclusion from the program creates incentives for them to take corrective action to improve the quality of audits and oversight.

The FDA's recognition program may have additional benefits in terms of participation, transparency and public accountability. Notice-and-comment rule making offers stakeholders an opportunity to participate in shaping the regulations governing audits and makes much of the process transparent. Under the program, the FDA will publish on its website a registry of recognized accreditation bodies and accredited auditors and will post notices when it revokes the recognition of any accreditation body or withdraws the accreditation of any auditor. The regulations require auditors to post on their websites a list of suppliers whom they have certified, the scope and duration of the certification, and the dates on which the supplier paid the auditor any fees associated with the audit. The regulations also require auditors and accreditation bodies to file with the FDA reports of all certification and accreditation decisions, ongoing surveillance and periodic self-assessments. All of this disclosure aims to make the agency and, by extension, the administration, publicly accountable for the success or failure of the program.[28]

Several aspects of the FDA's recognition program may blunt its comparative advantages. First, the scope of the program is not comprehensive – it covers only certification of imports, which constitute 15 per cent of the food consumed within the United States (although the percentage of imports may be much higher in particular sectors). Whether the federal government will eventually extend this approach to domestic food production remains to be seen. Additionally, the program's ability to encourage rigorous auditing and oversight, provide the FDA access to information about the quality of audits, and generate feedback and learning rests entirely upon the strength of the incentives it creates. Scott Rafferty, an expert on third-party certification, warns that the expedited review afforded by voluntary certification under the program 'may not be much of an incentive'. He points out that expedited review for food imports has been widely available under 'established programs that already streamline customs clearance for food importers'. Rafferty predicts that, '[g]iven fiscal constraints, the FDA is unlikely significantly to increase its own presence at ports of entry. So importers know that the overwhelming majority of

[28] For discussion of the democratic accountability of the administration for agency regulation, see Elena Kagan, 'Presidential Administration' (2001) 114 *Harvard Law Review* 2245.

shipments will not be refused, held, or even inspected at the port', thereby undermining the incentive of expedited review. Presumably, limited FDA inspection would also decrease the incentive under the program to obtain certification for high-risk foods.[29]

Moreover, one should not assume that government regulation is always more participatory, transparent or accountable than private alternatives. Notice-and-comment rule making by government agencies can be heavily influenced behind the scenes by industry stakeholders. For example, a recent study examined rule making by the US Environmental Protection Agency involving standards for the release of air toxins from major sources. The study found that, prior to publication of proposed rules for public comment, agency contacts with affected parties were 'extensive' and were 'dominated by regulated parties'. During the notice-and-comment period, formal comments came 'predominantly from regulated industry', and changes to the proposed rules reflected this imbalance and generally favored industry. After rules were promulgated as final, regulated parties frequently brought legal challenges and obtained additional revisions in non-public settlement negotiations. The breadth of public participation and its impact in rule making for the FDA's recognition program merits a similarly careful study.[30]

There are also clear disadvantages to the FDA's recognition program. Rule making proceeded at a slower pace than anticipated. FSMA mandated that the FDA promulgate final regulations for the recognition program by July 2013, but the agency did not publish the regulations until November 2015, and only after litigation against the FDA for this delay.[31] Whether delay is caused by insufficient FDA resources, technical complexity, the need for input from other agencies, political considerations, or some combination of these factors, the slow pace of administrative rule making suggests that the FDA's recognition program may not be as

---

[29] Michael Patoka, 'Three Food Safety Rules Grow Moldy at OIRA as Import-related Outbreaks Continue' Food Safety News (26 June 2013), accessed 25 November 2016 at www.foodsafetynews.com/2013/06/three-food-safety-rules-grow-moldy-at-oira-as-import-related-outbreaks-continue/#.UtQZ8ImA1i4; Scott Rafferty, 'FDA Moving Too Slowly to Promote Private Inspections' Food Safety News, accessed 25 November 2016 at www.foodsafetynews.com/2013/09/the-fda-is-moving-too-slowly-to-promote-private-inspections/#.Vt8rxpMrL6Z; Scott Rafferty, Comments on FDA-2011-N-1046 (RIN 0910-AG66) Third-party Certification of Food Import (29 July 2013) 1, 7–9, accessed 25 November 2016 at www.noticeandcomment.com/FDA-2011-N-0146-0029-fcod-325758.aspx.

[30] Wendy Wagner et al., 'Rulemaking in the Shade: An Empirical Study of EPA's Air Toxic Regulations' (2011) 63 *Admin. L. Rev.* 99, 113–14, 124, 128.

[31] Patoka (n 29).

capable of incorporating feedback in a timely manner to improve regulatory performance compared to private entities like auditing schemes and GFSI, which regularly revise their standards.

NETWORK CONFIGURATION

The different oversight mechanisms that address conflict of interest in private food safety auditing do not operate in isolation from one another. Instead, they comprise a network of institutional actors employing interrelated regulatory instruments. This network structure itself is part of the institutional architecture of oversight, and – like its component parts – it can be analysed in terms of its strengths and weaknesses relative to other configurations.[32]

We will focus on three particular structural attributes of this network: multiplicity, nesting and outsourcing. First, the network includes multiple oversight mechanisms. All of the mechanisms that we have surveyed counteract auditor conflict of interest. Second, some parts of the network have a nested structure. For example, GFSI benchmarks audit schemes that license auditors that conduct internal quality control. Third, some institutional actors outsource credentialing and oversight tasks to others. For instance, audit scheme owners rely on accreditation bodies to accredit auditors.

Each of these network attributes has comparative advantages. Multiplicity allows some oversight mechanisms to fill gaps left by others. Consider, for example, a buyer that did not require its domestic suppliers to obtain audits using benchmarked schemes or accredited auditors. Such audits would fall outside the purview of the FDA's regulation of import audits and the oversight provided by GFSI benchmarking, accreditation and scheme owner licensing. Tort litigation might fill this gap.[33] Multiple oversight mechanisms may also overlap. This can increase financial incentives that favor rigorous auditing. For example, an auditor who provides

---

[32] For a robust analysis of private food safety regulatory networks, see Fabrizio Cafaggi, 'Transnational Governance by Contract: Private Regulation and Contractual Networks in Food Safety' in Axel Marx et al. (eds), *Private Standards and Global Governance* (Edward Elgar 2012).

[33] See Spencer Henson and John Humphrey, 'The Impacts of Private Food Safety Standards on the Food Chain and on Public Standard-setting Processes' (May 2009) Prepared for FAO/WHO, vii (discussing how private food safety standards 'fill "voids"' in the regulatory system), accessed 25 November 2016 at www.fao.org/3/a-i1132e.pdf.

a substandard audit risks potential loss of accreditation, revocation of a license to provide certification under a food safety scheme and tort liability. Overlap may also reinforce professional norms and organizational commitment to food safety throughout the network. For example, professionalism among auditors is reinforced by audit firm policies, food safety scheme criteria, accreditation standards, benchmarks, tort doctrine and government regulations. Overlapping oversight mechanisms that generate similar information may increase the salience of the information, its framing or its importance within an organization.[34] For example, performance feedback from an accreditation inspection may include information already known to audit firm personnel, but an accreditation report may validate internal findings, highlight their importance, present them in a way that more clearly identifies the causes of shortcomings or attract the attention of top managers more effectively than the same information when generated by internal reviews. Finally, multiplicity also increases opportunities for stakeholder participation in the regulatory network.[35]

Nesting also has comparative advantages. By creating layers of oversight, nesting addresses the problem of conflict of interest at different levels of private regulation.[36] For example, just as audit fees give auditors incentive to reduce the rigor of audits, licensing fees give food safety scheme owners incentive to reduce the rigor of their oversight of auditors. GFSI benchmarking creates an additional layer of oversight that creates a financial incentive and cultivates norms to counteract the conflict of interest faced by scheme owners which, in turn, strengthens the effectiveness of their efforts to counteract the conflict of interest faced by auditors. The FDA's recognition program similarly addresses the conflict of interest faced by accreditation bodies in their oversight of auditors. Nesting also broadens participation by involving additional stakeholders in oversight, increases transparency through disclosure requirements and adds a layer or layers of accountability to institutional actors that grant recognition, accreditation or a license.

Outsourcing assigns specific oversight tasks, such as information collection, monitoring and sanctioning, to other institutional actors. Separating

---

[34] *See* Joanna C. Schwartz, 'Introspection through Litigation' (2015) 90 *Notre Dame Law Review* 1055, 1079 (fnn 123–5).

[35] See Errol Meidinger, 'The Administrative Law of Global Private-public Regulation: The Case of Forestry' (2006) 17 *European Journal of International Law* 47, 83.

[36] For a discussion of how nesting multiplies agency problems, see Susan P. Shapiro, 'The Social Control of Impersonal Trust' (1987) 93 *American Journal of Sociology* 623.

functions among different institutional actors may reduce the susceptibility of either actor to conflict of interest. For example, by relying on accreditation bodies to accredit auditors, an audit scheme limits its own ability to lower standards for licensing auditors, which it might be tempted to do in order to increase its income from licensing fees. Simultaneously, the accreditation body's desire to maintain its license from the audit scheme creates an incentive to apply rigorous accreditation standards to auditors, which counteracts the incentive to go easy on auditors in order to increase revenues from accreditation fees.[37] Outsourcing may also increase efficiency by assigning specific tasks to institutional actors best equipped to perform them. Finally, outsourcing increases opportunities for feedback and learning.

These network attributes also have disadvantages. Most notably, overlap and nested layers of oversight may produce inefficient duplication of effort.[38] Additionally, by contrast to a more linear and hierarchical system, a network diffuses responsibility and thereby reduces each institutional actor's accountability for its regulatory performance.[39] The buck does not stop anywhere. Instead, oversight and accountability are distributed throughout the system.

CONCLUSION

We have surveyed a variety of distinct oversight mechanisms that address auditor conflict of interest in private food safety certification audits. Our analysis identifies the institutional actors involved, describes the regulatory instruments that they use, and maps the network that connects their efforts. Our analysis also summarizes relative strengths and weaknesses of each mechanism.

Any evaluation of the effectiveness of the food safety system and its constituent parts would require analysis of performance goals, metrics and

---

[37] *See* Timothy D. Lytton, *Kosher: Private Regulation in the Age of Industrial Food* (Harvard University Press 2013) 127, 133 (discussing similar incentives that result from 'triangulation' between certifiers, food companies, and consumers).

[38] *See* National Research Council, *Standards, Conformity, Assessment, and Trade: Into the 21st Century* (National Academy Press 1995) 87–97 (discussing the costs of redundancy in the US standards setting system).

[39] For discussions of lack of accountability in networks of private regulation, see Anne Mette Kjær, *Governance* (Polity 2004) 14; Laurence Busch, 'Quasi-states? The Unexpected Rise of Private Food Law' in Bernd van der Meulen (ed.) *Private Food Law* (Wageningen Academic 2011) 64; Lesley K. McAllister, 'Regulation by Third-party Verification' (2012) 53 *Boston College Law Review* 1, 32.

outcomes – all of which are beyond the scope of this chapter. We have, however, disaggregated some of the complexity of the system in a way that can inform efforts to undertake such an evaluation. Moreover, we believe that this analysis can be helpful in thinking about regulatory design in other arenas where a multiplicity of institutional actors and regulatory instruments can be combined and configured in different ways to reduce conflict of interest in private auditing and, ultimately, improve regulatory outcomes.[40]

[40] For an empirical analysis of specific reforms aimed at reducing auditor conflict of interest in environmental auditing, see Esther Duflo et al., 'Truth-telling by Third Party Auditors and the Response of Polluting Firms: Experimental Evidence from India' (2013) 128 *The Quarterly Journal of Economics* 1499, 1504.

5 Hybridity in action: Accountability dilemmas of public and for-profit food safety inspectors in Switzerland[1]

Eva Thomann and Fritz Sager

1. ANALYSING HYBRIDITY IN ACTION

This chapter gives an empirical account of output performance in the hybrid implementation arrangement that characterizes the Swiss food safety sector. It makes three original contributions. First, as Havinga and Verbruggen[2] point out, 'governance is more than rule making'. We analyse how the interconnected processes of hybridized implementation, monitoring compliance and enforcement affect the achievement of policy goals at the frontline.[3] Second, conceptually, we highlight the importance of multiple roles and accountabilities of both public and for-profit frontline enforcement agents (street-level bureaucrats) for understanding the effects of hybridization. Third, we scrutinize the regulation of veterinary drugs use for livestock in primary production – an under-researched but crucial aspect in addressing the risks to food safety presented by animal diseases and antibiotic resistance.[4]

---

[1] This chapter is derived in part from an article published in (2014) 16(4) *Public Management Review*, copyright Taylor & Francis, available online: http://www.tandfonline.com/10.1080/14719037.2013.841979 (accessed 26 November 2016).

[2] T. Havinga and P. Verbruggen, 'Hybridization of Food Governance: An Analytical Framework', Chapter 1 in this volume.

[3] Havinga and Verbruggen (Chapter 1 in this volume) distinguish the regulatory processes of implementation (implementing standards within the operations of targets of regulation such as firms), monitoring compliance, and enforcement. In our study, we refer to 'implementation arrangements' or 'implementation structures' as the regulatory arrangements encompassing all these three processes (consistent with the policy implementation literature), while otherwise remaining faithful to the distinction.

[4] F. Sager, E. Thomann, C. Zollinger, and C. Mavrot, 'Confronting Theories

Hybridity can be understood as a complex interplay of state, market and societal actors at differing regulatory levels.[5] The network-like implementation setting under study involves the same actors in multiple regulatory activities: implementation, monitoring compliance and enforcement.[6] Given that the actors analysed here perform both monitoring and enforcement activities, we refer to them as 'enforcement agents'. By involving both public and private actors into monitoring compliance and enforcement, it is also situated at the intersection of different societal spheres: the private, for-profit and the public, non-profit sectors.[7] Each of these spheres imply distinct rationalities and differentiated task, legitimacy, and resource environments.[8] This chapter analyses how these two aspects of hybridity affect the degree to which the public and private actors assigned with these activities comply with their duties to help achieve safe food (output performance). As such, we apply a specific and limited focus on those aspects of output performance in the 'monitoring compliance' phase[9] that refer to enforcement agents' compliance with specific monitoring (inspection) targets. This neither entails enforcement in the sense of ensuring general compliance to rules, nor co-production in the sense of compliance to internalized professional standards.[10] Two research questions are explored: First, does it make a difference whether food safety regulation is enforced by public actors, or by private, for-profit actors who themselves are addressees of the policy? Second, what explains such (non-)differences?

The complexity prevailing between actors in hybrid implementation structures requires a specific analytical focus that is complementary to the usual analyses of command-and-control problems and regulatory

---

of Integration. A Comparison of Veterinary Drugs Regulations in Five European Countries' (2014) 15(5) *Journal of Comparative Policy Analysis* 457–474.

5 D. Levi-Faur, 'Regulation and Regulatory Governance' in D. Levi-Faur (ed.) *Handbook on the Politics of Regulation* (Edward Elgar 2011) 1–25.

6 Havinga and Verbruggen (n 2) 8.

7 C. Skelcher and S.R. Smith, 'Theorizing Hybridity: Institutional Logics, Complex Organizations, and Actor Identities: The case of Nonprofits' (2014) *Public Administration* DOI: 10.1111/padm.12105.

8 K. Fossestøl, E. Breit, T.A. Andreassen and L. Klemsdal, 'Managing Institutional Complexity in Public Sector Reform: Hybridization in Front-Line Service Organizations' (2015) *Public Administration* DOI: 10.1111/padm.12144 and M. Gulbrandsen, T. Thune, S. Brorstad Borlaug and J. Hanson, 'Emerging Hybrid Practices in Public-private Research Centres' (2015) *Public Administration* DOI: 10.1111/padm.12140.

9 Havinga and Verbruggen (n 2).

10 P. Hupe and M. Hill, 'Street-Level Bureaucracy and Public Accountability' (2007) 85(2) *Public Administration* 279–300, 294.

and economic incentives.[11] In this chapter we adopt a sociological, bottom-up implementation perspective that focuses on the interactions and accountabilities of implementing and enforcement agents instead.[12] While interacting with their environment, these agents take on social roles in which they feel the obligation to justify or explain their behavior to some significant other.[13] These roles generate requirements for behavior. Accountability describes 'a condition in which individuals who exercise power are constrained by external means and by internal norms'.[14] In hybrid environments, agents are 'called to be accountable to a multiplicity of actors, expectations, and in varying conditions'.[15] We propose an extended accountability regimes framework[16] that captures how accountability is simultaneously exercised toward the state, professional peers, the society, and customers or shareholders.[17]

The central argument we put forward is that as new roles and accountabilities are added to existing ones, role conflicts and accountability dilemmas for individual frontline workers can arise.[18] These dilemmas can negatively affect the agents' willingness to implement the policy.[19] Since

---

[11] For example T.D. Lytton and L.K. McAllister, 'Oversight in Private Food Safety Auditing: Addressing Auditor Conflict of Interest' (2014) *Wisconsin Law Review* 289–335 and C. Skelcher, 'Fishing in Muddy Waters: Principals, Agents, and Democratic Governance in Europe' (2009) 20(suppl 1) *Journal of Public Administration Research and Theory* i161–i175.

[12] Hupe and Hill (n 10), M. Lipsky, *Street-Level Bureaucracy. Dilemmas of the Individual in Public Services* (first published in 1980, Russell Sage 2010) and T. Parsons, 'Suggestions for a Sociological Approach to the Theory of Organizations' (1956) 1(2) *Administrative Science Quarterly*, 225–39.

[13] Hupe and Hill (n 10).

[14] J.G.S. Koppell, 'Pathologies of Accountability: ICANN and the Challenge of "Multiple Accountabilities Disorder"' (2005) 65(1) *Public Administration Review*, 94–108, 94.

[15] A. Buffat, '"Public on the Outside, Private on the Inside": the Organizational Hybridization, Sense of Belonging and Identity Strategies of the Employees of a Public Unemployment Insurance Fund in Switzerland' (2014) 80(1) *International Review of Administrative Sciences* 70–88, 81.

[16] E. Thomann, P. Hupe and F. Sager, 'Serving Many Masters: Public Accountability in Private Policy Implementation' (under review).

[17] J.L. Mashaw, 'Structuring a "Dense Complexity": Accountability and the Project of Administrative Law' (2005) 4 *Issues in Legal Scholarship* 1–38.

[18] Koppell (n 14), Mashaw (n 17) and B. Poulsen, 'Competing Traditions of Governance and Dilemmas of Administrative Accountability: The Case of Denmark' (2009) *Public Administration* DOI: 10.1111/j.1467-9299.2008.00727.

[19] Lipsky (n 12) and L. Tummers, B. Vermeeren, B. Steijn and V. Bekkers, 'Public Professionals and Policy Implementation. Conceptualizing and Measuring Three Types of Role Conflicts' (2012) 14(8) *Public Management Review* 1041–1059.

public and private agents have different goal orientations,[20] and these goal orientations influence their behavior, we expect this to be reflected in their decisions at the street level. The sociological perspective we adopt[21] supports and fruitfully illustrates empirically the argument of Hussein et al.[22] that under the economic relationship between the players, the regulatory process may be captured by the economically dominant player(s).

The case at hand is the national Swiss Ordinance on Veterinary Medicinal Products (OVMP), which regulates the supply and use of veterinary drugs for livestock. Within the OVMP's control system, enforcement tasks are shared between the public servants, that is the regional (cantonal) veterinary services, and the private veterinarians, that is the first target group of the policy. The private veterinarians have a control function on the farmers in their usage of veterinary drugs. This creates a double role: as the private veterinarians have to control their own customers, they are torn between the accountabilities of the state and the market. As we illustrate below, accountability rules (effective oversight) to counter these conflicts are lacking.

The study illustrates some in-built tensions that can arise from the hybridization of food governance and their practical implications. Our results suggest that the complex interaction patterns of hybrid settings can create multiple roles and contradictory accountabilities which, in the absence of effective oversight, may have detrimental effects on compliance on the ground. It is problematic if an actor is simultaneously the target group of a policy and its enforcement agent, and if the rationalities of the state and the market contradict each other. In a sector where a complete replacement of private regulation by public regulation is neither feasible nor desirable, regulators need to take such problems into account to ensure the regulatees' compliance with food safety regulations.[23]

Next we discuss the theoretical basics of hybrid implementation and enforcement and derive two hypotheses. After presenting our case, the data and methods employed as well as their limited reliability and generalizability, we present empirical findings from a survey that was done in the course of the evaluation of the OVMP.[24] Our empirical analysis is

---

[20] B.G. Peters, 'Institutional Theory' in M. Bevir (ed.), *The Sage Handbook of Governance* (London: Sage 2011).

[21] Parsons (n 12).

[22] M. Hussein, M.G. Martinez and A. Fearne, 'Management-based Regulation of Food Safety in The United Kingdom' (Chapter 7 in this volume).

[23] See Lytton and McAllister (n 11) for a discussion of possible remedies.

[24] F. Sager, N. van der Heiden, C. Mavrot, E. Thomann, C. Zollinger and M. Hinterleitner. *Formative Evaluation Tierarzneimittelverordnung (TAMV)*

structured along four aspects of the heuristic proposed by Havinga and Verbruggen:[25] the actors involved in the hybrid arrangement, the interaction of public and private actors, the results and effects of hybridization, and the character of their relationship. We conclude by discussing theoretical and practical implications.

2. PUBLIC ACCOUNTABILITY IN HYBRID IMPLEMENTATION ARRANGEMENTS

The last 40 years 'have seen a . . . shift from bureaucratic hierarchy to markets and networks . . . The identity and role of public servants has changed to emphasize these tasks'.[26] The collaboration between the public and private sector implies that private, for-profit actors are increasingly assigned tasks related to the implementation and enforcement of policies:[27] 'public food governance has been challenged, complemented or at times superseded by private governance systems', which gives rise to specific challenges.[28] Simultaneously, the state remains responsible and has typically focused on increasingly regulating private actors to safeguard the public interest.[29] To understand how hybridization works in practice,[30] Lipsky's[31] argument needs to be considered 'that the decisions of street-level bureaucrats, the routines they establish, and the devices they invent to cope with uncertainties and work pressures, effectively become the public policies they carry out'. The core determinant for output delivery is thus the situations in which frontline workers act: 'Street-level bureaucrats have discretion because the nature of service provision calls for human judgment.'[32]

(Bern: Kompetenzzentrum für Public Management der Universität Bern 2012) 35 and E. Thomann, 'Is Output Performance all about the Resources? A Fuzzy-Set Qualitative Comparative Analysis of Street-Level Bureaucrats in Switzerland' (2015) 93(1) *Public Administration* 177–94.

[25] Verbruggen and Havinga (n 2).

[26] M. Bevir, 'The New Governance and the Public Servant, cc. 1979–2011' Paper delivered at the *ECPR Joint Sessions* 2012, Antwerp, 10–15 April 2012, 1.

[27] C. Knill and J. Tosun, *Public Policy. A New Introduction* (Palgrave Macmillan 2012).

[28] Verbruggen and Havinga (n 2) 1.

[29] B.G. Peters and J. Pierre, *Governance, Politics and the State* (Palgrave Macmillan 2000).

[30] e.g. Hussein et al. (n 22).

[31] Lipsky (n 12) xii.

[32] Ibid (n 12) 161.

The concept of *accountability regimes* helps explain the use of discretion. It refers to a set of guidelines for action, which may include sanctions.[33] Accountability regimes involve six basic features:[34] who is accountable to whom, about what, through what processes, by what standards and with what effects? As enforcers of a policy, frontline workers are held accountable by formal rules stemming from *the state* (here: the food safety regulations). Second, frontline workers see themselves as *professionals* governed by 'occupational or professional' ideologies.[35] In this role, they are held accountable by the wider circle of professionals (here: the veterinary discipline). Third, frontline workers are also accountable to expectations from *society*. As Maynard-Moody and Musheno[36] point out, 'in their narratives . . . [they] define their work and to a large extent themselves in terms of relationships more than rules'. In this role, accountability is exercised toward the clientele (here: the livestock farmers). Finally, Thomann et al.[37] highlight that market mechanisms imply a fourth, essentially customer- and shareholder-driven type of accountability in policy implementation:

> In . . . markets, . . . producers are responsible to consumers . . . for their products' quality and price. The process or mechanism of accountability is market competition . . . The standards are customers' individual preferences. The effects of accountability to the market are, immediately, the willingness of consumers to buy the product at the offered price and, ultimately, a product's capacity to maintain itself in the market.[38]

The accountability regimes framework captures that in their various social roles, implementing and enforcement agents have multiple accountabilities that can create competing, incongruent demands and values – the dilemmas of street-level bureaucrats.[39] This notion has a special salience within hybrid implementation arrangements, whose institutional complexity 'is making matters increasingly complex for practitioners – especially with regard to the proliferation of expectations made of them'.[40] Combining and managing the complexity of multiple logics in hybrid arrangements

---

33 Hupe and Hill (n 10).
34 Mashaw (n 17).
35 Hupe and Hill (n 10) 282.
36 D. Maynard-Moody and M. Musheno, *Cops, Teachers, Counsellors* (University of Michigan Press 2003) 20.
37 Thomann et al. (n 16).
38 Mashaw (n 17) 21.
39 Lipsky (n 12).
40 Buffat (n 15) 71.

can be difficult.[41] The literature formulates contrasting expectations on the implications of hybridization for output delivery.

2.1 Hypotheses

Stoker[42] argues that new forms of governance are ultimately concerned with creating the conditions for ordered rule and collective action. Their outputs are supposedly no different from those of government: it 'is not what the state does that is different, but *how* he does it'.[43] Whether enforcement agents are public or private actors explains how they act,[44] but not what output they ultimately produce. Indeed, previous studies have not observed systematic differences between the performance of public and for-profit policy implementers,[45] and attributed this to the shared defining character of the nature of their work.[46] Our first hypothesis hence assumes that the main differences between the performance of public and private actors lie in the processes of policy implementation and enforcement rather than its results.

H1: *There are no differences between the output performance of public and private enforcement agents.*

Contrary to this, Smith et al.[47] argue that the 'problems of implementation have been magnified by a shift from hierarchy to networks and market forms of delivery'. First, hybrid governance modes 'involve actors with different goals and different values about the policy problems they are addressing'.[48] The multiple and complex interrelations generally

41 Fossestøl et al. (n 8).

42 G. Stoker, 'Governance as Theory: Five Propositions' (1998) 50(155) *International Social Science Journal* 17–28.

43 D. Richards and M.J. Smith, *Governance and Public Policy in the UK* (Oxford University Press 2002) 279, emphasis in the original.

44 For example M. Considine and J.M. Lewis, 'Governance at Ground Level: The Frontline Bureaucrat in the Age of Markets and Networks' (1999) 59(6) *Public Administration Review* 467–80.

45 M. Considine, J.M. Lewis and S. O'Sullivan, 'Quasi-markets and Service Delivery Flexibility Following a Decade of Employment Assistance Reform in Australia' (2011) 40(4) *Journal of Social Policy* 811–33.

46 Lipsky (n 12).

47 M.J. Smith, D. Richards, A. Geddes and H. Mathers, 'Analysing Policy Delivery in the United Kingdom: The Case of Street Crime and Anti-social Behaviour' (2011) 89(3) *Public Administration* 958.

48 Peters (n 20) 81.

imply an increased potential for competing demands.[49] Attempts at being accountable in multiple senses can create dilemmas for the individual frontline worker.[50]

Second, public and market actors may have distinct rationalities that guide their actions.[51] Public and private actors may diverge in their understandings of a 'good' output: whereas the public rationality focuses on public service objectives, market actors prioritize efficiency and results.[52] Their inherent interest in profits and customers[53] may be difficult to reconcile with the public interest.[54] As enforcement agents, private actors serve a public goal. It might not always be possible to fulfil both roles at once, if they are in conflict.[55] Accountability dilemmas might favour economic performance at the cost of, rather than in addition to central policy goals like equality, fairness and inclusion.[56] Whereas the literature often asserts a balancing effect of mixed governance modes,[57] we expect that accountability dilemmas will be reflected in the implementation and enforcement processes:

H2: *Due to divergent goal orientations and conflicting roles and accountabilities, implementation deficits of public enforcement agents are explained differently than those of private enforcement agents.*

We now present the hybrid implementation structure under study, our data and methods.

---

[49] Buffat (n 15) and Gulbrandsen et al. (n 8).

[50] Koppell (n 14) 95, 99 and Poulsen (n 18) 117.

[51] Considine and Lewis (n 44), Fossestøl et al. (n 8) and Skelcher and Smith (n 7).

[52] M. Considine and M.J. Lewis, 'Bureaucracy, Network of Enterprise? Comparing Models of Governance in Australia, Britain, The Netherlands, and New Zealand' (2003) 63(2) *Public Administration Review* 131–40.

[53] Ibid. (n 52).

[54] E. Lieberherr, 'Transformation of Water Governance and Legitimacy: Comparing Swiss, German and English Water Supply and Sanitation Service Providers' (2012) Doctoral degree, Swiss Federal Institute of Technology, Lausanne.

[55] Tummers et al. (n 19).

[56] Considine and Lewis (n 44) 471.

[57] Bevir (n 26).

3. RESEARCH DESIGN, DATA AND METHODS

This section depicts which actors are involved in the hybrid governance arrangement, and how they interact.[58] At the turn of the millennium, several animal diseases fostered the regulatory importance of food safety issues. The use of veterinary drugs for livestock is central to combatting and preventing such diseases, and plays a major role in the emergence of antibiotic resistance. Since 2004, the OVMP regulates the dispensing and use of veterinary drugs for livestock in Switzerland. It aims at ensuring the correct use of veterinary drugs, preventing drug residues in food products and protecting the animals. The ordinance regulates the type, the amount and the storage of drugs that may be given to which animals, under what circumstances and by whom. It addresses two main target groups: veterinarians prescribe and supply (dispense) veterinary drugs, whereas the livestock owners often apply (administer) the drugs to the animals single-handedly.

In federal Switzerland, the enforcement of the OVMP takes place at the cantonal level. Public inspectors of the 26 cantonal veterinary offices (public veterinarians) perform official controls of compliance through on-site inspections of veterinary practices and farms. These controls must take place every five years in veterinary practices and (until 2012) every ten years on farms. In addition to the latter, the farmers' compliance with the OVMP is partially controlled by the private veterinarians on a much more regular basis. The regulations foresee written agreements between veterinarians and livestock owners, which entail biannual visits to the farms. During these visits, the veterinarians are obligated to check the storage of drugs and the documentation of their use. Many veterinary drugs – especially antibiotics – are given to the animals via feed (medicated feedingstuffs). The On-Farm Manufacture (OFM) of medicated feedingstuffs by farmers must be supervised by a specially trained veterinarian (FTVP – usually the same dispensing vet), based on a written agreement. On site, the FTVP gives detailed instructions and supervises the processes of blending, feeding, and cleaning of the technical facilities. The FTVP is legally responsible for ensuring famers' compliance with regulations. A strong for-profit element characterizes this arrangement: the private veterinarians charge the farmers for their enforcement activities and depend economically upon this target group. These for-profit inspectors are hence likely to display the customer-driven type of accountability.

This complex implementation structure (summarized in Figure 5.1) is

---

58 Verbruggen and Havinga (n 2).

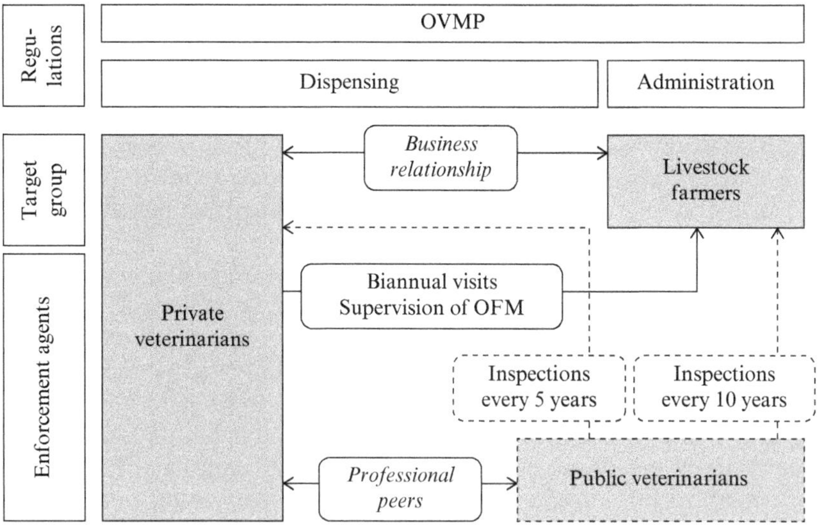

Note: Highlighted boxes indicate actors, two-directional arrows relationships between actors. Unidirectional arrows highlight prescribed enforcement activities, where dotted lines refer to public veterinarians and continuous lines to private veterinarians.

Source: Authors' own illustration.

Figure 5.1 Implementation structure of the OVMP

a system of regulated self-governance characterized by hierarchical intervention through legally binding rules, accompanied by cooperative relationships between public and private actors during implementation and enforcement.[59] Clearly formalized and institutionalized procedures delegate enforcement competencies to private market actors.[60] The hybridity of this arrangement has two components: first, the private veterinarians are involved at several regulatory levels, being simultaneously policy addressees and implementing agents.[61] Second, we can distinguish public and private enforcement agents. Both have discretional power, share the same professional background as trained veterinarians, and enforce the

[59] C. Knill and A. Lenschow, 'Modes of Regulation in the Governance of the European Union: Towards a Comprehensive Evaluation' in J. Jordana and D. Levi-Faur (eds), *The Politics of Regulation. Institutions and Regulatory Reforms for the Age of Governance* (Edward Elgar 2003).

[60] Knill and Tosun (n 27) 210f.

[61] Levi-Faur (n 5).

same overarching policy. This is the basis upon which their performance can be directly compared: both actor groups are assigned specific duties to monitor compliance, which can be compared through the output targets defined by the OVMP. Although these duties differ in their content (public on-site inspections vs. private biannual visits/OFM supervision), they do not differ in kind (monitoring compliance through physical controls of virtually the same regulatory contents) and their contributions to the goals of the OVMP are thus directly comparable.

The institutional design of (public) regulatory enforcement importantly helps private actors enforce regulation.[62] Effective monitoring crucially creates incentives for target groups to comply with policies.[63] Private actors might implement rules in a rather light-handed way if the threat of public enforcement is low.[64] However, regulatory oversight can be considered as low, and sanctions as absent, on both the public and the private veterinarians as enforcement agents. The official controls of the private veterinarians focus on how they dispense veterinary drugs in their role as policy addressees, rather than on the question as to whether they adequately monitor the farmers. Public veterinarians can impose monetary fines, additional inspections, enactments or penal sanctions,[65] but their use against the private veterinarians is uncommon. The Federal Veterinary Office collects the cantonal data on the frequency and results of inspections on farms (*Informationssystem für den öffentlichen Veterinärdienst*, ISVET), but neither is there a national database for the official controls of private veterinarians, nor any superordinate enforcement on public veterinarians who do not perform as required. Being only weakly held accountable by the state, we expect public and private veterinarians to respond strongly to accountabilities stemming from their social roles as professionals who interact with clients and need to respond to customer needs.

We rely on data gathered during the formative evaluation of the OVMP in early 2012. Semi-structured telephone interviews were conducted with cantonal public veterinarians from all except two cantons

---

[62] P. Verbruggen, 'Gorillas in the Closet? Public and Private Actors in the Enforcement of Transnational Private Regulation' (2013) 7(4) *Regulation & Governance* 512–32.

[63] S.C. Winter, 'Implementation Perspectives: Status and Reconsideration' in B.G. Peters and J. Pierre (eds), *Handbook of Public Administration* (Sage 2003) 220.

[64] R. Baldwin, M. Cave and M. Lodge, *Understanding Regulation: Theory, Strategy, and Practice* (Oxford University Press 2011) 35, 58.

[65] Sager et al. (n 24) 35.

(N = 22),[66] representatives of the cantonal (N = 24) and national (N = 11) agricultural producers' associations, producers of medicated feedingstuffs (N = 6), experts in animal health (N = 8), retailers (N = 4) and inspectors (N = 5) of food products, and national regulators (N = 3). Due to practical considerations of feasibility, an online questionnaire was sent to all Swiss private veterinarians (N = 373, response rate 25 per cent). Although the response rate could be higher, it enables us to gain valuable and rare large-N descriptive insights into private implementation. The results of inspections by public veterinarians on farms in 2010 stem from ISVET.

To juxtapose the output performance of public and private enforcement agents, we compare their delivery of inspections, sanctions and control results with the statutory provisions. When explaining these patterns, we qualitatively assess the accountabilities of private and public veterinarians in their social roles to identify possible dilemmas and the resulting incentives for implementation. Our causal conclusions are primarily based on qualitative information gained from the interviews and document analysis (legal regulations, official position papers by the federal administration and different stakeholder groups). We lack information about the criteria upon which the farms included in the ISVET data were selected for inspections, which are likely to differ between the cantons. Because neither the controlled farms nor the cantons represent a random sample, conclusions about the population cannot be drawn. The results of official inspections, for example the evaluations by cantonal veterinarians of the farmers' compliance with the different checkpoints, are likely to partly mirror different interpretations of the OVMP's rules by the public veterinarians. To put it in Lipsky's[67] words: 'Agency-generated statistics are likely to tell us little about the phenomena they purport to reflect, but a great deal about the agency behavior that produced the statistics'. Considering their methodological limitations and limited reliability, the data are analysed by means of descriptive statistics to illustrate and support our qualitative argumentation.

---

66 The cantons Uri, Schwyz, Nid- and Obwalden, as well as Appenzell Innerrhoden and Ausserrhoden, share one public veterinarian. Zug and Ticino did not participate in the interviews, but Liechtenstein is subject to the OVMP as a 'canton'.

67 Lipsky (n 12) 51.

4. PUBLIC AND PRIVATE PERFORMANCE: DOES HYBRIDITY MATTER?

We now analyse the results of hybridity, specifically, how the defined inspection goals were delivered. The output performance of the public veterinarians entails the inspections of veterinary dispensaries and farms. The public veterinarians should inspect 20 per cent of the veterinarians' dispensaries every year. Since there is no database for these inspections, we can only rely on the public veterinarians' own declarations about their control and sanction activities, which are unreliable, not available for all cantons, and limited in their comparability.

The available information indicates that the target of 20 per cent is met by many, but not by all cantons (Table 5.1, second column). Furthermore, the data reveal a clear implementation failure for the inspections on farms. Instead of 10 per cent, only 5.8 per cent of the livestock farms were actually controlled.[68] There is substantial variation in the output performance of the different cantonal public veterinarians. Interviewees mentioned the lack of money and personnel as the main reason for this implementation failure. However, simultaneously, only a minority (7 out of 22) of the public veterinarians complained about lacking resources – hence revealing an inconsistency. The available resources are not consistently related to output performance (Eta = 0.248). Clearly, and as we elaborate below, there must be an additional explanation for the deficient output performance of public veterinarians.[69]

The private veterinarians must perform biannual visits within written agreements, as well as their duties as FTVP. The ISVET (Table 5.2) indicates that most farmers have concluded at least one written agreement with a veterinarian. Yet, the biannual visits as the central duty within such an agreement were only carried out in half of the cases. Furthermore, in more than 50 per cent of the instances of OFM, private veterinarians dispensed the drugs to the farmers despite the absence of a written agreement with an FTVP – a clear breach of their monitoring duty. Finally, even if an FTVP was supposedly present on site, his or her instructions were often not followed (Table 5.2). This finding is not an artifact, but corresponds to the judgement of the public veterinarian who inspected the farm, checked the documentation of OFM, double-checked the amount of used drugs (usually antibiotics),

---

68 From 2004 to 2010, only 6.24% of Swiss livestock farms have been checked on average (ISVET). There are no substantial differences between years.

69 See Thomann 2015 (n 24) for an in-depth analysis of the role of resources in this setting.

Table 5.1 Output performance of public veterinarians

Canton[1]	% of veterinarians' dispensaries controlled per year[2] Required by OVMP: 20	% of farms controlled in 2010[3] Required by OVMP: 10
1	–	4.8
2	–	6.5
3	–	8.9
4	20	–
5	20	4.1
6	20	3.3
7	20	1.6
8	18	8.4
9	–	4.9
10	–	7.1
11	–	8.7
12	20	10.4
13	–	9.1
14	20	5.1
15	22.2	5.4
16	20	6.3
17	20	5.4
18	–	1.6
19	16.7	3.6
20	20	6.1
21	10	7.3
22	–	9.9

Notes:
1 The names of cantons are not displayed to ensure the respondents' anonymity.
2 Authors' own calculation according to self-indications by public veterinarians.
3 ISVET.
— No indications.

Source: Sager et al. (2014) (n 24) 491.

and sampled whether the feeding machines contained residues. It appears that a great number of the private veterinarians substantially neglect their obligation to ensure the farmers' compliance with the regulations.

Clearly, implementation failures exist both with public and with private veterinarians but are more severe with the latter.[70] The observed

[70] Policy addressees judged both public and private veterinarians to comply with the regulations to roughly the same extent, which, however, considerably

Table 5.2 Output performance of private veterinarians

Checkpoint	*CH*[1]	*Range*[2]	*Median*[2]	*IQR*[2]	*Dispersion*[3]
No formally correct written agreement exists	15.9	36.8	14.4	4.7–22.9	*6*; 6
Biannual visits are not carried out	50.1	100	48.2	28.6–66.9	*6*; 6
In case of OFM: No written agreement with FTVP exists	55.7	100	33.3	0.0–60.0	5
In case of OFM: Instructions of FTVP were not followed	49.1	100	0.0	0.0–54.6	5

Notes:
ISVET. 22 veterinary offices.
CH = Switzerland.
IQR = interquartile range.
1 % of controlled farms in Switzerland.
2 % of controlled farms in cantons.
3 Italics: Number of cantons above third quartile; others: below first quartile.

Source: Sager et al. (2012) (n 24) 491.

differences in the output performance of private and public veterinarians do not support our first hypothesis. In line with our second hypothesis, results indicate that private enforcement agents might perform worse than their public colleagues. To shed light on these patterns, we now assess the character of the relationship between public and private actors in more depth.[71]

4.1 The Relationship between Public and Private Veterinarians

Why are private veterinarians not always controlled and sanctioned as required by the public veterinarians? Our interviews indicate that the public veterinarians are somewhat reluctant to exert authority on private veterinarians. First, as professionals, the public veterinarians feel that they depend on the willingness of the private veterinarians to cooperate

exceeds the degree of compliance detected in the ISVET dataset (see in detail: F. Sager, E. Thomann, C. Zollinger, N. van der Heiden and C. Mavrot, 'Street-level Bureaucrats and New Modes of Governance – How Conflicting Roles Affect the Implementation of the Swiss Ordinance on Veterinary Medicinal Products' (2014) 16(4) *Public Management Review* 481–502).

71 Verbruggen and Havinga (n 2).

to effectively enforce the regulations on livestock farmers. Second, the public veterinarians used to be private veterinarians themselves and are professionally and personally interlinked with their former colleagues. These mechanisms are weaker when the inspections of veterinarians' dispensaries are outsourced to an external, independent veterinary office, as done by 11 cantons.[72] If a public veterinarian censures and/or sanctions a farmer, then this often also requires a change in behavior of the private veterinarian in charge who advised the farmer. Thus, public veterinarians might also avoid enforcing the OVMP on farms in order to maintain a good relationship with the private veterinarians. Indirectly, regulatory oversight on the private veterinarians is therefore even further weakened by the hybrid implementation structure.[73]

The different roles and accountabilities, the resulting dilemmas and incentives for policy enforcement of public and private veterinarians can be resumed as follows. Public veterinarians should control and sanction the private veterinarians as policy addressees. Simultaneously, they depend largely on the latter's cooperation as fellow policy enforcers. The private veterinarians' double role as policy addressees and enforcement agents alters their relationship with the public agent. The hybrid implementation structure limits the possibilities of public agents to effectively treat the private enforcement agents as target group. The public enforcement agent must trade off enforcing the policy vis-à-vis this first target group (veterinarians) against enforcing the policy vis-à-vis the second target group (the farmers). The resulting dilemma is a first effect of hybridization, created by the *simultaneous assignment of duties at differing regulatory levels.*

The relationship between the two groups is affected both by the private veterinarians' role as policy addressees and their role as professional peers. This second double role adds another dilemma for the public veterinarians and negatively affects their output performance. Both accountability dilemmas represent a conflict between the public enforcement agent's professional values and the need to comply with the regulations.

4.2 The Relationship between Private Veterinarians and Livestock Owners

Why are the farmers so poorly controlled by private veterinarians? Our qualitative evidence reveals that the key to this relationship could be that the farmers are not only a target group, but also the private veterinarians' main source of income. As service providers, the private veterinarians

---

[72] Sager et al. (n 24) 25.
[73] See also Hussein et al. (n 22).

depend on the farmers. Interviewees have stressed how important it is for the private veterinarians not to annoy their customers – which might not exactly be a good prerequisite to performing inspections.

The farmers grant the OVMP minor importance and mainly perceive it as restricting their freedom of action. Most farmers clearly prefer collaborating with a veterinarian who does not emphasize compliance too much. Some exert significant pressure on veterinarians to stretch the regulations in their own favor, for example to dispense high amounts of antibiotics. The biannual visits, as well as the supervision of OFM by FTVPs, are very unpopular amongst livestock owners – more than 50 per cent of them do not recognize the usefulness of these measures. Given that they have to pay for both, this is not surprising.

Our interviews as well as official statistics suggest that the easiest way for private veterinarians to avoid a loss of customers may be to bypass unfavorable provisions without having it discovered. An effective enforcement of the regulations is a potential threat to the veterinarians' business. This is reflected in the private veterinarians' general perception that the OVMP is too restrictive. Usually, the same veterinarian with whom the written agreement is concluded also assigns as FTVP. This means that the same private veterinarian first sells the drugs (usually antibiotics) and is then supposed to ensure the correctness of the process. Moreover, private veterinarians are locally rooted: a reputation of being 'strict' could potentially alienate other customers. In sum, private veterinarians have a significant economic interest in not carrying out their duties as policy enforcers. The interdependencies created by the business relationship with farmers have the potential to aggravate this effect.

We can hence identify the different roles of private veterinarians in their relationship with livestock owners, the resulting accountability dilemmas and incentives for enforcement. The private veterinarians are mainly held accountable by the livestock owners. They have a double role because they are simultaneously enforcement agents and for-profit service providers who depend economically on the target group.[74] These two roles create contrasting incentives which are difficult to reconcile. This accountability dilemma limits the private veterinarians' scope of action to effectively enforce the policy vis-à-vis the target group. Results suggest that economic motivations outweigh the responsibility as enforcement agents for many private veterinarians.

This second effect of hybridization prevails because of *the clash between the public and the private, for-profit logics* which the private veterinarians

---

[74] Lytton and McAllister (n 11).

are unable to reconcile. Contrary to the public veterinarians, the private veterinarians experience an accountability dilemma between market incentives and enforcement duties (state regime).

5. MULTIPLE ACCOUNTABILITIES AS A RESULT OF HYBRIDIZATION

The implementation structure of the OVMP illustrates that hybridization makes a difference to output delivery: contrary to Stoker's[75] assumption, the outputs of private enforcement agents are slightly worse and have different reasons than those of their public colleagues. Conforming to the expectations of Smith et al.,[76] the complexity of relations of the hybrid regime has created multiple and conflicting roles and accountabilities for both public and private enforcement agents.[77] Private veterinarians are simultaneously implementing agents, policy addressees, professionals and market actors. This produces additional dilemmas for and negatively affects the output delivery of both public and private enforcement agents.[78] This pattern suggests two possible limitations of the hybridization of food governance.

First, the fact that the private veterinarians perform tasks at several regulatory levels restricts the possibilities for the public veterinarians to effectively hold them accountable and enforce the regulations. This dilemma between rules and professional values is reinforced because the private agents are simultaneously clientele and professional peers for the public agents. For policy designers, this indicates that it can be problematic if an actor is simultaneously target group of a policy and enforcement agent.

Second, the output performance of private veterinarians is shaped by their double role and incompatible rationalities as 'public' monitoring and enforcement agents and private service providers. The livestock farmers are both clientele and their main source of income. This creates a dilemma where economic interests often impede the effective enforcement of the OVMP. This suggests that due to economic dependencies, private service providers may not always be interested in enforcing a public policy vis-à-vis their customers – which may be an in-built tension of this particular type of hybridity.[79]

---

75 Stoker (n 42).
76 Smith et al. (n 47).
77 Thomann et al. (n 16) and Tummers et al. (n 19).
78 Koppell (n 14).
79 Lytton and McAllister (n 11).

We do not claim that the hybridization of food safety policy enforcement inescapably worsens policy outputs. The implementing agents we observed are only weakly held accountable by the state, and particularly likely to refer to market incentives. In other populations, different responses to hybridization might emerge.[80] However, our results do suggest that regulators should take possible accountability dilemmas in hybrid arrangements into account. This goes beyond an analysis of incentives to include social roles and accountabilities of implementing agents. As an analytic complement to the insightful heuristic proposed by Havinga and Verbruggen,[81] the accountability regimes framework[82] provides a useful tool to model and anticipate such problems.

Indeed, our results very much support Verbruggen's[83] assertions that effective regulatory enforcement and overlapping interests of the public and the private sector are crucial to make private governance work. As to the former, Lytton and McAllister[84] propose several control mechanisms to counter tensions such as the ones encountered in our case – which might, however, not be a panacea in practice.[85] As to the latter, Thomann et al.[86] note that hybrid arrangements demonstrably respond to competing demands by developing strategies and practices that integrate different rationalities over time.[87] As Poulsen[88] points out, 'it is through the occurrence of dilemmas that agency constantly transforms and reinvents existing traditions'. In a sector like food safety regulation where a complete replacement of private regulation by public regulation is neither feasible nor desirable, it is crucial that the differing rationalities of the public and private sector can be reconciled. The contribution of our case study lies in showing that hybridity can have concrete and negative effects in practice. Regulators need to take such problems seriously to ensure the regulatees' compliance with food safety regulations.

---

80 For example Fossestøl et al. (n 8) and Gulbrandsen et al. (n 8).
81 Verbruggen and Havinga (n 2).
82 Hupe and Hill (n 10) and Thomann et al (n 16).
83 Verbruggen (n 62).
84 Lytton and McAllister (n 11).
85 Lipsky (n 12).
86 Thomann et al (n 16).
87 Fossestøl et al. (n 8) and Gulbrandsen et al. (n 8) and Skelcher and Smith (n 7).
88 Poulsen (n 18) 121–2.

PART II

Hybridization of EU food law

6 Responsibility in EU food law

Bernd M.J. van der Meulen

1. INTRODUCTION

This chapter focuses on hybrid arrangements in EU food hygiene law. In the European Union 'food hygiene' is legally defined as: 'the measures and conditions necessary to control hazards and to ensure fitness for human consumption of a foodstuff taking into account its intended use'.[1] Hygiene is that part of food safety law that focusses on what businesses producing, handling or selling food have to do to meet food safety objectives.[2] EU food hygiene legislation imposes upon food business operators the obligation to self-regulate their business processes using the principles of Hazard Analysis and Critical Control Point (HACCP).[3] By imposing legal obligations to design systems based on HACCP, the EU legislature sets the agenda as regards the objectives of food safety legislation and defines broad-brush principles of food safety. The implementation of these objectives and principles in detailed rules and procedures, however, is left to

[1] Article 2(1)(a) of Regulation (EC) 852/2004 on the hygiene of foodstuffs. The definition in Codex Alimentarius is similar: 'All conditions and measures necessary to ensure the safety and suitability of food at all stages of the food chain.' See: Recommended International Code of Practice. General Principles of Food Hygiene, CAC/RCP 1-1969 at 2.3, accessed 26 November 2016 at ftp://ftp.fao.org/codex/Publications/Booklets/Hygiene/FoodHygiene_2009e.pdf. 'In the United States, the term "hygiene" is not used in the context of food regulation. Rather, the concept of sanitation is embedded in regulations governing current good manufacturing practices (CGMP), codified at 21 CFR Part 110.' R. Carvajal in B.M.J. van der Meulen, et al. (2016) 444–5.

[2] Other parts of food safety law regard the setting of food safety objectives (for example maximum limits for residues of plant protection products, veterinary drugs, for natural contaminants or microorganisms) and the authorisation of innovative foods such as food additives, food supplements, genetically modified organisms or (other) novel foods. See B.M.J. van der Meulen and H. Schebesta (2014).

[3] Again in the USA the approach is slightly different. The Food Safety Modernization Act requires firms to apply HAPCP (Hazard Analysis and Preventive Control Plan).

the food industry, either the individual food business operators or their representative organizations. Thus while for private food safety standards the rule making is done by private actors, the impact of EU legislation in this process is unmistakable.

The increasing trend of regulating food chains through private standards has been described and analysed in an ever-growing body of literature.[4] The emergence of dominant retail standards often has been assigned a starting year of 1997 and a frontrunner position to the British Retail Consortium (BRC).[5] The introduction in food law of responsibility of food business operators has been identified as a catalyst to this trend.[6] This responsibility in turn is said to have inspired a need among businesses to protect themselves from liability by organising due diligence.[7] The concept of responsibility is included in Regulation (EC) 178/2002 (here after: the 'General Food Law' or 'GFL').[8] Its drafters had on their desk as example the 1990 UK Food Safety Act. For this reason it is not beyond plausibility that both the need for due diligence and the form it took in private standards originated in the United Kingdom and have been exported into the General Food Law and into the European Union.

In this chapter I want to explore the public law imposition of responsibility on food business operators and a possible relation to private regulation by food businesses. The emerging picture is one of interrelatedness between public food law and private food law.[9] As will be contended, this interrelatedness is of a symbiotic nature.

The argument is organised as follows: section 2 addresses the concept of responsibility in EU food law; section 3 addresses imposed self-regulation in food hygiene both by businesses individually (sub-section 3.1) and by

---

[4] For our own contribution and sources, see B.M.J. van der Meulen (ed.) (2011).

[5] See for example, L. Busch (2011).

[6] See e.g. C. Scott (1990); L. Fulponi (2006).

[7] See for example, L. Busch (2011).

[8] Regulation 178/2002/EC of the European Parliament and of the Council of 28 January 2002 laying down the general principles and requirements of food law, establishing the European Food Safety Authority and laying down procedures in matters of food safety.

[9] In this chapter the expression 'private food law' relates to systems of requirements on food businesses (i.e. food law) which systems have been made by private actors by using private law instruments such as contract law and property. Most commonly these systems consist of private standards and certification schemes. The label 'private food law' conveys the pervasiveness of these systems. See for this concept: Van der Meulen (ed.) (2011). In other words, the label is not used to refer to those parts of the legislation that are referred to as private law or civil law (such as the Civil Code; including concepts like contract, tort, property, and law of associations).

businesses collectively (subsection 3.2). As this section is the largest of the chapter it has its own in-between conclusion (subsection 3.3) on imposed self-regulation and responsibility. Section 4 addresses private regulation imposed by businesses upon other businesses – in particular businesses upstream. As this private regulation does not address the 'self' but other businesses, in the title to the section I have labelled it 'external'. Section 5 concludes the discussion.

2. RESPONSIBILITY

The General Food Law imposes on food business operators responsibility for the safety of the food they bring to the market. Article 17, which bears the title 'Responsibilities',[10] states in its first paragraph that food business operators must ensure compliance with food law.

Article 17(1) GFL on Compliance with Food Law

ARTICLE 17(1) GFL

Food and feed business operators at all stages of production, processing and distribution within the businesses under their control shall ensure that foods or feeds satisfy the requirements of food law which are relevant to their activities and shall verify that such requirements are met.

To some extent this may sound like stating the obvious: 'one should comply with the law', but there is more to it than this. Food law is full of

[10] This title is worded rather differently in the different language versions. As a consequence it is also understood differently in different EU Member States. The Dutch ('Verantwoordelijkheden') and French ('Responsabilités') language versions seem close to the English one. In the UK Article 17 tends to be understood in terms of liability. In German ('Zuständigkeiten') it seems to be more on the distribution of tasks and obligations (in Italian 'Obblighi'). This example shows that the fact the EU has 24 different official languages, contributes to the complexity of achieving uniformity in EU law. On these language differences in Article 17 GFL, see F. Albisinni (2003). Antonio Sciaudone seems to embrace all these different meanings when he writes: 'The boundaries of responsibility transcend the traditional limits of liability, and impose positive behavioural obligations that are independent from fault and damage. Participation in the chain of production is in itself a source of responsibility, which is also reflected in the assumption of direct obligations of intervention and in the duty to cooperate with the Authority.' A. Sciaudone (2012).

open and vague norms. Moreover, it addresses the conditions of *products*. Article 17(1) GFL transforms requirements on products into the behavioural requirement to ensure. Article 14 GFL forbids bringing food to the market if it is unsafe. Food is deemed to be unsafe if it is injurious to health or unfit for human consumption.[11] Together the Articles 17 and 14 GFL contribute to a general responsibility to ensure the safety of any food brought to the market. This implies a general risk for the food business operator in case a food that has been brought to the market turns out to have been injurious to health. Even the effects on the health of subsequent generations are taken into consideration.[12] In other words Article 17(1) GFL can be understood to imply that adverse effects of food may constitute an infringement[13] committed by the food business operator. The relevance of this will become apparent in section 4.

Article 17(1) GFL may also be of relevance for the further development of food legislation. If food business operators are to be responsible, food legislation should be drafted in such a way that they can indeed take their responsibility. In the explanatory memorandum to the initial proposal[14] for what became the General Food Law, the European Commission put it this way:

> Responsibilities
> In some areas of European food law, notably in hygiene legislation, the primary responsibility for ensuring compliance with food law, and in particular the safety of the food, rests with the food business. To complement and support this principle there must be adequate and effective controls organised by the competent authorities of the Member States. In other areas of food law this principle is not so widely applicable. This proposal will extend this principle to all food law, and lead to a general review of food law to establish if this principle is respected or whether there are rules where Community legislation has unnecessarily taken responsibility away from the feed or food business by prescribing how a given objective has to be achieved instead of fixing the objective.

In other words, according to the drafters of the provision on responsibility, given the choice the legislator should formulate norms in terms of

11 On the concept of unsafe food, see: B.M.J. van der Meulen (2012).

12 See Article 14(4)(a) GFL.

13 At this point, the nature of this infringement (civil, criminal or administrative) is open.

14 Proposal for a Regulation of the European Parliament and of the Council laying down the general principles and requirements of food law, establishing the European Food Authority, and laying down procedures in matters of food, 8.11.2000, COM(2000) 716 final, pp. 10–11.

objectives to achieve rather than in terms of ways to behave.[15] In this way of thinking responsibility has two faces. With the obligation to act, comes the right to decide how to act (in order to achieve that for which the actor is responsible – here: food safety).[16]

3. IMPOSED BUSINESS SELF-REGULATION

3.1 HACCP

We see responsibility understood in this way reflected in hygiene legislation. Where the GFL gives the general principles of food law in the European Union, this legislation focusses on the obligations of food business operators related to the production, processing and handling of food.[17] Indeed, it seems that for the EU legislature 'responsibility' is an issue of such paramount importance, that in this legislation it reiterates as a principle that 'primary responsibility for food safety rests with the food business operator'.[18]

This responsibility has been operationalized through the so-called HACCP system (Hazard Analysis and Critical Control Point).[19] Within this system the production process is analysed to establish what

---

[15] What the European Commission advocates here, is in line with what is currently discussed under the heading of principles based regulation. On this concept see inter alia J. Black, M. Hopper and C. Band (2007); B.M.J. van der Meulen et al. (2014).

[16] Indeed, Sciaudone (2012) derives from the concept of responsibility that the entrepreneur cannot choose between a strategy based on prevention and a strategy based on indemnification. 'The entrepreneur is obliged to pursue legally defined standards in the organisation of his or her business.'

[17] Sciaudone (2012) connects the hygiene requirements to the overarching concept of responsibility as follows: 'The more the attention of the law-maker focuses on the stages prior to marketing the product and requires the use of business organization models aimed at avoiding the damage, the more active the business owner's role becomes in the process of generating regulations for the establishment of a "safe" food system. When the law lays down general principles, or requires the pursuit of safety, without specifying the conduct to be observed, and there is no appropriate technical standard for the sector, the effectiveness of preventive measures can only be tested on the basis of practical experience.'

[18] Article 1(1)(a) of Regulation (EC) 852/2004 of the European Parliament and of the Council of 29 April 2004 on the hygiene of foodstuffs.

[19] HACCP has been promoted by the Codex Alimentarius Committee of the World Health Organization and Food and Agricultural Organization since 1969. See: Codex Alimentarius Commission, Recommended International Code of Practice General Principle of Food Hygiene (CAC/RCP 1-1969, Rev. 4-2003).

kind of hazards may enter the product in which part of the process. Procedures must be developed to prevent hazards or to deal with the consequences. Meticulous application of such a system in combination with testing of products is believed to achieve the highest possible level of food safety.

Article 5 of the GFL requires food business operators to put in place, implement and maintain a HACCP system. The application of HACCP is mandatory for virtually all food businesses in the European Union.[20] As a consequence, food business operators have to analyse their processes, to establish procedures to ensure hygiene and to exercise self-control on the functioning of these systems. In other words: the businesses themselves have to formulate and uphold the rules that apply to their processes. Public food law engages with this form of private regulation in that it requires business to set self-made rules in place to achieve the public law objectives.[21]

By imposing HACCP as a requirement the European Union sets food business operators on a course to take control over the processes for which they are responsible, to acquire more information on what goes on and what goes wrong in their businesses and hence to shape the tools to guarantee food hygiene and to improve on standards already achieved. The application of HACCP is a continuing and circular process that is founded on the efforts already made, on changes in the food business organization internally, and in the outside business environment. The responsible food business operator is approached 'top-down' but in a way that is very different from a set of rules specified in advance and applied to situations that must be isolated to determine whether a certain rule has been applied correctly. The HACCP approach does not offer such a specified set of rules on what is allowed but a method to achieve what is allowed, and an incentive to do even better.

The food business operators applying HACCP have to analyse their own processes; have to identify the hazards and have to decide on the measures to deal with them. For this reason HACCP is often referred to as 'imposed' (or even 'enforced'[22]) self-regulation.[23] '*Self*-regulation' because ultimately the rules applying to the production process have to be formulated by the food business operator. 'Imposed' because unlike other types

---

[20] There are some exceptions. Article 5(3) GFL exempts primary producers from the obligation. However, on the basis of private standards such as GlobalGAP, HACCP requirements may also apply to primary production.

[21] C. Coglianese and D. Lazer (2003); F. Wendler (2007).

[22] See: R. Fairman and C. Yapp (2005).

[23] The expression is probably coined by J. Braithwaite (1982).

of self-regulation to do so is not a free choice, not even in theory. This, in my view, makes it a hybrid form of regulation.

3.2 Guides to Good Hygiene Practice

The aforementioned Regulation 852/2004 on the hygiene of foodstuffs,[24] offers an alternative to the application of HACCP by individual food business operators in the form of guides to good hygiene practice. It is not stated explicitly, but for all practical purposes it must be assumed that compliance with an approved guide equals compliance with the HACCP obligation.

Article 4(6) Regulation 852/2004 on Guides to Good Hygiene Practice

> ARTICLE 4(6) REGULATION 852/2004
>
> Food business operators may use the guides provided for in Articles 7, 8 and 9 as an aid to compliance with their obligations under this Regulation.

National guides to good hygiene practices are drafted by the food business sectors on their own initiative.[25] Chapter III of Regulation 852/2004 gives a set of rules that have to be applied when a guide is made, that instruct the Member States to assess the national guides and to forward the approved guides to the European Commission. Guides can also be made at the EU level. The legislation for the European guides makes it possible for the European Commission to take the initiative at the EU level, if the Member States allow it. The Commission can only encourage, not impose on, businesses and sector organisations to create guides.

National guides

National guides are developed by the food business sectors themselves. The persons or organisations in the food business sectors who take the initiative to develop a guide have to meet some conditions, among which to consult representatives of the persons and organisations whose interest may be substantially affected. The regulation mentions competent authorities and consumer groups explicitly.[26] The legislator recommends

---

[24] Regulation 852/2004.

[25] At least, that is the theory. Empirical research has revealed that sometimes public authorities take the initiative. See T. Havinga (2014).

[26] Article 8(1)(a) Regulation 852/2004. Further they have to use the relevant codes of practice of the Codex Alimentarius.

each initiative to seek the support of their national standards institute to benefit from its authority to set standards.

The Member States have to assess the national guides to ensure that the conditions set for their development have been observed.[27] In addition the Member States have to test the guides on two other aspects, their practicality and potential to help food business operators to fulfil a part of their food hygiene obligations. The Member States have to send the guides that have passed the test to the European Commission who will place them in a register without further testing.

The European Commission has set up a register of national guides which is available to all Member States.[28] The Commission has made the 'Register of national guides to good hygiene practice' publicly available on a webpage of DG SANTE.[29] The Register lists hundreds of national guides, giving for each one the following information: title in the original language, title in English, country, language, author, edition, and ISBN or ISSN. It presents a list of keywords on good hygiene practices with an internet address or other contact details in the Member States.

European guides

The European Commission takes a more active part in the creation of guides at EU level than governments do at Member State level. Unlike the Member States, the Commission can take the initiative to create a guide. The Commission has to use the Comitology procedure to decide with the Member States' representatives whether European guides will be made, and what scope and subject matter they will have.[30]

When the Member States have agreed on the need to establish a European guide, it is for the Commission to take action. The Commission will perform tasks that are comparable with the tasks of the Member States in the development process of the national guides, but has to act in a markedly more active manner. European guides are published in the Official Journal of the European Union.[31] The Commission has published guidelines for the development of community guides to good practice for hygiene and for the application of the HACCP principles.[32]

---

[27] Article 8(3)(a) Regulation 852/2004.

[28] Article 8(4) Regulation 852/2004.

[29] For the register, see http://ec.europa.eu/food/food/biosafety/hygienelegislation/docs/register_national_guides_en.pdf (accessed 26 November 2016).

[30] Article 9 Regulation 852/2004.

[31] See http://ec.europa.eu/food/food/biosafety/hygienelegislation/good_practice_en.htm (accessed 26 November 2016).

[32] Guidelines for the development of community guides to good practice for

National and European guides

When the law for EU voluntary guides to good hygiene practice is compared with the law on the national guides there are a number of marked differences. Two main points are the dominance of the European Union in the procedure for developing European guides, and the position of the Member States. Subsidiarity explains part of the elaborate testing that has to be done before guides at EU level are even contemplated. This means that it has to be shown that action at the national level does not suffice.

On the other hand the more active position of the Commission can be explained by a shortage of representative partners across the full range of affected interests due to weaker civil society representation at the EU level when compared with the national level. That the Commission is required to be more active on the EU level seems fair to compensate for the missing aspects of civil society.

3.3 Hygiene Self-regulation and Responsibility Before the European Court of Justice

In section 2 above it has been stated that with the proposal for the GFL, the European Commission argued that public law should leave businesses room to actually take their own responsibility in delivering safe food. In relation to hygiene self-regulation, this notion has been put to the test of the Court of Justice of the European Union (CJEU) in the *Albrecht and others v. Landeshauptmann von Wien* case.[33]

Austrian food safety inspectors acted against businesses that sold bread through self-service retail. Consumers could take unprepackaged bread out of plastic containers. It was also possible to place the selected bread after removal back into the container. The inspectors considered this practice unhygienic and fines were imposed. The Austrian court dealing with the case raised preliminary questions before the CJEU. It wished to be informed about whether a food business operator violates hygiene requirements where it offers food for sale that could conceivably

---

hygiene and for the application of the HACCP principles, in accordance with Article 9 of Regulation (EC) No 852/2004 on the hygiene of foodstuffs and Article 22 of Regulation (EC) No 183/2005 laying down requirements for feed hygiene. In the latest version at the time of writing, the version of 1 December 2015, the title is simplified to: Guidelines on the registration of national guides to good practice – regarding Regulation (EC) No 852/2004. See: http://ec.europa.eu/food/food/biosafety/hygienelegislation/docs/national_guides_register_15-07-2008.pdf (accessed 26 November 2016).

[33] CJEU 6 October 2011, Case C-382/10.

have been touched or sneezed upon by a would-be purchaser. The Court based its answer to this question on the concept of responsibility:

> It follows that, in a situation such as that in the main proceedings, where the competent authorities do not appear to have concluded that there was actual contamination, it cannot be concluded that food business operators have infringed the abovementioned paragraph 3 on the basis only of the finding that a potential purchaser could conceivably have touched the foodstuffs by hand or sneezed on them, without considering the measures taken by those operators under Article 5 of the regulation [852/2004] in order to prevent, eliminate or reduce to acceptable levels the hazard which the contamination referred to in paragraph 3 of Chapter IX of Annex II to the regulation [852/2004] may present and without determining that the measures taken in that regard were insufficient in the light of all the available relevant data.[34]

The essence is in the last sentence of this extract. In assessing compliance, the inspector has to take account of the measures taken by the business to implement its HACCP obligation. This finding is of crucial importance. In this situation of imposed self-regulation the self-made requirements are the ones against which compliance has to be assessed. Inspectors cannot simply override the self-regulatory system by their own assessment of what the hygiene situation requires. It stands to reason that the same is true in case businesses use jointly made hygiene guides. Accordingly, the hybrid regulatory arrangement as prescribed by EU food hygiene law received strong support from the CJEU.

4. EXTERNAL PRIVATE REGULATION

Not only can businesses apply food safety systems within their own processes, they can also require other businesses – their suppliers in particular – to apply such systems.

EU public food law requires private regulation only with a view to businesses' responsibilities regarding their own internal processes. Ultimately, however, businesses have to ensure that products they place on the market are compliant and safe. This depends on more than the internal processes. It also depends on the condition of the inputs (such as purchased ingredients and other raw materials) which in turn depends (among others) on the processes applied by businesses upstream. This responsibility for the outcome of the consecutive contributions in the food chain, is sometimes

---

[34] Ibid, para 22.

referred to as 'chain-responsibility'.[35] EU public food law nowhere directly requires private regulation to ensure this chain responsibility.

The potential scope of chain responsibility has become visible in the case law of the CJEU. The first case that needs to be mentioned in this respect is a ruling of the CJEU in the case *Lidl v. Italy*.[36] In short the case concerned the following. Inspectors found in a Lidl supermarket an A-brand (that is, not a Lidl brand) liquor that in laboratory testing was revealed to have a lower alcohol content than indicated on the label. Lidl was fined, but contested this because it had not been involved in the labelling that had been found to be incorrect. According to the text of the ruling of the CJEU, Lidl argued: 'The distributor cannot know whether or not the label affixed to the packaging by the producer contains true information, and in any event could not do anything either in respect of the production of the product or the label under which it is sold to the ultimate consumer.'[37]

The referring Italian Court asked for a preliminary ruling on the question whether a national law that allows for punitive measures against the trader for infringements by the producer runs against EU law. According to the CJEU, the provisions of EU law at issue:

> are to be interpreted as not precluding legislation of a Member State, such as that at issue in the main proceedings, which makes it possible for an operator, established in that Member State, which distributes a pre-packaged alcoholic beverage to be delivered as such within the meaning of Article 1 of that directive [2000/13 on labelling[38]], produced by an operator established in another Member State, to be held liable for an infringement of that provision, established by a public authority, resulting from the producer's inaccurate statement on the product label of the alcoholic strength by volume of the product and, consequently, to be penalised by an administrative fine, even where, as the mere distributor, it simply markets the product as delivered to it by the producer.[39]

After the Lidl case concerning a labelling issue, the question as to whether the same line of reasoning applies to matters of food safety came to the

---

[35] For example: P. Hahn and K. Pichhardt (2008); M. Girnau (2007). Chain responsibility implies the accountability of a food business operator for the results of actions performed by players up the chain. In product liability law we see that a brand owner is considered as producer and is held liable while the actual manufacturer is another business. See Directive 85/374/EEC on the approximation of the laws, regulations and administrative provisions of the Member States concerning liability for defective products.

[36] CJEU 23 November 2006, Case C-315/05.

[37] Ibid., para 32.

[38] Now succeeded by Regulation (EU) 1169/2011 on food information to consumers.

[39] Ibid., para 61.

table in the second case that needs to be mentioned here. This is the ruling of the CJEU in the case *Ute Reindl v. Bezirkshauptmannschaft Innsbruck*.[40] In this case, the Austrian Food Safety Authority in Innsbruck had taken a sample during an on-the-spot check in a retail company of a vacuum-packed fresh turkey breast produced and packed by another undertaking. After microbiological examination, a contamination by Salmonella Typhimurium was found and, in turn, the retailer was fined. The retailer challenged this fine before the administrative court of Tirol, which turned to the CJEU with preliminary questions to assess whether the fine was imposed correctly. The CJEU pointed to Article 17(1) GFL which provides that food business operators at all stages of production, processing and distribution within the businesses under their control must ensure that foods satisfy the requirements of food law relevant to their activities. The Court did not find the fine to be contrary to EU law, considering that the GFL must be interpreted as meaning that, in principle, it does not preclude national law, which imposes a penalty on a food business operator active only at the distribution stage for placing a foodstuff on the market, on account of the failure to comply with microbiological criteria.[41]

It follows from these two rulings that ultimately, chain responsibility in terms of liability for situations caused by players upstream is largely a matter of Member State law. It may not be directly required by EU law but it fits well with the EU law system in general and its attribution of responsibility in particular. Another Member State other than Italy and Austria which goes a long way in attaching liability to chain responsibility is the United Kingdom. The limit to this liability under UK law is due diligence.

The due diligence defence in the United Kingdom implies that (legal) persons charged with infringing food law with regard to safety or fraud, escape punishment if they establish that the following conditions have been met: they neither prepared the food nor imported it; the offence was due to an act or default of another person who was not under their control; they carried out all such checks of the food in question as were reasonable in all the circumstances; and they did not know and had no reason to suspect at the time of the commission of the offence that their act or omission would amount to an offence.[42]

---

40 CJEU 13 November 2014, Case C-443/13.

41 Ibid., paras. 18 and 34.

42 MacMaoláin (2015) has the following to say on the concept: 'The . . . defence is that due diligence was exercised, provided that the accused can demonstrate that he took all reasonable precautions to avoid the commission of the

It is said that private standards on food safety reinforced with audits and certification systems have been put in place to ensure that in case of a food safety problem, all elements of this defence are fulfilled.

BRC was the first, but the approach has spread like wild-fire.[43] Up to a point, the approach is comparable to HACCP and hygiene guides. The crucial difference is that these private standards are designed to be applied not by the involved businesses themselves, but by businesses upstream. While such businesses upstream from the retailers who initially took the initiative are increasingly involved in the formulation of the obligations they derive from private standards, the purpose of these standards with their certification schemes is to ensure and provide evidence that business processes comply with customer (that is, retailer) requirements.[44] The standards are often referred to as 'private *voluntary* standards'.[45] The only thing voluntary about them is that compliance with them is only legally required after they have been accepted as part of a contractual obligation. For all practical purposes, however, they are imposed top-down. This top-down imposition is not in any way based on a legal power, but on the factual control over market access, that is, over inclusion and exclusion of food business operators from the market.

Because these private standards are not self-regulation in the sense of rules made to be used by the rule-makers themselves, additional instruments are put in place to ensure compliance. These are the third party audits and certifications.[46]

---

offence by himself or by a person under his control. Due diligence can also be demonstrated by those who did not prepare or import the offending food if it can be shown that the food was made unsafe by someone else and that all reasonable safety checks were carried out. Due diligence can only be used as a defence where the accused identifies, or takes all reasonable steps to identify, the other party involved, that is the one who it is claimed is responsible for making the food unsafe.'

See The Society of Food Hygiene and Technology, Food Law and Due Diligence Defence (2009) accessed 26 November 2016 at http://www.sofht.co.uk/wp-content/uploads/2016/09/W-food-law-due-diligence-defence.pdf.

[43] For an overview, see T. Appelhof and R. van den Heuvel (2011).

[44] In this respect they differ from hygiene guides that are primarily designed to comply with government requirements. Obviously, in practice also customers can require compliance with hygiene guides – or with legal requirements for that matter.

[45] For example by Appelhof and Van den Heuvel (2011).

[46] See: M. Hatanaka, C. Bain and L. Busch (2005); P. Verbruggen (2014); and Fagotto, Chapter 3 in this volume.

5. CONCLUSION

It seems that a case can be made for the hypothesis that the assignment of responsibility in public EU food law contributes to the emergence of private food law at the EU level of governance. In situations where the legislator itself requires private regulation, this results in true *self*-regulation; that is, where private regulators set requirements on their own behaviour.[47] In the case of HACCP at the individual business level, rules are set for the businesses' own behaviour; in the case of hygiene guides, the group of businesses set rules to be applied by the members. Either way, the actors involved are the businesses that at the same time are the regulators and the regulatees. Inspection and enforcement of compliance with the self-formulated hygiene obligations are in the hands of public authorities. In the case of hygiene guides, there is prior control by public authorities. HACCP systems do not require approval, but may be checked in the context of inspections.

Where the legislator leaves the initiative completely to the stakeholders, we observe that private regulation addresses the behaviour of stakeholders further up the chain, rather than addressing businesses' own behaviour. In this situation, regulator and regulatee are no longer the same. The private regulation acquires a top-down characteristic and is imposed by more powerful businesses in the chain on others constituting that chain. Inspection (audits) and enforcement (certification with its possible refusal and withdrawal) are then typically outsourced and put in the hands of accredited third-party certification bodies. Thus, in EU food safety law, responsibility for food safety implies regulation by businesses of business processes, regulation of own processes if imposed, and regulation of others' processes shifting the burden of compliance to them if possible.

In the domain of EU food hygiene law public and private rules set the legal limits for business activities in concert and provide a yardstick against which compliance is measured. From the perspective of the regulated business, undoubtedly, this will come across as a stacking of obligations. From the perspective of regulation, however, we observe a strong symbiosis of public and private rules that jointly contribute to the attainment of the public law objective of food safety.

47 Although in the case discussed in this chapter, this self-regulation is enforced. See also J. Black (1996).

REFERENCES

Literature

Albisinni, F. (2003), 'Commento all'art. 21 del reg. Ce n. 178/2002', Instituto di Diritto Agrario Internazionale e Comparato.

Appelhof, T. and R. van den Heuvel (2011), 'Private Food Law'; Part III in Irene Scholten-Verheijen et al., *Roadmap to EU Food Law* (Sdu/Eleven International Publishing) 123–68.

Black, J. (1996), 'Constitutionalising Self-Regulation' 59(1) *Modern Law Review* 24–55.

Black, J., M. Hopper and C. Band (2007), 'Making a Success of Principles-based Regulation', *Law and Financial Markets Review* 191–206.

Braithwaite, J. (1982) 'Enforced Self-regulation: A new Strategy for Corporate Crime Control', *Michigan Law Review* 1466–507.

Busch, L. (2011) 'Quasi-states? The Unexpected Rise of Private Food Law', in B.M.J. Van der Meulen (ed.), 'Private Food Law: Governing Food Chains through Contract Law Self-Regulation, Private Standards, Audits and Certification Schemes' (Wageningen Academic Publishers), accessed 26 November 2016 at http://www.wageningenacademic.com/EIFL-06

Coglianese, C. and D. Lazer (2003), 'Management-based Regulation: Prescribing Private Management to Achieve Public Goals' 37(4) *Law and Society Review* 691–730.

Costato, L. and F. Albisinni (eds) (2012), *European Food Law* (Cedam/Kluwer Milano).

Fairman, R. and C. Yapp (2005), 'Enforced Self-regulation, Prescription, and Conceptions of Compliance within Small Businesses: The Impact of Enforcement' 27(4) *Law and Policy* 491–519.

Fulponi, L. (2006), 'Private Voluntary Standards in the Food System: The Perspective of Major Food Retailers in OECD Countries' 31(1) *Food Policy* 1–13.

Girnau, M. (2007), 'Das neue Lebensmittelrecht – Kompetenzen und Verfahren', *Zeitschrift für das gesamte Lebensmittelrecht*, 309–24.

Hahn, P. and K. Pichhardt (2008), 'Lebensmittelsicherheit. Haftung, Rückruf, Rückverfolgbarkeit' (Behr's Germany).

Hatanaka, M., C. Bain and L. Busch (2005), 'Third Party Certification in the Global Agrifood System' 30(3) *Food Policy* 354–69.

Havinga, T. (2014), 'National Variations in the Implementation and Enforcement of European Food Hygiene Regulations. Comparing the Structure of Food Controls and Regulations between Scotland and the Netherlands', *Recht der Werkelijkheid* 32–53.

MacMaoláin, C. (2015), 'Food Law. European, Domestic and International Frameworks' (Hart Publishing).

Sciaudone, A. (2012), 'Responsibilities of Food Business Operators', chapter IX in L. Costato and F. Albisinni (eds), *European Food Law* (Cedam/Kluwer).

Scott, C. (1990), 'Continuity and Change in British Food Law' 56(6) *Modern Law Review* 785–801.

van der Meulen, B.M.J. (ed.) (2011), 'Private Food Law: Governing Food Chains through Contract Law Self-regulation, Private Standards, Audits

and Certification Schemes' (Wageningen Academic Publishers), accessed 26 November 2016 at http://www.wageningenacademic.com/EIFL-06.
van der Meulen, B.M.J. (2012), 'The Core of Food Law. A Critical Reflection on the Single Most Important Provision in all of EU Food Law', *EFFL* 117–25.
van der Meulen, B.M.J., H.J. Bremmers, K.P. Purnhagen, N. Gupta, H. Bouwmeester, L.L. Geyer (2014), 'Governing Nanofoods: Principles-based Responsive Regulation' *EFFoST Critical Reviews* #3 (Elsevier).
van der Meulen, B.M.J. and H. Schebesta (2014), 'Onveilig voedsel op de markt: Kwalificatie en actie' *Ars Aequi* 136–45.
van der Meulen, B.M.J., Sun Juanjuan, R. Carvajal, J. Kite, T. Costa Dias (2016), 'Food Safety Regulations Applied to Traditional and Ethnic Foods', Chapter 23 in V. Prakash et al. *Regulating Safety in Traditional and Ethnic Foods* (Elsevier).
Verbruggen, P. (2014). *Enforcing Transnational Private Regulation: A Comparative Analysis of Advertising and Food Safety* (Edward Elgar).
Wendler, F. (2007), 'The Public-private Regulation of Food Safety through HACCP: What Does it Mean for the Governance Capacity of Public and Private Actors?' in E. Vos (ed.), 'European Risk Governance: Its Science, its Inclusiveness and its Effectiveness' CONNEX Report Series Nr 06, Mannheim, 223–55.

Sources of Law

CJEU 13 November 2014, case C-443/13 *Ute Reindl v. Bezirkshauptmannschaft Innsbruck*.
Directive 85/374/EEC on the approximation of the laws, regulations and administrative provisions of the Member States concerning liability for defective products [1985] OJ L210/29.
ECJ 23 November 2006, case C-315/05 *Lidl v. Italy*.
ECJ 6 October 2011, case C-382/10 *Albrecht and others v. Landeshauptmann von Wien*.
Guidelines for the development of community guides to good practice for hygiene and for the application of the HACCP principles, in accordance with Article 9 of Regulation (EC) No 852/2004 on the hygiene of foodstuffs and Article 22 of Regulation (EC) No 183/2005 laying down requirements for feed hygiene.
Proposal for a Regulation of the European Parliament and of the Council laying down the general principles and requirements of food law, establishing the European Food Authority, and laying down procedures in matters of food, 8.11.2000, COM(2000) 716 final. Recommended International Code of Practice. General Principles of Food Hygiene, CAC/RCP 1-1969 at 2.3, accessed 27 November 2016 at ftp://ftp.fao.org/codex/Publications/Booklets/Hygiene/FoodHygiene_2009e.pdf.
Regulation (EC) 178/2002 of the European Parliament and of the Council of 28 January 2002 laying down the general principles and requirements of food law, establishing the European Food Safety Authority and laying down procedures in matters of food safety ([2002] OJ L31/1).
Regulation (EC) 852/2004 on the hygiene of foodstuffs [2004] OJ L139/1.
Regulation (EU) 1169/2011 on food information to consumers [2011] OJ L304/18.

7 Management-based regulation of food safety in the United Kingdom

Mohamud Hussein, Marian Garcia Martinez and Andrew Fearne

INTRODUCTION

Over the past two decades, there has been a growing interface between public and private controls of food safety governance systems due to a marked shift from the traditional command-and-control regulation by government towards alternative flexible forms of regulation, such as self-regulation, management-based regulation and co-regulation systems of governance.[1] In particular, regulatory approaches combining public and private control activities have enjoyed a degree of popularity both in Europe and North America. A number of existing regulations in environmental protection[2] and media[3] and food safety controls[4] now include features that are either partly designed and/or enforced by industry bodies to supplement official controls by public authorities. Such reliance on

[1] Bardach, Eugene and Kagan, Robert, *Going by the Book: The Problem of Regulatory Unreasonableness* (Temple Univ. Press 1982); Ayres, Ian and Braithwaite, John, *Responsive Regulation:Transcending the Deregulation Debate* (Oxford University Press 1992); Ogus, Anthony I., *Regulation: Legal Form and Economic Theory* (Clarendon Press 1994); Coglianese, Cary and Lazer, David, 'Management-Based Regulation. Prescribing Private Management to Achieve Public Goals' 37 *Law & Society Review* 691; Havinga, T., Casey, D. and Van Waarden, F., 'Changing Regulatory Arrangements in Food Governance,' in F. Van Waarden, T. Havinga and D. Casey (eds), *The Changing Landscape of Food Governance* (Edward Elgar 2015); Verbruggen, P. and Havinga, T., 'Patterns of Interplay between Public and Private Food Regulators – An Introduction' 6 *European Journal of Risk Regulation*.

[2] Coglianese and Lazer (n 1).

[3] Verbruggen, Paul, 'Does Co-Regulation Strengthen EU Legitimacy?' 15 *European Law Journal* 425.

[4] Coglianese and Lazer (n 1); Ollinger, Michael and Moore, Danna *The Interplay of Regulation and Marketing Incentives in Providing Food Safety* (U.S. Dept. of Agriculture, Economic Research Service 2009).

industry actors to achieve regulatory policy objectives almost always occurs at least partly as a means of reducing the administrative and compliance costs of regulation, and sometimes reflects antagonism towards the use of state power.[5]

Verbruggen and Havinga (Chapter 1 in this volume) set out key characteristics of coordinated public-private governance systems and discuss how, where and why these governance systems have emerged. In general, the coordination of private regulatory capacity has more recently become attractive for regulators around the world as a result of a number of interlinked factors, including increasing globalization of food chains, the internationalization of public food safety controls and growing budgetary pressures on national food authorities. However, regulatory outcomes under such 'hybrid' governance models would largely depend upon a combination of different factors that reflect both the regulatory and industrial capacity to administer these models and henceforth resulting incentives for compliance at a firm level. These factors include the extent to which the regulated firms have the administrative capacity, resources, and ethos necessary to implement the regulatory schemes, as well as the regulators' ability to monitor their compliance effectively.[6]

In this chapter we examine the hybrid governance approach of 'management-based regulation' that has gained popularity in food safety policymaking in recent years, with specific example on its application in the UK inspection regime for the fresh poultry meat sector. This approach requires regulated entities to engage in their own internal planning and rulemaking efforts aimed at delivering food safety objectives.[7] In effect, management-based approaches allow state regulators to prescribe private food safety management systems, such as HACCP, to achieve the goal of a safe public food supply.[8] Thus, in prescribing food systems that are managed by the firm and which in some cases include the internal

---

[5] Balleisen, Edward J., 'The Prospects for Effective "Co-Regulation" in the United States: An Historian's View from the Early Twenty-First Century' in Edward Balleisen and David Moss (eds), *Government and Markets: Toward a New Theory of Regulation* (Cambridge University Press 2009).

[6] Ibid. See also Kirezieva and Luning, Chapter 8 in this volume.

[7] Yapp, Charlotte and Fairman, Robyn 'Assessing Compliance with Food Safety Legislation in Small Businesses' 107 *British Food Journal* 150; Balleisen Coglianese, Cary, 'Management-based Regulation: Implications for Public Policy' in *OECD Reviews of Regulatory Reform: Risk and Regulatory Policy – Improving the Governance of Risk* (OECD Publishing; Pap/Psc edition 2010); Gilad, Sharon, 'It Runs in the Family: Meta-regulation and Its Siblings' 4 *Regulation & Governance* 485.

[8] Coglianese and Lazer (n 1).

monitoring of its compliance, the regulatory authorities implicitly vest responsibility in the industry actors who possess the information necessary to design effective controls and therefore may be best placed to efficiently improve food safety.[9]

In this regard, management-based regulation can be viewed as a hybrid form of governance as it involves both public (state) and private (firm) actors in controls intended to ensure food safety. In the case of fresh poultry meat inspection, the hybrid approach is specifically concerned with compliance with EU food hygiene standards (legislative enactment), which are overseen by both public and firm hygiene inspectors. Considering that regulatory regimes comprise elements of standard setting, implementation, monitoring and enforcement,[10] hybridity manifests mainly in the latter two components of management-based regulation as it is primarily concerned with enforcing the prescribed legal requirements intended to direct a firm's internal planning and rulemaking toward the social goal of a safe food supply. However, hybridity also emerges in the standard-setting and implementation stages since management-based regulation requires firms to set internal safety standards and protocols that are derived from public law requirements and subsequently implemented at firm-level.

Such a hybrid governance approach implies that firms are afforded considerable administrative flexibility in their planning and rulemaking efforts and so allows for sufficient incentives to tailor internal systems that reflect the specific features of individual processes. If successful, this form of hybrid governance regime is then expected to align firms' commercial objectives with the socially orientated objective of ensuring the safety of the food supply by inducing compliance beyond what would be possible under traditional forms of regulation. Our contention is that there are practical challenges to aligning the objectives of the state regulator with those of the regulated food firm due to potential incentive problems related to the often limited ability of regulators to verify the food safety outcomes of firms' internal efforts.

We examine the key features of the management-based governance regime using, as an example, a delivery model for the enforcement of EU meat hygiene controls in poultry abattoirs in the United Kingdom. We first provide an overview of the evolution of EU legislation that applies

---

[9] See also Van der Meulen, Chapter 6 in this volume.

[10] Christopher Hood, et al., *The Government of Risk: Understanding Risk Regulation Regimes* (Oxford University Press 2001) and Kenneth W. Abbott and Duncan Snidal, *The Governance Triangle: Regulatory Standards Institutions and The Shadow of the State*, in Walter Mattli and Ngaire Woods (eds), *The Politics of Global Regulation* (Princeton University Press 2009).

to the fresh poultry meat sector, highlighting salient historic and recent reforms that have enabled the use of hybrid governance models such as management-based regulation in Europe. We then highlight the challenges that the hybrid governance regime may face, drawing upon existing evidence of its cost-effectiveness in protecting public health. The goal is to set an appropriate legal and administrative context and then assess the conditions necessary for this type of hybrid governance model to deliver the social goals of safe food supply at minimal regulatory cost.

A broader conclusion that we draw from our analysis is that, under a management-based approach, food safety is largely an outcome of the interaction between the strategic behaviour of regulated firms and the effectiveness of official enforcement oversight in terms of verification and monitoring compliance of regulated entities. Consequently, without a well-crafted regulatory incentive mechanism capable of committing firms to ensuring a safe meat supply, the management-based regulation may be sub-optimal. This would be especially problematic when such regimes involve outdated official visual inspection practices and financial incentives, as is the case in the UK regime. Indeed, existing evidence suggests that the poultry meat inspection regime is unable to protect public health despite the considerable public and industry resources it absorbs.

EVOLUTION OF THE EU FOOD HYGIENE REGIME

Historically, EU legislation on food hygiene and the organisation of official controls were based on no fewer than 17 directives, some of which dated back to 1964.[11] The multiplicity of these directives, the intermingling of different disciplines (hygiene, animal health, official controls) and the existence of different hygiene regimes for products of animal origin have all led to a complex administrative situation. In addition to being product-specific, the requirements under the old legislation were also prescriptive in their approach, leaving little room for national regulators to take account of the heterogeneity of regulated entities when implementing the

---

[11] The EU hygiene regulation has evolved considerably since Council Directive 64/433/EEC of 26 June 1964 on health conditions for the production and marketing of fresh meat (4). More recently, Directive 2004/41/EC of the European Parliament and of the Council of 21 April 2004 repealed previous Directives concerning food hygiene and health conditions for the production and marketing of certain products of animal origin intended for human consumption and amended Council Directives 89/662/EEC and 92/118/EEC and Council Decision 95/408/EC (2004).

legislation.[12] In the late 1990s the European Commission initiated reform of the legislation with a view to regrouping it into one legislative package that now applies horizontally across all sectors of the food supply chain. To this end, in 2000, the Commission proposed a new package for consolidation of food hygiene legislation that emphasized the need to 'make [controls] more coherent, more flexible, better suited to the evolution of the market and of scientific knowledge and better able to meet the increasing public demand for better food safety and consumer protection'.[13]

The BSE crisis was particularly instrumental in bringing to light significant dysfunctions both in industrial practices and in their supervision by governments, and so undermined public trust in food safety governance and supply chains.[14] On the one hand, although it was known for many years that BSE in cattle was probably spread by infected bonemeal feed,[15] UK farmers had little incentive to take the necessary but voluntary precautionary measures, even after emerging scientific evidence linked CJD with infected beef consumption.[16] In effect, the voluntary measures would have involved cattle farmers switching to more expensive vegetarian concentrate feed with potentially higher production costs which consumers might not have been willing to pay for at the time. On the other hand, the UK government's BSE controls and actions taken to tackle the outbreak were seen by many to be slow and inconsistent with the scientific evidence available at the time.[17]

---

[12] Howard, Michael T., 'Food Hygiene Regulation and Enforcement Policy in the UK: The Underlying Philosophy and Comparisons with Occupational Health And Safety Law' 4 *Food Service Technology* 69.

[13] European Commission, *Daily notebook: Better food safety rules* (2004).

[14] Borraz, Olivier, Besancon, Julien and Clergeau, Christophe, 'Is it just about Trust? The Partial Reform of French Food Safety Regulation' in Christopher Ansell and David Vogel (eds), *What's the beef: The Contested Governance of the European Food Safety Regulation* (MIT Press 2006).

[15] Hennessy, David A., Roosen, Jutta and Jensen, Helen H., 'Systemic Failure in the Provision of Safe Food' 28 *Food Policy* 77; Chalmers, Damian, 'Food for Thought: Reconciling European Risks and Traditional Ways of Life' 66(4) *Modern Law Review* 532–62; Rothstein, Henry, 'Precautionary Bans or Sacrificial Lamb? Participative Regulation and the Reforms of the UK Food Safety Regime' 82 *Public Administration* 857.

[16] Ansell, Christopher and Vogel, David, 'The Contested Governance of European Food Safety Regulation' in Christopher Ansell and David Vogel (eds), *What's the Beef: The Contested Governance of European Food Safety Regulation* (MIT Press 2006)

[17] Rothstein, Henry, 'From Precautionary Bans to DIY Poison Tasting: Reform of the UK Food Safety Regulation' in Christopher Ansell and David Vogel (eds), *What's the Beef: The Contested Governance of European Food Safety*

The public outrage that resulted from the BSE crisis had profound implications for both EU and UK food safety governance regimes. In a report to the European Parliament, the then President of the European Commission, Jacques Santer,[18] acknowledged that the BSE crisis in Europe was partly a result of the European Commission's role in food policymaking that the public perceived to predominantly support producer interests. He acknowledged numerous shortcomings in the existing EU food safety governance regime and called for urgent remedial action in the form of wide-ranging reforms of the administrative structures including the system for scientific advice on food safety, the regulatory decision-making machinery, inspection methods and the legal basis for food safety regulation. In particular, following the White Paper on Food Safety and the resulting Regulation (EC) 178/2002, which instituted these reforms, it became clear that EU food hygiene controls needed updating so that they reflected these institutional changes – namely, greater incentives for proactive compliance that resulted from explicit allocation of the legal responsibility for ensuring food safety to industry operators. In this setting, the public regulators' role becomes clearly more focused on verifying and monitoring the effectiveness of the industry controls as opposed to operational enforcement of the rules.[19] Therefore, there was an implicit expectation that the new legislation would be more effective and efficient than the fragmented legislation that existed under the old hygiene regime. In fact, in its proposal for repealing the old legislation, the EU Commission argued that '[t]he leitmotif throughout the recast of the (old) hygiene rules is that (now) food operators bear full responsibility for the safety of the food they produce'.[20]

Specifically, the Commission emphasized that the implementation of hazard analysis and control principles and the observance of hygiene rules must ensure food safety in line with the internationally accepted HACCP

Policy (MIT Press 2006); House of Commons, Mr Douglas Hogg, Parliamentary statement by the Minister of Agriculture, Fisheries and Food: BSE (Agriculture) HC Deb 25 March 1996 vol 274 cc724-37 724 4.27 pm (1996).

[18] Speech by Jacques Santer, President of the European Commission at the Debate in the European Parliament on the Report into BSE by the Committee of Enquiry of the European Parliament, 18 February 1997, Speech 97/39 (1997).

[19] Food Standards Agency, *Meat Establishment Audit Categories* (2008); Garcia Martinez, M. et al., 'Co-regulation as a Possible Model for Food Safety Governance: Opportunities for Public-Private Partnerships' 32 *Food Policy* 299.

[20] European Commission, Proposal for a Council Regulation laying down the animal-health rules governing the production, placing on the market and importation of products of animal origin intended for human consumption /* COM/2000/0438 final – CNS 2000/0181 */ [2000] OJ C365E/58.

approach advocated by the Codex Alimentarius.[21] Thus, the Commission envisaged that placing primary responsibility on operators and ensuring these risk-based control measures are both necessary to ensure food safety under the new and more enlightened EU regulatory regime.

THE NEW EU FOOD HYGIENE REGIME

The new EU food hygiene legislation was adopted and applied on 1 January 2006 in the United Kingdom.[22] The regulations include:

- Regulation 852/2004 of the European Parliament and of the Council of 29 April 2004 on the hygiene of foodstuffs.[23]
- Regulation 853/2004 of the European Parliament and of the Council of 29 April 2004 laying down specific hygiene rules for food of animal origin.[24]
- Regulation 854/2004 of the European Parliament and of the Council of 29 April 2004 laying down specific hygiene rules for the organisation of official controls on products of animal origin intended for human consumption.[25]
- Directive 2004/41/EC of the European Parliament and of the Council of 29 April 2004 repealing certain directives concerning food hygiene and health conditions for the production and placing on the market of certain products of animal origin intended for human consumption, and amending Directives 89/662/EEC and 91/67/EEC and Council Decision 95/408/EC.[26]

---

21 European Commission, Regulation (EC) No 852/2004 of the European Parliament and of Council of 29 April 2004 on the hygiene of foodstuffs [2004] OJ L139/1.

22 Food Standards Agency, 'Full Regulatory Impact Assessment: Consolidation of EU food hygiene regulations' (2005), accessed 30 November 2016 at http://tna.europarchive.org/20110912091909/http://www.food.gov.uk/multimedia/pdfs/EURegulationsRIA.pdf.

23 Regulation 852/2004.

24 European Commission, Regulation (EC) No 854/2004 of the European Parliament and of the Council laying down specific rules for the organisation of official controls on products of animal origin intended for human consumption [2004] OJ L 139/206.

25 Ibid.

26 European Commission, Directive 2004/41/EC of the European Parliament and of the Council of 21 April 2004 repealing certain Directives concerning food hygiene and health conditions for the production and placing on the market of certain products of animal origin intended for human consumption and amending

These new hygiene regulations are implemented and enforced under the broader legal framework for food safety underpinned by the General Food Law (Regulation (EC) No 178/2002), which set out the general obligations to provide safe food.

Thus, the comprehensive regulatory reforms following the BSE crisis provide a legal framework that now enables food regulators to adopt more flexible governance systems, such as management-based regulation. Indeed, the new hygiene regulation has shifted the emphasis of official control from the traditional physical inspections of production processes toward audit and verification of firms' food safety management systems. For example, following the adoption of the consolidated EU hygiene legislation set out above, the Hygiene Assessment Scheme (HAS) system used by UK official inspectors to monitor compliance in the fresh meat sectors has been replaced by a new more risk-based audit system.[27] Under HAS, official veterinarians, based at meat premises,[28] had to look at various hygiene aspects of a premise's structure, equipment and operation and awarded each aspect a mark according to a published set of guidance notes from which an overall compliance score was determined.

On the other hand, the new audit system is more concerned with food safety outcomes and makes explicit that the hygienic production of fresh meat is the primary responsibility of the food business operators by focusing the efforts of the inspection regime on two types of risk.[29] The first type relates to meat establishments in relation to production activities and the nature of the food business, and as such covers some aspects that were included in the old scheme. The second type of risk is related to control actions undertaken by the individual firms and their food safety management systems.[30] A score of up to 120 points is awarded for each of the risk factors, with the total score determining the appropriate audit category (there are five categories in total) and frequency of auditing for a firm can range from every two to twelve months.

Council Directives 89/662/EEC and 92/118/EEC and Council Decision 95/408/EC [2004] OJ L157/33.

[27] Food Standards Agency, *Meat Establishment Audit Categories.*

[28] These include all approved slaughterhouses, game handling establishments and cutting plants. See more at https://www.food.gov.uk/enforcement/approved-premises-official-controls#sthash.Y0jPKhnL.dpuf (accessed 26 November 2016).

[29] European Commission, Regulation (EC) No 178/2002 of the European Parliament and of the Council of 28 January 2002 laying down the general principles and requirements of food law, establishing the European Food Safety Authority and laying down procedures in matters of food safety [2002] OJ L31/1.

[30] Food Standards Agency, *Meat Establishment Audit Categories.*

In effect, under the new audit scheme, the operational control of meat safety unambiguously rests on the shoulders of operators, whilst the role of the official inspectors becomes one of verifying compliance. Thus, the new audit scheme indeed enables the use of the management-based approaches based on HACCP. However, Regulation 854/2004, which governs the organisation of official controls on products of animal origin, does not apply across meat sectors symmetrically. For example, whilst a partial firm devolvement of official controls under a management-based regime is permitted in the poultry sector, the inspection regime does not offer red meat operators any such opportunity, largely due to historic incidents like BSE. This constitutes a major legal hurdle to adopting a more efficient approach to delivering official controls of food hygiene across the meat sectors, notwithstanding the relatively lower public health risks currently posed by the consumption of red meat compared to poultry.

A key question that we are trying to answer is whether the management-based regulation in the poultry meat sector, which is intended to align a firm's commercial goal of designing a flexible regulatory regime with its implementation of HACCP-based controls, offers poultry firms sufficient incentives to safeguard meat safety under a minimal official supervision. And if it does not do so, a further question is: What other considerations need to be included to commit firms effectively to this social goal?

KEY INCENTIVES FOR COMPLIANCE UNDER THE NEW HYGIENE REGIME ACROSS DIFFERENT REGULATED ENTITIES

Different meta-regulatory approaches may be necessary in some cases if the regulated entities differ widely in economic scale, technical capability and incentives to comply with rules. The heterogeneity of regulated food businesses, including the potential unequitable compliance cost implications for different sized firms and the associated food safety outcomes of the mandatory HACCP systems, has been the subject of numerous empirical studies over the past decade.[31] These studies showed that first time implementation of HACCP requires a large upfront investment in developing and implementing the system[32] and this investment cost is lower on

[31] Unnevehr, Laurian J. (ed.), *The Economics of HACCP* (Eagan Press 2000); Unnevehr, Laurian J. and Jensen, H., 'Industry Costs to Make Food Safe' in Hoffmann, Sandra A. and Taylor, Michael R. (eds), *Toward Safer Food: Perspectives on Risk and Priority Setting* (Resources for the Future Press 2005).

[32] Unnevehr and Jensen (n 31).

a per unit basis for larger processors.[33] Thus, small firms' costs increase proportionally faster than larger firms' costs with the implementation of HACCP, which constitutes a competitive advantage for larger firms. In effect, while larger firms often have in-house human and capital resources at their disposal for the design and implementation of HACCP, small firms may go out of business as result of their relatively higher compliance costs. To minimize this disadvantage, small firms are often given a longer period to comply with the new regulations.[34]

Although the flexibility offered to smaller firms can help them to spread their compliance costs over longer periods, it can also result in heterogeneous compliance or even non-compliance if such differential regulatory approaches are not carefully managed. In effect, the flexibility in conjunction with some less transparent waivers and grace periods allowed to national authorities to implement and enforce rules can potentially be used to protect an inefficient national industry rather than facilitating smooth implementation of rules.[35] Therefore, discretions given to EU Member States' regulators can be exploited by industry to 'capture' regulation, for example, in the presence of strong industry interests.[36] Capture of regulation refers in this case to industry's ability to politically influence regulatory law-making and enforcement processes for their own commercial advantage – an issue that may ultimately result in regulation not being able to achieve its stated social objectives where such political influence is effective.[37]

In addition to the above incentive problems related to heterogeneity in management-based regulation, there are other governance issues related to the unduly restrictive nature of the EU official controls which, despite the reform, still enshrine outdated practices involving visual inspections with little impact on microbial safety of meat.[38] Under the current EU regulations, the official auxiliaries (known in the United Kingdom as Meat

---

[33] Unnevehr (n 31).

[34] Unnevehr and Jensen (n 31).

[35] Caduff, Ladina and Barnaeuer, Thomas, 'Managing Risk and Regulation in European Food Safety Governance' 23 *Review of Policy Research* 153.

[36] Stigler, George J. (ed.), *Chicago Studies in Political Economy* (University of Chicago Press 1988); Laffont, Jean-Jacques and Tirole, Jean, *A Theory of Incentives in Procurement and Regulation* (MIT Press 1993).

[37] Buchanan, James M. and Tullock, Gordon, *The Calculus of Consent: Logical Foundations of Constitutional Democracy* (Ann Arbor 1962); Stevens, Joe, *Economics of Collective Choice* (Westview Press 1993).

[38] Dyckman, Lawrence J., 'The Current State of Play: Federal and State Expenditures on Food Safety' in Hoffmann, Sandra A. and Taylor, Michael R. (eds), *Toward Safer Food: Perspectives on Risk and Priority Setting* (Resources for the Future 2005); Food Standards Agency, *Progress Report: Food Safety,* accessed

Hygiene Inspectors) can assist the official veterinarians in poultry abattoirs to carry out some control activities, but they cannot carry out ante-mortem inspections of animals because animal health is within the remit of the official veterinarians.[39] The same official auxiliary tasks performed by official meat inspectors can also be carried by firms' own staff, known as Plant Inspection Assistants (PIAs). These tasks include auditing activities to collect information regarding good hygienic practices and HACCP-based procedures of the production plant; ante-mortem inspection and checks concerning the welfare of animals and to conduct initial ante-mortem checks of animals and post-mortem inspections of carcasses.[40] In relation to post-mortem inspections, the official veterinarian must regularly check the work of official auxiliaries and, in the case of animals having undergone emergency slaughter outside the slaughterhouse, carry out the inspection personally.

Thus, despite the residual restrictions they enshrine, the regulations provide a relatively permissive legal framework to facilitate the use of hybrid governance: not only does it allow regulators to encourage firms to design their own HACCP-based food safety management system according to their individual business circumstances but, as discussed below, they also permit regulators to delegate substantial responsibilities for the delivery of official controls of food hygiene to food business operators in the poultry meat sector. An added complication is that state regulators can provide financial compensation for the delegated auxiliary tasks performed by PIAs – which can potentially weaken the incentives for the firm to shoulder its legal responsibility to safeguard meat safety. In line with the language used in the economic literature, the word 'delegation' in this context refers to the implicit recognition by the state regulators to compensate the firm for the cost associated with the auxiliary tasks.[41] Such payment scheme in effect implies that the regulator values the meat safety outcome of the auxiliary tasks more than the firm, and therefore the latter should be incentivized to perform these tasks which presumably are necessary to ensure the safety of its products.

---

26 November 2016 at http://www.foodstandards.gov.uk/multimedia/pdfs/board/fsa080207.pdf (2008).

[39] Food Standards Agency, Review of models for delivering official controls in approved meat premises: report phase 1, presented by Programme Manager, G. Tierney, Options Review Team for Meat Hygiene Controls, Agenda item 3.2 for Board meeting, 15 February 2007, London (2007).

[40] Regulation 854/2004.

[41] Laffont and Tirole (n 36); Laffont, Jean-Jacques and Martimort, David, *The Theory of Incentives: The Principal-Agent Model* (Princeton University Press 2002).

MANAGEMENT-BASED REGULATION IN THE UK POULTRY SECTOR

Regardless of whether inspections are carried out by a veterinarian or a meat inspector, poultry operators are required to partially pay for costs of official inspections of meat hygiene and animal welfare at the abattoirs, as set out in Articles 26 and 27 of Regulation (EC) No. 882/2004 (the EC Regulation). However, the operator can reduce their partial charges by choosing who performs the auxiliary tasks. Typically, a poultry meat firm capable of meeting pre-specified risk-based criteria can seek permission for its PIAs to perform the official auxiliary tasks.[42] In effect, a firm with an established HACCP system and appropriately trained PIA staff is permitted to carry out the hygiene controls entailed by the auxiliary tasks under the supervision of official veterinarian.[43] As part of this arrangement, the approved firm can then receive full financial compensation for the time cost associated with PIAs performing the delegated tasks.[44] At the same time, the state regulator retains substantial oversight of the firm's controls through a combination of mandatory requirements for approval of its internal rules and the veterinary supervision to ascertain compliance – in effect a management-based enforcement regime.[45]

What is as yet unknown is whether this hybrid governance regime is capable of committing management-based regulated firms to the social goal of safe meat supply. In particular, two key features of the enforcement regime that is currently used in the United Kingdom and some other European countries, albeit with variations, to enforce EU meat hygiene legislation[46] raise doubts about its ability to efficiently safeguard meat safety. First, this management-based strategy essentially entails a principal-agent relationship since substantive official inspection responsibilities are delegated to firms operating under the regulators' supervision and compensation.[47] The imperfect nature of meat safety outcomes of the delegated tasks

---

42 Regulation 854/2004.

43 Food Standards Agency, Review of models for delivering official controls in approved meat premises (n 39).

44 Regulation 854/2004; Food Standards Agency, Review of models for delivering official controls in approved meat premises (n 39).

45 Coglianese and Lazer (n 1); Balleisen, Edward J. and Eisner, Marc, 'The Promise and Pitfalls of Co-Regulation: How Governments Can Draw on Private Governance for Public Purpose' in David Moss and John M. Cowden Cisternino (eds), *New Perspectives on Regulation* (The Tobin Project, Cambridge 2009).

46 Food Standards Agency, Review of models for delivering official controls in approved meat premises (n 39).

47 Laffont and Martimort (n 41); Laffont and Tirole (n 36).

and the practical difficulties for the regulator in devising a cost effective monitoring strategy may reduce the efficiency of the enforcement regimes.[48]

Second, the PIA-performed auxiliary tasks are likely to yield different meat safety outcomes across the poultry sector given that the regulated firms differ in their ability and (possibly) willingness to satisfactorily perform the delegated tasks. Thus, a heterogeneous compliance outcome of the hybrid governance system in this sector is likely. Large meat firms with sufficient in-house technical expertise and resources are likely to be more able to efficiently implement preventive food safety management systems such as HACCP and thus find it less onerous to comply with rules compared to smaller firms.[49] Therefore, the combination of imperfect meat safety and the heterogeneity across regulated firms raises fundamental questions as to whether a management-based enforcement strategy can efficiently deliver meat safety across the UK poultry sector. And if it cannot, we need to consider what needs to be changed in the existing incentive structures to improve the efficiency of the regime.

Answering these questions clearly requires substantive quantitative analysis based on hard data relating to compliance behaviour of the regulated firms, administrative cost of delivery of the model and associated public health outcomes; a task that is beyond the scope of this chapter. Instead, we provide a contextual assessment of the effectiveness of the regime based on existing evidence. Nevertheless, we hope that such an assessment provides an informative illustration of the management-based hybrid governance regime at work as well as insights that are pertinent to EU food policymaking. This is particularly important as abattoirs governed by the regime are a critical 'choke point' through which all poultry products move before entering the food chain;[50] therefore, effective controls (or lack of them) at this segment of the supply chain are likely to have significant implications for public health.

---

48 Henson, S. and Traill, B., 'The Demand for Food Safety: Market Imperfections and the Role of Government' 18 *Food Policy* 152–62; Starbird, S. Andrew, 'Moral Hazard, Inspection Policy and Food Safety' 87(1)(Feb.) *American Journal of Agricultural Economics* 15–27.

49 Unnevehr and Jensen (n 31); Antle, J.M., 'No Such Thing as Free Safe Lunch: The Cost of Safety Regulation in Meat Industry' 82(2) *American Journal of Agricultural Economics* 310–22.

50 Morris, J. Glenn, 'Opportunity for Risk Reduction: A Public Health Perspective' in Sandra A. Hoffmann and Michael R. Taylor (eds), *Toward Safer Food: Perspectives on Risk Priority Setting* (Resources for the Future 2005).

EVIDENCE REGARDING THE EFFECTIVENESS OF THE MANAGEMENT-BASED REGIME

Existing evidence suggests that poultry meat-bone disease has long been and remains a major public health concern in the United Kingdom[51] and other EU Member States.[52] Figure 7.1 summarizes the reported zoonotic disease cases, in particular, disease caused by salmonella, campylobacter and E. coli. In the United Kingdom, these are closely associated with consumption of animal products, including meats, and are the

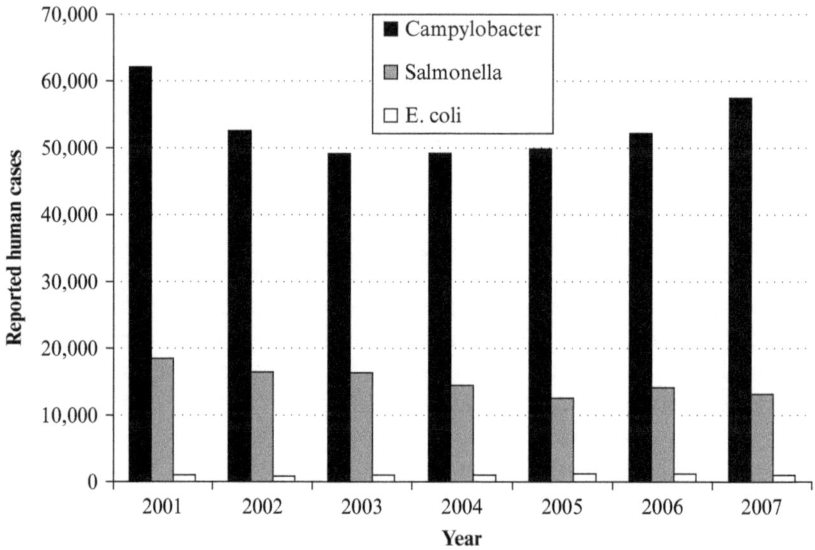

Source: Defra, https://www.gov.uk/government/organisations/department-for-environ ment-food-rural-affairs

Figure 7.1 Zoonotic disease in the United Kingdom 2001–2007

---

[51] Data reported is for England and Wales. Unfortunately, we have not been able to collect more recent data.

[52] European Food Safety Authority (EFSA), 'Scientific Opinion on the Public Health Hazards to be Covered by Inspection of Meat (Poultry)' (2012) 10(6) *EFSA Journal* 2741; Food Standards Agency (n 39); EFSA, 'Scientific Opinion on Campylobacter in Broiler Meat Production: Control Options and Performance Objectives and/or Targets at Different Stages of the Food Chain, EFSA Panel on Biological Hazards (BIOHAZ)' (2011) 9(4) *EFSA Journal* 2105; Food Standards Agency, *Annual Report of the Chief Scientist 2012/13* (2013).

subject of monitoring by various zoonoses surveillance programmes.[53] Campylobacter is not only linked to the highest rate of zoonotic diseases, as shown in Figure 7.1 for the years 2001 to 2007, but it still continues to pose considerable challenges for UK food safety regulators. In fact, poultry meat consumption accounted for 90 and 26 per cent of all confirmed foodborne disease outbreaks caused by campylobacter and salmonella, respectively, in 2009 in England and Wales.[54] Campylobacter alone caused sickness in over 300,000 people each year in the United Kingdom, with around 15,000 people admitted to hospital for treatment and 80 deaths.[55]

Given that the primary purpose of hygiene controls is to prevent unsafe meat entering the food chain, these findings indicate significant weakness in the current poultry inspection regime. Existing evidence linking the poultry-borne disease to poor husbandry and hygiene practices at production and abattoir levels, respectively, indeed suggests that the regime is ineffective. The Food Standards Agency (FSA) carried out a survey of campylobacter in chicken on retail sale in the United Kingdom between May 2007 and September 2008, and reported that campylobacter was present in 65 per cent of the fresh chicken samples tested.[56] Furthermore, although there are some differences in the way EU Member States enforce hygiene rules,[57] poultry-borne disease is pervasive in Europe, suggesting that there is a common underlying weakness in the enforcement of hygiene controls. The European Food Safety Authority[58] has estimated that there are approximately nine million cases of human *campylobacteriosis* linked to poultry products each year across the 27 EU Member States.

Evidence from analysis of UK food safety strategies also further supports our conclusion. As a result of the continued under-compliance right through the period leading up to 2008, the FSA's Chief Scientist reported to the Agency's Board of Governors in February 2008 that the Agency

---

53 BPEX, *Zoonoses Action Plan: Annual Report July 2007–March 2008*, accessed 26 November 2016 at http://www.bpex-zncp.org.uk/resources/000/320/206/ZAP_Annual_Report_2007-2008_.pdf (2008); Defra, *Zoonoses report 2007* (2008) Food Standards Agency.

54 Health Protection Agency, 'eFOSS- electronic Foodborne and non-Foodborne Gastrointestinal Outbreak Surveillance System, England and Wales: Report 2: Foodborne Outbreaks in 2009'.

55 UK Research and Innovation Strategy for Campylobacter – in the food chain 2010–2015.

56 See https://www.food.gov.uk/science/microbiology/campylobacterevidence programme#sthash.VjQWXUaL.dpuf (accessed 27 November 2016).

57 Food Standards Agency, Review of models for delivering official controls in approved meat premises (n 39).

58 EFSA, 'Scientific Opinion on Campylobacter in broiler meat production' (n 52).

was unable to meet this target to improve food safety due to a large number of foodborne disease cases increasingly caused by campylobacter and salmonella.[59] The report singled out a mismatch between the control activities that would have been necessary to improve food safety at abattoir level and the actual operational requirements by the EU meat hygiene regulations. The Chief Scientist argued that EU hygiene legislation contains prescriptive requirements with no basis in science and, despite the reforms, it unduly requires officials to visually inspect meat carcasses when there is very little of public health significance that can be seen with the eye. He pointed out that, by requiring the constant presence of officials tasked with enforcing compliance with regulations rather than securing food safety, the prescriptive controls perversely inhibit slaughterhouse operators from taking their legal responsibility for food safety as implied by the EU food law. Further evidence from a risk factor analysis of data collected during the EU baseline study for campylobacter in 2008 links regulatory incentives with underperformance of delegated tasks at firm level. The study found that there were differences in the levels of campylobacter on carcasses from different slaughterhouses and these were independent of the level of campylobacter carried in chickens' guts before processing.[60] In particular, the study has shown that the control activities adopted by different plants, such as washing and chilling, have a variable effect on campylobacter levels. Although it is reasonable to expect heterogeneous compliance behaviour across any sector, it is clear that either most poultry plants or a relative small number of plants producing a high volume of contaminated meat are underperforming the delegated tasks in this case, given the high prevalence of campylobacter in retail chicken and the considerable burdens of foodborne disease linked to poultry consumption.

In addition to the public health impact, there is also an economic aspect to the misplaced EU requirements. The meat hygiene controls, as a whole, paradoxically absorb considerable public and industry resources as shown in Figure 7.2. Although the cost of official meat hygiene controls has been gradually transferred to the industry over the past decade, the proportion of cost borne by the UK taxpayer is larger than industry costs. In 2008/09 the industry costs recovered through the partial statutory charges only covered the cost of official inspection staff, whilst other significant administrative costs were met by the taxpayer. In the financial year 2009/10 the operational costs of the Meat Hygiene Service (MHS), the agency responsible for the enforcement of EU official controls in the UK fresh

---

59 Food Standards Agency (n 39).

60 Food Standards Agency, *Annual Report of the Chief Scientist 2012/13*.

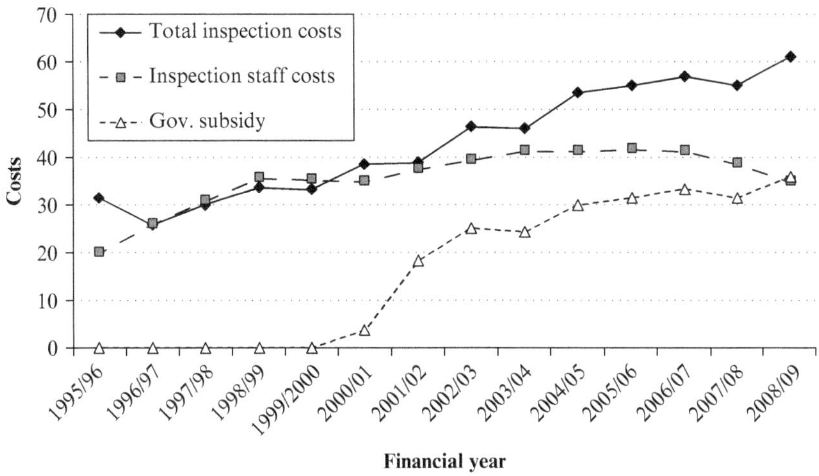

Source: Food Standards Agency, Annual Accounts and reports of MHS.

Figure 7.2 MHS total inspection and staff costs

meat industry, were £68.1 million.[61] About 35 per cent (approximately £24 million) of the overall costs have been recovered from industry through partial service charges set by EU law, whilst the remainder is paid for by the taxpayer as a subsidy to the operational deficit of the MHS.

Although it has not been possible to identify the exact figure of the overall official controls cost attributed to poultry sectors, it is reasonable to expect that a substantial part of the cost has been, and continues to be, spent in the poultry sector given that under the management-based regime the operators can claim the full costs associated with the auxiliary tasks performed by their PIAs. In fact, a review of UK delivery models for EU hygiene controls in fresh meat sectors found that 75 per cent of large and medium abattoirs used PIAs in 2007 to perform auxiliary tasks. Thus, the incentive problems associated with financial compensation paid to operators for auxiliary tasks performed under the supervision of official veterinary controls – perceived to be unduly restrictive in this case – appear to limit considerably the scope for possible efficiency gains from management-based regulation.

[61] Meat Hygiene Service, *Annual Report & Accounts 2008/09: Protecting Public Health and Animal Health and Welfare* (2010).

CONCLUDING REMARKS

These foregoing discussions suggest that, due to the incentive problems associated with the veterinary supervision coupled with partial payment system, the current hybrid regime for the enforcement of EU meat hygiene controls in UK poultry abattoirs may not be rigorous enough to commit firms to the social goal of safe meat supply. They also point to the regulators' limited ability to verify the meat safety outcome of the hybrid regime and consequently inefficiency allocation of the regulatory and industry resources. Evidence linking poor governance of the regime and under-compliance in the poultry sector corroborates the findings of the case study. Both UK and EU food safety regulatory agencies recognized in major reports that the regime does not provide strong incentives for hygiene controls at abattoir level and as such is unable to prevent contaminated meat entering the food chain, linking under-compliance to the reported high incidents of poultry disease.

Two broader conclusions can be drawn from this analysis. First, under a management-based approach, food safety is largely an outcome of the interaction between strategic firm behaviour related to the delegated auxiliary tasks and the inspection practices encompassed by the official veterinary oversight. Therefore, without a well-crafted regulatory incentive mechanism capable of committing firms to the social goal of safe meat supply, management-based regulation is likely to be sub-optimal.

Second, the analysis shows that flexible regulatory strategies, such as management-based approaches, may not necessarily deliver better outcomes than the traditional prescriptive (command-and-control) regulation they were intended to improve upon. In particular, the flexibility afforded to regulated firms through delegated auxiliary tasks may not translate into regulatory efficiency gains where the outcome cannot be verified easily – typically where the information on the outcome is imperfect and it is costly to ascertain it. Thus, a key prerequisite for effective implementation of this form of regulation is to ensure that regulated firms not only possess sufficient administrative capacity and resources for approval for flexible regulation but also have appropriate incentives to comply with the rules. Our findings mirror those of Lytton and McAllister and of Thomann and Sager (Chapters 4 and 5 respectively in this volume), and all point toward a common pattern of failing hybrid governance systems in the absence of strong legal and administrative frameworks capable of safeguarding the social goals they intend to deliver.

The evidence presented by this chapter in particular calls for further research assessing the effectiveness of the management-based approach more formally, ideally based on real data on the relevant industry and regulatory costs and compliance outcomes. Such research should try to establish a clear causal link between the effects of enforcement activities undertaken by both the official and the PIA inspectors and the resulting regulatory costs and food safety outcomes at the firm level.

ACKNOWLEDGEMENTS

The authors wish to acknowledge the funding from the UK Food Standards Agency for the research upon which this chapter is based. The views expressed in the chapter are entirely those of the authors and do not necessarily represent the views of the FSA.

8 The influence of context on food safety governance: Bridging the gap between policy and quality management

Klementina Kirezieva and Pieternel Luning

INTRODUCTION

Food safety is an ongoing concern for the food industry, agribusinesses, competent food authorities and consumers. Food safety governance is aimed at controlling food safety risks and protecting human health.[1] It involves the establishment of a legal framework and the enforcement of food safety policies, with the goal to induce compliance by companies in the food supply chain. They have to set-up and implement food safety management systems (FSMS). Next to the public requirements, many private standards emerged, such as British Retail Consortium (BRC) and GlobalGAP, which pose additional demands for food companies and agribusinesses.[2] FSMS are thus the result of the translation of all these various standards and guidelines and legal requirements into a company specific system.[3]

Food safety governance is exercised in various contexts – that is, different countries, sectors and/or supply chain management structures. This is relevant for all food sectors, but especially challenging for fresh produce, which is increasingly produced, traded and distributed across the world, thereby being confronted with different context characteristics wherein the FSMS need to operate. In Europe, in the last few decades, the focus

---

[1] FAO/WHO, *Risk management and food safety. Report of the Joint FAO/WHO Expert Consultation* (FAO/WHO 1997).

[2] A.G. da Cruz, S.A. Cenci and M.C.A. Maia, 'Quality Assurance Requirements in Produce Processing' (2006) 17 *Trends in Food Science & Technology* 406.

[3] P.A. Luning and W.J. Marcelis, 'A Food Quality Management Research Methodology Integrating Technological and Managerial Theories' (2009) 20 *Trends in Food Science & Technology* 35.

of food safety management at company level has been mainly on animal products.[4] However, foodborne outbreak data reveal an increasing number of incidences in fresh produce and derived food products in Europe and beyond.[5] This indicates weaknesses in current FSMS in this sector.[6] Fresh produce are vulnerable products, commonly consumed raw, fresh cut or minimally processed. The production usually occurs in diverse climates around the globe, under different administrative conditions, in differently structured food systems ranging from traditional to highly industrialized. Moreover, chain actors range from very small to very large.[7]

Most studies focus on investigating either the implementation and performance of FSMS,[8] or the mechanisms of establishing public and private enforcement of food safety policies.[9] Although very few studies have investigated the role of enforcement practices on HACCP based systems,[10] there is still a need to gain a deeper understanding of the link

---

4 P.A. Luning and others, 'Performance Assessment of Food Safety Management Systems in Animal-Based Food Companies in view of their Context Characteristics: A European Study' (2015) 49 *Food Control* 11.

5 L. Baert and others, 'Review: Norovirus prevalence in Belgian, Canadian and French Fresh Produce: A Threat to Human Health?' (2011) 151 *International Journal of Food Microbiology* 216; R.V. Tauxe and others, 'Evolving Public Health Approaches to the Global Challenge of Foodborne Infections' (2010) 139 *International Journal of Food Microbiology* 16–28; M.F. Lynch and others, 'The Growing Burden of Foodborne Outbreaks due to Contaminated Fresh Produce: Risks and Opportunities' (2009) 137 *Epidemiology and Infection* 307.

6 S.J. Ilic and others, 'Coliforms and Prevalence of Escherichia coli and Foodborne Pathogens on Minimally Processed Spinach in Two Packing Plants' (2008) 71 *Journal of Food Protection* 2398; L.M. Johnston and others, 'A Field Study of the Microbiological Quality of Fresh Produce of Domestic and Mexican Origin' (2006) 112 *International Journal of Food Microbiology* 83.

7 E.B. McCullough, P.L. Prabhu and K.G. Kostas, 'Small Farms and the Transformation of Food Systems: An Overview' in E.B. McCullough and others (eds), in *The Transformation of Agri-Food Systems: Globalization, Supply Chains and Smallholder Farmers* (Routledge 2008).

8 E.g. SM Osés and others, 'Food Safety Management System Performance in the Lamb Chain' (2012) 25 *Food Control* 493; Luning, 'Performance Assessment of Food Safety Management Systems' (n 4).

9 E.g. E. Rouvière and J.A. Caswell, 'From Punishment to Prevention: A French Case Study of the Introduction of Co-regulation in Enforcing Food Safety' (2012) 37 *Food Policy* 246; C. Jia and D. Jukes 'The National Food Safety Control System of China – A Systematic Review' (2013) 32 *Food Control* 236; J Lundén, 'Reasons for using Enforcement Measures in Food Premises in Finland' (2013) 31 *Food Control* 84.

10 E.g. R. Fairman and C. Yapp, 'Enforced Self-Regulation, Prescription, and Conceptions of Compliance within Small Businesses: The Impact of Enforcement' (2005) 27 *Law & Policy* 491.

between FSMS performance and public and private enforcement as part of the broader systems context. Further studies are needed to bridge the gap between policy and quality management.

This chapter provides a synopsis of particular research done in the frame of a large European project on safety in global fresh produce chains.[11] The research was aimed at gaining a deeper understanding of the impact of context characteristics on FSMS performance in (inter)national fresh produce chains. Though the studies were not specifically designed to bridge the gap between policy and quality management, findings of several empirical studies provided interesting insights that can help to narrow this gap.

The chapter is structured as follows. First, food safety governance is described from multiple perspectives, followed by a brief discussion of private standards in view of food safety governance. Subsequently, concepts and theories used as the basis for the empirical research are outlined followed by major findings, and an overall discussion and conclusions. The research followed an interdisciplinary approach, integrating technological and managerial theories and models.[12] Moreover, connections were established with the social sciences disciplines of public policy and supply chain management to explore the influence of context on food safety governance.

FOOD SAFETY GOVERNANCE

The general concept of governance has been described as the structures and processes of collective decision-making, including public and private actors.[13] For food safety governance, particular structures are put into place to provide human health protection. Food safety governance includes the three conventionally recognized elements of risk analysis, comprising risk assessment, risk management and risk communication.[14]

---

[11] http://veg-i-trade.org (accessed 26 November 2016); K Kirezieva, *Impact of Context on Food Safety Management Systems in Fresh Produce Chains* (Wageningen University 2015); J. Sentongo Nanyunja, *Food Safety Management Systems in the East African Community: Empirical Evidence from the Fresh Produce Sector in Kenya and Uganda* (Ghent University 2015).

[12] P.A. Luning and W.J. Marcelis, 'A Techno-Managerial Approach in Food Quality Management Research' (2006) 17 *Trends in Food Science & Technology* 378.

[13] J.S. Nye and J.D. Donahue, *Governance in a Globalizing World* (Brookings Institution Press 2000).

[14] Codex Alimentarius Commission 'Principles and Guidelines for the Conduct of Microbiological Risk Management' CAC/GL 63-2007, accessed 26

Commonly, risk management is put into the hands of food companies, and their behaviour is steered by different public and private stakeholders. In practice, however, the process of food safety governance is not that straightforward and may involve several public, private and hybrid organizations that are involved in inspection and auditing of legal requirements and or private standards as translated and implemented into companies' FSMS. Examples are sector organizations which work closely with government to facilitate the enforcement of the national food safety law, or NGOs in developing countries promoting the Codex Alimentarius Commission. Such organizations are common in the European Union, which follows the principles of subsidiarity resulting in multi-level governance. The adoption of the General Food Law in the European Union in 2002[15] was 'driven by the need to guarantee high and uniform level of food safety'.[16] Furthermore, several Regulations have been promulgated to harmonize food safety and hygiene laws of EU Member States.[17] Nevertheless, much room is left for the Member States in the interpretation and enforcement of the food safety policy.[18] Some countries define their own standards and guidelines, while others leave it to market self-regulation. In fact, public and private standards are not discrete, and they operate intertwined.[19] Figure 8.1 schematically presents food safety governance in the European Union. Even though all Member States operate under the same General Food Law, the transposition into national

---

November 2016 at http://www.fao.org/fao-who-codexalimentarius/standards/list-of-standards/en/?provide=standards&orderField=fullReference&sort=asc&num1=CODEX (Codex Alimentarius, 2007).

[15] Regulation 178/2002/EC of the European Parliament and of the Council of 28 January 2002 laying down the general principles and requirements of food law, establishing the European Food Safety Authority and laying down procedures in matters of food safety ([2002] OJ L31/1).

[16] A. Szajkowska, *Regulating Food Law: Risk Analysis and the Precautionary Principle as General Principles of EU Food Law* (Wageningen University 2012).

[17] Regulation (EC) No 852/2004 of the European Parliament and of the Council of 29 April 2004 on the hygiene of foodstuffs ([2004] OJ L139/1); Regulation (EC) No 853/2004 of the European Parliament and the Council laying down specific hygiene rules for foodstuffs ([2004] OJ L139/55; and Regulation (EC) No 854/2004 of the European Parliament and of the Council of 29 April 2004 laying down specific rules for the organisation of official controls on products of animal origin intended for human consumption ([2004] OJ L226/83).

[18] J.R. Houghton and others, 'The Quality of Food Risk Management in Europe: Perspectives and Priorities' (2008) 33 *Food Policy* 13.

[19] A. Fearne and M. Garcia Martinez, 'Opportunities for the Coregulation of Food Safety: Insights from the United Kingdom' (2005) 20 *Choices* 109.

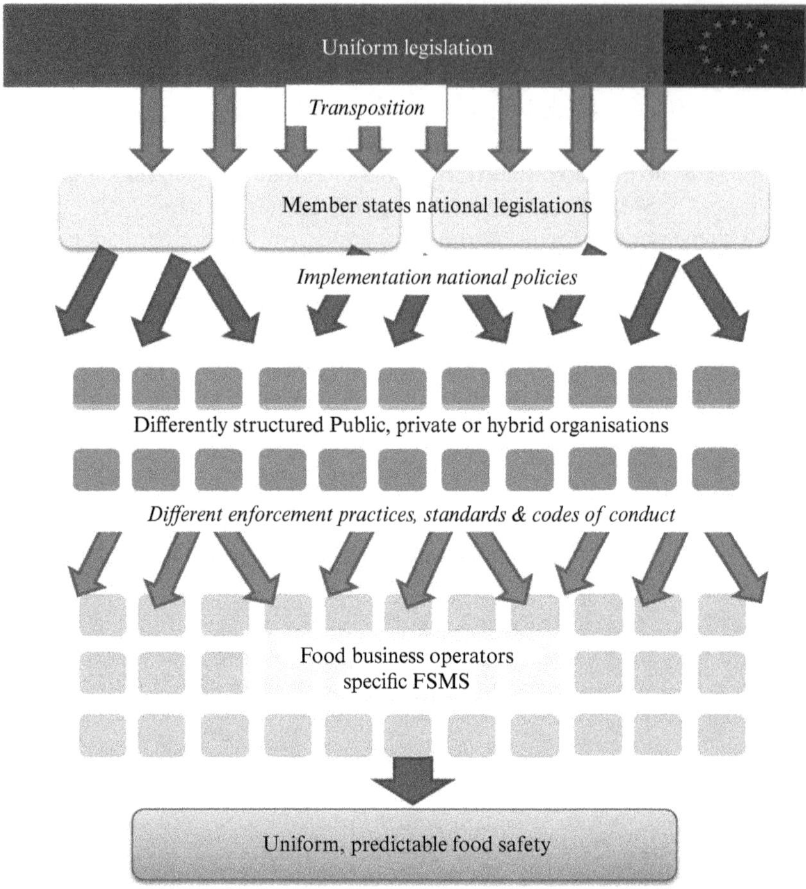

Figure 8.1 Food safety governance in the European Union showing the enforcement of the legislation and the link to the standards

legislation, followed by the implementation of food safety policies into country specific structures (being public, private and or hybrid organizations) result in a broad variety of enforcement practices (through codes of conduct such as standards, guidelines, and so on) to evaluate implemented FSMS that finally should achieve the common goal of uniform and predictable safe food.

From a global perspective, general codes of practices are put forward by the Codex Alimentarius Commission, with the goal of protecting the health of consumers and assuring fair trade practices around the globe.[20] These codes serve as a reference point in international disputes regarding food safety and consumer protection.[21] Compliance with these codex guidelines is compulsory for World Trade Organization (WTO) members. The sanitary and phytosanitary (SPS) agreement of the WTO sets out the rules that members are presumed to follow, when they set SPS-based measures to govern food and feed safety, animal health and plant health. Similarly as in the European Union, next to these international guidelines, governments can enforce their own safety policies, or leave it to market self-regulation via private standards.[22]

PRIVATE STANDARDS AND FOOD SAFETY GOVERNANCE

The increased prevalence of private standards in the last few years has raised questions regarding their legitimacy.[23] However, conclusions were difficult as private standards differ in their content and institutional arrangements. They address food safety but also other non-food safety attributes, and represent different interests.[24] In practice, standards are actually checklists of very detailed technical requirements against which companies are audited.[25] These requirements have been criticized for lacking scientific basis and importance ranking,[26] which creates possibilities for exceeding the core requisites for food safety or for not addressing them sufficiently. For instance, huge differences were identified in the recommendations for irrigation water control, none of which was

---

20 Codex Alimentarius Commission, *Food Hygiene* (Basic texts, 4th edn, WHO/FAO 2009).

21 Szajkowska (n 16).

22 M. Garcia Martinez and others, 'Co-regulation as a Possible Model for Food Safety Governance: Opportunities for Public-Private Partnerships' (2007) 32 *Food Policy* 299.

23 S. Henson, 'The Role of Public and Private Standards in Regulating International Food Markets' (2008) 4 *Journal of International Agricultural Trade and Development* 63.

24 S. Henson and J. Humphrey, 'Understanding the Complexities of Private Standards in Global Agri-Food Chains as They Impact Developing Countries' (2010) 46 *The Journal of Development Studies* 1628.

25 F. Albersmeier, H. Schulze, G. Jahn and A. Spiller, 'The Reliability of Third-Party Certification in the Food Chain: From Checklists to Risk-Oriented Auditing' (2009) 20 *Food Control* 927.

26 L. Fulponi, 'Private Voluntary Standards in the Food System: The Perspective of Major Food Retailers in OECD Countries' (2006) 31 *Food Policy* 1.

actually based on scientific evidence.[27] Such core food safety activities clearly need scientific input, and to be translated into guidelines or even public standards. What is more, not all private standards are updated systematically. Only those which are benchmarked against the Global Food Safety Initiatives (GFSI) need to be regularly reviewed.[28]

Another issue with private standards is that in anticipation of food safety incidences the common response is to increase the number of requirements in the checklist, whereas new challenges and systemic risks are not systematically addressed.[29] A systems-based approach to upgrading standards would improve their adaptive capacity regarding new threats.[30]

Last but not least, private standards are heavily dependent on third-party audits. Audits and inspections are demonstrated not to be sufficient to consistently prove the effectiveness of FSMS, as they are people-dependent and prone to subjectivity and influences.[31] They should be paired with other controls, such as sampling and in-house checks.[32] Neither the content of standards nor requirements for audits or auditors is yet commonly regulated by governments or independent (international) organizations, although GFSI is working to intensify international requirements on auditor competences.[33] Moreover, state actors increasingly seek to influence the content of private food safety standards, in particular their auditing mechanisms.[34]

---

27 Y. Pachepsky and others, 'Irrigation Waters as a Source of Pathogenic Microorganisms in Produce: A Review' (2011) 113 *Advances in Agronomy* 73–138.

28 See also the contributions of Fagotto (Chapter 3) and Havinga and Verbruggen (Chapter 9) in this volume.

29 J. Kleboth, P.A. Luning and F Fogliano, 'Risk-Based Integrity Audits in the Food Chain – A Framework for Complex Systems' (2016) 56 *Trends in Food Science & Technology* 167–74.

30 Kirezieva, *Impact of Context on Food Safety Management Systems in Fresh Produce Chains* (n 11); Kleboth and others (n 29).

31 Albersmeier and others (n 25); D.A. Powell and others, 'Audits and Inspections are Never Enough: A Critique to Enhance Food Safety' (2013) 30 *Food Control* 686.

32 Powell and others (n 31) 686.

33 See also the contributions of Fagotto (Chapter 3) and Havinga and Verbruggen (Chapter 9) in this volume.

34 See for examples the contributions in this volume and in the Special Issue of the *European Journal of Risk Regulation* on Patterns of Interplay between Public and Private Food Regulators (2015) 6(4) edited by Paul Verbruggen and Tetty Havinga.

FOOD SAFETY GOVERNANCE FROM A BROADER PERSPECTIVE

Food safety governance used to be primarily focused on food safety risks. However, nowadays the tendency is for it to move towards a broader scope requiring input from multiple stakeholders and scientific disciplines to cope with other (emerging) food-related issues, such as fraud mitigation, food safety culture and risk-based auditing. To incorporate these elements Ely et al. provide a broad notion of food safety governance, including also institutional design, technical methodology, administrative consultation, legislative procedures, political accountability of public bodies, and social or corporate responsibility of private enterprises.[35] Food safety governance thus includes input from government, commercial and civil society actors to build and use scientific knowledge for fostering innovation and technical competences to develop effective strategies and promote social and organizational learning.

According to Motarjemi and Lelieveld,[36] food safety governance is realized in cooperation with several stakeholders, which are: governments, industry, science and consumers, each of them having its role and responsibilities. Figure 8.2 depicts a general overview of food safety management in society, as proposed by Motarjemi and Lelieveld,[37] which we have modified by also including the public, private and hybrid organizations involved via development and implementation of standards and guidelines. Governments and governmental agencies set risk-management priorities and promulgate legislation. However, they follow a certain enforcement philosophy, which commonly follows the public policy traditions.[38] Governmental agencies are also responsible for communicating the risk. They need to select strategies to achieve effective communication based on how risks are assessed scientifically and how they are perceived

---

[35] A. Ely and others, 'The Need for Change' in M. Dreyer and O. Ortwin (eds), *Food Safety Governance: Integrating Science, Precaution, and Public Involvement* (Springer 2009) 28–250.

[36] Y. Motarjemi and H. Lelieveld, 'Fundamentals in Management of Food Safety in the Industrial Setting: Challenges and Outlook of the 21st Century' in Y. Motarjemi and H. Lelieveld (eds), *Food Safety Management* (Academic Press 2014) 1–20.

[37] Motarjemi and Lelieveld (n 36).

[38] M. Bevir, R.A.W. Rhodes and P. Weller, 'Traditions of Governance: Interpreting the Changing Role of the Public Sector' (2003) 81 *Public Administration* 191.

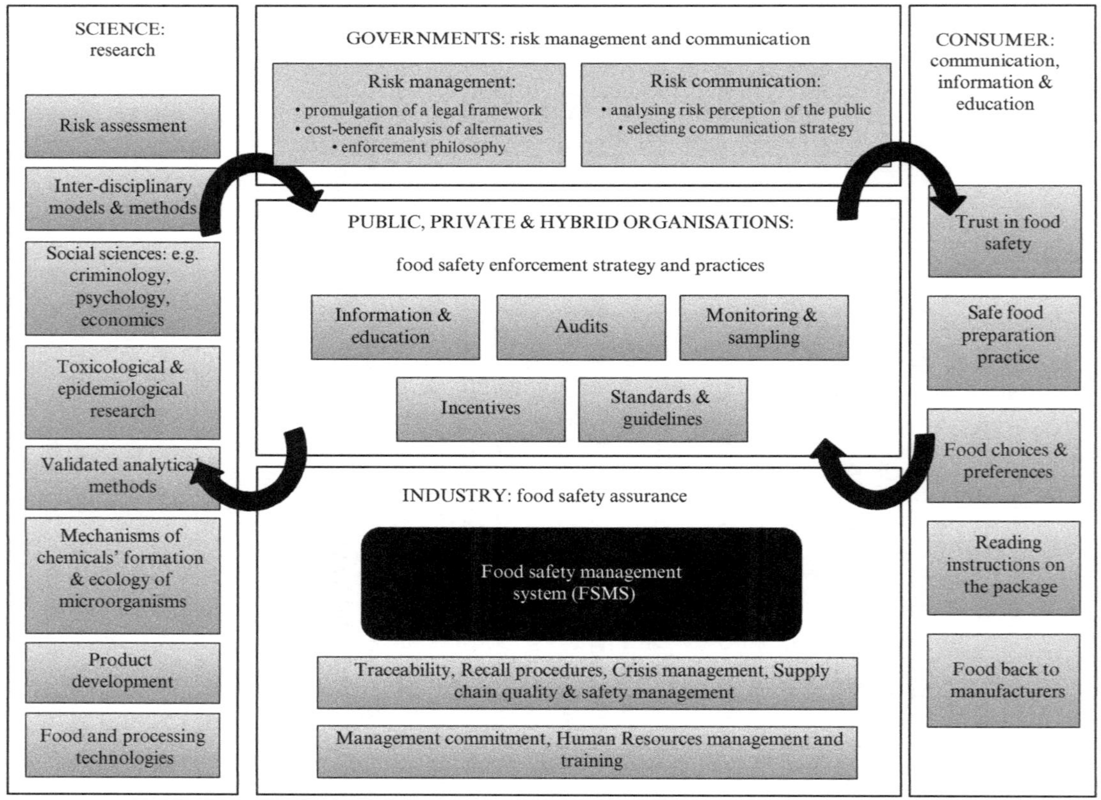

Source: Adapted from Motarjemi and Lelieveld (n 36).

Figure 8.2 General overview of the organization of food safety management in society

by the public in different contexts.[39] Risk perceptions obviously differ amongst countries due to cultural differences.[40]

The role of science in food safety management and governance has been traditionally seen to explain occurrence of hazards, propose new production methods and products, and search for patterns, causes and effects of health and disease conditions on the population.[41] However, this perspective overlooks the contribution of social sciences and the abilities they have to inform governments on risk management and risk communication. For instance, challenges to food safety management related to food fraud and food safety culture would benefit from insights from criminology and psychology.[42] Economic disciplines would contribute to finding, for example, the most effective and efficient enforcement strategies and practices, and integration of the supply chain, operations and food safety management. Inter-disciplinary models and methods are needed to link social and natural science disciplines and enable goal-oriented research to address the complex issues in food safety management.[43] Consumers should also be taken into account, not only as final users of the food, but also as formally and informally setting requirements on policy and industry.

Furthermore, the traditional risk analysis approach has been criticized for its inability to handle new challenges and systemic risks, because it ignores the 'broad context' of social and economic systems.[44] It has been argued that any type of risk governance, including food safety governance, should recognize and deal with systemic risks. The concept of systemic risk was created in the last decade to describe the risks affecting the systems on which society depends, such as food, health, transport, environment, and so on.[45] The concept recognizes the fact that risks to human health

---

[39] J. Kennedy and others, 'Public Perceptions of the Dioxin Incident in Irish Pork' (2010) 13 *Journal of Risk Research* 937; M. de Vocht and others, 'Affective and Cognitive Reactions towards Emerging Food Safety Risks in Europe' (2014) *Journal of Risk Research* 1.

[40] K.T. Chou and H.M. Liou, '"System destroys trust?": Regulatory Institutions and Public Perceptions of Food Risks in Taiwan' (2010) 96 *Social Indicators Research* 41.

[41] Motarjemi and Lelieveld (n 36) 1–20.

[42] C.J. Griffith, K.M. Livesey and D. Clayton, 'The Assessment of Food Safety Culture' (2010) 112 *British Food Journal* 439; P. Shears, 'Food Fraud – A Current Issue but an Old Problem' (2010) 112 *British Food Journal* 198.

[43] P.A. Luning and W.J. Marcelis (n 3).

[44] O. Renn and others, 'Risks' in P. Pechan and others (eds), *Safe or Not Safe* (Springer 2011) 1–41.

[45] Organisation for Economic Cooperation and Development, *Emerging systemic risks in the 21st century: An agenda for action* (OECD 2003).

and environment are embedded in a broad context of social, financial and economic systems.[46] There are strong interconnections between these different systems and systemic risks can occur at the junction between them.[47] Systemic risks can be the result of interaction between natural events (affected or not by humans), economic, social and technological systems, and policy actions both at national or international level.[48] Climate change is such a natural event. It can create pressures on food safety management at a company and regional level.[49] The pressures are created because the variability of climate can lead firms to exceed microbial and or chemical contamination criteria, which set additional requirements on coping and or adaptive strategies within the FSMS.[50] So, when trying to understand FSMS performance one needs to consider the context wherein the systems operate to gain a better understanding of differences in food safety outputs amongst sectors, countries and supply chains.

CONCEPTS, THEORIES AND TOOLS TO EXPLORE ROLE OF FSMS' CONTEXT

Systems Thinking

Systems thinking is aimed at understanding the behaviour of systems constituted of different components, and their interaction with context and other systems.[51] At the core of systems thinking are the concepts of hierarchy and emergence. Systems can be expressed as a hierarchy of levels of organization, each level more complex than the one preceding it, and each level having emergent properties arising from the way its

---

46 Renn and others (n 44).

47 OECD (n 45); O. Renn and A. Klinke, 'Systemic Risks: A New Challenge for Risk Management' (2004) 5 *EMBO Reports* 541; International Risk Governance Council, *White paper on risk governance. Towards an integrative approach* (IRGC 2005).

48 Renn and others (n 44).

49 K Kirezieva and others, 'Towards Strategies to Adapt to Pressures on Safety of Fresh Produce due to Climate Change' (2015) 68 *Food Research International* 94.

50 D.A. Hennessy, J. Roosen and H.H. Jensen, 'Systemic Failure in the Provision of Safe Food' (2013) 28 *Food Policy* 77; K. Kirezieva and others, 'Factors Affecting the Status of Food Safety Management Systems in the Global Fresh Produce Chain' (2015) 52 *Food Control* 85.

51 L. Von Bertalanffy, *General System Theory: Foundations, Development, Applications* (George Braziller Inc, 1969).

parts are organized.[52] Systems can be embedded parts in larger systems, called supra-systems.[53] Emergence represents the synergetic effect of the system as a whole, which is lost when the system is dismantled into its parts.[54] Problem solving based on the systems thinking approach seeks to understand the fundamental differences between one complexity level and the other, and to explain the relationships between these different levels. To achieve that, systems-based approaches commonly search for patterns, to increase understanding of the problem and enable response. Systems thinking has been introduced in food quality management research by Luning and Marcelis.[55] They defined FSMS with their respective components and narrow FSMS context.[56] Narrow context factors were defined as structural elements that affect decision-making activities in the FSMS and the food safety output.[57]

Systems Theory and Broad Context

Another major concept of systems theory is communication and control, related to the imposition of constraints from an upper to a lower level of hierarchy. The lower level should exhibit specific emergent properties as a result of the imposed constraints.[58] The design and actual operation of a FSMS result from the company's translation of legal requirements and private standards into its unique system, as well as from internal audits and public and private enforcement to assess compliance to these requirements. A FSMS is considered as the lower level of the supra-system of food

---

[52] M.C. Jackson, *Systems Approaches to Management* (Springer 2002); L. Skyttner, *General Systems Theory: Problems, Perspectives and Practice* (World Scientific 2005).

[53] Skyttner (n 52).

[54] Jackson (n 52).

[55] P.A. Luning and W.J. Marcelis (n 12).

[56] P.A. Luning and others, 'Comprehensive Analysis and Differentiated Assessment of Food Safety Control Systems: A Diagnostic Instrument' (2008) 19 *Trends in Food Science & Technology* 522; Luning and Marcelis (n 3); P.A. Luning, W.J. Marcelis, J. Rovira, M. Van der Spiegel, M. Uyttendaele and L. Jacxsens, 'Systematic Assessment of Core Assurance Activities in a Company Specific Food Safety Management System' (2009) 20 *Trends in Food Science & Technology* 300; P.A. Luning, W.J. Marcelis, J. Rovira, M.A.J.S. van Boekel, M. Uyttendaele and L. Jacxsens, 'A Tool to Diagnose Context Riskiness in View of Food Safety Activities and Microbiological Safety Output' (2011) 22 *Trends in Food Science &Technology* 67–79.

[57] Luning and others 'A Tool to Diagnose Context Riskiness' (n 56).

[58] P. Checkland, *Systems Thinking, Systems Practice: includes a 30-year retrospective* (Wiley 1999).

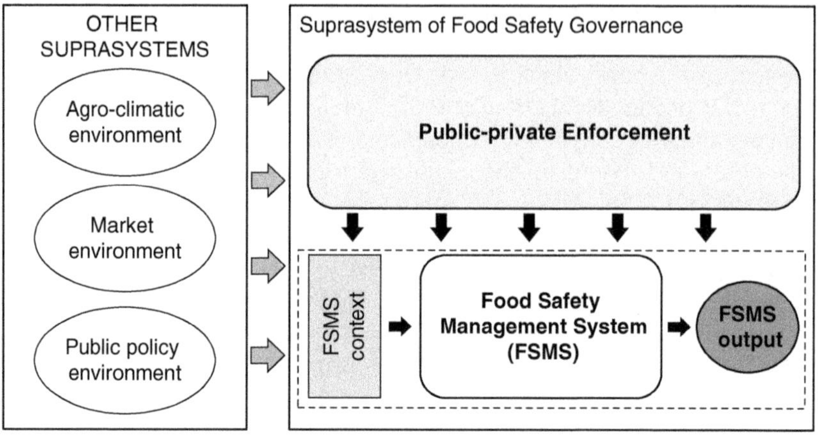

Figure 8.3 Schematic presentation of the interaction between the systems (FSMS, narrow context, food safety governance context, and other broader context factors (like agro-climate, market environment), which are here called supra-systems)

safety governance. Enforcement aims to induce FSMS implementation in companies, by control and communication, with the final goal of achieving food safety. Thus, food safety can be seen as the emergent property of the FSMS and food safety governance as a whole. Control as defined in the systems theory requires four conditions: goal, action, model and observability.[59] These conditions were also included in defining enforcement practices of food safety. The goal is the implementation of FSMS. The actions to affect the state of the FSMS are realized through various incentives, including sanctions, stimulus, information and education. The 'model' condition is provided through setting standards and guidelines. Audits and sampling plans are aimed at achieving observability of this status. Of even higher level of complexity are the other three systems discussed in the 'broad context': agro-climatic, market and 'public-policy' environments. Supra-systems show greater variation in their organization and behaviour than their separate sub-systems.[60] Figure 8.3 shows the different systems (context) perspectives, which have been studied in the empirical studies presented below.

---

59 W.R. Ashby, *An Introduction to Cybernetics 2* (Chapman and Hall 1956).
60 L. Skyttner (n 52).

Principles of Diagnostic Tool to Assess FSMS in View of Context

To study the FSMS from a systems perspective within a company specific context, a diagnostic tool was developed and adapted for different food sectors.[61] The tool enables a differentiated assessment of performance levels of core control measures (such as hygienic design, sanitation programme design and practices) and assurance activities (such as validation, verification practices) in a FSMS, apart from the quality assurance guidelines, standards and legal requirements used to set up the system. It also allows for a systematic assessment of the riskiness of multiple context characteristics, including of product, process, organization and chain environment characteristics that affect food safety and put requirements on the systems design and operation.[62] Product characteristics refer to vulnerability to chemical and microbial contamination due to the particular product features; processes characteristics concern features of the production system and environment that create vulnerability to contamination. Organization characteristics concern the administrative conditions in a company that enable decision-making in a FSMS, whereas the chain environment refers to supplier and customer relationships, the company position in the chain that can create vulnerabilities towards safety issues.[63] The tool consists of sets of indicators and corresponding grids representing different levels of respectively design and operation of FSMS activities (basic, average and advanced), context riskiness (low, moderate and high), and system output (poor, moderate and good). Table 8.1 shows examples of grids reflecting different situational descriptions. Each situation corresponds with a score, ranging from 1–3 for low to high context riskiness; from 1–4 for basic to advanced control and assurance activities; ranging from 1–4 for poor to good safety output.

The basic principle behind the diagnostic tool is that a more risky

---

[61] Luning and others, 'Comprehensive Analysis and Differentiated Assessment' (n 56); Luning and Marcelis (n 3); Luning and others, 'Systematic Assessment of Core Assurance Activities' (n 56); Luning and others, 'A Tool to Diagnose Context Riskiness' (n 56); Liesbeth Jacxsens, Mieke Uyttendaele, Frank Devlieghere, Jordi Rovira, S. Oses Gomez and P.A. Luning, 'Food Safety Performance Indicators to Benchmark Food Safety Output of Food Safety Management Systems' (2010) 141 *International Journal of Food Microbiology* 180–7; K. Kirezieva and others, 'Context Factors Affecting Design and Operation of Food Safety Management Systems in the Fresh Produce Chain' (2013) 23 *Trends in Food Science & Technology* 108; K. Kirezieva and others, 'Assessment of Food Safety Management Systems in the Global Fresh Produce Chain' (2013) 52 *Food Research International* 230.

[62] Luning and others, 'A Tool to Diagnose Context Riskiness' (n 56).

[63] Ibid; Kirezieva and others, 'Context Factors' (n 61).

Table 8.1 *Examples of indicators and corresponding grids to analyse and assess respectively context riskiness (Example I), FSMS performance level (Example II), and system output (Example III)*

Example I: Indicator and grid to analyse and assess the context factor process characteristics: Risk of water supply

Situation 1 (low risk)	Situation 2 (moderate risk)	Situation 3 (high risk)
• No association of water supply with contamination	• Occasional association of water supply with contamination	• Common association of water supply with contamination
• Potable water supply, coming from approved sources (e.g. municipal water, artesian well water, water from drilled deep wells)	• Water controlled at the company/farm (e.g. recycled/re-used water, water stored in open reservoirs, water from dug or driven wells, rain water)	• Uncontrolled surface water (e.g. from rivers, canals, ponds, lakes, creeks, etc.)

Example II: Indicator and grid to analyse and assess preventive control measures in the FSMS: Extent of personal hygiene requirements

Situation 1 (low level)	Situation 2 (basic level)	Situation 3 (average level)	Situation 4 (advanced level)
Personal hygiene requirements are not implemented (i.e. absence of washing facilities and toilets and no emphasis on personal care and hygiene)	• Standard requirements for all employees on clothing (gloves, jackets); • The same for personal care and health; • Common washing facilities and toilets with no washing stations • No specific hygiene instructions.	• Additional task-specific requirements on clothing (own clothing, specific storage conditions); • The same for personal care and health; • Special hand washing facilities and toilets with washing stations; • Basic hygiene instructions;	• High and specific requirements, for all food operators, on clothing; • The same for personal care and health; • Tailored facilities to support personal hygiene; • Specific hygiene instructions implemented in daily practice

Example III: Indicator and grid to analyse and assess the system output: Advancedness of sampling for pesticide residues

Situation 1 (no info)	Situation 2 (poor output)	Situation 3 (moderate output)	Situation 4 (good output)
No samples are taken and no chemical analyses are performed	• Ad-hoc sampling (on demand of customers or legislation) on particular lot(s)/ batch(es)	• Structured sampling (with fixed frequency) at company level	• Structured sampling, on company level, and regular monitoring on a sector level (statistically underpinned)

context requires more advanced FSMS activities to mitigate the actual risk on food safety hazards (FSMS output), which is based on the widely acknowledged contingency theory.[64] Multiple, empirical studies using the various tools to measure FSMS in multiple food sectors by own and other researchers have provided evidence for the principle behind the tools and the validity.[65]

The outcome of the assessment on the total set of indicators can be depicted in radar diagrams (Figure 8.4). The 'Context riskiness' profile (with higher scores for riskiness) represents a more risky context, whereas the 'FSMS performance' profile (with higher scores for how far advanced the systems activities are) reveals a more advanced system, which is the same for the food safety output profile.

[64] For details see Luning and others, 'A Tool to Diagnose Context Riskiness' (n 56).

[65] E.g. I. Sampers and others, 'Performance of Food Safety Management Systems In Poultry Meat Preparation Processing Plants in Relation to Campylobacter spp. Contamination' (2010) 73 *Journal of Food Protection* 1447; P.A. Luning and others, 'A Concurrent Diagnosis of Microbiological Food Safety Output and Food Safety Management System Performance: Cases from Meat Processing Industries' (2011) 22 *Food Control* 555; Luning and others, 'Performance Assessment of Food Safety Management Systems' (n 4); J. Nanyunja and others, 'Shift in Performance of Food Safety Management Systems in Supply Chains: Case of Green Bean Chain in Kenya versus Hot Pepper Chain in Uganda' (2016) 96 *Journal of the Science of Food and Agriculture* 3380.

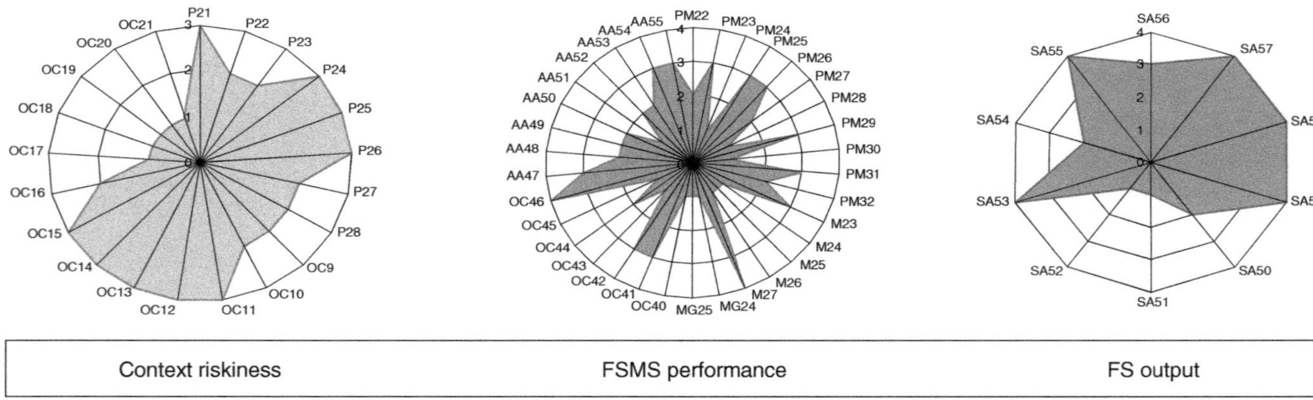

Figure 8.4 Example of a company profile based on results from the diagnostic tool

INSIGHTS FROM EMPIRICAL STUDIES

FSMS Performance of European Fresh Produce Farmers Differing in Broad Context

The role of the broad context (as depicted in Figure 8.3) was investigated through an explorative case study in European fresh produce companies all operating under the same EU food legislation.[66] The performance of implemented FSMS in view of their broad context characteristics was analysed in three regions of leafy greens-growing in Murcia (Spain), Lier (Norway) and Flanders (Belgium). These regions differ in agro-climatic characteristics (that is, typical climate and methods of production) and market chain structure. The study assessed main agricultural policy interventions by government in the sector, such as subsidies and import tariffs through conducting a literature review and expert interviews from the three regions. Food safety governance was characterized by examining literature, reports and information bulletins of the national food safety agencies (FASFC in Belgium; Mattilsynet in Norway; AESAN in Spain) and produce organizations, which are involved in enforcement of the food safety policy (Vegaplan in Belgium; Matmerk in Norway; Proexport in Spain), and by interviewing 27 experts. The FSMS performance of in total 27 leafy greens production companies was analysed by using the diagnostic tool for fresh produce.[67]

The study reveals that, unless the fact that all companies operate under the same European legal framework (that is, the GFL and associated EU Regulations), obvious distinctions in FSMS performance were linked to differences in the broad context. The Spanish fresh produce companies overall demonstrated advanced FSMS (science-based, modified and tested in own production). They operate in a favourable climate for leafy greens and are typically large companies operating in integrated supply chains. The enforcement strategy is based on market self-regulation, as the companies have been following many voluntary private standards and retailer's quality assurance schemes. The Norwegian companies, by contrast, demonstrated average level FSMS (that is, based on standards but not adapted and tested for own circumstances). They produce in a humid continental climate (open field

[66] Kirezieva and others, 'Exploring the Influence of Context on Food Safety Management: Case Studies of Leafy Greens Production in Europe' (2015) 51 *Food Policy* 158.

[67] Kirezieva and others, 'Assessment of Food Safety Management Systems (n 61); Kirezieva and others, 'Context Factors' (n 61).

and greenhouse), are mostly small companies producing for local markets and are protected by public policy from international market pressures through direct subsidy transfers and seasonal import tariffs. The Norwegian enforcement strategy has been identified as generally following the traditional approach of direct command-and-control intervention by the state, because companies mainly follow the national public standards. Still, a sign of co-regulation has been observed in the joint management of the standards by state and industry. The Belgian fresh produce companies, in turn, demonstrated more basic performing FSMS (based on own knowledge and experience). They produce in a maritime temperate climate (both open field and greenhouse), are micro family-owned farms, supplying to the local market and exporting to the neighbouring countries via an auction. The enforcement strategy in Belgium was typified as following the principles of co-regulation. In Belgium public and private standards are used that are jointly managed by the sector organization.[68]

These findings can be explained by the traditions of governance in the countries.[69] Napoleonic tradition with central state and many regional bodies has been historically established in Spain,[70] but with time has led to significant differences between national regions.[71] Scandinavian countries traditionally have a very strong state role.[72] Neo-corporatist democracy is typical for Belgium, and is based on consensus, compromise, and representation by a few well-organized groups recognized by the state.[73]

---

[68] L. Jacxsens and others, 'Measuring Microbial Food Safety Output and Comparing Self-Checking Systems of Food Business Operators in Belgium' (2015) 49 *Food Control* 59.

[69] Bevir, Rhodes and Weller (n 38).

[70] G.B. Peters, 'The Napoleonic Tradition' (2008) 21 *International Journal of Public Sector Management* 118.

[71] L. Torres and V. Pina, 'Reshaping Public Administration: The Spanish Experience Compared to the UK' (2004) 82 *Public Administration* 445; S. Parrado, 'Failed Policies but Institutional Innovation through "Layering" and "Diffusion" in Spanish Central Administration' (2008) 21 *International Journal of Public Sector Management* 230.

[72] T. Christensen, 'Narratives of Norwegian Governance: Elaborating the Strong State Tradition' (2003) 81 *Public Administration* 163.

[73] W.J.M. Kickert, 'Public Governance in Small Continental European States' (2002) 25 *International Journal of Public Administration* 1471.

FSMS Performance from a Global Perspective: The Role of Public and Private Standards

Kirezieva et al. investigated FSMS performance in fresh produce companies (n=118) operating in EU and non-EU countries (including developing and emerging states) to explore what factors could explain differences in FSMS performance.[74] System performance was assessed by using the previously discussed diagnostic tool for fresh produce chains[75] via workshops, face-to-face interviews, experts' interviews, and on-site visits in Belgium, China, Egypt, India, Kenya, the Netherlands, Norway, South Africa, Spain and Uganda. Hierarchical cluster analysis of the data provided three main clusters of companies, differing in FSMS performance level ranging from advanced (cluster one) to basic/low (cluster three) (Figure 8.5). FSMS activities of the companies in cluster 1 were mostly at level 3, design according to the standards and using standard equipment and methods. Even more advanced level 4 was given for storage facilities, fertilization program, pesticide management, and sampling for pesticide residues and microorganisms. Level 4 is attributed when activities are adapted to fit-for-purpose and tested for specific farm/company situation. Companies in cluster 2 scored mostly at 3 (average level), but several activities such as hygienic design of equipment, material control and irrigation method demonstrated even lower level (2). This score was given to activities designed according to historical knowledge and own experience. Companies in cluster 3 had basic control activities. Only few activities (these are, maintenance program, personal hygiene requirements, and pesticide program) were actually implemented in these companies.

Cluster 1 consists of companies in both EU and non-EU countries. These companies have implemented and are certified against multiple private standards, such as GlobalGAP, BRC, ISO, and standards developed by major individual brand companies. Also in cluster 2, companies from both EU and non-EU countries were grouped. However, these were certified only against national standards and GlobalGAP, and no other private standards were included. In the last cluster 3, companies were mostly small and only from non-EU countries. These companies were not certified against any standard.

Several factors have a dominant effect on the FSMS performance in the

---

[74] Kirezieva and others, 'Factors Affecting the Status of Food Safety Management Systems' (n 50).

[75] Kirezieva and others, 'Assessment of Food Safety Management Systems' (n 61); Kirezieva and others, 'Context Factors' (n 61).

Product and process characteristics[a]

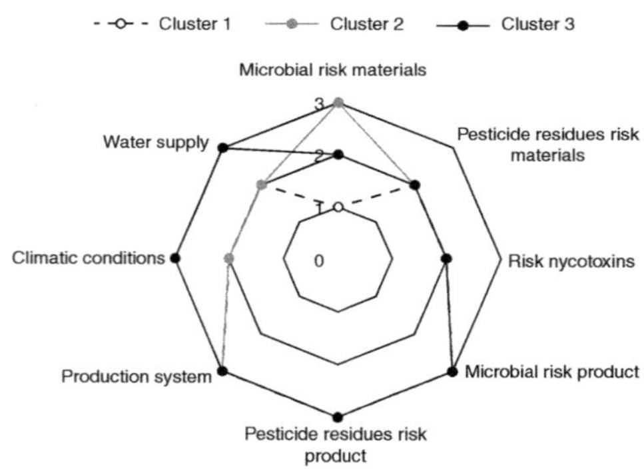

Organisational and chain characteristics[b]

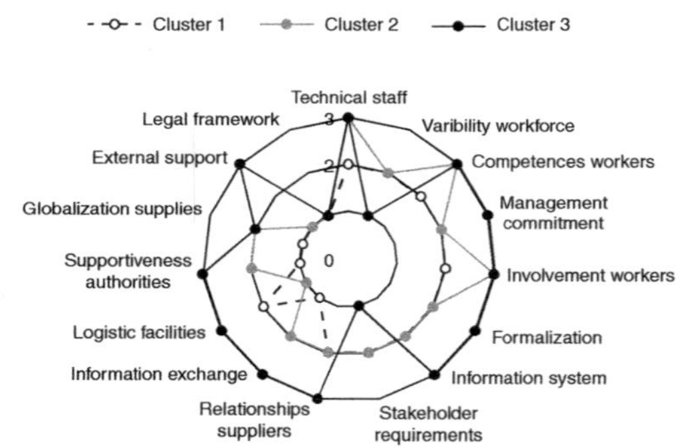

Control activities design[c]

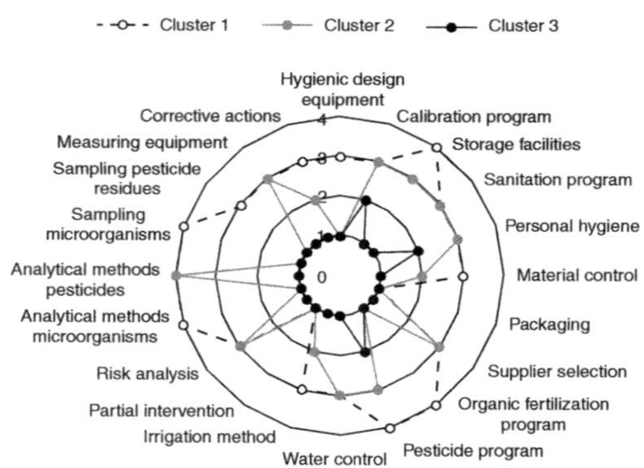

Control activities operation

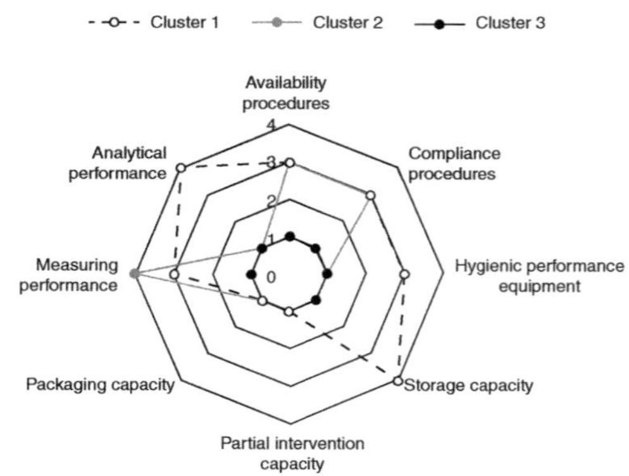

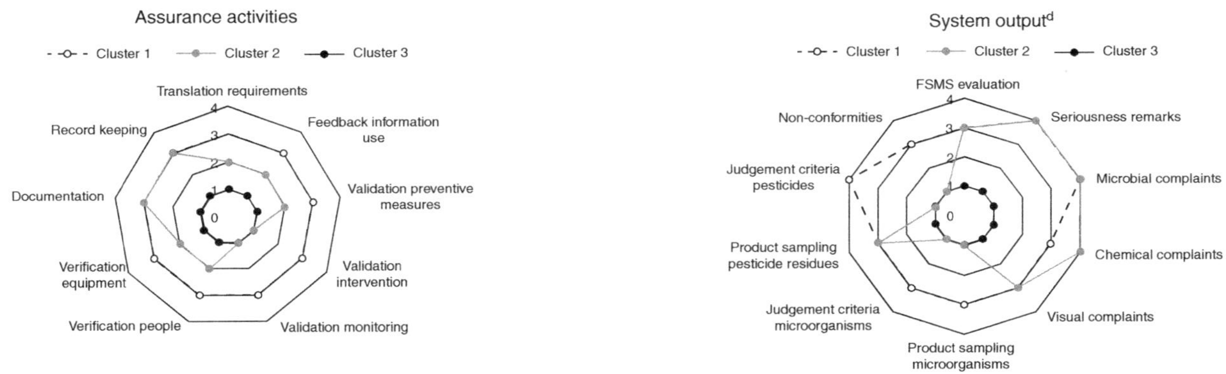

Notes:

[a] Low (1), medium (2) and high (3) risk situations for product and process characteristics correspond to low, potential and high chance of microbiological or chemical contamination.

[b] Low (1), medium (2) and high (3) risk situations for organizational and chain characteristics they correspond to supportive, constrained and lacking administrative chain conditions or low, restricted and high dependence on other chain actors.

[c] Situations 1, 2, 3, and 4 for control and assurance activities correspond to: low level (1) → absent, not applicable, unknown; basic level (2) → lack of scientific evidence, use of company experience/history, variable, unknown, unpredictable, based on common materials/equipment; average level (3) → best practice knowledge/equipment, sometimes variable, not always predictable, based on generic information/guidelines for the product sector; advanced level (4) → scientifically underpinned (accurate, complete), stable, predictable, and tailored for the specific food production situation.

[d] Situations 1, 2, 3, and 4 for system output correspond to: no information (1) → absent, not applied, unknown; poor output (2) → ad-hoc sampling, minimal criteria used for evaluation, various food safety problems due to different problems in the activities; moderate output (3) → regular sampling, several criteria used for evaluation, restricted food safety problems mainly due to one (restricted) type of problem in the activities; good output (4) → systematic evaluation, using specific criteria, no safety problems.

Figure 8.5 Median score results for the indicators in the diagnostic instrument for cluster 1 (n=46), cluster 2 (n=42) and cluster 3 (n=29) of farms active in fresh produce production

global fresh produce chain. International export-oriented supply chains seem to promote capacity building within companies in the chain, to answer to the stringent requirements of private brand standards. This was also demonstrated in a study comparing fresh produce farmers (in total n=60) in Uganda and Kenya showing more advanced systems in Kenya due to the private standards of Western importing retailers, and more elaborated food safety enforcement.[76] The stringent private standards and third-party auditing of these standards seems to be an important factor in advancing the FSMS of companies in emerging and developing countries, where local institutional environments often fail to support companies in setting, implementing and evaluating their FSMS. However, the role and usefulness of such standards for food safety governance in emerging countries is differently perceived in view of food sovereignty.[77] Moreover, the legislative framework in these countries still requires improvements in the establishment and enforcement,[78] which has negative consequences for the FSMS in companies supplying the local markets. Currently, only the export-oriented companies that have to comply with the strict private standards are able to control and assure the safety of food. However, companies producing for local markets suffer from poorly elaborated FSMS or no systems at all, because of the absence or weakly elaborated food safety governance system.

In companies located in the European Union, sector and other produce organizations facilitate the sampling for pesticide residues and collaboration in the sector. Overall, farmers showed less knowledge and awareness regarding microbiological hazards, which is related to the less attention paid to these in the current legislation and standards. Furthermore, standards are an important tool in triggering the maturation of FSMS as companies that were lacking any pressure to comply to standards operated at a very basic level, with only few activities implemented. The insights from this global comparative study indicate the need for stratified measures and policies to support individual companies in the fresh produce chain in designing and operating their FSMS according to the institutional environment in which they operate.

---

76 Nanyunja and others (n 65).

77 L. Jacxsens and others, 'Opinions on Fresh Produce Food Safety and Quality Standards by Fresh Produce Supply Chain Experts from the Global South and North' (2015) 78 *Journal of Food Protection* 1914.

78 J.B. Kussaga and others, 'Food Safety Management Systems Performance in African Food Processing Companies: A Review of Deficiencies and Possible Improvement Strategies' (2014) 94 *Journal of the Science of Food and Agriculture* 2154; Nanyunja (n 65).

OVERALL DISCUSSION AND CONCLUSIONS

The results from our studies reveal that food safety governance is increasingly involving both private and hybrid forms. Public agencies collaborate with private (industrial) organizations in issuing national standards and their enforcement or rely on private standards to reduce the number of inspections and audits. However, these third-party private audits have been criticized for being ineffective and partial as companies pay for the certification.[79] Audits and inspections should provide an independent, objective and transparent evaluation, and this is where the public sector may exercise more control and intervene.[80]

The various standards that are put into place differ not only in their public or private character, but also in the way they are set up. Some authors mention the so-called baseline standards, which aim at assuring the minimum requirements for addressing food safety.[81] At the same time, stringent (mostly private) standards put additional requirements on specific elements of the FSMS, thus, creating high entry costs.[82] Henson and Humphrey raised the issue that previous studies have not sufficiently addressed the institutional forms standards assume.[83] Our studies linked differences in the performance of FSMS to various standard types and enforcement practices. However, further empirical research is needed to explore whether and how institutional mechanisms lead to different forms of food safety governance, and how this interplay between public and private parties can affect the content of standards, the set-up and operation of FSMS, and their food safety output. We also suggested undertaking studies to determine the most effective and efficient institutional arrangement to deliver safe food, and the role of the public sector as a regulator. Moreover, food safety governance can be affected by other social systems such as market and public policy. Systems interact with each other, connected via causal relationships and (complex) feedback loops. These also need to be studied in further detail to determine how policy measures and tools can be made more effective in ensuring quality and safety in the food supply chain without impeding economic growth.

---

79 Albersmeier and others (n 25); Powell and others (n 31).

80 Lytton and McAllister (Chapter 4) in this volume discuss several oversight mechanisms to address auditor conflict of interest.

81 Fearne and Garcia Martinez (n 19).

82 Henson (n 23).

83 Henson and Humphrey (n 24).

PART III

Hybridization in transnational food governance

9 The Global Food Safety Initiative and state actors: Paving the way for hybrid food safety governance

Tetty Havinga and Paul Verbruggen

> Increasingly, government officials around the world are recognizing the role that GFSI, and other third-party food safety certification programs, can play in facilitating compliance with their national food safety regimes. (Karil Kochenderfer, North American Representative of the Global Food Safety Initiative).[1]

1. INTRODUCTION

The Global Food Safety Initiative (GFSI) plays a central role in the adoption and coordination of private food safety standards.[2] Major food retailers, manufacturers and their representative organizations seek to have their standards and accompanying certification schemes 'benchmarked' by GFSI as a sign of authority and robustness. Since its establishment in May 2000, GFSI's influence on both the material and procedural aspects of food safety governance has grown steadily. Currently, 13 private food safety schemes owned by nine organizations have been recognized by GFSI. These schemes relate to different stages of food and feed production, including farming, processing, production, packaging, storage and distribution.[3]

A recent development concerns GFSI's activities in engaging with international government organizations, such as the Codex Alimentarius Commission and the World Trade Organization (WTO) and with national food safety authorities via its 'Global Regulatory Affairs Working

---

[1] http://www.mygfsi.com/news-resources/news/411-debunking-5-gfsi-myths-food-online-interview.html, accessed 28 November 2016.

[2] See on GFSI also the contributions by Fagotto (Chapter 3), Lytton and McAllister (Chapter 4), and Kottenstede (Chapter 10) in this volume.

[3] GFSI, 'Recognised Schemes', accessed 28 November 2016 at http://www.mygfsi.com/schemes-certification/recognised-schemes.html.

Group'. This working group is developing a 'strategy for engagement with governments and international organizations' and pursues the following objectives:

- To encourage governments to understand and recognise the credibility of the GFSI process.
- Specifically, the Group seeks to gain US and EU recognition by 2017 of GFSI benchmarked schemes as an accepted tool to help them prioritise their food safety compliance resources and factory inspection.
- To build a relationship with Codex and the World Trade Organisation (WTO) to ensure ongoing alignment of approach between the private and public sectors.[4]

These aims suggest increasing coordination and collaboration between public and private actors engaged in the governance of food safety. At the same time, public food authorities in countries such as Canada, China, the Netherlands and the United States are exploring the possibilities of cooperation with private food governance arrangements. They appear to be primarily interested in enrolling GFSI benchmarked private food safety schemes in their risk-based monitoring and enforcement policies to economize on official inspection costs. As part of this hybrid governance approach to food safety controls, however, national authorities submit GFSI benchmarked schemes to specific criteria and engage with GFSI to exert influence on its benchmarking requirements.

In this chapter we discuss and analyse the strategy of GFSI to engage with national and international governmental actors and *vice versa*. In the literature on transnational governance, attention has been called to the indirect and soft modes of governance employed by international governmental organizations (IGOs) in pursuit of their regulatory objectives. In particular, Abbott and others have recently developed the concept of 'orchestration' to study and assess the ways in which IGOs enlist intermediary actors to address target actors in the pursuit of their goals.[5] In this chapter we contend that GFSI, as an international non-state private body, is also deploying an orchestration strategy when engaging with governmental organizations to better achieve its regulatory goals. Moreover, we argue that the governmental organizations being enlisted also deploy a

---

[4] GFSI, 'Technical Working Groups', accessed 28 November 2016 at http://www.mygfsi.com/about-us/technical-working-groups.html.

[5] Kenneth W. Abbott, Phillip Genschel, Duncan Snidal and Bernard Zangl (eds), *International Organizations as Orchestrators* (Cambridge University Press 2015).

strategy of orchestration by enlisting GFSI in their risk-based monitoring and enforcement policies. We thus observe an ever denser, networked and hybrid regulatory space of transnational food governance.

To substantiate these claims we address the following questions: (i) why do IGOs, national food authorities and GFSI wish to align their activities regarding food safety governance; (ii) what strategies do they employ to ensure coordination, cooperation and integration with other actors; and (iii) what has been achieved so far? In doing so, we discuss the incentives and obstacles for the different actors involved in aligning public and private transnational food governance. To answer the questions we draw on publicly available documentary evidence (for example, documents and press releases from GFSI, public food authorities and international organizations, legislation, and private standards), and three open-ended interviews with representatives of the GFSI Global Regulatory Affairs Working Group and the public food authority in the Netherlands.[6] These interviews aimed to gain information to clarify statements in policy documents and to update insights into ongoing activities. Where statements from the interviews could be confirmed by publicly available documents, we refer to these public sources.

The chapter is structured as follows. Section 2 discusses the rise of GFSI as a key actor in the (global) governance of food safety risks, its activities and achievements. Section 3 deals with the GFSI vision and activities towards engagement with public regulatory affairs. In Section 4 we analyse how the relationship between international and national governmental organizations and GFSI has evolved over time. While public actors were initially very suspicious of international private standards and related certification schemes, several forms of collaboration were eventually created. More specifically, a limited number of national food authorities developed policy frameworks detailing conditions under which they could integrate GFSI benchmarked schemes in their monitoring and enforcement policies. We discuss existing and developing frameworks in the Netherlands, Canada, the United States and China, which are the principal countries with some form of cooperation with GFSI. Section 5 then recapitulates why and how GFSI engages with government organizations and *vice versa*, and discusses how to conceptualize the relationships observed between these two categories of actors.

[6] More specifically, we interviewed the chairperson and a member of the GFSI Global Regulatory Affairs Working Group, and had one interview with two staff members of the public food authority in the Netherlands. The interviews lasted between one and two hours and were transcribed.

2. THE RISE OF GFSI

2.1 A Growing Need for Coordination

Since the 1990s, food governance has developed from a predominantly state-centered system to a transnational hybrid system involving many public and private actors pursuing regulatory functions at the local, national and/or transnational level. A series of major food crises (BSE, dioxin), the adoption of more stringent liability regimes, the increasing globalization of food supply chains, and the perception of inadequate government food regulation among both businesses and consumers, have been identified as relevant circumstances leading to the adoption of private food safety standards by large firms in food manufacturing, processing, retail, and trade. Particularly favourable to this development was the existence of large multinational corporations with a dominant market position created by mergers and acquisitions in the food industry, specifically in food retail.[7]

Soon after their adoption, these private food safety standards and accompanying certification schemes started to undergo a process of harmonization and standardization. Companies adopting standards joined forces and merged their individual standards into national standards. In the United Kingdom, for example, it was recognized in the mid-1990s that suppliers were subject to multiple certification audits thanks to divergent food safety standards that individual retailers had put in place.[8] Negotiations on a common, unified industry standard for food safety took place under the auspices of the British Retail Consortium (BRC), a pre-existing trade organization for retailers in the United Kingdom. The first version of the BRC Standard was adopted in 1998.

As a subsequent step leading to the creation of GFSI, harmonized national standards and individual retailer standards started to cross borders.[9] These standards gained a transnational reach first of all because

---

[7] Lawrence Busch and Carmen Bain, 'New! Improved? The Transformation of the Global Agrifood System' (2004) 69 *Rural Sociology* 3321–46; Tetty Havinga, 'Private Regulation of Food Safety by Supermarkets' (2006) 28 *Law and Policy* 515; Terry Marsden, Robert Lee, Andrew Flynn and Samarthia Thankappan, *The New Regulation and Governance of Food. Beyond the Food Crisis?* (Routledge 2010).

[8] Spencer Henson and James Northen, 'Economic Determinants of Food Safety Controls in the Supply of Retailer Own-branded Products in the UK' (1998) 14 *Agribusiness* 113.

[9] Paul Verbruggen, *Enforcing Transnational Private Regulation: A Comparative Analysis of Advertising and Food Safety* (Edward Elgar 2014) 166.

retailers required their foreign subsidiaries and franchisees to ensure that the food products sold, including those that were locally sourced, were produced according to these standards. Furthermore, foreign suppliers were also required to comply with these standards as part of the supply agreements they concluded with the retailers. Finally, retailers also adopted standards developed abroad. For example, in 2001 the Dutch association of retailers decided to adopt the BRC Standard as the common standard for retailers' own-branded food products.[10]

Heeding these developments in the British retail sector and elsewhere in Europe, retailers and producers across Europe set out to establish collective transnational schemes. A key example is the Euro-Retailer Produce Working Group (EUREP), a consortium of some 13 leading European retailers that was established in 1997. By 1999, this group had developed a collective scheme – EUREPGAP – for the application of 'good agricultural practices' (GAP) with the purpose of warranting the safety and quality of primary products. The EUREPGAP standards were rapidly adopted by the agricultural sector in Europe and beyond. In order to give a more accurate reflection of its global impact and application, EUREPGAP was re-branded 'GLOBALGAP' in 2007.[11]

Whereas GLOBALGAP concerned a uniform standard for good agricultural practices, the world's largest retailers also established a forum through which food safety standards could converge. In 2000, the Global Food Safety Initiative was established with that goal in mind. Today's mission of GFSI is the 'continuous improvement in food safety management systems to ensure confidence in the delivery of safe food to consumers'.[12] Rather than developing one single global food safety standard, GFSI benchmarks pre-existing food safety standards based on the so-called GFSI Guidance Document.[13] GFSI itself therefore does not represent a specific food safety standard, nor does it own one. It facilitates a benchmarking exercise for food safety standards, setting baseline requirements for these standards and their accompanying certification schemes. As such, GFSI seeks to improve efficiency and reduce the costs of auditing

---

10 Havinga (n 7) 522.

11 See for a detailed discussion of GLOBALGAP Casey in this volume.

12 GFSI, Enhancing Food Safety Through Third Party Certification (2011), accessed 28 November 2016 at http://www.mygfsi.com/gfsifiles/GFSI_White_Paper_-_Enhancing_Food_Safety_Through_Third_Party_Certification.pdf.

13 http://www.mygfsi.com/news-resources/faq.html, accessed 28 November 2016.

and certification throughout the value chain.[14] Initially GFSI focused on standards for manufactured food (in particular retailers' private labels), but standards for primary produce were also included later.[15]

2.2 Organizational Structure

GFSI was established in 2000, initially as a membership organization. Its membership consisted exclusively of retailers.[16] Currently, GFSI is no longer a membership organization, but a non-profit foundation established under Belgian law and managed by the Consumer Goods Forum.[17] This forum is a membership organization and includes as its members over 400 retailers, manufacturers, service providers and other stakeholders across 70 countries.[18] Figure 9.1 illustrates GFSI's organizational structure.

The GFSI Board is concerned, inter alia, with overseeing and steering the Initiative's strategy and implementation, the effective governance of GFSI, and overseeing the benchmarking process. The Board is composed of representatives of major retailers, manufacturers and food service operators. A balanced stakeholder and geographical representation is sought, but there is no set distribution of Board seats among different categories.[19] Retailers thus increasingly share decision-making powers with other actors in the food supply chain.

---

[14] Paul Verbruggen and Tetty Havinga, 'The Rise of Transnational Private Meta-regulators' (2016) 21 *Tilburg Law Review*, 116–43; Fabrizio Cafaggi and Andrea Renda, 'Measuring the Effectiveness of Transnational Private Regulation', accessed 28 November 2016 at http://ssrn.com/abstract=2508684, 58–9; Fabrizio Cafaggi, 'Transnational Private Regulation: Regulating Global Private Regulators' in Sabino Cassese (ed.), *Research Handbook on Global Administrative Law* (Edward Elgar 2016) 212, 231–3.

[15] Benchmarking of pre-farm gate standards was first included in version 4 of the GFSI guidance document, September 2004.

[16] The retailers establishing GFSI were Ahold, Carrefour, Delhaize, ICA, Metro, Migros, Tesco and Wal-Mart. Havinga (n 7) 524.

[17] GFSI Foundation created July 2005. See more elaborately Verbruggen and Havinga (n 14) 7–10; Cafaggi (n 14) 231.

[18] GFSI, 'GFSI Governance Model and Rules of Procedure' (February 2015), accessed 28 November 2016 at http://www.mygfsi.com/files/GFSI_Governance_Model.pdf.

[19] The Governance Model 2015 (n 18) introduced this rule on the composition of the GFSI Board. The Board may be made up of representatives from retail/wholesale, distribution, food service/catering, manufacturing and primary production companies. In May 2016, the GFSI Board comprised representatives of major retailers (50%) and branded manufacturers and food service operators (50%). See

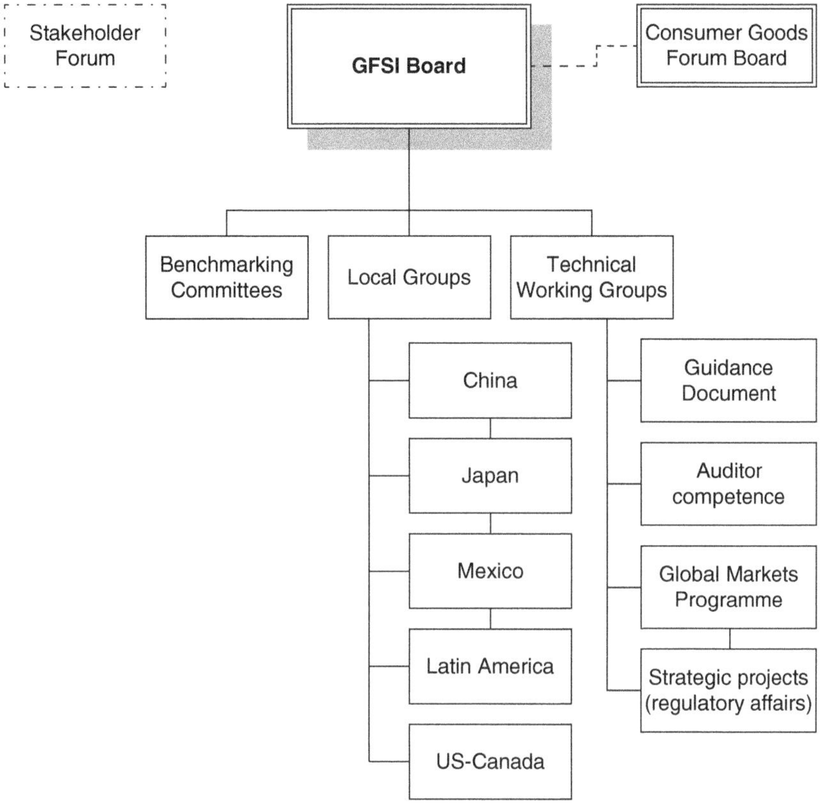

Figure 9.1 GFSI's organizational structure

Technical Working Groups (TWGs) provide technical expertise and advice to the GFSI Board.[20] They are made up of experts from retailers, manufacturers, food service operators, standard owners, certification bodies, accreditation bodies, and industry associations. There are TWGs specifically concerned with the revision of the GFSI Guidance Document, auditor competency, food service and catering, regional outreach, food safety culture, and capacity building among small and less-developed manufacturers and primary producers to achieve certification against a

also Doris Fuchs, Agni Kalfagianni and Tetty Havinga, 'Actors in Private Food Governance: The Legitimacy of Retail Standards and Multistakeholder Initiatives with Civil Society Participation' (2011) 28 *Agriculture and Human Values* 360–1.

[20] Ibid, 16.

GFSI recognized scheme. To this end, the Global Markets Programme was introduced, which involves a step-by-step approach by gradually bringing the companies' quality management system to a higher level.[21]

Local Groups are concerned with the implementation of GFSI's global policies at local level, the communication of GFSI's activities among companies, and the building of relationships with government bodies.[22] Local Groups are composed of representatives from various stakeholders and a balanced representation is sought. There are local groups in China, Japan, Mexico, Latin-America and US-Canada.[23] The creation of a European Local Group is anticipated. The Board, TWGs and Local Groups are supported in their operations by the GFSI Team, funded by the Consumer Goods Forum.[24] Finally, GFSI hosts a Stakeholder Forum yearly for 'any organisation or individual with an interest in the GFSI and its activities'.[25]

2.3 Benchmarking

GFSI's main regulatory preoccupation is benchmarking. In February 2016, 13 food safety schemes owned by nine different organizations were recognized by GFSI.[26] The benchmarking is carried out by the Benchmarking Committee, which is composed of food safety experts trained and approved by the GFSI Team.[27] Benchmarking involves comparing a food safety scheme to the GFSI Guidance Document.[28] This document has evolved from a set of basic principles into a detailed guide covering many issues and procedures. The document now specifies the (procedural) requirements that a scheme must implement (for example, governance structure, requirements for auditing and certification) and the basic (material) elements for the production of safe food that must

---

21 http://www.mygfsi.com/market-access/global-markets-programme/overview.html, accessed 28 November 2016.

22 GFSI Governance Model (n 18) 21.

23 http://www.mygfsi.com/about-us/local-groups.html, accessed 28 November 2016.

24 GFSI Governance Model (n 18) 7.

25 Ibid, 15.

26 BRC (3 schemes), IFS (3 schemes), GlobalGAP, CanadaGap, FSSC22000, SQF, Primus, GRMS, Alliance aquaculture, accessed 28 November 2016 at http://www.mygfsi.com/schemes-certification/recognised-schemes.html.

27 GFSI Governance Model (n 18) 25.

28 GFSI, 'GFSI Benchmarking Requirements/Guidance Document', (Version 6.4), accessed 28 November 2016 at http://www.mygfsi.com/schemes-certification/benchmarking/gfsi-guidance-document.html. See for a detailed description of the Guidance Document the contribution by Fagotto, Chapter 3 in this volume.

be included in the standard (content and procedures of food safety management systems). It also specifies the procedure for benchmarking. The requirements, according to GFSI, 'are firmly based on the food safety principles laid down by the Codex Alimentarius Commission (Codex), the National Advisory Committee on Microbiological Criteria for Foods (NACMCF), relevant ISO standards, and International Codes of Practice where appropriate'.[29] The 7th edition of the GFSI Guidance Document (renamed 'GFSI Benchmarking Requirements' and to be published in the summer of 2016) is expected to include new requirements for auditor competences, unannounced audits and food fraud.[30]

One of the priorities of GFSI since its inception has been to enhance confidence among relevant stakeholders in third-party certification. Over the years, certification schemes and their reliability had been heavily criticized by businesses in the supply chain, governments and NGOs. Following the policy of most of its retailer members, GFSI has promoted third-party certification as the most reliable institutional mechanism for assessing compliance with transnational private food safety standards.[31] GFSI-benchmarked schemes all apply third-party certification. This implies that certification bodies that have been accredited by a competent accreditation body verify compliance of food business operators with the applicable private food safety standard. Scheme owners have put in place audit integrity programmes, requirements for auditor expertise and training, options for unannounced audits, and requirements for senior management commitment and the management of certification bodies. Compliance with these conditions is assessed by scheme owners as part of the licence agreements they conclude with certification bodies. Accreditation bodies, in turn, assess the competence, impartiality and performance capability of certification bodies and their staff in order to certify against particular food safety standards.[32]

As a result of the process of globalization and convergence of private food safety standards, only a few schemes currently dominate the global

---

[29] GFSI, 'What is the GFSI Guidance Document Sixth Edition?, accessed 28 November 2916 at http://www.mygfsi.com/gfsifiles/What_is_the_GFSI_Guidance_Document_Sixth_Edition.pdf.

[30] Chris Anstey, 'GFSI: "Safe Food for consumers everywhere", the Food World's Biggest Story of Technical Cooperation' (2014) *Food Quality Magazine* 2, 10–12; Presentation Hugo Byrnes at the FSSC22000 Harmonization event, 21 October 2015, Amsterdam.

[31] GFSI White paper (n 12).

[32] See on accreditation Casey (Chapter 2), and Lytton and McAllister (Chapter 4) in this volume. See for a comprehensive discussion of the network of actors and contracts involved in third party certification: Verbruggen (n 9), 168–70.

food supply market. For processed foods in Europe these are the BRC's Global Standard for Food Safety, the International Featured Standards (IFS) Food Standard, and Food Safety System Certification 22000 (FSSC 22000). For primary produce, GLOBALGAP is the world's leading standard. In the United States, the SQF (Safe Quality Food) Code is the principal retail-driven standard for both food processing and primary produce.[33]

A large share of the groceries, vegetables, fruits and meat sold in supermarkets in Western countries such as France, Germany, the Netherlands, the United Kingdom and the United States, has been certified under GFSI benchmarked schemes. As early as 2006, a survey of the world's leading supermarkets found that an estimated 75–99 per cent of food supplies sold by supermarket chains were certified against GFSI benchmarked schemes.[34] Most major international food retailers currently support certification against a food safety scheme recognized by GFSI.[35] Because these retailers and many large food manufacturing firms require from their suppliers and subsidiaries compliance with such a scheme as part of their commercial contracts or procurement policies, its adoption and implementation is in fact mandatory for many farmers, food processors and food manufacturers around the world.

Nevertheless, there appear to be major obstacles to achieving the objective of GFSI as expressed by its motto 'once certified, accepted everywhere'.[36] At present, many major retailers and other buyers do not accept certification against all GFSI recognized schemes, but simply the scheme specified in contractual arrangements or procurement policies. For example, most British retailers only accept BRC, while many German retailers require IFS.[37]

Arguably, GFSI has the characteristics of an exclusive club. GFSI Board members are appointed by the Board itself only after careful nomination through GFSI bodies.[38] Currently, the Board is comprised exclusively

---

33 Fuchs (n 19); Tetty Havinga, 'Retail Driven Food Safety Regulation' in Abdelhakim Hammoudi, Christina Grazia, Yves Surry and Jean-Baptiste Traversac (eds), *Food Safety, Market Organization, Trade and Development* (Springer 2015) 59.

34 Linda Fulponi, 'Private Voluntary Standards in the Food System: The Perspective of Major Food Retailers in OECD Countries' (2006) 31 *Food Policy* 1.

35 Havinga (n 33) 64, 67.

36 Compare Kottenstede (Chapter 10) in this volume, who is more optimistic.

37 Interview GFSI working group member; Maureen Olewnik, Global Food Safety Initiative Overview, accessed 28 November 2016 at http://www.grains.k-state.edu/spirel/docs/conferences/mb-alternatives/presentation/m%20olewnik.pdf.

38 GFSI Governance Model (n 18) 9–10.

of members of the world's leading food businesses.[39] This reinforces the powers of these firms to impose ever more stringent demands on their suppliers. Moreover, the benefits generated by GFSI are said to serve only an exclusive part of the food industry. More specifically, GFSI has been criticized for being tailored to the top end of the market. Participation of small and medium sized enterprises (SMEs), consumers and NGOs in the GFSI organization is constrained by (insufficient) resources in terms of the time and (travel) costs needed to attend meetings of TWGs and Local Groups, and the annual 'Global Food Safety Conference'. Moreover, the requirements of GFSI-recognized schemes are said to be extremely severe to comply with for SMEs and food business on local (non-Western) markets. In the course of time it has become increasingly difficult for a food business to step into the world of GFSI and meet the requirements of its benchmarked schemes, because these requirements have expanded and become more rigid with every new edition of the GFSI Guidance Document. The 'Global Market Program' should be seen as a response by GFSI to such criticism, with the aim of ensuring attainable solutions for small, developing companies in local markets. It remains to be seen, however, how successful this program will be in delivering that objective.

As a meta-regulator of business-to-business food standards, GFSI's legitimacy is first and foremost based on its widespread acceptance in the market.[40] Its legitimacy is bolstered by building on generally accepted global public and private norms, providing opportunities for multi-stakeholder participation and being responsive to critiques from international organizations such as the United Nations Food and Agricultural Organization (FAO) and the World Trade Organization (WTO).[41] GFSI has created a global forum for the exchange of knowledge and best practices, promoting third-party certification and the GFSI initiative. By engaging with public regulatory affairs and state actors, it further seeks to bolster its legitimacy, as we explore below.

---

[39] GFSI Board members are affiliated to, inter alia, Aeon, Albert Heijn, Cargill, Coca-Cola, Danone, McDonalds, Metro, Nestlé, and Walmart.

[40] See in general on market-based legitimacy of standards Colin Scott, 'Standard-setting in Regulatory Regimes' in Robert Baldwin, Martin Cave and Martin Lodge (eds), *The Oxford Handbook of Regulation* (Oxford University Press 2010) 104, 116.

[41] Verbruggen and Havinga (n 14).

3. GFSI'S ENGAGEMENT WITH PUBLIC REGULATORY AFFAIRS

While GFSI was established in 2000 as a private sector initiative concerned with the development and convergence of private food safety standards, it soon recognized the importance of engaging with the public sector as a strategy that could help to achieve that objective. In 2003, GFSI stated that cooperation between the global food sector and national and supranational governments is one of its five key priorities.[42] A few years later, in 2008, the new GFSI Board member Mike Robach noted:

> One of our priorities will be to engage with the public authorities around the world to encourage a wider understanding and implementation of the GFSI approach to food safety. An alignment of policy between the public and private sector will enable the consistency to which we all aspire.[43]

From 2009 on, GFSI organized targeted activities for a continued and better alignment with international and national government agencies, and to support these activities it created the Global Regulatory Affairs Working Group. This working group was mandated to 'actively engage governments in recognizing and accepting GFSI benchmarked schemes', to further align industry and government efforts in food safety, and to integrate GFSI with requirements set under the Sanitary and Phytosanitary (SPS) Agreement of the WTO, and by the Codex Alimentarius Commission (Codex) of FAO and WHO.[44] The working group employs three strategies to achieve better alignment with governments: (i) communication on GFSI activities and explaining what it actually does to government actors; (ii) comparing national legislation with GFSI requirements set out in its Guidance Document; and (iii) improving weaknesses in third-party certification and auditor competences.

GFSI aims to gain recognition of its activities by state governments and relevant IGOs. The 2013 working plan of the Global Regulatory Affairs Working Group stipulates four objectives:

---

[42] 'Arrangement between IAF and GFSI for the GFSI program' MLA-2003/5, 17 September 2003 (on file with the authors).

[43] GFSI Newsletter December 2008, 2.

[44] GFSI Newsletter November 2012, 3, accessed 28 November 2016 at http://www.mygfsi.com/images/mygfsi/gfsifiles/newsletters/GFSI_Newsletter_November_2012_FINAL.pdf.

1. Within five years obtain recognition by five governments that third party accredited certification against GFSI benchmarked schemes as a credible and reliable tool that the governments will use as part of their risk assessment in determining deployment of food safety compliance resources and plant inspections
2. Obtain feedback by ten governments and IGOs to optimize the implementation of the Global Markets Program
3. Seek to develop opportunities to collaborate with governments and IGOs in gaining alignment in the building of regulatory oversight capacity; and
4. Seek to harmonize global food safety standards by participating in Codex as an observer and dialoguing with relevant national authorities.[45]

The first priority of the Global Regulatory Affairs Working Group in 2009 was to draft a position paper on why government agencies should give serious consideration to GFSI-benchmarked schemes.[46] The working group focused on the role and benefits of third-party certification and several case studies to show how governments and industry are working together to use the GFSI principles as a risk prioritization tool for monitoring companies.[47]

In 2015, GFSI's governance structure was reorganized and as part of that effort the position of the Working Groups was also revised. In this organizational overhaul, much of the effort of the Global Regulatory Affairs Working Group was transposed to and divided among the relevant Local Working Groups. The reason for this shift is that these local groups maintain the relationships with the government actors in the region concerned.[48] As a result, however, the Global Regulatory Affairs Working Group has acquired a less prominent status. The working group still meets, yet the frequency of the meetings has been reduced to once a year at the GFSI annual Global Food Safety Conference.

---

[45] 'The GFSI Global Regulatory Working Group: What is it and what is it doing?', accessed 28 November 2016 at www.ifofs.org/whatsnew/2013-04-04/58.html.

[46] GFSI Newsletter December 2009, 2.

[47] GFSI Newsletter July 2010, 6.

[48] Global Regulatory Affairs is included in the organizational structure as a sector-specific working group (See GFSI Governance Model (n 18) 6), but is no longer listed as Technical Working Group on the website. See http://www.mygfsi.com/about-us/technical-working-groups.html, accessed 28 November 2016. This change was confirmed by our interviewees.

4. COLLABORATION WITH GOVERNMENT ACTORS

4.1 Collaboration with IGOs

One of the objectives of GFSI and the Global Regulatory Affairs Working Group is to build strong relationships with IGOs. Within this scope, GFSI representatives met with many international organizations principally to explain what GFSI is doing and to develop opportunities for collaboration.[49] From the perspective of GFSI, a main obstacle to cooperation between IGOs and GFSI is the lack of understanding on the part of these international organizations of what GFSI stands for and how it works. A clear example of this is the discussion about the impact of GFSI and private food standards for developing countries. IGOs such as FAO and WTO see private standards such as those supported by GFSI as trade barriers, in particular for firms from emerging markets. There are concerns over the negative effects of private standards in developing countries and in international trade.[50] GFSI, however, views itself as a representative body of industry that is enabling trade and facilitating markets for it aims to harness the capacity of food businesses to access global markets, including SMEs and food businesses in developing countries. To ensure its activities would also benefit food business in developing countries, GFSI developed the Global Markets Programme and in that context sought collaboration with the United Nations Industrial Development Organization (UNIDO).[51]

---

[49] This includes meetings with representatives of Codex, WHO, FAO, WTO, the World Organization for Animal Health (OIE), International Organization for Standardization (ISO) and the World Bank, and cooperation with the United Nations Industrial Development Organization (UNIDO). Soon after its inception in 2000, GFSI also sought cooperation with the International Accreditation Forum to strengthen the system of accredited third party certification. See: IAF, 'Arrangement between IAF and GFSI for the GFSI program', Multilateral Agreement 2003/5, 17 September 2003 (on file with authors).

[50] See the conclusions on private standards (Report on the 18th session of the FAO/WHO coordinating committee for Latin America and the Caribbean, Costa Rica, 19–23 November 2012, 17 (on files with the authors)); Gretchen H. Stanton, 'Food Safety-related Private Standards: The WTO Perspective' and Miet Martens and Johan Swinnen, 'Private Standards, Global Food Supply Chains and the Implications for Developing Countries' in Axel Marx and others (eds), *Private Standards And Global Governance. Economic, Legal and Political Perspectives* (Edward Elgar 2012), 235–54 and 153–71.

[51] GFSI and UNIDO signed a Memorandum of Understanding on 15 June 2016 to signal their joint commitment to 'a large-scale partnership for

As a result of the strategy of the Global Regulatory Affairs Working Group to explain GFSI's activities and objectives to IGOs, GFSI is increasingly recognized as a relevant actor in the field. GFSI is now participating in discussions on food governance at Codex and the World Organization for Animal Health (OIE). While this is a sign of structural communication, it would be false to claim that GFSI's regulatory activities are now accepted by IGOs. From the perspective of IGOs, the participation of private standard-setting bodies in their meetings as observers is considered an important strategy, given their concerns about private standards creating barriers to trade for SMEs and food businesses in developing countries, the lack of scientific justification for the stricter requirements set by private standard owners, and the perceived lack of transparency in private standard-setting, monitoring and enforcement activities. By inviting GFSI to participate in their meetings, IGOs create a communication channel through which they can stress the prevalence of public standards over private standards in international trade and convey their concerns as regards the governance of private standards.

Distrust, misunderstanding and sheer ignorance regarding GFSI and its activities is considered an important obstacle for cooperation and alignment with national and EU authorities as well. Government actors are generally suspicious of the information provided by GFSI benchmarked schemes. And as a GFSI respondent acknowledged, it takes a long time to overcome this distrust.

4.2 Collaboration with National Governments

One of the factors that motivated the food industry to take the initiative to develop private food safety standards in the 1990s was the perception that government regulation had failed. Critical observers found government food regulations to be out of date and inadequate to deal with new risks; the critique applied to both the laws concerning food safety and the organization and effectiveness of official controls and enforcement of these laws. Busch and Bain found that:

> . . . the diminishing ability of the public sector to regulate trade has provided an opportunity for the private sector to reorganize aspects of the market to better

food safety' between government and global business. GFSI and UNIDO will develop large-scale food safety capability building projects based on the GFSI Global Markets Programme. See http://www.mygfsi.com/news-resources/news/news-releases/500-gfsi-and-unido-sign-mou-to-solidify-strategic-partnership-for-food-safety-capability-building.html accessed 28 November 2016.

> suit its needs. This is not to say that public regulations are obsolete; in fact, they continue to form the basis from which many private regulations operate.[52]

Initially, government responses to these private food safety standards and initiatives were rather reserved. However, changes in the legal framework governing food safety in the European Union, and more recently those in Canada and the United States, have introduced the statutory requirement for food businesses to have in place a food safety management system. Food safety management systems were already employed within the food industry and constitute a core component of the major private schemes, in particular those benchmarked by GFSI. This alignment between public legal frameworks and private management systems signals a two-sided relationship. Public authorities build on the experiences of private actors and lend an ear to the lobby from the food industry and private food safety initiatives regarding the industry's capacity to deal with food safety risks themselves, while at the same time they promote the use of food safety management systems as a statutory requirement that boosts the further adoption of private food safety schemes in the industry.

GFSI activities

As noted, the Global Regulatory Affairs Working Group saw the recognition and adoption of accredited third-party certification by national governments as one of its core deliverables. To deliver on its aims, the working group first identified 20 countries on which to focus their activities. One of the criteria for selection was the willingness of national governments to engage with GFSI. High-priority countries included Brazil, Canada, Chile, China, Mexico, South Africa, the Netherlands and the United States.[53] Alignment with the European Union as a whole was also considered a priority. In 2009, representatives of GFSI met with EU officials as a 'first step in permitting a review of the relationship of food safety schemes to current legislation'.[54] EU officials appeared as invited speakers at GFSI conferences. Moreover, members of the Global Regulatory Affairs Working Group engaged regularly with representatives of the Canadian, Dutch and US governments. The activities included meetings at the national offices in these countries, invitations of senior officers of

---

[52] Busch and Bain (n 7) 322.

[53] Other focus countries: Australia, Belgium, Colombia, France, India, Japan, Korea, New Zealand, Peru, Thailand, Turkey and the UK, Global Regulatory Affairs TWG Progress (Sept 2014) <www.mygfsi.com> accessed 28 November 2016. GFSI Newsletter 2013 speaks of 15 countries.

[54] GFSI Newsletter Summer 2009, 4.

national food agencies to GFSI conferences and meetings with the GFSI Board, and the sharing of written information about GFSI. The chair of the working group described this effort as:

> . . . a long process of informing the government and officials, getting them to understand more about these standards and GFSI and the fact that it is a global standard and the process that GFSI uses to benchmark the various schemes.

At several GFSI conferences the issue of public-private collaboration was put on the agenda. A panel discussion at the annual Global Food Safety Conference organized by GFSI in 2013 included officials of the national food safety authorities of Canada, Chile, China, the Netherlands, the United Kingdom and the United States.[55]

In preparing the ground for collaboration with public authorities, the Global Regulatory Affairs Working Group identified two major concerns: building confidence in third-party certification and the equivalence of the GFSI benchmarking requirements to government regulation. As regards the first concern, the working group and GFSI have sought to address the ongoing criticism about the reliability and transparency of third-party certification. These efforts include the introduction of requirements of unannounced inspections,[56] and auditor integrity and competence. A special working group has been developing an auditor competence scheme. It is expected that both issues will be included in the 2016 edition of the GFSI Guidance Document. Another issue that is perceived as a barrier to the acceptance of third party certification by public authorities is the obstacles to the mutual exchange of information. Audit reports are confidential and certification bodies are contractually prohibited from sharing information with public authorities. Public authorities also have to deal with legal obstacles relating to the sharing of information about food safety incidents and non-compliance at inspection sites. Finally, the development of the Global Markets Programme, now supported by UNIDO, is also part of GFSI's strategy to build confidence in third-party certification.

To address the second major concern, namely the question whether GFSI's benchmarking requirements meet the level of protection awarded by standards in national government regulation, GFSI hired an external party to review the national regulations of focus countries and the GFSI requirements for equivalence. The results are expected to be made publicly available in 2016.

---

[55] GFSI Newsletter February 2013, 17.

[56] Recommendation of the working group to the GFSI Board, GFSI Newsletter Summer 2013, 4.

In the following we will deal with the developments between GFSI and national governments in relation to four countries: the Netherlands, Canada, the United States, and China. In the first three countries, concrete progress has been made as regards the integration of GFSI benchmarked schemes in public monitoring and enforcement policies. Our respondents expected the Global Regulatory Affairs Working Group to make significant progress in gaining recognition from other national governments in the short to medium term.[57] We also discuss developments in China because Chinese state agencies and GFSI have entered into several formal public-private partnerships. Moreover, GFSI introduced a new section in its Guidance Document on what is called 'Standard Equivalence' to resolve structural problems with the benchmarking of Chinese food safety standards, which are effectively owned by public, rather than private actors. The 'Standard Equivalence' process has been developed to evaluate and assess the technical requirements of government certification schemes against the existing Key Elements from the GFSI Guidance Documents.[58] Thus it is a tool to benchmark public food safety requirements against GFSI's harmonized standards. The public scheme's governance or operational management is not assessed. This means that GFSI now offers its benchmarking services not only to private standard owners, but also to government organizations. Applications by governments are reviewed by a GFSI Expert Team. The GFSI Board decides on equivalence. The Standard Equivalence process is presented as:

> . . . a positive initiative for building public-private partnerships providing a mechanism for governments to become familiar with the fundamental requirements and principles of the GFSI Guidance Document. It is also hoped that government certification systems will come forward to GFSI to undertake the standard equivalence process enhancing the relationships government and the private sector, in the hope that there is a positive move toward global harmonisation and continuous improvement for food safety systems.[59]

Clearly, this is a new strategy pursued by GFSI to engage with government organizations. It not only seeks to obtain public recognition of its

---

57 Our respondents also mention significant progress in Japan and Thailand.

58 GFSI news 2015/08/16, accessed 28 November 2016 at http://www.mygfsi.com/news-resources/news/413-government-standard-equivalence-process-gfsi-guidance-document-version-6-4-part-iii.html; GFSI Guidance document Version 6.4, October 2015, Part III Government Standard Equivalence Process.

59 Government Standard Equivalence Process, GFSI Guidance Document Version 6.4 Part III, 2015/08/16, accessed 28 November 2016 at http://www.mygfsi.com/news-resources/news/413-government-standard-equivalence-process-gfsi-guidance-document-version-6-4-part-iii.html.

benchmarking activities by communicating and discussing with these organizations, but now it also invites governments to submit their public regulatory frameworks to its private benchmarking assessment.

The Netherlands

The Netherlands is said to be one of the most successful countries in achieving integration with GFSI benchmarked schemes and official food safety controls. The Dutch government, its Ministry of Economic Affairs (including its institutional predecessors) and the Netherlands Food and Consumer Product Safety Authority (*Nederlandse Voedsel-en Warenautoriteit* – NVWA) share a rich history of engagements with private organizations concerned with food safety management at the national level.[60] Also internationally, the Dutch government has been involved in the development and implementation of transnational private food safety schemes, for example the abovementioned EUREPGAP certification scheme for fruits and vegetables. The Dutch government also provided funds for the promotion and training of farmers,[61] and accepted parts of the EUREPGAP scheme as the officially recognized guide for good hygienic practice for the agri-food sector.[62]

The Dutch government has also been engaged in the development of Dutch HACCP, which was among the first private food safety management schemes to be benchmarked by GFSI. The (institutional predecessor of the) NVWA has been a consultative member of the National Board of Food Safety Experts, which provides scientific input to the private

---

60 An example is the RiskPlaza scheme, which is a multi-stakeholder initiative established in 2005 with the aim of controlling food safety hazards in raw materials and ingredients for food production. See in detail: Paul Verbruggen and Tetty Havinga 'Food Safety Meta-controls in the Netherlands' (2015) 6 *European Journal of Risk Regulation* 512. While RiskPlaza offers a case of rather successful public-private collaboration in the Netherlands, other initiatives have failed. An example is provided by the early policy framework called 'Monitoring Control' (*Toezicht op controle*), which sought to incorporate private assurance systems into the public food controls. See in detail: Haiko van der Voort, 'Co-regulatory Failure in the Food Industry. Explaining Regulatory Failure by means of Two Contrasting Interpretations of Governance' (2015) 6 *EJRR* 502.

61 The Dutch government also provided funding for training projects in African countries such as Kenya and Senegal (see http://www.passievoorfood.nl/detail/article/wat-je-van-ver-haalt/, https://www.cbi.eu/news/Dutch-minister-seeks-expansion-of-EurepGAP-imports-from-Africa/125895/ accessed 28 November 2016).

62 http://www.tuinbouw.nl/artikel/hygi%C3%ABnecodes-en-globalgap-ifa-plantaardige-productie and http://www.gfactueel.nl/Home/Achtergrond/2007/1/EurepGAP-IFA-goedgekeurd-als-hygienecode-GFA106227W/ accessed 28 November 2016.

scheme.[63] Initially, Dutch HACCP did not perform very well. Inspections in 2004 showed that 30 per cent of HACCP certificates should never have been issued.[64] In response, the Foundation for Food Safety Systems (*Stichting Certificatie Veiligheid, Kwaliteit en Duurzaamheid*), the owner of Dutch HACCP (and the secretariat to FSSC 22000), initiated a pilot project with the NVWA aimed at harmonizing audits and registering HACCP certified organizations leading to a lower inspection frequency.[65] In 2008, Dutch HAACP proudly announced that it would be the first GFSI-recognized scheme formally used by a public authority in its official inspection policy.[66] However, the pilot failed as the national authority still found Dutch HACCP certificates too unreliable.[67]

The NVWA has sought to expand its engagement with Dutch HACCP to other GFSI-recognized schemes. After assessing such schemes in 2011, it concluded that the food safety norms cover the important public norms, but food safety certificates do not guarantee that the food business is compliant with all requirements. The main cause of these apparent mismatches, the NVWA held, is that some firms just want to get the certificate and are not intrinsically motivated to maintain and improve food safety. Moreover, auditor competence and independence also needed to be improved, according to the authority.[68]

Furthermore, in September 2012 the NVWA concluded a covenant with US-based food producer Cargill stating that Cargill Netherlands will perform internal and external audits with the objective of complying with Dutch legislation and regulations, and communicate the results to the NVWA. If these results meet the standards of the NVWA, the public authority will amend the form and intensity of its inspection activities accordingly.[69] This policy agreement has been mentioned as a success case

---

63 Verbruggen (n 9) 241. Dutch HACCP was recognized by GFSI between 2004 and 2012.

64 'VWA-inspecties straks niet meer nodig' (24 January 2008) VMT, accessed 28 November 2016 at www.vmt.nl/nieuws/vwa_inspecties_straks_niet_meer_nodig-0800124120000.

65 Ibid.

66 GFSI Newsletter December 2008, 5.

67 'GFSI licht "third party" certificatie toe' (29 March 2011) VMT, accessed 30 November 2016 at http://www.vmt.nl/nieuws/GFSI_licht_third_party_certificatie_toe-110329122433.

68 Hans Beuger, 'Overheidstoezicht en certificatie. Verhogen betrouwbaarheid vergt inspanning van alle betrokkenen', (2012) *Voedingsmiddelentechnologie* 20–1; Elena Fagotto, 'Industry Food Safety Standards: Public and Private Interest in Global Food Safety' (PhD thesis, Rotterdam 2015) 121ff.

69 Covenant for Horizontal Supervision between Cargill BV and the Dutch Food

in the alignment of GFSI benchmarking with national food controls. The GFSI Global Regulatory Affairs Working Group 'identified a few case studies that demonstrate success in gaining government recognition of GFSI-benchmarked certification, like the covenant between the Dutch NVWA and Cargill'.[70]

More recently, the NVWA is (again) considering engaging with GFSI-recognized schemes. Budgetary constraints at the authority only account for part of this development. A more specific impetus to this policy was the Dutch government's creation in March 2013 of a Taskforce on Food Safety as a response to the EU horsemeat scandal, with a view to restoring consumer confidence in food and food production. The Taskforce consisted of food industry representatives and government officials. The Taskforce presented its action plan in June 2013. The establishment of criteria for the acceptance of private quality assurance systems was an important part of that plan.[71] The experience the NVWA had with its engagement with domestic private food safety assurance systems was important in framing these criteria, together with discussions with corporate regulatory affairs officers, representatives of private food safety schemes, and indeed GFSI. The action plan of the Taskforce refers to ISO standards for certification and auditing as one of the criteria for acceptance. The NVWA takes GFSI-benchmarked schemes as a basis for the acceptance of transnational private food safety schemes. Four GFSI schemes applied for acceptance under this policy.[72] In September 2016 the NVWA recognized the GFSI-benchmarked schemes of BRC and IFS as meeting the criteria set out in the action plan. The NVWA did not finalize its assessment of the other systems in 2016.[73]

Finally, to discuss its activities in relation to (inter alia) GFSI

---

and Consumer Product Safety Authority, accessed 30 November 2016 at https://www.nvwa.nl/documenten/communicatie/over-de-nvwa/convenanten/2016/convenant-tussen-cargill-bv-en-de-nvwa.

[70] 'Dr. Joseph Scimeca will join 2013 International Forum on Food Safety', accessed 28 November 2016 at http://www.ifofs.org/WhatsNew/2013-04-04/58.html; see also http://www.cargill.com/corporate-responsibility/responsible-supply-chains/food-safety/ accessed 28 November 2016.

[71] NVWA 'Requirements for the acceptance of quality systems by the Netherlands Food and Consumer Product Safety Authority' (4 June 2014), accessed 28 November 2016 at http://ketenborging.nl/wp-content/uploads/Criteria-voor-acceptatie-Engels.pdf.

[72] These are BRC, FSSC22000, GLOBALGAP and IFS. See http://ketenborging.nl/kwaliteitsschemas-en-status/, accessed 28 November 2016.

[73] NVWA 'Kwaliteitsschema's en status', accessed 4 January 2017 at http://ketenborging.nl/kwaliteitsschemas-en-status/.

benchmarked schemes, the NVWA has also initiated a working group at the European level to deal with the 'Value of Private Assurance Schemes', under the auspices of the Heads of European Food Safety Agencies. In this working group representatives from nine national food safety authorities discuss the value of certification schemes for official food safety controls.[74] The working group has drafted a quick scan to gain an overview of the activities currently ongoing in EU Member States regarding the integration of public and private food controls.[75] A total of ten national authorities reported they would take food business operators membership of private assurance schemes into account when planning official controls. The reliability of private schemes is most often mentioned as a challenge to integrating private assurance schemes in official food safety controls. Members of the working group together with representatives of non-European government agencies met with the GFSI Board at the annual Global Food Safety Conference in 2016. Both GFSI and the NVWA chair of the working group have claimed that this meeting was groundbreaking.[76] In 2017 the Canadian and Dutch food safety authorities are to organize a meeting of government agencies to further discuss public-private cooperation.[77]

Canada

It follows from the previous discussion that Canada is also perceived as a frontrunner in engaging with private food standards and GFSI more specifically. GFSI's activities in Canada started in 2010 with its recognition of CanadaGap, a private food safety scheme for fresh fruits and vegetables governed by a private, not-for-profit organization. Federal and provincial governments were involved in reviewing the HACCP model and manuals of CanadaGap.[78]

In more recent years, the Canadian Food Inspection Agency (CFIA) has been working on the modernization of its inspection policy. During

---

[74] Belgium, Denmark, Finland, France, Germany, Norway, Sweden, the United Kingdom and the Netherlands attended the first meeting.

[75] Head of Food Safety Agencies (Working Group on the Value of Private Assurance Schemes), 'Quickscan' (2015) (on file with authors).

[76] http://www.mygfsi.com/newsresources/lates-news/476-gfsc-2016-round-up-the-food-safety-journey.html accessed 28 November 2016; Hans Beuger, 'Dialoog private kwaliteitssystemen komt los', (4 March 2016) VMT, accessed 28 November at http://www.vmt.nl/Nieuws/Column_Hans_Beuger_dialoog_private_kwaliteitssystem_komt_los-160304120830.

[77] Beuger (n 76).

[78] Between 2002–2008; see http://www.canadagap.ca/about-us/history/ accessed 28 November 2016.

this process, the CFIA consulted many stakeholders, including representatives of GFSI. In 2015, the CFIA presented its so-called 'integrated agency inspection model', through which it promotes a more preventive and systems-based approach for food safety inspections. This also includes the application of globally recognized risk management concepts.[79] A key element of the new model is that certain food businesses will need a Preventive Control Plan (PCP). Such a plan describes a systems-based approach developed by regulated parties that focuses on prevention as a way to achieve compliance. This approach provides flexibility for the regulated business to opt for a private certification scheme (GFSI is explicitly mentioned), which will typically facilitate setting a PCP in place.

It is expected that many food facilities in Canada will seek certification from a GFSI-benchmarked scheme in order to comply with the new Safe Food for Canadians Act.[80] In January 2016, the CFIA published a guidance document entitled 'Private Certification Policy'.[81] In this document, CFIA notes that it 'recognizes that private certification schemes may play an important role in helping industry achieve food safety regulatory objectives, provided they can be assessed as being effective, credible and aligned with public policy objectives'. The CFIA will furthermore use private certification data to inform risk-based prioritization. Certification under a scheme that meets regulatory requirements should positively impact the risk profile of the regulated party, according to the CFIA. The agency thus places a fair amount of confidence in certification under a scheme recognized by GFSI and schemes certifying against a relevant ISO food safety standard and HACCP certification. This policy came into effect on 3 September 2015. The CFIA assessed the level to which the GFSI guidance document and the accredited certification process meet federal legislative requirements. In the words of one of our respondents:

> As the CFIA is modernizing its regulation under the Safe Food for Canadians Act, they looked at the GFSI standards and recognized that they were very

---

[79] CFIA, Integrated Agency Inspection Model (Final Version 11 February 2015), accessed 28 November 2016 at http://www.inspection.gc.ca/about-the-cfia/accountability/inspection-modernization/integrated-agency-inspection-model/eng/1439998189223/1439998242489.

[80] GFSI Focus Days Come to Canada, accessed 28 November 2016 at http://www.mygfsi.com/news-resources/news/425-gfsi-focus-days-come-to-canada-key-time-in-food-safety-regulatory-landscape.html.

[81] CFIA, Private Certification Policy, accessed 28 November 2016 at http://www.inspection.gc.ca/about-the-cfia/accountability/consultations/regulatory-risk-based-oversight/private-certification-policy/eng/1452808755126/1452808821799?chap=0.

> well constructed . . . We now know and are discussing with the Canadian government that the GFSI standard would totally meet the Canadian proposed modernized role.

In parallel to this development, GFSI established a Local Group 'US-Canada' in 2013. Key objectives of the group included creating links with government agencies and driving greater regulatory acceptance of GFSI-benchmarked schemes.[82] GFSI has welcomed the recent CFIA policy framework on private certification schemes.[83] It sees this framework as a result of its work and engagement with the Canadian government.[84] Canada and the Netherlands are taking the lead in the continuation of meetings about public cooperation with private quality assurance systems, including meetings with GFSI representatives.

United States

Not only Canada, but also the United States has recently modernized its food regulations with the new Food Safety Modernization Act (FSMA), which was signed into law 4 January 2011. The act indicates a shift from reactive to a more proactive approach to food safety assurance and draws on policy alternatives that have been developed in private governance systems, such as the GFSI benchmarked schemes.[85] The adoption of these GFSI schemes in the United States was stimulated by the decision of Wal-Mart in 2008 to require GFSI recognized audits of its suppliers.[86] However, outbreaks of foodborne illness raised profound concerns among consumers about the quality of private audits, as well as of public controls. The food industry, consumer representatives, and the Food and Drug Administration (FDA) agreed that reliance on private audits was

---

[82] GFSI Newsletter December 2013, 16.

[83] GFSI applauds New Canadian Policy on Private Certification of Food Facilities, accessed 28 November 2016 at http://www.mygfsi.com/news-resources/latest-news/454-gfsi-applauds-new-canadian-policy-on-private-certification-of-food-facilities.html.

[84] Interview, chair GFSI Global Regulatory Affairs Working Group.

[85] Neal Fortin, 'The U.S. Food Safety Modernization Act: Implications in Transnational Governance of Food Safety, Food System Sustainability, and the Tension with Free Trade' (2015) 25 *Duke Environmental Law & Policy Forum* 313, 321 and 327; Michaela Tarr Oldfield, 'Enactment of the Food Safety Modernization Act' (2015) 6 *European Journal of Risk Regulation* 488, 501; Alexia Brunet Marks, 'A New Governance Recipe for Food Safety Regulation' (2016) 47 *Loyola University Chicago Law Journal* 907; Ching-Fu Lin 'Public-private Regime Interactions in Global Food Safety Governance' (2013) Osgood Hall Law School Research paper series 41/2013, 17.

[86] Oldfield (n 85) 491.

necessary, but they disagreed on the role of public and private actors in ensuring safe food.[87]

Since the adoption of the FSMA in 2011, the FDA may require certifications to assure that particular imported foods comply with US requirements. These certifications can be issued by a government representative designated by the FDA or by third parties accredited in accordance with provisions in the FSMA. Certifications are also used in determining whether an importer is eligible to participate in the so-called 'fast track program'.[88] The FDA issued guidelines for accreditation bodies seeking recognition by the FDA and for third-party certification bodies seeking accreditation, as well as FDA procedures relating to the monitoring and oversight of participating accreditation bodies and certification bodies.[89] Undeniably, the result is an increasingly integrated public-private regulatory arrangement.

Our analysis suggests that GFSI was involved in discussions regarding the design of this system of accredited third-party certifications for imported food under the Food Safety Modernization Act. In 2010 the Chair of the Global Regulatory Affairs Working Group met with several US government agencies involved in food regulation to share information about GFSI's activities and results.[90] GFSI representatives also explained the value of third-party accredited certification and the work that GFSI is doing to US congressional staff.[91] Furthermore, GFSI claims to have provided technical support to the US government to evaluate third-party certification and to have discussed with government the current regulatory landscape impacting third-party certification.[92] In addition, the GFSI Local Group on US-Canada worked with the US accreditation body ANSI to strengthen third-party certification. One of our interviewees recalled that the FDA initially wanted private auditors to act like a public inspector and forward any findings on non-compliance to the FDA.

---

87 Oldfield (n 85) 492.

88 Fortin (n 85) 325–26; Lesley K. McAllister 'Third party programs to assess regulatory compliance' (Report for the Administrative Conference of the United States, October 22, 2012), 10–15.

89 'FSMA Final Rule on Accredited Third Party Certification', accessed 28 November 2016 at http://www.fda.gov/Food/GuidanceRegulation/FSMA/ucm361903.htm.

90 These included the US Department of Agriculture (USDA), Food and Drug Administration (FDA), CDC (Centers for Disease Control and Prevention), American National Standards Institute (ANSI) and US Government Accountability Office (GAO).

91 Interview, chair GFSI Global Regulatory Affairs Working Group.

92 GFSI Newsletter April 2010, 5; GFSI Newsletter July 2010, 3.

Clearly, the certification bodies were not prepared to take on this role as delegated public officials.

China

After several major food safety incidents, the Chinese government has invested a great deal in designing new food safety laws and systems for effective food controls.[93] Food businesses are required to have food safety experts and procedures, and compliance with good manufacturing practices and HACCP principles is encouraged. As of December 2016, businesses having a GMP or HACCP certificate may be seen as representing a lower level of risk food safety. Accordingly, they may benefit from less frequent official inspections.[94]

GFSI has developed a close relationship with China and Chinese government actors.[95] China is important for GFSI and its corporate stakeholders, as it is a significant market for the production of food and food ingredients, and many food manufacturers in Europe and North America source raw materials from China.

There are several linkages between GFSI and the Chinese government. First of all, the ChinaGAP scheme, which is a government-led certification scheme for primary produce, is remotely linked to GFSI, since this scheme is recognized by GLOBALGAP as being equivalent to a specific GLOBALGAP module of fruit and vegetables. GLOBALGAP, in turn, is itself benchmarked by GFSI for primary produce. Second, the China HACCP scheme, which is a government-led scheme for food processing, has applied for GFSI recognition. Third, GFSI has signed several memoranda of understanding with Chinese accreditation agencies.[96] These memoranda allowed GFSI to proceed with benchmarking the China HACCP scheme. In 2014, China HACCP had completed most steps of the benchmarking process; only stakeholder consultation and the GFSI Board decision remained to be done. However, since China HACCP effectively

---

[93] Neil Collins and Jörn-Carsten Gottwald, 'Being Well Fed: Food Safety Regimes in China' in Tetty Havinga, Frans van Waarden and Donal Casey (eds), *The Changing Landscape of Food Governance* (Edward Elgar 2015) 79; John P. Burns, Jing Li and Xiaoqi Wang 'The Political Economy of Chinese Food Safety Regulation: Distributing Adulterated Milk Powder in Mainland China and Taiwan', in Havinga et al., ibid, 96–113.

[94] Food Safety Law 2009 (as amended in 2015) and Administrative Measures on Determination of Risk Levels of Food Businesses, (CFDA Sep. 2016). Information provided by Yongkang An.

[95] See the contribution of Kottenstede in this volume for a more detailed account of the relationship between GFSI and China.

[96] In 2011, 2012 and 2015.

is government-owned it did not (and could not) meet all requirements specified in the GFSI Guidance Document. As a result, the benchmarking process of China HACCP came to a halt.

Since 2012, GFSI Focus Days have taken place in China annually to explain what GFSI stands for and how food safety in China can be advanced through a global food safety culture. GFSI has been present at major food safety events and conferences in China. Furthermore, it has developed a Chinese website and it established a Local Group called the China Food Safety Initiative (CFSI). The proposed governance structure of the CFSI consists of a Board, an Advisory committee and a Steering committee (with enterprise members). A Memorandum of Understanding between GFSI and CFSI structures the relationship between the two.[97]

In November 2015, the collaboration between GFSI and the Chinese government was further strengthened with the establishment of three new public private partnerships to enhance food safety in China. GFSI and the Chinese government also announced that China submitted its China HACCP scheme to GFSI for assessment. This could be seen as a strategic answer to the halted process of GFSI benchmarking in 2014. China HACCP has now been considered 'technically' equivalent with the GFSI requirements.[98] This equivalence applies only to the technical food safety requirements (Part III of the GFSI Guidance Document) and does not include the scheme's governance and operational management components (Part II).[99] This is justified by the different governance structure of a government-owned scheme like China HACCP, given that these schemes usually do not comply with requirements of separation between rule making, auditing and decision-making on certificates. Requirements related to auditing (frequency, duration and reporting),

---

97 Presentation Yves Rey (former chair GFSI Board), accessed 28 November 2016 at http://www.slideshare.net/Jane20150115/gfsi-fbif2-shanghai-april-may-2104.

98 Partnerships with the Certification and Accreditation Administration of China, China Nutrition and Health Food Association and UNIDO, see http://www.mygfsi.com/news-resources/news/news-releases/435-leveraging-the-global-food-safety-initiative-to-meet-china-food-safety-challenges.html accessed 28 November 2016; 'GFSI embarks on public-private partnership with China's CNCA to accelerate food safety development', accessed 28 November 2016 at http://www.mygfsi.com/news-resources/news/432-gfsi-embarks-on-public-private-partnership-with-china-s-cnca-to-accelerate-food-safety-development.html.

99 This seems to be contrary to the Guidance document ed. 6, which reads: 'The types of scheme that can be recognized by GFSI are schemes owned by non-governmental bodies or government bodies. Irrespective of ownership, schemes must meet the requirements for application specified in Part II Section 2.' (Part II 1.1, Guidance document 6th ed, version 6.3).

auditor competences and relations with accreditation and certification bodies are also outside the scope of this equivalence test.

The 'technical equivalence' status may be considered a political compromise, as one of our respondents noted. GFSI needed China to be on board to gain more global scope and did not want to disrupt its fragile relationship with the Chinese government by insisting on compliance with the requirements for private certification under the GFSI Guidance Document, which China HACCP by its very nature could not meet. The public-private partnerships and the technical equivalence of China HACCP were realized at the level of the GFSI Board, not the Regulatory Affairs Working Group or the Local Working Group (CFSI).[100] GFSI, however, frames this recognition as a new step in its strategy to improve global food safety. Now, not only private food safety schemes but also public standards can be benchmarked by GFSI. Consequently, GFSI not only strives for public recognition of the value of certification against GFSI benchmarked schemes, it also seeks alignment in the other direction.

GFSI clearly plays a fundamentally different role in China than in the other countries addressed here. This could be attributed to the different economic and political system in China, which is state-dominated and authoritarian. In analysing the access of new regulatory actors in China's environmental regulation, Van Rooij and others observe that public authorities remain at the centre of the regulatory landscape. The Chinese party-state only supports new actors insofar as they remain controllable.[101] Next to the dominant position of the state, the underdeveloped private sector and public distrust of private commercial entities to safeguard in public interests has also seriously impeded industry from engaging in regulatory processes in China. Alternatively, the difference could be attributed to the different phases of engagement with private standards organizations by national government. Initially, governments in the Netherlands and the United States also wanted to stay in control, but this longing for control decreased over time as recognition and trust in these private sector bodies grew.

---

[100] Interview, chair GFSI Global Regulatory Affairs Working Group.

[101] Benjamin van Rooij, Rachel E. Stern and Kathinka Fürst, 'The Authoritarian Logic of Regulatory Pluralism: Understanding China's New Environmental Actors' (2016) 10 *Regulation & Governance* 3. See also Kottenstede, Chapter 10 in this volume.

5. DISCUSSION: WHY, HOW AND WHAT HAS BEEN ACHIEVED?

What are the reasons for state actors at international and national levels to engage with GFSI? State actors have two main arguments to engage with GFSI and related private governance arrangements in the food industry. First, and this is the initial response for most of the government organizations, they engage with private regulators because they are worried about the development and increased importance of private food safety standards and related certification schemes. They want to communicate with central actors in the private sector in particular to stress the importance and prevalence of public laws and enforcement. IGOs and national governments, in particular from developing countries, argue that private food standards constitute barriers to trade and should meet the applicable legal framework and not go beyond it. The European Union and governments such as those of the United States and the Netherlands also stress the primacy of state law and try to superimpose a legal framework on private standards. In other words, by engaging with GFSI they engage with a central actor in the domain of private food standards in order to exert control over the scope and depth of private standards. In discussing opportunities for collaboration with private assurance systems, the representatives of 20 countries agreed that private systems could support public oversight but could not replace it.[102]

A second reason for state actors to engage with GFSI is to exploit the potential of private food safety schemes to contribute to public policy goals by improving food safety management systems, by ratcheting up training and auditing standards for the food safety assurance industry, and by promoting a stronger professional food safety culture within industry. This argument for engaging with private actors hints at a more positive evaluation of private food governance that moves beyond initial attitudes of resentment from government officials. However, both perspectives can be observed in parallel in government organizations: some state officials may be in favour of collaboration, while others remain suspicious of the private sector. For example, in the Netherlands, which (as noted) is a country that is perceived to be a frontrunner and success story when it comes to integrating GFSI-benchmarked schemes in public inspection policies, there are clear indications of persistent resistance inside the food authority, even at the top level.[103]

---

[102] Beuger (n 76).

[103] At the 2015 annual meeting of the food retailers trade association in the Netherlands, the Inspector General of the NVWA stated: 'We have to get rid of

From the perspective of GFSI, the principal reason for engagement with IGOs, national government and public authorities, is to gain broad acceptance of its benchmarking process and recognized schemes. Engagement with state actors adds to the legitimacy of GFSI and as such is expected to contribute to the further rollout of GFSI's approach using a soft-handed coordination of competing private food safety standards and GFSI-recognized food safety schemes themselves. More specifically, it is in the interest of industry stakeholders that the requirements for benchmarking set out in the GFSI Guidance Document are consistent with public food laws. Compliance with a GFSI-recognized scheme should, at a minimum, be equivalent to legal compliance. The more public food safety authorities appreciate and trust the system and benchmarking process of GFSI, the less intrusive and burdensome public food controls will be for food businesses. The ultimate goal is that governments will recognize or adopt GFSI third-party certification as an accepted tool to assist in the prioritization of food safety compliance resources and inspection.[104]

What strategies did GFSI employ to ensure coordination, cooperation and (the partial) integration of public and private food safety regimes? The main strategy pursued by GFSI has been to provide information about its organization, activities and achievements to government officials, at all possible national and international meetings and conferences, and by preparing and translating documents on food safety and providing information on the website. Besides these extensive communication strategies, GFSI specifically sought to address and respond to public concerns about GFSI, its benchmarked schemes and its industry stakeholders.[105] Two main concerns relate to auditor competency in third-party certification schemes and the equivalence of GFSI guidelines with public food regulations. To address these concerns, private food safety schemes have been working on strengthening weaknesses in the accreditation process, the auditing process and auditor competences. GFSI has also defined quality standards for the auditors and added optional unannounced audits in

---

ticking the box. We really need to move to a situation in which quality assurance systems support a riskbased approach [to food safety inspections]. (. . .) We need to deal with these private quality assurance systems. That we as a public regulator can trust them, and that the consumer knows that these systems can really be trusted. That all has to do with this word: trust.' Speech by Harry Paul, Inspector General NVWA at the CBL 2015 annual meeting, 18 June 2015 (translation TH/PV) accessed 30 November 2016 at http://145.12.37.103/actueel/bestanden/bestand/2208877/speech-inspecteur-generaal-harry-paul-cbl-18-juni-2015.

[104] Interview chair GFSI Global Regulatory Affairs Working Group.

[105] GFSI, Addressing Perceived Barriers to Acceptance of Third Party Certification, February 2014.

its forthcoming GFSI Guidance Document. Furthermore, GFSI has reviewed the national regulations of focus countries and the GFSI standards for equivalency. The results of both efforts have not been presented at the time of writing. The Global Markets Programme was developed in response to critiques about trade barriers to developing countries and small food businesses. Finally, GFSI also initiated efforts to prevent fraud and strengthen food safety culture.

Finally, what has been achieved so far? The most important achievement has been a growing public awareness of what GFSI stands for and that it could contribute to the public interest. As one of our respondents put it:

> I am not sure what you would deem as successful. In some regard the mere fact that they [IGOs] are willing to have these discussions and engage on this, yes. We have come a long way, I would say; five years ago, private standards were a dirty word to these organizations. So they have gotten past that. They recognized the need for the importance of private standards. And so we have made some successful inroads there. But there is still work to be done. There is still some skepticism on barriers to trade. But we are getting there.

The new food laws in Canada and the United States have benefited from the experience of GFSI and other private actors. Accredited third-party certification has been accepted as part of the national policy framework for official controls. Both Canadian and US authorities have issued guidelines for accredited certification. The Netherlands has set criteria for private food quality systems to be accepted as part of the risk assessment for the food authority. China too has issued new food safety legislation and has vowed to work with GFSI to further improve its food safety regulation. Therefore, little by little, various forms of hybrid food governance arrangements are developing and GFSI (and its engagement with state actors) is playing a leading role in paving the way for these increasingly hybrid system of food governance.

In the literature on transnational governance, Abbott and others have called attention to the way IGOs strategically enlist intermediary actors to pursue their own regulatory objectives in transnational governance, thereby orchestrating (and not governing in the traditional sense) a specific regulatory domain.[106] We observe that GFSI, too, as an industry-driven, private actor, deploys an orchestration strategy by seeking to enroll intermediaries to deliver on its regulatory objectives, with considerable success. These intermediaries might be IGOs, national governments

---

[106] Abbott et al. (n 5).

or semi-public organizations such as accreditation bodies. In fact, the analysis in this chapter shows that both public and private actors try to enrol each other in the pursuit of their objectives.[107] IGOs and national governments enlist GFSI and its recognized schemes to strengthen their grip on private third-party certification, to enlarge their inspection capacity, and to use their own resources more efficiently. On the other hand, GFSI and its recognized schemes actively support this development since this also lends them a degree of legitimacy and assists them in enhancing the uptake of their standards by the market. Consequently, the interactions between GFSI and national and international state actors are not adequately captured by the picture of an IGO as single orchestrator of an international network of actors. Rather, several of the actors involved try to orchestrate and enlist other actors to suit their own goals and interests. Ultimately, the result is that food governance is increasingly multilevelled, networked and thus hybrid in nature.

---

[107] See on enrolment in food safety governance: Paul Verbruggen, 'Understanding the "New Governance" of Food Safety: Regulatory Enrolment as a Response to Change in Public and Private Power', 5 *Cambridge Journal of International and Comparative Law* 3 (forthcoming).

10 Transnational private food standards in the People's Republic: Hybridization with Chinese characteristics

Kai Kottenstede

INTRODUCTION

Despite its economic importance and intense linkage to the world economy, China has rarely been a topic within the growing academic debate about the characteristics of transnational private regulation in the food sector so far. This case study contributes to closing this gap. It discusses transnational private food safety standards (TPS) in China, the development and the rationale behind it, and explores the nature of the hybridization of food safety regulation in the People's Republic. It finds hybridization with Chinese characteristics, so to speak, in which the government makes use of the benchmarking mechanism to keep control over TPS.

One central motivation for retailers to invest in the establishment of private standards was to safeguard themselves against the increased risks and potentially new risks that derived from globally spread supply chains.[1] Retailers (and increasingly producers) therefore request certification against a private standard from their suppliers regardless of where they are located, whether in developed countries or developing countries.[2] This way, private standards project regulation across national borders.

[1] Frans van Waarden, 'Taste, Traditions, and Transactions: The Public and Private Regulation of Food' in Christopher K. Ansell and David Vogel (eds), *What's the Beef?: The Contested Governance of European Food Safety* (MIT Press 2006) 55; Spencer Henson and John Humphrey, 'The Impacts of Private Food Safety Standards on the Food Chain and on Public Standard-Setting Processes: Paper prepared for FAO/WHO' (2009) 8–14; Linda Fulponi, 'Private Voluntary Standards in the Food System: The Perspective of Major Food Retailers in OECD Countries' (2006) 31(1) *Food Policy* 1.

[2] Tetty Havinga, 'Retail Driven Food Safety Regulation' in Abdelhakim

This establishes the transnational dimension of private standards, as regulatory governance has a transnational dimension when 'regulation can have behavioural effects across territorial borders, while being driven by private constituents'.[3] Therefore, such private standards will be referred to as *transnational* private standards. This chapter focuses on collective international food safety standards that apply third party certification.[4] This, however, does not imply that TPS float freely in the air, unconnected and unaffected by public regulation. Rather, these standards need to be interpreted within the respective domestic settings.[5]

From all that we know about TPS in various specific domestic settings and their relation to global regulation, there is little, if anything, we can readily assume to hold true in the People's Republic of China given its different political, regulatory and economic system. Most importantly, due to the strong influence of the government in companies, firms may not behave as market actors but follow some other, often opaque rationale. For example, the China National Cereals, Oils and Foodstuffs Corporation, China's largest food company, is state-owned. Despite this, or maybe even because of it, China has yet to be included in the discussion about the transnational dimensions of food safety standards. Jensen and Zhou provide clarity about food safety standards within China, but they bracket out the role of TPS.[6] Similarly, Shen briefly discusses recent development of third-party certification with no differentiation between Chinese voluntary standards and TPS.[7]

Hammoudi and others (eds), *Food Safety, Market Organization, Trade and Development* (Springer 2015) 72.

[3] Paul Verbruggen, 'Gorillas in the Closet? Public and Private Actors in the Enforcement of Transnational Private Regulation' (2013) 7(4) *Regulation & Governance* 512, 514; see also Fulponi (n 1) 4.

[4] For a characterization of the different types of food safety standards see Spencer Henson and John Humphrey, 'Private Standards in Global Agri-Food Chains' in Axel Marx and others (eds), *Private Standards and Global Governance: Legal and Economic Perspectives* (Leuven global governance. Edward Elgar 2012) 99.

[5] Tim Bartley, 'Transnational Governance as the Layering of Rules: Intersections of Public and Private Standards' (2011) 12(2) *Theoretical Inquiries in Law*. See also Kalfagianni and Andrade Roche, Chapter 11 in this volume.

[6] Helen H. Jensen and Jiehong Zhou, 'Food Safety Regulation and Private Standards in China' in Abdelhakim Hammoudi and others (eds), *Food Safety, Market Organization, Trade and Development* (Springer 2015).

[7] Yuanyuan Shen, 'The Development of and Challenges Facing Food Safety Law in the People's Republic of China' in Wayne Ellefson, Lorna Zach and Darryl M. Sullivan (eds), *Improving Import Food Safety* (IFT Press series. Wiley-Blackwell 2013).

China is an especially interesting case for studying the implementation of TPS because it combines two characteristics. First, it has become a superpower on the global food market. The economic boom starting in the 1980s made China the biggest producer of agricultural products, the largest grocery market and the world's fourth biggest food exporter by 2011.[8] Second, China has experienced massive food safety problems.[9] Food safety problems cover the whole range of food safety issues: microbiological contamination (for example due to lack of hygiene and imperfect cool chains), extremely high residue levels of harmful substances (due to misuse or overuse of pesticides, fertilizers and veterinary drugs, poor knowledge of safe usage and environmental degradation), and purposely adulterated foodstuff (for example using melamine to pretend sufficient level of protein in milk).[10] For liberalized food trade and strongly globalized food supply chains, this unfortunate combination poses potentially severe risks: '[w]ith China's increasing engagement in global agricultural markets, food safety is no longer just a domestic issue [for China – KK] – it is now a global one'.[11] This raises the question of how transnational private food standards respond to China, and in particular, how TPS function in China. This includes two sub-questions. First, what role do private standards play in the Chinese market? Second, how do private standards in China interact with public regulations and what character of hybridization emerges in China, if any?

This chapter focuses on the Global Food Safety Initiative (GFSI) and the TPS recognized by it. It draws upon 38 interviews with European and Chinese experts from food safety standards, certification bodies, government bodies and academia (Table 10.3). The interviews were conducted between April 2014 and June 2015 in China, Europe and at the Global

---

8 WTO, *Trade Profiles 2012* (World Trade Organization 2012) 69.

9 Neil Collins and Jörn-Carsten Gottwald, 'The Chinese Model of the Regulatory State' in David Levi-Faur (ed.), *Handbook on the Politics of Regulation* (Edward Elgar 2011) 147; Thomas N. Thompson, 'Glowing Pork, Exploding Watermelons: Why China Can't Keep Its Food Safe' (2012), accessed 28 November 2016 at http://www.foreignaffairs.com/articles/137329/thomas-n-thompson/glowing-pork-exploding-watermelons?cid=nlc-this_week_on_foreignaffairs_co-031512-glowing_pork_exploding_waterme_3-031512#; Fred Gale and Jean C. Buzby, 'Imports From China and Food Safety Issues' (Washington, D.C., July 2009), Economic Information Bulletin, accessed 28 November 2016 at https://www.ers.usda.gov/publications/pub-details?pubid=44392.

10 Yunxiang Yan, 'Food Safety and Social Risk in Contemporary China' (2012) 71(03) *The Journal of Asian Studies* 705; FORHEAD, 'Food Safety in China: A Mapping of Problems, Governance and Research' (2014), accessed 28 November 2016 at www.forhead.org/uploads/soft/140306/1-140306103309.pdf.

11 The Lancet, 'China's Food Safety: A Continuing Global Problem' (2014) 384(9941) *The Lancet* 377.

Food Safety Conference in Kuala Lumpur, Malaysia. The remainder of the chapter is organized as follows: First, the research framework is presented based on the concept of hybridization. Following this, the emergence of private standards in China since 2000 is described. Third, the development of public-private interactions is analysed, differentiated between the rules on paper and regulation in practice. Fourth, the findings are discussed to specify the nature of hybridization of food safety regulation in China. Finally, the conclusion sums up the findings and points to future areas of research.

RESEARCH FRAMEWORK

TPS in China will be discussed along the lines of the analytical framework for hybridization proposed by Verbruggen and Havinga.[12] While adopting their understanding of hybridization which goes beyond a focus on standard setting, for the purpose of this chapter it is sufficient to differentiate between the rules of regulation and the same regulation in practice with the latter including elements of implementation and enforcement (as the monitoring of compliance and response to non-compliance). This follows Bartley's research approach for analysing TPS within domestic circumstances.[13] As he explains, 'the implementation of those standards always occurs within a particular nation-state, where domestic law still holds sway'.[14] Therefore, to understand the operation of TPS at domestic level it should be analysed by following its implementation within the local regulatory contexts, of which national public laws constitute an important element.[15] Therefore, the relationship between the content of TPS and that of public regulation as well as the implementation of both in practice need to be analysed.

The content of TPS, the standard itself, is a document specifying the obligations a food business applying for certification has to meet. TPS recognized by GFSI have to cover matters of food safety management, good practice, HACCP principles[16] and certification of multi-site

---

[12] Verbruggen and Havinga, Chapter 1 in this volume.

[13] Bartley (n 5).

[14] Ibid, 521.

[15] Ibid, 525.

[16] Hazard Analysis and Critical Control Points is a widely accepted concept for preventive food safety measures, for details see Steve Hathaway, 'Harmonization of International Requirements under HACCP-based Food Control Systems' (1995) 6(5) *Food Control* 267.

organizations.[17] TPS do not only provide their own substantive rules and criteria, however. They also set in place a specific system for implementation, monitoring and enforcement in the form of third-party certification. Accordingly, TPS may differ from domestic public regulation not only with respect to rule content, but also in relation to strategies for implementation and enforcement. Interaction between public and private regulation may occur at all of these stages in the regulatory cycle. Thus, each of these elements provide opportunities for public-private interaction and deserve attention in the empirical analysis of the hybridization of food governance in China.

Another important element of such hybridization concerns the institutional dimension of TPS. TPS are typically owned by a private organization, which acts as standard or scheme owner. For example, the FSSC 22000 scheme is owned by a private legal entity established under Dutch law called Foundation FSSC 22000. Such entities are owned and/or controlled by private industry actors, which also have the final say on the content of the scheme itself. These scheme owners delegate the monitoring and enforcement of TPS to (typically private) certification bodies. These certification bodies, in most cases, need to conclude a license contract with the scheme owner, which allows them to issue certificates for TPS and use its copyright protected logos and certificates. In China, by contrast, the ownership and governance of private standards differs strongly and is principally in the government's hands. This shapes the way in which hybridization of food governance is currently occurring in China and this aspect thus is included in the empirical analysis.

TRANSNATIONAL PRIVATE FOOD SAFETY STANDARDS IN CHINA

In 1999, leading retailers from Europe met to discuss a solution to problems created by the 'plethora of private food safety and quality standards'.[18] This meeting led to the founding of GFSI in May 2000.[19] According to GFSI, its main goal is to '[p]rovide continuous improvement

---

[17] GFSI, 'Guidance Document: Sixth Edition Version 6.3' (Issy-les-Moulineaux 2013); see also Fagotto (Chapter 3), Havinga and Verbruggen (Chapter 9) in this volume.

[18] Spencer Henson and Thomas Reardon, 'Private Agri-Food Standards: Implications for Food Policy and the Agri-Food System' (2005) 30(3) *Food Policy* 241, 242.

[19] Interview 26.

in food safety management systems to ensure confidence in the delivery of safe food to consumers worldwide'.[20] GFSI does not create a new TPS, but benchmarks existing TPS. The general idea behind GFSI's benchmarking activities is that if a food business gains certification for a TPS benchmarked by GFSI, that certificate is treated as equivalent to certification for other GFSI recognized schemes. When benchmarking TPS, GFSI assesses whether or not the applicant standard fulfils all criteria set out in the GFSI guidance document. The process is conducted by a benchmarking committee with support from the GFSI's secretariat. Additionally, an open consultation process is conducted in which all GFSI stakeholders can comment on the preliminary proposal of the committee.

The GFSI board, which is composed of corporate representatives of retailers, manufacturers and food service operators, decides whether or not the applicant TPS will be recognized.[21] If recognized as being equivalent, certification for the benchmarked scheme can be substituted against any other scheme recognized by GFSI. Thus, the benchmarking mechanism aims at eliminating competition between private standards. 'Certified once, accepted everywhere', as GFSI communicates its mission.[22] There are some preliminary signs that companies are increasingly willing to accept the equivalence in practice. For example, at the 2015 Global Food Safety Conference in Kuala Lumpur, US food producer Cargill announced that it would do so. An important step in GFSI's development was that from 2005 onwards, GFSI succeeded in convincing food manufacturers to join in the initiative. Before that, TPS, and GFSI specifically, were retailer-driven. This limited the reach of GFSI to retailer-owned brands only. When the FSSC 22000 standard was successfully benchmarked in 2009, a TPS which met food producers' needs became part of GFSI's scope.[23] Currently, 13 private standards from nine private standard organizations are recognized by GFSI (Table 10.1).

As a general rule, producers apply for certification against one of the GFSI recognized schemes when buyers demand such certification. Consequently, private standards go where companies go, or where companies source that demand the respective standard from their

---

[20] GFSI, 'What is GFSI?' 1.

[21] GFSI, 'Structure and Governance', accessed 28 November 2016 at http://www.mygfsi.com/about-us/about-gfsi/structure-and-governance.html.

[22] Interview 26; see for example GFSI, 'Newsletter June 2008' (2008), accessed 28 November 2016 at http://www.mygfsi.com/news-resources/news/newsletter.html.

[23] Interviews 26 and 29.

Table 10.1 GFSI recognized certifications worldwide and in China

Transnational private standard	Geographical origin	Global number of certifications	Number of countries with certified sites	Number of certifications in P.R. China
FS22000[1]	The Netherlands	10,915	109	852
GlobalGAP[2]	Germany	130,000	113	300
IFS Food Standard[3]	Germany	14,000	96	272
BRC[4]	UK	17,289	113	1329
PrimusGFS[5]	USA	12,947	North America	0
GRMS[6]	Denmark	27	Europe	0
Global Aquaculture Alliance	USA	No information available	No information available	No information available
CanadaGAP[7]	Canada	954	Canada	0
SQF[8]	USA	6910	30	6
(ChinaGAP)[9]	(China)	(2000)	(P.R. China)	(2000)

Sources:

1 Tetty Havinga (n 2); FSSC, 'FSSC 22000 Certificates Directory', accessed 30 November 2016 at https://viasyst.net/fssc.
2 Information provided by GlobalGAP on request.
3 IFS, 'FAQ', accessed 30 November 2016 at https://www.ifs-certification.com/images/ifs/faq/documents/IFS_FAQs_EN.pdf.
4 BRC (n 26); BRC, 'BRC Directory', accessed 30 November 2016 at http://www.brcdirectory.co.uk.
5 Primus GFS, 'Certification Register', accessed 30 November 2016 at http://www.primusgfs.com/certificationRegister.aspx.
6 GRMS, 'Approved Sites', accessed 30 November 2016 at http://www.grms.org/approved-sites.
7 CanadaGAP, 'Certified Companies', accessed 30 November 2016 at http://www.canadagap.ca/becoming-certified/certified-companies.
8 SQF, 'Certified Supplier Search', accessed 30 November 2016 at http://www.sqfi.com/suppliers/sqf-certified-suppliers; additional information provided by SQF on request.
9 Standard Maps, 'China GAP', accessed 30 November 2016 at http://www.standardsmap.org/identify; for comparison only, indirectly recognized by GFSI through benchmarking against GlobalGAP.

suppliers.[24] Scheme owners learn about a growing demand in a market through the companies using their scheme and through the board of the organizations or certification bodies. Typically following this, scheme owners become active with regard to this market. In China, the demand for private standard certification predominantly comes from western

[24] Interviews 26 and 27.

businesses, either companies sourcing in China for overseas markets or companies sourcing in China for the Chinese market.[25] The British Retail Consortium (BRC), a prominent scheme owner, reports that 'Chinese sample site assessments were generally in response to overseas customer requirements'.[26] Sourcing in China for western markets is more relevant for food producers. Western supermarkets rarely put Chinese fresh produce on their shelves.[27] There is virtually no demand for certification against GFSI recognized TPS from Chinese companies trading domestically.[28] This situation is reflected in the client base of international certification bodies, which mainly consists of international companies working or sourcing in China. China's companies use international certification bodies mainly because their international customers require them to, as a certification body expert confirms.[29] Likewise, GlobalGAP reports that Chinese retailers do not use GlobalGAP.[30]

GlobalGAP was one of the first GFSI recognized TPS to arrive in China when the first certificates were issued in 2003.[31] The BRC started in China in 2005.[32] Compared to the international scale, however, the number of food production facilities certified against these TPS is low. Based on available data, roughly 2,800 certified facilities exist in China as of 2014 (Table 10.1). In comparison, around 195,000 certifications had been issued worldwide. Thus, China makes up roughly 1.4 per cent of all private standard certificates.

To facilitate further market uptake of TPS in China the industry collectively mandated GFSI. Individual scheme owners have no strategic focus on China.[33] GFSI's growing engagement with China can be traced through the GFSI newsletters, which have been available since 2008. In April 2008, GFSI held a first event in Shanghai. This was repeated in Beijing in 2009. From this point onwards, GFSI has shown sustained engagement in China (Table 10.2).[34] A major milestone in this development is the memorandum of understanding between the GFSI and the Certification and Accreditation Administration of the People's Republic of China (CNCA)

---

25 Interviews 5 and 27.
26 BRC, 'Food Safety: A Global View' (2014), 35.
27 Interview 6.
28 Interviews 33 and 34.
29 Interview 9.
30 Interview 4.
31 Interview 4.
32 Interview 24.
33 Interviews 5, 10, 11, 26, 27, 29.
34 See also Havinga and Verbruggen, Chapter 9 in this volume.

Table 10.2 GFSI activities in China 2008–2015

Year	GFSI activity in China
2008	April: first Asia road show with event in Shanghai Start of partnership with China Chain Story & Franchise Association (CCFA)
2009	April: 2nd Asia road show with Beijing event
2010	April: GFSI delegation one week in China for meetings, including with members of the Chinese government April: co-branded conference with CCFA November: Participation of GFSI in China International Food Safety and Quality Conference (CIFSQC) GFSI team has China coordinator
2011	April: 7th CCFA China Food Safety Annual Conference in Hangzhou in cooperation with GFSI April: GFSI workshop with Chinese food company Cofco, meeting with CNCA, Beijing November: GFSI official partner of CIFSQC November: Memorandum of Understanding between GFSI and CNCA
2012	March: GFSI Food Safety workshop at the 18th Franco-Chinese economic forum, Beijing March: Memorandum of Understanding between GFSI and the China Certification & Accreditation Institute (CCAI) July: 1st GFSI China Focus Day, speakers from AQSIQ, CNCA, Chinese Center for Disease Control and Prevention (CDC) March: official announcement of GFSI China Local Group November: GFSI partner of CIFSQC
2013	April: GFSI session at international Forum on Food Safety (IFOFS), Beijing June: 2nd GFSI China Focus Day, Beijing, with speakers from China Food and Drug Administration (CFDA), CNCA, CDC, China Inspection and Quarantine (CIQ) June: official launch of local GFSI China Local Group July: GFSI presentation at International Dairy Development Forum, Hohhot, Inner Mongolia July: GFSI presentations at 9th CCFA Food Safety Annual Conference November: 4th meeting of GFSI China local group November: GFSI partner of CIFSQC
2014	3rd GFSI China Focus Day GFSI, Beijing, with speakers from CFDA, CNCA, China National Center For Food Safety Risk Assessment (CFSA, former CDC) GFSI China local group office set up in Shanghai
2015	November: GFSI announces technical equivalence of China HACCP GFSI reveals new partnerships with CNCA, China Nutrition and Health Food Association (CNHFA) and UNIDO during 4th GFSI Focus Day China, Beijing

Source: GFSI, 'GFSI Newsletter' (2008–2015), accessed 30 November 2016 at http://www.mygfsi.com/news-resources/news/newsletter.html.

in 2011. Located under the ministry-level General Administration of Quality Supervision, Inspection and Quarantine (AQSIQ), CNCA is responsible for supervision of China's conformity assessments policies including the regulation of the certification system. In 2012, a GFSI local group in China was announced and a further memorandum was signed. The local group, also referred to as China Food Safety Initiative, was initiated by over 100 companies. Its aim is to motivate China's food industry to 'follow GFSI principles'.[35] GFSI clearly has an interest in pushing for wider usage of the benchmarked schemes: '[T]he aim was to have as many companies as possible becoming certified against one of the GFSI benchmarked schemes. This was mainly a task of communication in order to inform food businesses around the world to know about and to make use of the GFSI's approach.'[36]

FOOD SAFETY RULES IN CHINA AND TPS

There are two separate developments relevant to the analysis of the interaction between public and private regulation at the level of the content of formal food safety rules. First, China's food safety regulation has changed fundamentally over the past decade, altering the relationship between private food safety standards and public laws, at least on paper. In the early 2000s, China's public food safety laws were clearly lagging behind internationally accepted standards for food safety.[37] The first steps to develop food safety legislation in a new direction had been taken earlier, but it was in 2009 with the new Food Safety Law (FSL) that China made a major step by introducing a comprehensive set of rules resembling an internationally established understanding of food safety regulation.[38] The World Health Organization (WHO) described China's food safety regula-

---

35 GFSI, 'GFSI Focus Day China 2012: Post Event Report' (19 July 2012), 12.

36 Interview 29.

37 Yongmin Bian, 'The Challenges for Food Safety in China: Current Legislation is Unable to Protect Consumers from the Consequences of Unscrupulous Food Production' (2004), accessed 28 November 2016 at http://chinaperspectives.revues.org/819; Waikeung Tam and Dali L. Yang, 'Food Safety and the Development of Regulatory Institutions in China' (2005) 29(4) *Asian Perspective* 5.

38 Hon-Ming Lam and others, 'Food Supply and Food Safety Issues in China' (2013) 381(9882) *The Lancet* 2044, 2049; Collins and Gottwald (n 9) 151; Chenhao Jia and David Jukes, 'The National Food Safety Control System of China – A Systematic Review' (2013) 32(1) *Food Control* 236.

tion after 2009 as 'modern'.[39] Despite this substantial improvement, there are still numerous shortcomings with regard to the rules. In particular, public food safety standards for specific substances in food often do not meet the level of safety set by Codex Alimentarius and the development, unification and revision of public food safety standards continued for many years after the FSL was introduced.[40] From a purely formal perspective, TPS thus were substantially different from public regulation as they already reflect requirements of international food safety regulation: they were stricter and incorporated more sophisticated concepts (like HACCP) compared to Chinese public regulation. After 2009, this difference has become less clear and the gap between the two has narrowed, at least on paper. In terms of residue limits and similar substance-specific standards, however, TPS still exceeds standards of public regulation.

Second, elements of western concepts were introduced in China before the development of the FSL, through benchmarking activities. Much like GFSI, the scheme of GlobalGAP uses a benchmarking process to assess the equivalence of private food standards. In 2006, GlobalGAP and CNCA signed a memorandum of understanding to benchmark the newly established Chinese standard ChinaGAP for primary production.[41] The benchmarking process was initiated as early as 2003 when the CNCA visited GlobalGAP in Cologne.[42] There was at least one follow-up, high level, meeting in 2005 in China.[43] With the introduction of ChinaGAP, the concept of Good Agricultural Practice (GAP) was introduced in China before the FSL was in force.[44] ChinaGAP is a voluntary standard owned by the CNCA. Thus, it is effectively a publicly owned voluntary standard put in the market like a private standard. ChinaGAP consists of two distinct certificates indicating two levels of compliance. GlobalGAP has twice recognized the first class certification, the stricter version, as being equivalent to GlobalGAP's standards for fruit and vegetables through its benchmarking process. The benchmarking status achieved by ChinaGAP is termed approved modified checklist, which indicates the technical requirements

---

[39] WHO, 'China – Food Safety', accessed 28 November 2016 at http://www.wpro.who.int/china/mediacentre/factsheets/food_safety/en/.

[40] Jia and Jukes (n 38) 243.

[41] FAO, 'A Practical manual for Producers and Exporters from Asia' (2007) 46–47, accessed 28 November 2016 at http://www.fao.org/docrep/010/ag130e/AG130E00.htm#Contents.

[42] Interview 11.

[43] Cora Dankers, *Private Standards in the United States and the European Union Markets for Fruit and Vegetables: Implications for developing countries* (FAO Commodity Studies, FAO 2007).

[44] Interview 11.

by ChinaGAP are considered be equivalent with GlobalGAP. As of 2015, GlobalGAP has not benchmarked ChinaGAP's complete system: it has only benchmarked the technical requirements set out by the standard. ChinaGAP's administration and management of certification bodies and the training of auditors has not been benchmarked.[45] GlobalGAP supported and consulted the CNCA in developing ChinaGAP. The cooperation between them almost led to the establishment of a joint venture company, but the Chinese stopped this project in 2011.[46]

GFSI and CNCA replicated this benchmarking process in principle for the ISO 22000 standard. This food safety standard, published in 2005 by the International Organization for Standardization (ISO), is especially tailored for food manufacturers. CNCA used it to develop a standard called China HACCP. This marks an extension of scope of China's voluntary standards as ChinaGAP only covers pre-farm gate production. GFSI and CNCA engaged in intense exchanges during the development of China HACCP.[47] Two related issues were discussed: the establishment of a local GFSI group and the benchmarking of China HACCP against the GFSI guidance document. Foreign companies involved in GFSI supported the CNCA in developing China HACCP.[48] For example, foreign certification bodies were part of the technical working group of the CNCA that supports the development and benchmarking of China HACCP against the GFSI guidance document.[49] The 2011 memorandum of understanding expressed the will to proceed with the benchmarking, as publicly announced by GFSI.[50] The intensity of interest from both sides is documented by GFSI's continuous presence in China since 2008 and the Chinese government's constant involvement and active participation in GFSI events during this period. In 2013, CNCA and GFSI institutionalized their cooperation by establishing the China Food Safety Initiative with a representative office in Shanghai. Finally, in 2015, GFSI announced that it granted China HACCP the newly created status of technical equivalence. By this, the GFSI acknowledged that China HACCP is 'equivalent with the GFSI technical requirements as laid out in the GFSI Guidance Document'.[51]

---

45 Interview 10.
46 Interview 11.
47 Interview 36.
48 Interview 24.
49 Interviews 24 and 33.
50 GFSI, 'Newsletter Spring 2012' (2012), accessed 28 November 2016 at http://www.mygfsi.com/news-resources/news/newsletter.html.
51 GFSI, 'China embarks on Public-Private Partnership with China's CNCA to Accelerate Food Safety Development' (3 November 2015), accessed 28 November

This is not a full benchmarking, however, as it excludes an assessment on the equivalence of the governance structure of the standard and its owner. Like GlobalGAP, GFSI thus refrained from fully benchmarking Chinese public voluntary standards.

TPS AND FOOD SAFETY REGULATION IN PRACTICE

On paper, China narrowed the gap between public regulation and TPS requirements by updating mandatory regulation and introducing voluntary standards. In practice, however, there is an enduring lack of implementation and enforcement of food safety regulation in China.[52] Implementation and enforcement of China's food safety regulation are uneven across provinces and types of food.[53] The FSL did not fundamentally change the situation. International certification bodies were 'very concerned' about potential integrity problems, as one of their representatives pointed out.[54] As observed by others, there remains 'an obvious need to improve monitoring, inspection and law enforcement'.[55]

Reports about the food safety situation point to misuse and overuse of chemicals in food production, despite the fact that pesticide regulation became stricter and concepts of good agricultural practice were introduced.[56] Official data from testing food that would provide information of actual compliance with food safety regulation is patchy, if available at all.[57] However, monitoring data provided by TPS scheme owners reflects implementation and enforcement deficits. In its 2014 report, the BRC disclosed that in China only 25.5 per cent of all inspected sites achieved the A grade, which is the 'lowest percentage across all regions and countries' in which BRC certification is granted.[58] China accounted for 31 per cent of all major nonconformities worldwide and in two criteria it represents the

2016 at http://www.mygfsi.com/news-resources/news/432-gfsi-embarks-on-public-private-partnership-with-china-s-cnca-to-accelerate-food-safety-development.html.

[52] Lam and others (n 38); FORHEAD (n 10) 42.

[53] Ibid; Collins and Gottwald (n 9) 149.

[54] Interview 27.

[55] S. Chung and C.K.C. Wong, 'Regulatory and Policy Control on Food Safety in China' (2013) 67(6) *Journal of Epidemiology & Community Health* 476, 477.

[56] FORHEAD (n 10) 32; Lam and others (n 38) 2048.

[57] FORHEAD (n 10) 80.

[58] BRC (n 26) 35.

vast majority of cases of major nonconformity with BRC requirements.[59] These figures illustrate a substantial gap between standard requirements and actual implementation even for food producers who applied for a certificate. There is little reason to believe that companies that did not even apply for certification do better than that.

The fragmentation of the Chinese food market is a major obstacle on the road to safe food. It implies that many businesses in the supply chain are very small. There are an estimated 200 million farms, which cultivate on average 0.6 hectare of land.[60] Similarly, of the estimated 400,000–450,000 food processors, as many as 350,000 have no more than ten employees.[61] The small size of food producers is considered a strong contributing factor to the low degree of professionalization, insufficient facilities, and poor knowledge and training.[62] The fragmentation also has implications for governmental oversight and enforcement. Reaching out to all food producers to inform them about changes in food safety regulation itself is a challenge.[63] Arguably, the same holds true for inspections and monitoring.[64] Implementation and enforcement is further complicated by the fragmentation of Chinese governmental oversight for food safety, resulting in unclear responsibilities between the numerous authorities involved.[65] Multiple reform and reorganizations have been undertaken to improve this situation, including the establishment of the China Food and Drug Administration as a new authority, but limitations remain.[66] Connected to the issue of fragmentation is a lack of capabilities and capability building on the governmental side. The Chinese authorities lack trained inspectors, who could also support especially small-scale food manufacturers in implementing food safety practices.[67] Reportedly, 'duty-dodging public agencies' and

---

[59] Ibid. As regards the criterion of 'managing supplier services', 30 out of a total of 33 nonconformities and as regards 'metal control', 18 out of 26 in total.

[60] FORHEAD (n 10) 23.

[61] United Nations, 'Advancing Food Safety in China' (Peking 2008). Occasional Paper, 6, accessed 28 November 2016 at http://s3.documentcloud.org/documents/365292/advanicng-food-safety-in-china.pdf.

[62] Linda Calvin and others, 'Food Safety Improvements Underway in China' (2006) 4(5) *Ambers Waves* 16, 18.

[63] Gale and Buzby (n 9) 3.

[64] Chung and Wong (n 55) 476.

[65] Bian (n 37) 11; United Nations (n 61) 13; Linden J. Ellis and Jennifer L. Turner, *Sowing the Seeds: Opportunities for U.S.-China Cooperation on Food Safety* (Woodrow Wilson International Center for Scholars 2008) 24.

[66] Lam and others (n 38) 4049.

[67] United Nations (n 61) 17.

unwillingness to enforce properly contributes to the lack of compliance.[68] In sum, improving the practice of regulation seems to be a more pressing task compared to improving the formal rules of China's food safety regulation.[69]

The lack of implementation and enforcement is reflected in the practice of TPS in China. Statements from various interviewees indicate deep scepticism by foreign experts with regard to the reliability of certifications in China.[70] Auditors repeatedly come across instances in which officially certified Chinese food producers did not comply with the obligations. One European business expert put it bluntly: 'They are all certified. When we audit them, they lose any certification they had.'[71] In the experience of another European business expert who previously worked in European countries as auditor, this is a specific Chinese phenomenon.[72] One reason is a lack of understanding by Chinese food producers about the objective of auditing. Deviations from the requirements are perceived as failure and are often not accepted by the audited parties, who then sometimes attempt to forge auditing results.[73] In this regard, ChinaGAP was mentioned particularly. While officially recognized as being equal to GlobalGAP, food businesses with a ChinaGAP certificate often do not fulfil all requirements of GlobalGAP.[74] However, the two different levels of ChinaGAP certificates, of which GlobalGAP only recognizes one, might contribute to this impression.[75] GlobalGAP claims to have never received any complaint about ChinaGAP.[76] Yet, a private standard expert argued that due to the negative experiences with the integrity of standards benchmarked against GlobalGAP in China, he would not encourage the use of benchmarking as a mechanism to assess equivalence between Chinese and western TPS.[77] The GlobalGAP board itself perceives China as high risk for the brand

---

68 Chung and Wong (n 55) 477; Austin Ramzy, 'Will China's New Food-Safety Laws Work?' (2009), accessed 28 November 2016 at http://www.time.com/time/world/article/0,8599,1882711,00.html; Yanzhong Huang, 'China's Corrupt Food Chain' (17 August 2012), accessed 28 November 2016 at http://www.nytimes.com/2012/08/18/opinion/chinas-corrupt-food-chain.html?pagewanted=all&_r=1&; interview 9.

69 Collins and Gottwald (n 9) 151.

70 Interviews 7, 9, 10, 14, 26 and 27.

71 Interview 7.

72 Interview 14.

73 Interviews 14 and 27.

74 Interviews 7 and 9.

75 Interview 11.

76 Interview 10.

77 Interview 26.

'GlobalGAP' and therefore is reluctant to push for more activities in China.[78]

The Chinese government tightly regulates implementation of TPS.[79] According to a European business expert based in China, the Chinese government wants to control private standards and the certification business 'extremely carefully'.[80] To be legal in China, any private standard needs to be licensed by the CNCA.[81] Accordingly, certification bodies can only certify standards also approved by the CNCA.[82] Certification bodies operating in China themselves are also under strict control of the Chinese government. They need to be accredited by the China National Accreditation Service for Conformity Assessment (CNAS), a government organization authorized by the CNCA.[83] Only certification bodies accredited by CNAS are allowed to issue certifications. This is inconsistent with international practice. Many countries do not require the accreditation of certification bodies. Accreditation is typically required by TPS scheme owners and under the GFSI benchmarking requirements for certification bodies to obtain a license agreement with the scheme owner.[84] It is also contrary to the principle of the International Accreditations Forum to accept accreditation across countries mutually.[85] Thus, in comparison, the Chinese regulation of certification bodies is much stricter compared to international standards.[86]

In practice, the restrictive stance on TPS was undermined by a de facto usage of standards. Most GFSI standards did not make the effort to register with the CNCA (the BRC is a notable exception).[87] Chinese companies which want to export to western, especially European markets, still need certification for schemes recognized by GFSI. Therefore, the demand for such certifications nevertheless remained. This has led to a

---

78 Interview 11.

79 Interviews 11, 14 and 27.

80 Interview 9.

81 Interview 36.

82 Interview 33.

83 Interview 33, see also CNAS, 'CNAS Introduction' (2015), accessed 28 November 2016 at https://www.cnas.org.cn/english/introduction/12/718683.shtml.

84 IAF, 'Why use an accredited certification body?' (2011) 2, accessed 28 November 2016 at http://www.iaf.nu/upFiles/IAF_Why_use_accredited_CB_0112.pdf?pdf=PD-Why-use-ac-cert-body. See also Casey, Chapter 2 in this volume.

85 See for example DAKKS, 'Internationales Netzwerk', accessed 28 November 2016 at http://www.dakks.de/content/internationales-netzwerk.

86 Interviews 9, 14, 27 and 28.

87 Interview 33.

situation in which official regulation of standards and business practice has diverged. Chinese suppliers ask an international certification body to issue a certificate for a specific GFSI recognized TPS, which has not been licensed by the CNCA.[88] The certification body sends an auditor to the facility to be certified and sometimes auditors are even flown in. The certificate is then issued by the legal entity of the certification body, which is accredited outside of China. This way, Chinese businesses can obtain GFSI endorsed private certifications in China, which are accepted by their customers, even though the standard is not licensed by the CNCA. While this is not against international principles, as explained above, the CNCA disapproves of this situation.[89] The Chinese government has the intention to exert more control over TPS. However, a forceful ending to this practice would hamper food exports.[90] In addition, the government may also lack the means and capacities to put an end to this practice, and enforce the existing rules for TPS in China.[91] As one interviewee summarized the development, the Chinese government has lost considerable influence in comparison to 2003 when no foreign certification body was active on the Chinese market.[92]

So far, GFSI has only recognized the technical equivalence of China HACCP with its benchmarking requirements. It has not benchmarked the governance design of this standard, which plays a central role in the implementation and enforcement, and hence its integrity. With regard to this point, GFSI requires that the scheme owner, certification body and accreditation body are separate organizations.[93] In the case of China HACCP, CNCA is the standard owner and CNAS is the authority responsible for accreditation. However, CNAS is authorized by CNCA. It seems this lack of organizational separation (and thus independence in compliance assessment) is a major reason for GFSI not to fully recognize China HACCP as equivalent to other TPS and only award it 'technical equivalence', as did GlobalGAP in the case of ChinaGAP.[94] Arguably, this indicates a lack of trust in the integrity of the Chinese public voluntary standards system.

---

88 Interview 24.
89 Interviews 28 and 33.
90 Interview 28.
91 Interview 33.
92 Interview 11.
93 GFSI, 'Guidance Document' (n 17).
94 Interviews 26 and 29.

DISCUSSION: DIMENSIONS OF HYBRIDIZATION IN CHINA

The analysis highlights four instances of hybridity: First, the approval of TPS by CNCA; second, the accreditation of certification bodies by CNAS; third the benchmarking of ChinaGAP by GlobalGAP and fourth the benchmarking of China HACCP by GFSI. This hybridization will now be deepened by discussing the six dimensions of the hybridization research framework proposed by Verbruggen and Havinga.[95]

Who are the Actors?

The key organization representing TPS in China and interacting with the Chinese government is the GFSI. It is important to note that the GFSI Board consists of executive managers from major western food corporations. Thus, western company representatives interact on behalf of GFSI with the Chinese government. GFSI most intensively interacted – that is met, discussed and cooperated – with the CNCA because it is the responsible authority for licensing voluntary standards and regulating the certification market in China. However, GFSI also interacted frequently with Chinese governmental actors that play a more important role in regulating food safety. Representatives of the CFDA and the AQSIQ took part as speakers at GFSI events (Table 10.2). As interviewees pointed out, exchanges with governmental actors other than CNCA were important in proceeding with the establishment of GFSI in China and its benchmarking activities. CNCA alone does not have all the competencies needed. Reportedly, exchanges with the National Health and Family Planning Commission (NHFPC) were more complicated in this regard.[96] It appears China's fragmented governmental oversight affected the emergence of hybrid food safety regulation.

What are the Drivers and Motivations?

For western companies representing GFSI, the prime motivation is the same for which TPS have been set up in general: ensuring the safety of their supply while keeping costs at bay by means of harmonizing standards.[97] As one interviewee explained his company's interest in

[95] Havinga and Verbruggen, Chapter 9 in this volume.
[96] Interview 37.
[97] Interview 26.

supporting GFSI's expansion to China: '[W]e want to maintain our high quality in the Chinese market as well. This is why we have an interest in safe food supply in China. On top of that comes food supply from China to other parts of the world.'[98] GFSI accordingly argues that it needs to be present in China because of an increasing demand for certification of Chinese suppliers against GFSI standards.[99] GFSI's engagement with the CNCA can be interpreted as a way to find a solution that allows for private certification while avoiding the unsecure situation of operating in a legal grey zone. This is especially important for those western companies, which source in China for the Chinese market. The fact that since 2005 manufacturers are also represented on the board of GFSI can explain the high motivation to gain a stronger foothold in the Chinese market, as sourcing on the Chinese market is more relevant for manufacturers compared to retailers. A full benchmarking of China HACCP would have made a more substantial impact in this regard. However, credibility is a fundamentally important factor for GFSI: the organization and the companies participating in its governance seem reluctant to risk it by fully benchmarking China HACCP.

For the Chinese government, there are three separate motivations for interacting with GFSI. First, benchmarking seems to be the government's strategy to overcome the situation of unlicensed TPS in China. By benchmarking its own standards, the Chinese government potentially regains control over the usage and proliferation of TPS in China – a level of control that was initially envisaged by the respective national law.[100] Second, TPS support the improvement of the food safety situation in the market.[101] TPS are a source for improved rule setting and third-party certification is a way to improve implementation and enforcement as audits can complement state inspections. The introduction of third-party certification for Chinese voluntary standards indicates the motivation to make use of this mechanism.[102] Further supporting this argument is the fact that the CNCA initially approached GlobalGAP as part of the government's attempt to improve food safety.[103] The revision of the FSL

---

[98] Interview 29.

[99] GFSI, 'GFSI Focus Day: June 26, 2013 – Beijing, China' (2013), accessed 28 November 2016 at http://www.infoexevents.com.cn/gfsichina/; similar points have been made in interviews 24, 26 and 29.

[100] Especially State Council of the People's Republic of China 1.11.2003 #1403.

[101] Interview 29.

[102] Shen (n 7).

[103] Interview 32.

in 2014 confirmed this trend by introducing the concept of shared responsibility, highlighting also food businesses' obligation to ensure the safety of food.[104] A Chinese government official pointed out a third motivation, namely that the acceptance of China HACCP by GFSI facilitates exports by Chinese food producers to international markets.[105] The interest of the Chinese government and the private actors behind GFSI thus converge on the issue of the transfer of standards on a rule level to China, and they agree on an increased private involvement in implementation and enforcement. However, their interests diverge on the question of governmental control over the certification system.

What are the Mechanisms and Instruments?

The central mechanism is the benchmarking of Chinese standards organized by GlobalGAP and more recently by GFSI. To understand how this hybridization works as well as its degree, the fact that a government authority owns the Chinese standards is of central importance. While the Chinese government seeks recognition of voluntary standards it has set itself through foreign private organizations (that is, GlobalGAP and GFSI), the degree to which these organizations recognize these standards is limited.[106] GFSI and GlobalGAP interacted quite intensively with CNCA during the respective benchmarking processes. In both cases, private western organizations supported the CNCA in developing new voluntary public standards. It is important to note that in neither of the two cases had the governance system behind the Chinese voluntary standards been accepted by 2015. Somewhat ironically, this limitation is due to the two other hybridization mechanisms – the licensing of TPS by CNCA and the accreditation of certification bodies by CNAS.

What is the Character of Interaction?

Hybridization in China includes elements of competition, coordination and co-option.[107] Without the recognition of technical equivalence, TPS

---

[104] Kai Kottenstede, '食品安全监管是政府和企业共同的责任 (Food safety regulation is the shared responsibility of the government and business)' *China Social Sciences Today* (21 November 2014), accessed 28 November 2016 at http://sub.cssn.cn/xk/xk_tp/201411/t20141121_1409544.shtml.

[105] Interview 36.

[106] Interview 36.

[107] For a discussion of these characteristics see Verbruggen and Havinga, Chapter 1 in this volume and Burkard Eberlein and others, 'Transnational Business

and Chinese voluntary standards competed with each other. The technical benchmarking includes aspects of coordination and co-option. It is a form of coordination as both sides work together to develop robust Chinese voluntary standards based on internationally accepted standards for food safety. At the same time, it represents a co-option of a public standard by a private institution *on request of the public side.* ChinaGAP and China HACCP purposely adopt standards and procedures set by GlobalGAP and GFSI, respectively. This co-option is potentially temporary though. GFSI can withdraw the recognition of China HACCP as being technically equivalent if, for example, China HACCP does not adopt changes contained in the regularly revised GFSI guidance document.[108] CNCA thus has some pressure to maintain the status of China HACCP as being technically equivalent. Likewise, whenever the guidance document is updated, GFSI has to re-evaluate China HACCP. Thus, the benchmarking process binds both sides together.

Outside of this interaction, however, an element of competition between public and private regulation remains as the Chinese government keeps the public food safety standards in national laws completely separate from the system of voluntary standards. All market participants have to comply with public regulation, but differences in effectivity of implementation and enforcement carry the potential of a competition over trustworthiness of food safety regulation in the market.

What are the Results and Effects?

Foremost, the benchmarking procedures and associated interactions have led to a transfer of standards and food safety concepts from GlobalGAP and GFSI to China's public voluntary standards. With the status of technically equivalent, China's voluntary public standards become more attractive for Chinese food businesses because it enhances the international recognition of the standard. Chinese certification bodies are likely to offer certifications for China HACCP, rather than for GFSI recognized schemes, as obtaining the required license agreement with the respective scheme owner is more difficult and costly. This may in effect lead to an increased usage of third-party certification within the Chinese market, supporting the government's approach of increased shared responsibility for food safety between government and businesses.

Governance Interactions: Conceptualization and Framework for Analysis' (2014) 8(1) *Regulation & Governance* 1.

[108] GFSI, 'Guidance Document' (n 17).

However, the success of China HACCP will be limited to the domestic Chinese market. Given the scepticism about the quality of audits in China and lack of a full benchmarking, western companies may simply not accept China HACCP.[109] As with ChinaGAP, these companies are still likely to demand certifications for schemes fully recognized by GFSI from Chinese suppliers. Alternatively, they may organize their own auditing procedures to complement China HACCP certification. Therefore, the acceptance as technical equivalent will not push TPS from the Chinese market. However, it may limit the further development of TPS within the Chinese market – that is between Chinese suppliers and buyers – because for these market actors, China HACCP might be more attractive. The stagnation of GlobalGAP certificates in China, and the comparably successful rise of ChinaGAP point to this direction (Table 10.1). Yet another result of the situation is that the Chinese government is likely to long for full recognition of its voluntary standards. The CNCA's recent request for a full benchmarking of ChinaGAP by GlobalGAP indicates this. This has the consequence that GlobalGAP, and potentially GFSI, will need to balance carefully their organizational interests in guarding their credibility with the interest of Board members to expand their presence on the Chinese market.

What are the Changes over Time?

Interaction in terms of exchanges between the GFSI personnel and Chinese officials overall has intensified. Public regulation in China has increasingly put more emphasis on business responsibility, which provided the foundation for public-private interactions. However, the most important change over time is the change in the character of interaction, which changed from competition to coordination and at times co-option through the benchmarking activities of GlobalGAP and GFSI in relation to ChinaGAP and China HACCP respectively.

CONCLUSION: CROSSING THE RIVER BY FEELING THE STONES

Hybridization of food safety regulation in China is limited to public voluntary standards, which are an important part of China's strategy to improve food safety locally. The hybridization in this restricted area,

---

[109] Interview 26.

however, has become intense. The Chinese government asks private actors to accept their public standard to be treated as equal to TPS. This way, China potentially gets some of the credibility that GFSI recognized schemes enjoy, while at the same time limiting western industry involvement in the governance of private standards within China. Thus, the type of hybridization identified for China's food safety regulation differs from the types of hybridization identified elsewhere, such as in Europe and the United States.[110] The specific points of difference are the public ownership of voluntary standards and the strict regulation of and control over certification bodies. So, while there are signs of hybridization, it should be seen as hybridization with Chinese characteristics.

From the viewpoint of the theoretical debate, a number of points stand out. First, the analysis confirms that transnational regulatory governance needs to be interpreted in national regulatory contexts to gain effect. Looking at the benchmarking mechanism only with regard to the technical rules included in the standards would be misleading. The critical point is the integrity of the enforcement. In this context, this chapter also illustrated the analytical advantage of unpacking TPS into its separate elements. The character of public-private interaction differs depending on whether the substantive rules, the scheme owner or related certification bodies are analysed. Here, analysing the role of certification bodies provides deeper insights into the motivations and interests of hybridization.[111] While the analysis highlighted some aspects, additional research on the role and interests of certification bodies seems to be necessary. Also the mechanism of benchmarking invites further research. It accumulates power at organizations like the GFSI that conduct benchmarking. Understanding the (conflicts of) interests and the governance system better would greatly help in judging the development and limits of regulatory hybridization.

This, of course, is not the end of the story of TPS in China and the question about the changes in public-private interaction over time may in fact be the most interesting. China's governmental actors have an interest in full recognition of their standards by the global market players.

---

[110] Terry Marsden and others, *The New Regulation and Governance of Food: Beyond the Food Crisis?* (vol 29, Routledge 2010) and Lytton and McAllister, Chapter 4 in this volume.

[111] See also David Levi-Faur and Shana M. Starobin, 'Transnational Politics and Policy: From Two-Way to Three-Way Interactions' (Jerusalem 2014). Jerusalem Papers in Regulation & Governance Working 62 and Fagotto, Chapter 3 in this volume.

Table 10.3 Expert interviews

No.	Affiliation	Year	Place
1	EU public organisation	2014	Beijing
2	EU public organisation	2014	Beijing
3	EU public organisation	2014	Beijing
4	Private standard organisation	2014	Beijing
5	Private standard organisation	2014	Cologne
6	European retailer	2014	Düsseldorf (by phone)
7	European retailer	2014	Shanghai
8	German public organisation	2014	Frankfurt (by phone)
9	European certification body	2014	Shanghai (by phone)
10	Private standard organisation	2014	Cologne (by phone)
11	Private standard organisation	2014	Shanghai
12	Expert from EU member state government	2014	Shanghai
13	Chinese government	2014	Shanghai
14	European food producer	2014	Shanghai
15	Chinese university	2014	Beijing
16	European industry association	2014	Shanghai
17	EU member state government	2014	Berlin
18	Chinese government	2015	Beijing
19	Chinese government	2015	Beijing
20	Chinese university	2015	Beijing
21	Chinese government	2015	Beijing
22	German public organisation	2015	Beijing
23	German public organisation	2015	Beijing
24	European certification body	2015	Kuala Lumpur
25	EU Commission	2015	Kuala Lumpur
26	Private standard organisation	2015	Kuala Lumpur
27	Private standard organisation	2015	Kuala Lumpur
28	German public organisation	2015	Kuala Lumpur
29	Private standard organisation	2015	Paris (by phone)
30	EU commission	2015	Brussels
31	EU commission	2015	Brussels
32	Chinese university	2015	Beijing
33	Chinese certification body	2015	Beijing
34	Chinese retailer organisation	2015	Beijing
35	International governmental organisation	2015	Beijing
36	Chinese government	2015	Beijing
37	European retailer	2015	Shanghai
38	German public organisation	2016	Bremen (by phone)

Source: Authors' own.

Technical equivalence may only have been a first step, following a strategy the former president of China, Deng Xiaoping, famously described as 'crossing the river by feeling the stones'.[112]

[112] Anonymous, 'Cross the River by Feeling the Stones', China Radio International (31 October 2008), accessed 28 November 2016 at http://english.cri.cn/3126/2008/10/31/53s419839.htm.

11 Domestic responses to transnational private governance: The Marine Stewardship Council in Alaska, Australia and Ecuador

Agni Kalfagianni and Tiffany Andrade Roche

1. INTRODUCTION

Private transnational governance, the rules and standards developed by non-state actors of more than two countries in order to address challenges in a particular issue area, has proliferated in recent years particularly in the sustainability domain.[1] Yet while earlier efforts have focused on the particular characteristics of transnational private governance institutions in order to understand their potential to contribute to the provision of sustainability objectives, more recently scholars have started to examine their interaction with public actors and institutions. Indeed, far from existing and functioning independently from states, private institutions interact synergistically or antagonistically with them.

The concept of 'hybridization of governance' refers particularly to the interplay between public and private actors in institutional arrangements emerging in a particular sector.[2] Hybridization can be visualized in the form of the 'governance triangle' proposed by Abbott and Snidal[3] which

[1] Tim Bartley, 'Certification as a Mode of Social Regulation', in D. Levi-Faur (ed.), *Handbook on the Politics of Regulation* (Edward Elgar 2011); Axel Marx, 'Global Governance and the Certification Revolution: Types, Trends and Challenges' in Levi-Faur 2011 (op. cit); Boudewijn Derkx and Pieter Glasbergen, 'Elaborating Global Private Meta-Governance: An Inventory in the Realm of Voluntary Sustainability Standards' (2014) 27 *Global Environmental Change* 41.

[2] Paul Verbruggen and Tetty Havinga, Chapter 1 in this volume.

[3] Kenneth Abbott and Duncan Snidal, 'The Governance Triangle: Regulatory Standards Institutions in the Shadow of the State' in W. Mattli and N. Woods (eds), *The Politics of Global Regulation* (Princeton University Press 2009) 44–88, 50.

depicts a combination of institutional arrangements based on the actors involved in regulatory standard setting (states, civil society and firms). As this chapter focuses on the Marine Stewardship Council (MSC), our analysis refers in particular to zone 6 of this triangle including institutions that involve collaboration between firms and civil society organizations. The chapter explores how this hybridity in standard setting gains an additional or deeper lever of hybridity when implemented at domestic level, where it interacts with state regulation and policies.

The central question of this chapter is how state actors respond, that is, support or constrain, private transnational governance institutions (such as those situated in Zone 6 of the governance triangle) and what explains these responses. The chapter focuses on the MSC as the world's leading transnational certification program for sustainable wild capture fish.[4] MSC fisheries account for 10 per cent of the annual global harvest with 8.8 million metric tons of seafood.[5] The objective of the MSC is to promote socio-economic incentives for sustainable fisheries and to address declining fish stocks.[6] In 2011, 61 per cent of fisheries were fully fished and 29 per cent were overfished.[7,8]

Via a selection of cases, and on the basis of a literature review and interviews with selected stakeholders, this chapter examines state responses to the MSC standard and their variation on the basis of three main indicators: (a) creation of public funds to support certification with the MSC; (b) cooption of the MSC standard within public policies; and (c) development of domestic certification schemes as a reaction to the MSC supported by states.

In order to explain variation the chapter uses a number of criteria derived from the literature of transnational governance:[9] (a) the standard's

---

[4] Lars H. Gulbrandsen, 'The Emergence and Effectiveness of the Marine Stewardship Council' (2009) 33 *Marine Policy* 654.

[5] Marine Stewardship Council, 'The MSC in Numbers' (2015), accessed 28 November 2016 at https://www.msc.org/business-support/key-facts-about-msc.

[6] Fred Gale and Marcus Haward, 'Public Accountability in Private Regulation: Contrasting Models of the Forest Stewardship Council (FSC) and Marine Stewardship Council (MSC)', *Australasian Political Studies Association Conference* (2004), accessed 28 November 2016 at https://www.adelaide.edu.au/apsa/docs_papers/Pub%20Pol/Gale-Haward.pdf.

[7] Overfished: fish stocks fished at a biologically unsustainable level [Food and Agricultural Organization (FAO) *The State of the World Fisheries and Aquaculture: Opportunities and Challenges* (FAO 2014)].

[8] Food and Agricultural Organization (FAO) *The State of the World Fisheries and Aquaculture: Opportunities and Challenges* (FAO 2014).

[9] Agni Kalfagianni and others, 'National Responses to Transnational Governance: The Regulatory Effects of Fisheries and Aquaculture Certification in Sweden, Norway and Iceland', *General ECPR Conference* (2013); Lars H.

perceived credibility; (b) complementarity to public regulation; and (c) the importance of the standard for international trade and market access.

Empirically the chapter focuses on Alaska (USA), Australia and Ecuador. These states provide sufficient variation regarding their responses to the MSC certification and are themselves sufficiently diverse, thus allowing us to better understand both the observed variation and the reasons behind it.

Alaska was included in this study given that it has two major MSC certified fisheries: pollock and salmon. However, in recent years, there has been a lot of discussion about the relevance of the MSC standard for Alaska, to the extent that in 2012, salmon fisheries dropped MSC certification in favor of the state-based Alaska's Marketing Seafood Institute Responsible Fisheries Program. In contrast, in Australia and specifically Western Australia the MSC certification has experienced an increasing acceptance and support from state actors. The inclusion of Ecuador gives some insight into the current situation of developing countries which struggle to become MSC certified.

For this study 13 semi-structured interviews were conducted during the months of May and June 2014. These were targeted at staff from local governments, WWF, industry associations and Regional Fisheries Management Organizations (RFMOs).[10] Specifically, we conducted interviews with three representatives from industry associations in Alaska, and more specifically from the Alaskan Seafood Market Institute (ASMI), At-Sea Processors Association (APA) and the Alaska Fisheries Development Foundation (AFDF). In addition, we conducted three interviews with representatives from the National Oceanic and Atmospheric Administration (NOAA) in Alaska, and the Alaska Department of Fish and Game (ADF&G). We were not able to reach as many stakeholders in Australia and Ecuador. For the Australian case we carried out one interview with a representative from Austral Fisheries (industry) and one with the Western Australian Department of Fisheries representative. For Ecuador, we conducted one interview with an RFMO representative from the Inter-American Tropical Tuna Commission (IATTC) and a former employee from the Ministry of Agriculture, Livestock, Aquaculture and Fisheries. In all cases interviews were conducted with regional WWF representatives as well.

Gulbrandsen, 'Dynamic Governance Interactions: Evolutionary Effects of State Responses to Non-State Certification Programs' (2014) 8 *Regulation & Governance* 74.

[10] We tried to contact RFMOs in all regions but we only got a response from the Inter-American Tropical Tuna Commission (IATTC).

The rest of the chapter is structured as follows. Section 2 presents the analytical framework that is used to identify and explain the responses of state actors to private transnational governance. Section 3 applies this framework to identify and explain the effects of the MSC in three selected cases, namely Alaska (USA), Australia and Ecuador. Conclusions are drawn in Section 4.

2. ANALYTICAL FRAMEWORK

The relationship between public and private governance is complex. Scholars have initially explained this relationship following two main lines: first, 'crowding out' of government regulation and obstruction of the expansion of citizenship rights[11] and second, strengthening of state regulation as a result of private rules and standards.[12] More recently, other scholars have explored this subject from more varied perspectives, levels, and empirical foci.[13] In this context, Abbott and Snidal examine how international (rather than state) regulation may be strengthened by transnational forms of governance.[14] Conversely, Verbruggen examines how the presence of state regulatory capacity may be a basic condition for the effectiveness of private transnational governance.[15] Gulbrandsen uses a historical perspective to analyse different state responses to fisheries and forestry transnational standard schemes along different stages of the regulatory process.[16] From a legal perspective Bartley examines 'layering', that is, the interrelation of domestic law, with labor and private forestry standards in Indonesia.[17] Similarly, Black explores legitimacy and

---

[11] Tim Bartley, 'Certification as a Mode of Social Regulation', in David Levi-Faur (ed.), *Handbook on the Politics of Regulations* (Edward Elgar 2016).

[12] David Vogel, 'The Private Regulation of Global Corporate Conduct: Achievements and Limitations' (2009) 49 *Business & Society* 68.

[13] Kalfagianni and others, 'National Responses to Transnational Governance' (n 9).

[14] Kenneth Abbott and Duncan Snidal, 'Strengthening International Regulation through Transnational New Governance: Overcoming the Orchestration Deficit' (2009) *Vanderbilt Journal of International Law* 501.

[15] Paul Verbruggen 'Gorillas in the Closet? Public and Private Actors in the Enforcement of Transnational Private Regulation' (2013) 7 *Regulation & Governance* 512.

[16] Lars H. Gulbrandsen, 'Dynamic Governance Interactions: Evolutionary Effects of State Responses to Non-State Certification Programs' (2014) 8 *Regulation & Governance* 74.

[17] Tim Bartley, 'Transnational Governance as the Layering of Rules: Intersections of Public and Private Standards' (2011) *Theoretical Inquiries in Law* 517.

accountability relationships by focusing on the institutional environment; the dialectical nature of accountability relationships; and the structures of communication through which accountability and legitimacy are created.[18]

In this context, we are particularly interested in the extent to which state responses to transnational private governance enable or constrain the latter's authority and the reasons behind variation in such responses. The framework elaborated in order to systematically examine state responses to the MSC is explained in some detail below.

2.1 State Responses

We use the following indicators in order to examine state responses that support or constrain the authority of transnational private governance: (a) development of public funds; (b) cooption of private standards within public regulation; and (c) development of domestic standards as a counter reaction supported by states.[19] Additionally, states can influence the demand side through public procurement policies that promote the purchase of certified products.[20] However, our interviews reveal that this did not play a role in the cases under study; hence it is excluded from our analysis.

Development of public funds

Costs of certification have been identified as one of the major constraints for the adoption of transnational private governance. Regarding the MSC in particular, a report from FAO indicates that costs can range from around US$ 10,000 for a small fishery to US$ 250,000 for a large one.[21] For instance, the Alaska pollock fishery, one of the largest certified fisheries worldwide, paid approximately US$ 500,000 in order to obtain the MSC certification.[22] The Small Cornish hand-line mackerel fishery paid US$ 15,000,[23] and the full assessment of the South African hake trawl

---

[18] Julia Black, 'Constructing and Contesting Legitimacy and Accountability in Polycentric Regulatory Regimes' (2008) 2 *Regulation & Governance* 137.

[19] See also Kalfagianni and others, 'National Responses to Transnational Governance' (n 9); Paul Foley, 'National Government Responses to Marine Stewardship Council (MSC) Fisheries Certification: Insights from Atlantic Canada' (2013) 18 *New Political Economy* 284.

[20] Gulbrandsen, 'Dynamic Governance Interactions' (n 16).

[21] FAO, *The State of the World Fisheries and Aquaculture* (n 7).

[22] ibid.

[23] Food and Water Europe, 'De-Coding Seafood Eco-Labels: How the European Commission Can Help' (2011) <http://www.foodandwaterwatch.org/reports/de-coding-seafood-eco-labels-europe/> accessed 4 August 2012.

industry cost GBP 50,000 (around US$ 78,000).[24] To estimate the overall costs of certification one also needs to add annual audits and management expenses.[25] For instance, the South African hake trawl industry annual assessments cost GBP 20,000 (approximately US$ 31,000).[26]

Accordingly, public actors may decide to support private standards by providing public funds for certification. Indicatively, in the mid-2000s the UK government offered direct financial support to the MSC.[27] More recently, New Zealand created the 'Environmental Certification Fund' paying up to 75 per cent of the costs of certification for the MSC or Friend of the Sea (a competitive fisheries certification program). Moreover, taking advantage of the resources provided for environmental projects by the European Union, some countries have supported their fisheries certification. In particular, the Dutch Parliament approved in 2009 €1.5 million for fishery certification seeking MSC certification for all the fisheries in the North Sea by 2012.[28]

Cooption of private standards within public regulation

The authority of private standards relies to some extent on how well they are integrated in governmental policy making.[29] Indeed, the inclusion of private standards into public policies can provide them with legitimacy. Likewise, governments can use standards as benchmarks or as best practice references in their on-going policy development.[30]

---

[24] Andre Standing, *The Growth In Certification Of Marine Fisheries In Southern Africa* (Institute for Security Studies 2009).

[25] Wendy Goyert, Raphael Sagarin and John Annala, 'The Promise and Pitfalls of Marine Stewardship Council Certification: Maine Lobster as a Case Study' (2010) 34 *Marine Policy* 1103.

[26] Standing (n 24).

[27] Paul Foley, 'National Government Responses to Marine Stewardship Council (MSC) Fisheries Certification: Insights from Atlantic Canada' (2013) 18 *New Political Economy* 284.

[28] Kalfagianni, 'National Responses to Transnational Governance' (n 9).

[29] Ian Bartle and Peter Vass, 'Self-regulation within the Regulatory State: Towards a New Regulatory Paradigm?' (2007) 85 *Public Administration* 885; Marc Allen Eisner, 'Private Environmental Governance in Hard Times: Markets For Virtue And The Dynamics Of Regulatory Change' (2011) 12 *Theoretical Inquiries in Law* 489; Bryne Purchase, 'The Political Economy Of Voluntary Codes, *Voluntary Codes: Private Governance, the Public Interest and Innovation* (Carleton Research Unit for Innovation, Science and Environment, Carleton University 2004); Dara O'Rourke, 'Outsourcing Regulation: Analyzing Nongovernmental Systems of Labor Standards and Monitoring' (2003) 31 *Policy Studies Journal* 1; Vogel (n 12).

[30] Foley (n 27).

For example, in the mid-2000s, several European governments shifted from skepticism to support of the MSC program. Norway, the United Kingdom, Denmark, the Netherlands and Sweden have included the certification as part of their sea food policy and have also provided funding for certification.[31] In 2007, the Canadian federal Department of Fisheries and Oceans (DFO) made eco-labelling and certification a basis of its Oceans to Plate policy strategy which objective was to assure that sustainable management systems were adopted to secure eco-certifications. This was accompanied by government documents which, more or less, were officially endorsing the MSC.[32] We see similar developments in forestry. In Sweden where certification is considered vital for the achievement of public policy objectives, for example, due to the implementation of forest certification standards the Parliament reached its goal of preserving half million hectares of high conservation value five years before its original deadline of 2010.[33]

Development of domestic standards as counter reaction

States may react against transnational private standards and may cooperate with national private actors in the development of territorial alternatives.[34] A number of examples illustrate this case. Scandinavian countries, for example, were initially skeptical of the MSC because they believed it 'was undermining countries' regulatory jurisdiction over marine resources'.[35] Consequently, the Nordic Council of Ministers created a working group in the late 1990s that was in charge of the development of the Guidelines for the Eco-labelling of Fish and Fishery Products from Marine Wild Capture Fisheries adopted by the UN FAO in 2005. This represented an effort by governments to gain back control from non-governmental actors. In Sweden, state and industry rejected MSC and encouraged the development of an alternative eco-label created in 2004 and administrated by the NGO KRAV (Association for Control of Organic Production). Iceland followed a similar path, and in 2005 used the FAO guidelines as reference for the development of their own eco-label program.[36] In Japan and Alaska

---

31 Gulbrandsen, 'Dynamic Governance Interactions' (n 16).

32 Foley (n 27).

33 Gulbrandsen 'The Emergence and Effectiveness of the Marine Stewardship Council' (n 4).

34 Kalfagianni, 'National Responses to Transnational Governance' (n 9).

35 Graeme Auld, 'The Origins and Growth of Social and Environmental Certification Programs in the Fisheries Sector', *11th Annual Conference of the International Society for New Institutional Economics* (2007), accessed 28 November 2016 at http://www.isnie.org/assets/files/papers2007/auld.pdf, 29.

36 Foley (n 27).

(USA) certifications schemes for wild capture fisheries have emerged with the support of the government.[37]

2.2 Explaining State Responses

Based on the literature on transnational governance we identify the following explanatory factors for state responses to private standards: (a) the standard's perceived credibility by public actors; (b) complementarity to public regulation; and (c) importance of the standard for international trade and market access.[38] We turn to these criteria in some detail below.

Perceived credibility of the standard

We hypothesize that states support standards according to their perceived credibility, that is, the recognition conferred to standard systems as a result of their effectiveness in delivering their objectives.[39] Standards rely on their credibility to gain legitimacy and to maintain authority to govern production and consumption practices in global production networks.[40] Credibility of the claims embedded in sustainability standards has become fundamental due to increasing demand for products meeting new standards and the expansion of markets and competition.[41] Practices such as inclusiveness, scientific rigor, independence and transparency contribute to label credibility.[42] Miller and Bush also underline the traceability of

---

[37] Gulbrandsen, 'Dynamic Governance Interactions' (n 16).

[38] We further inquired about the perceived relevance of the standard for the implementation of international agreements on fisheries. However, we found no evidence in favor, thus it is excluded from our analysis.

[39] ISEAL Alliance, 'Principles for Credible and Effective Sustainability Standards Systems. ISEAL Credibility Principles' (2013), accessed 28 November 2016 at http://www.isealalliance.org/sites/default/files/Credibility%20Principles%20v1.0%20low%20res.pdf.

[40] Alice M.M. Miller and Simon R. Bush, 'Authority without Credibility? Competition and Conflict Between Ecolabels in Tuna Fisheries' (2015) 107 *Journal of Cleaner Production* 137.

[41] Daniele Giovannucci and Stefano Ponte, 'Standards as a New Form of Social Contract? Sustainability Initiatives in the Coffee Industry' (2005) 30 *Food Policy* 284.

[42] Magnus Boström, 'Establishing Credibility: Practicing Standard-Setting Ideals in a Swedish Seafood-Labelling Case' (2006) 8 *Journal of Environmental Policy & Planning* 135; Sally Eden, 'The Work of Environmental Governance Networks: Traceability, Credibility and Certification by the Forest Stewardship Council' (2009) 40 *Geoforum* 383; Simon R. Bush and others, 'The "Devils Triangle" of MSC Certification: Balancing Credibility, Accessibility and Continuous Improvement' (2013) 37 *Marine Policy* 288; Miller and Bush (n 40).

fishing operations through the chain of custody certification as an important element of credibility.[43]

To gain credibility, the MSC became an independent organization from its founding partners (WWF and Unilever). For this, the MSC established an international Board of Trustees and started to seek funds from charities, trusts and private organizations. This allowed the standard to be seen as an essential step for gaining credibility as a neutral body in a multi-stakeholder industry.[44] The MSC, in particular, has managed to a large extent to present itself as a promoter of strictly managed fisheries. Currently, it is seen as the best fisheries ecolabel available,[45] is considered trustworthy,[46] and is taken more seriously by scientists in relation to alternatives.[47]

More recently, however, MSC's credibility is at risk of being undermined because of two main reasons. The first one is the low representation of small fisheries or fisheries from developing countries.[48] The second is that the MSC has not led to quantifiable reduction of fish stock decline.[49] Furthermore, in the long term, problems with compliance might affect credibility of the scheme, reducing its attractiveness to stakeholders committed to sustainability.[50]

The question pursued below is to what extent credibility matters in the decision of public actors to support a private transnational standard.

Complementarity to public regulation

We hypothesize further that states are more likely to support private standards which complement rather than antagonize public regulation, for example, when the state relies on the private standards for the

---

[43] Miller and Bush (n 40).

[44] Gulbrandsen, 'The Emergence and Effectiveness of the Marine Stewardship Council' (n 4).

[45] Jennifer Jacquet and Daniel Pauly, 'Funding Priorities: Big Barriers to Small-Scale Fisheries' (2008) 22 *Conservation Biology* 309.

[46] Claire Christian and others, 'A Review of Formal Objections to Marine Stewardship Council Fisheries Certifications' (2013) 161 *Biological Conservation* 10.

[47] Jacquet and Pauly (n 45).

[48] Simon R. Bush and others, 'The "Devils Triangle" of MSC Certification: Balancing Credibility, Accessibility and Continuous Improvement' (2013) 37 *Marine Policy* 288; Miller and Bush (n 40).

[49] Simon R. Bush and others, 'The "Devils Triangle" of MSC Certification' (n 48).

[50] Agni Kalfagianni and Philipp Pattberg, 'Fishing In Muddy Waters: Exploring The Conditions For Effective Governance of Fisheries and Aquaculture' (2013) 38 *Marine Policy* 124.

implementation of public policy or for the attainment of public policy objectives.[51]

In the case of fisheries, for instance, Foley highlights that governments in seafood producing countries have become interested in the MSC certification within their jurisdictions because the MSC has not promoted itself as an alternative to state management but integrated its environmental standards into the management frameworks in place.[52] Similar observations are made by Gulbrandsen who demonstrates that through the years, several governments (for example, the United Kingdom, Norway, Sweden, the Netherlands and Denmark) have decided to support the MSC program because they consider it is a useful supplement to domestic, regional and international management regimes.[53] Likewise, Ponte underlines the importance of the third core MSC principle requiring compliance with local, national and international laws and standards.[54] In addition, the development of the MSC on the basis of the FAO Code of Conduct for Responsible Fisheries was considered instrumental for its support by public actors as well.[55]

Importance for international trade and markets

We hypothesize that states will support the MSC, as they seek to secure, maintain and expand exports of domestic seafood products. Indeed, private standards have become a paramount requirement for global market access, mainly via their endorsement by global retail chains, putting pressure on governments to assign resources for the endorsement and compliance with such standards.[56] Currently, more than 35 European retailers offer MSC products and the top five retailers in North America, including Walmart, have committed to provide MSC products in the future.[57] In this regard, governments in seafood producing countries have an interest in easing commercial development of the domestic seafood industry operating within their jurisdictions.[58] For instance, one of the main reasons backing the MSC certification of Western Rock Lobster

---

[51] Gulbrandsen, 'Dynamic Governance Interactions' (n 16).

[52] Foley (n 27).

[53] Gulbrandsen, 'Dynamic Governance Interactions' (n 16).

[54] Stefano Ponte, 'The Marine Stewardship Council (MSC) and the Making of a Market for "Sustainable Fish"' (2012) 12 *Journal of Agrarian Change* 300.

[55] Gale and Haward (n 6).

[56] Kalfagianni, 'National Responses to Transnational Governance' (n 9); Ponte (n 54).

[57] Kalfagianni, 'National Responses to Transnational Governance (n 9).

[58] Foley (n 27).

Fishery in 2001, was precisely the support for market access in Europe which had been difficult for Australian producers.[59] Consumer countries are also supporting more sustainable fishing practices. For instance, the Common Fisheries Policy of the European Union aims at ensuring sustainable fishing. In this context, the MSC ecolabel is one of the paths towards a more sustainable industry.[60] In particular, the Dutch government encourages consumers to support sustainable fishing practices by buying MSC or Aquaculture Stewardship Council (ASC) certified fish.[61] More generally, the growing movement towards sustainable seafood, pressure from retailers and fear of losing markets if not certified is a major driver for supporting transnational certification.[62]

It should be noted that it is extremely difficult to estimate the amount of MSC certified fish sold in a given country or continent. The MSC's annual report 2014–15 includes consumer demand data obtained through surveys to seafood buyers from 15 countries across Asia, Australasia, Europe and North America. Accordingly, 60 per cent agree that buying sustainable seafood ensures fish stocks for future generations, 41 per cent look for fish products from sustainable sources and 33 per cent recognize the MSC ecolabel. The highest recognition was in Germany (58 per cent) and Switzerland (57 per cent).[63]

3. CASE STUDIES

3.1 Alaska

In Alaska a total of 21 fisheries are MSC certified, at the time of writing this chapter. Two of them are Pollock, one in the Eastern Bering Sea[64] and

---

59 Marcus Haward, 'State, Market and Community: Managing Australia's Fisheries' (2009) 21 *Dialogue* (Academy of the Social Sciences in Australia).

60 European Youth Portal, see https://europa.eu/youth/EU/voluntary-activities/european-voluntary-service_en, accessed 28 November 2016.

61 Government of the Netherlands, 'Dutch Fisheries Policy', accessed 28 November 2016 at https://www.government.nl/topics/fisheries/contents/dutch-fisheries-policy.

62 Goyert, Sagarin and Annala (n 25).

63 Marine Stewardship Council, 'Annual Report 2014–2015' (2015), accessed 28 November 2016 at https://www.msc.org/business-support/msc-annual-report.

64 Marine Stewardship Council, 'Alaska Pollock – Bering Sea and Aleutian Islands' (2015), accessed 28 November 2016 at https://fisheries.msc.org/en/fisheries/.

the other one in the Gulf of Alaska.[65] Salmon includes six certified fisheries, with sockeye, chum, chinook, coho and pink.[66] In the Gulf of Alaska there are five flatfish certified fisheries: flathead sole, arrowtooth flounder, rex sole, Northern rock sole and Southern rock sole.[67] In the Bering Sea and Aleutian Island there are six additional flatfish certified fisheries (yellowfin sole, flathead sole, arrowtooth flounder, Alaska plaice, Kamchatka flounder and Northern rock sole.[68] There are two cod certified fisheries, one in the Gulf of Alaska and the other one in the Pacific Ocean.[69,70]

Responses to the MSC

Development of public funds In 1998, the MSC was interested in certifying the Alaska salmon fishery as it needed a high profile fishery to gain recognition around the world.[71] The State of Alaska was not very receptive initially but finally agreed to undergo certification with the condition that the MSC had to certify the entire Alaska salmon fishery; it was either all, or nothing.[72] In 2000 all five species of Alaska salmon[73] were certified and recertified in 2005. When Alaska salmon was first certified, the government paid US$ 300,000–$ 400,000 on behalf of the industry.[74]

---

65 Marine Stewardship Council, 'Alaska Pollock – Gulf of Alaska' (2015), accessed 28 November 2016 at https://fisheries.msc.org/en/fisheries/.

66 Marine Stewardship Council, 'Alaska Salmon' (2015), accessed 28 November 2016 at https://fisheries.msc.org/en/fisheries/.

67 Marine Stewardship Council, 'Alaska Flatfish – Gulf of Alaska' (2015), accessed 28 November 2016 at https://fisheries.msc.org/en/fisheries/.

68 Marine Stewardship Council, 'Alaska Flatfish – Bering Sea and Aleutian Islands' (2015), accessed 28 November 2016 at https://fisheries.msc.org/en/fisheries/.

69 Marine Stewardship Council, 'Alaska Pacific Cod – Gulf of Alaska' (2016), accessed 28 November 2016 at https://fisheries.msc.org/en/fisheries/.

70 Marine Stewardship Council, 'Alaska Pacific Cod – Bering Sea and Aleutian Islands' (2015), accessed 28 November 2016 at https://fisheries.msc.org/en/fisheries/.

71 Interview with James Browning, Alaska Fisheries Development Foundation (Amsterdam, The Netherlands, 20 May 2014).

72 Ibid.

73 Sockeye, Chum, Chinook, Coho and Pink (Marine Stewardship Council, 'Net Benefits the first ten years of MSC certified sustainable fisheries', available 28 November 2016 at https://www.msc.org/documents/fisheries-factsheets/net-benefits-report/net-benefits-introduction-web.pdf/view?searchterm=Net%20Benefits%20the%20first%20ten%20years%20of%20MSC%20certified%20sustainable%20fisheries.

74 Interview with Glenn Haight, Alaska Department of Fish and Game (Amsterdam, The Netherlands, 27 May 2014).

In 2008, however, the client for this fishery (ADF&G) decided to step back, and the following year the clientship was taken over by the Alaska Fisheries Development Foundation (AFDF).[75] The AFDF is a non-profit organization that represents harvesters, processors and businesses in the seafood industry. Back in 1976, after the Magnuson-Stevens Fisheries Conservation and Management Act was passed, six fishery development corporations were created with the objective of building infrastructure for the American fishery resources; the AFDF was among them.[76] The AFDF was in charge of collecting the funds for certification from the companies participating in the AFDF Salmon Coalition. These funds had to be paid to the certifier, Intertek Moody Marine (IMM). After a commitment made by the MSC in July 2011, 75 per cent of the certifiers costs would be reimbursed to the AFDF if the second certification audit was successful.[77] However, the MSC certification was not renewed in 2012.[78]

Development of domestic standards as counter reaction As previously mentioned, the certification lapsed in 2012, when eight major fish processors,[79] handling 70 per cent of the total harvest in the state, decided to pull out from the MSC in favor of a territorial certification program.[80] This decision was taken in favor of the Responsible Fisheries Management (RFM), an ecolabel created by Global Trust in collaboration with the Alaska Seafood Marketing Institute[81] (ASMI).[82] Alaska's wild salmon

---

75 Alaska Fisheries Development Foundation, 'MSC Salmon Program' (2012), accessed 28 November 2016 at http://www.afdf.org/msc-salmon-press-release/; Browning (n 71).

76 Alaska Fisheries Development Foundation, Inc., 'About AFDF', accessed 28 November 2016 at http://www.afdf.org/about/.

77 Alaska Fisheries Development Foundation, 'MSC Certification Updates-December 2011' (2011) < http://www.afdf.org/sustainabilityupdate12232011/ > accessed 30 November 2016

78 Hall Bernton, 'Alaska Salmon Industry pulls out of Sustainable Fisheries Certification Program' *The Seattle Times* (2016) <http://www.seattletimes.com/business/alaska-salmon-industry-pulls-out-of-sustainable-fisheries-certification-program/> accessed 8 February 2016.

79 Trident Seafoods, Icicle Seafoods, Ocean Beauty Seafoods, Peter Pan Seafoods, Alaska General Seafoods, E & E Foods, Kwikpak Fisheries and North Pacific Seafood (AFDF, 2012).

80 Bernton (n 78).

81 ASMI is a marketing organization with the mission of increasing the economic value of the Alaska seafood resource (Alaska Seafood 'About', accessed 28 November 2016 at http://pressroom.alaskaseafood.org/about/.

82 David Jolly, 'Salmon Fishermen Battle Walmart on Certification' *The New York Times* (2013), accessed 28 November 2016 at http://www.nytimes.

fishing industry argued that this decision would save money and reduce the 'outside' interference in business since they did not need any *European* NGO to confirm the sustainability status of their fisheries[83] (our emphasis). In other words, there was a concern that private transnational standards, such as the MSC, were undermining the mandate of the competent authority managing the fisheries.[84] Accordingly, the MSC's role was considered more constructive in fisheries where appropriate governance tools were not in place.[85]

Supporting this perspective, in June 2014, the US Senate Appropriations Committee passed the Commerce, Justice and Science 2015 funding bill, including a number of provisions regarding Alaska's fishing industry. The bill maintains funding of US$ 30.2 million for salmon management activities, and includes US$ 72.2 million in expanded stock assessments and US$ 24.4 million for survey and monitoring projects within the fisheries research and management account. Importantly, the bill does not support transnational certification programs like the MSC as it forbids federal agencies from using outside groups to certify fish caught in US waters.[86] Senator Lisa Murkowski in particular argued that:

> The committee (US Senate Appropriations Committee) acknowledges that some U.S. fisheries voluntarily utilize third-party seafood sustainability certification schemes but believes it is not the (federal government's) role to adopt such certification schemes when doing so could result in the (government) arbitrarily influencing the domestic seafood market.[87]

In fact, according to our interviews the state is trying to demonstrate that refraining from the MSC certification does not imply the fishery is not sustainably managed.[88]

In addition to the ASMI label, fisheries from the East Coast of the United States have been pressing the National Marine Fisheries Service

---

com/2013/10/22/business/salmon-fishermen-battle-walmart-on-certification.html?_r=3&.

[83] Interview with Alison Cross, WWF (Amsterdam, The Netherlands, 15 May 2014).

[84] Interview with Randy Rice, WWF (Amsterdam, The Netherlands, 6 June 2014).

[85] Interview with C Oliver (Amsterdam, The Netherlands, 22 May 2014).

[86] Seafood Source, 'Senate Committee Passes Alaska Fisheries Funding' (2014), accessed 28 November 2016 at http://www.seafoodsource.com/news/supply-trade/26270-senate-committee-passes-alaska-fisheries-funding.

[87] Seafood Source (n 86); Jolly (n 82).

[88] Haight (n 74).

to develop a public certification program, where the Federal Fishery Management Agency will certify any fishery managed by the US Fisheries Management Act (Magnuson-Stevens Act). This is not supported by everybody – there have been bills put forward to try to get this process going but a big portion of the industry and NGOs raised concerns about the costs and credibility of this program.[89] Supporters highlight, however, that from an industry perspective a governmental stamp of approval carries a lot of weight; it is expected to be cheaper and better than transnational certification because it is recognized by the local customers.[90] At the time of writing this chapter, we have no further information about further developments in this regard.

In sum, while the MSC remains an option for Alaskan fisheries, Alaska salmon, in particular, has been at the center of a heated debate regarding the desirability of transnational certification. This case demonstrates clearly that when a domestic alternative is available, supported by public actors, in a strong local market, the authority of transnational private certification is not necessarily guaranteed.

Explaining responses

Perceived credibility of the standard The MSC standard has been criticized by client fisheries, APA, and NGOs for inconsistent fishery assessments.[91] In particular, the Alaskan seafood industry has accused the MSC of lack of transparency, high costs and inconsistent standards.[92] Discontent started with the Alaska Pollock fishery which was certified in 2005 despite an ongoing litigation regarding the endangered Steller sea lion population.[93] Furthermore, the MSC certified Russian Pollock against the objection of At-Sea Processor Association in 2013.[94]

Criticism about compliance with the MSC principles in Alaska further discredited the standard in the eyes of the critics. More specifically, MSC's Principle 1 states that a 'fishery must be conducted in a manner that does

---

89 Cross (n 83).

90 Oliver (n 85).

91 Jim Gilmore, 'Case Study 3: MSC Certification Of The Alaska Pollock Fishery', *Seafood Ecolabelling: Principles and Practice* (Wiley-Blackwell 2008).

92 'MSC Hits Back to ASMI for "Negative and Inaccurate Statements" accessed 28 November 2016 at http://www.atuna.com/index.php/environment/43-environmental-news/73-msc-hits-back-to-asmi-for-negative-and-inaccurate-statements.

93 Gilmore (n 91).

94 Browning (71).

not lead to over-fishing or depletion of the exploited populations and, for those populations that are depleted, the fishery must be conducted in a manner that demonstrably leads to their recovery'.[95] Nevertheless, the Bering Sea Pollock fishery, certified in 2005, experienced a decreased population by 64 per cent by 2009.[96] In addition, MSC's Principle 3 requires fisheries to respect local, national and international law.[97] Yet several court rulings have indicated that the Gulf of Alaska Pollock fishery has not been in compliance with the national law.[98] In fact, after certification of the Gulf of Alaska and Bering Sea Pollock fisheries, bycatch of Chinook salmon exceeded the legal limits several times. In 2007, more than 35,000 Chinook salmon were caught as bycatch in the Gulf of Alaska Pollock fishery and 120,000 in the Bering Sea Pollock fishery.[99]

These developments resulted in the MSC losing some of its credibility among its relevant target group.[100] Despite voices arguing that the domestic Responsible Fisheries Management standard is not necessarily more credible as it is an industry developed and controlled program,[101] critics claim that the MSC is 'not the Holy Grail'; and that 'it should undergo some quality control to determine whether or not it is an appropriate verification standard'.[102] These arguments, were utilized by the salmon processors in order to support their decision to exit the program. However, this is only part of the explanation. Indeed, as explained below MSC's expansive demands to include salmon hatcheries in the assessment process and a large domestic market for salmon sympathetic to national interests provide further reasoning.

Complementarity to public regulation In the United States the management of fisheries follows a federal approach, so in each region or state fisheries are managed by separate organizations which develop management regulations that are then submitted to the US Secretary of Commerce

---

[95] MSC, 'MSC Fishery Standard: Principles & Criteria and Criteria for Sustainable Fishing' (2010) < https://www.msc.org/documents/scheme-documents/msc-standards/MSC_environmental_standard_for_sustainable_fishing.pdf> accessed 30 November 2016.

[96] Jacquet and Pauly (n 45).

[97] https://www.msc.org/documents/quality-and-consistency-in-assessments/Guide%20to%20P-Cs-SC-PIs.pdf/view?searchterm=PRINCIPL (22/05/2015).

[98] Christian and others (n 46).

[99] ibid.

[100] Oliver (n 85).

[101] Atuna, 'MSC Hits Back to ASMI for Negative and Inaccurate Statements' (n 92).

[102] Haight (n 74).

for approval, in compliance with national laws.[103] The US Fisheries Management Act (2006), also known as the Magnuson-Stevens Act, set rules for the management of fisheries in the country.[104] It is the primary law governing marine fisheries management in US federal waters. It mandates annual catch limits and accountability measures to end overfishing, calls for bigger international cooperation and provides for market-based fishery management.[105]

The Constitution of Alaska mandates all state resources like coal, timber, fish and mining to be managed on a sustainable basis; this is because, as was pointed out in our interviews, no other state in the United States includes sustainability laws in its constitution.[106] Accordingly, the Constitution of Alaska states that: ‘Fish, forests, wildlife, grasslands, and all other replenishable resources belonging to the State shall be utilized, developed, and maintained on the sustained yield principle, subject to preferences among beneficial uses’[107] The inclusion of sustainable yield in a Constitution written in 1959 demonstrates according to our interviews the innovative character of state legislation in Alaska.[108] This, in combination with annual catch allowances based on scientific research conducted by NOAA are considered to remove incentives for capitalizing fisheries beyond what is needed to harvest individual allocations, according to experts.[109]

In addition, in Alaska there is a system of regional fishing game advisory committees. The latter collect public concerns and requests about fisheries’ status, for example, reduction of commercial or sport fishing in places with reported low stock.[110] Once a request is received, the committees discuss and recommend regulatory changes to the Board of Fisheries, which analyses the proposals and passes the corresponding regulation.[111] Furthermore, there are very complex fishery management plans and regulations for catch monitoring and accounting which are extremely critical for the sustainability.[112] This information allows the alerting of vessels

---

[103] Gilmore (n 91).
[104] Cross (n 83); Oliver (n 85); Rice (n 84).
[105] NOAA Fisheries, ‘State/federal partnerships’ (2014), accessed 28 November 2016 at http://www.nmfs.noaa.gov/sfa/management/state_federal/index.html.
[106] Haight (n 74); Browning (n 71); Rice (n 84).
[107] Constitution of Alaska, article 8.4.
[108] Haight (n 74).
[109] Gilmore (n 91).
[110] Browning (n 71).
[111] Browning (n 71); Haight (n 74).
[112] Oliver (n 85).

about areas with bycatch and the exclusion of poor performers from specific areas for a certain period of time.[113]

Turning to the complementarity of the MSC to public regulation, detractors of the standard highlight that in Alaska, management authorities rely on legislative and constitutional mandates, science, and fisheries' expertise to manage fisheries and not on private standards.[114] Interviewees underline that Alaskan fisheries are not managed in a sustainable fashion because of a certification program, rather certification programs tend to model what has always been done in Alaska.[115] To exemplify, they argue that back in 1998, when the MSC was a brand new standard, in need of a high profile fishery for a higher market, Alaska salmon was quickly certified because the fishery had healthy stocks and was sustainably managed.[116] Furthermore, none of the federally managed Alaska fisheries included in the program needed to change their management practices to meet the standard, MSC critics argue.[117]

However, regarding salmon more specifically, the MSC is considered to have raised the bar.[118] More specifically, when the standard decided to include hatcheries as part of the assessment, during the re-certification of Alaska salmon in 2007, several conditions were levied against the fisheries, 19 of which centered on hatchery impacts on wild stock. Likewise, in 2012, it was not certain which Alaska salmon fisheries were going to be re-certified due to concerns with hatcheries. While the scientific community in Alaska had already recognized the problem, the MSC was the key element to accelerate research on and recognition of salmon hatchery concerns.[119]

In this regard, there is no agreement as to whether the MSC complements the public regulation in place. On the one hand, the MSC is considered redundant to the already stringent public regulation. On the other, it is seen as an opportunity to identify and improve deficiencies in government regulation.

Importance for international trade and market access All of the interviewees consider market access as the cornerstone for certification. Approximately two-thirds of Alaska seafood are exported to over 100

113 Gilmore (n 91).
114 Rice (n 84).
115 Haight (n 74).
116 Browning (n 71); Haight (n 74).
117 Gilmore (n 91).
118 Interview with Jim Gilmore, At-Sea Processors Association (Amsterdam, The Netherlands, 22 May 2014).
119 Rice (n 84).

countries. In 2014, seafood in Alaska accounted for 55 per cent of US seafood exports (US$ 3.2 billion).[120] The main markets for Alaska seafood are China, Japan and Europe. China is the largest primary importer; however, Alaska seafood products are not entirely consumed in the country; they are re-processed and re-exported to Europe, Japan or the United States. This leaves Japan as the major end-user consumer. Since 2011, the country has bought between US$ 682 to 786 million of Alaska seafood per year, equivalent to 20–23 per cent of the entire industry's production. Another important market is Europe; in 2013, most of the 27 EU member countries imported US$ 798 million of Alaska seafood.[121]

Salmon and Pollock have been the most relevant MSC certified fisheries in Alaska. Alaska Pollock is the largest MSC certified fishery with 60 per cent of the total certified volume.[122] After it was certified, in 2005, the MSC became a major player in the whitefish industry, supplying one-fifth of the world traded volume.[123] In 2013, Pollock accounted for 34 per cent of all Alaska seafood exports, followed by salmon, with a third of total export value.[124]

While the majority of Alaska seafood is exported, the majority of Alaska salmon is consumed in the United States.[125] In 2013, out of 1,049,705 thousand of pounds (476 thousand tons) of harvested salmon,[126] approximately 43 per cent was exported (203 thousand tons).[127] In 2012, Alaska salmon fisheries' total harvest represented 44 per cent of the global salmon volume.[128] However, the MSC certified volume decreased to 34 per cent when, in 2013, the Prince William Sound unit was excluded from

---

[120] Alaska Seafood Marketing Institute 'Economic Value of Alaska Seafood Industry' (2015) <http://ebooks.alaskaseafood.org/ASMI_Seafood_Impacts_Dec2015/pubData/source/ASMI%20Alaska%20Seafood%20Impacts%20Final%20Dec2015%20-%20low%20res.pdf > accessed 30 November 2016.

[121] Alaska Seafood, 'Alaska Seafood Export Market Analysis' (2016) < http://www.alaskaseafood.org/wp-content/uploads/2015/10/Spring2016-Alaska-Seafood-Exports-Final.pdf> accessed 30 November 2016.

[122] Jacquet and Pauly (n 45); Ponte (n 54); Gulbrandsen, 'The Emergence and Effectiveness of the Marine Stewardship Council' (n 4).

[123] Gulbrandsen, 'The Emergence and Effectiveness of the Marine Stewardship Council' (n 4).

[124] (n 121).

[125] http://www.sustainablefish.org/fisheries-improvement/supply-chain-roundtables/salmon/alaska-salmon, accessed 28 November 2016.

[126] http://www.adfg.alaska.gov/index.cfm?adfg=CommercialByFisherySalmon.exvesselquery (27-1-2016)

[127] (n 121).

[128] Pacific States Marine Fisheries Commission, 'Global Sustainability Overview of Pacific Salmon Fisheries' (2013) <http://www.psmfc.org/wp-content/

re-certification awaiting further analysis on the impact on hatcheries.[129] It is estimated that if all Alaska salmon fisheries decided to leave the MSC program, only 7 per cent of the total global salmon harvest volume would be MSC certified.[130]

The eight major processors[131] of Alaska Salmon which withdrew from the MSC salmon represented 70 per cent of the total wild salmon harvest as mentioned earlier.[132] The decision to leave the MSC program was initially threatened when Walmart decided to stop sourcing Alaska salmon not certified by the MSC. In turn, the Alaska fish industry portrayed itself as a victim of the 'anti-American purchasing policy' of Walmart and of the foreign interference of the MSC certification.[133] Fishermen put a lot of pressure on Walmart to change its sourcing policy; they involved the State Fisheries Managers, the Senate and the Congress. The disputes scaled up to the point that Senator Lisa Murkowski introduced a bill to ban federal agencies from requiring seafood to be third-party certified.[134] As previously mentioned, the US Senate Appropriations Committee passed the Commerce, Justice and Science 2015 funding bill, which forbade federal agencies from using outside groups to certify fish caught in US waters.[135] Additionally, Senator Mark Begich summoned a hearing to question companies that were threatening to stop buying Alaska salmon. There is little publicly available information about how the MSC reacted to these combined efforts. In a statement to the Seafood Business Magazine, the Vice President of Fisheries at WWF in Washington, D.C. at the time defended the MSC standard arguing that that: 'Everyone knows that, for seafood, MSC is the only credible standard, though we wish more certifications

---

uploads/2013/08/GlobalSustainabilityOverviewOfPacificSalmon.pdf> accessed 9 February 2016.

129 https://www.msc.org/track-a-fishery/fisheries-in-the-program/certified/pacific/alaska-salmon/reassessment-prince-william-sound (25-1-2015).

130 Pacific States Marine Fisheries Commission (n 128).

131 Trident Seafoods, Icicle Seafoods, Ocean Beauty Seafoods, Peter Pan Seafoods, Alaska General Seafoods, Kiwk'pak Fisheries, E&E Foods, and North Pacific Seafoods (Margaret Bauman (2012), 'Marine Stewardship Council losing ground with wild salmon fisheries' accessed 28 November 2016 at http://www.alaskadispatch.com/article/marine-stewardship-council-losing-ground-wild-salmon-fisheries.

132 Margaret Bauman (2012) <http://www.alaskadispatch.com/article/marine-stewardship-council-losing-ground-wild-salmon-fisheries> accessed 8 February 2016; Bernton (n 78).

133 Jolly (n 82).

134 Jolly (n 82).

135 Seafood Source, 'Senate Committee Passes Alaska Fisheries Funding' (2014), accessed 28 November 2016 at http://www.seafoodsource.com/news/supply-trade/26270-senate-committee-passes-alaska-fisheries-funding.

were as credible'.[136] While environmental interest groups were supportive of MSC certification, the combination of fierce campaigns and the leverage of the Alaska salmon industry as a provider of one of the most important products for major retailers in the country, led Walmart to decide to source Alaska salmon RFM certified in January 2014.[137]

3.2 Australia

Six fisheries are MSC-certified in Australia: the Macquarie Island toothfish,[138] Spencer Gulf king prawn,[139] Lakes and Coorong Fisheries,[140] Australian Western rock lobster,[141] Heard Island and McDonald Islands (HIMI) toothfish[142] and Mackerel icefish.[143] Furthermore, as of March 20, 2014, Walker Seafoods Australia is seeking certification for yellowfin tuna, Albacore tuna, swordfish and mahi mahi.[144]

Responses to the MSC in Australia

Development of public funds In 2012, the Western Australian Government in partnership with the Western Australian Fishing Industry Council (WAFIC) funded AUS$ 14.5 million for Western Australian fisheries to gain the MSC certification. This funding was split into 6.5 million for

---

136 Seafood Source, 'Beyond the Stamp' (2013), accessed 28 November 2016 at http://www.seafoodsource.com/news/supply-trade/27227-top-story-beyond-the-stamp.

137 Margaret Bauman, 'Talks begin to keep Alaska seafood on Walmart shelves' (2013) http://www.fishermensnews.com/story/2013/10/01/features/talks-begin-to-keep-alaska-seafood-on-walmart-shelves/212.html accessed 30 November 2016.

138 Marine Stewardship Council, 'Macquarie Island Toothfish' (2015), accessed 28 November 2016 at https://fisheries.msc.org/en/fisheries/.

139 Marine Stewardship Council, 'Spencer Gulf King Prawn Marine Stewardship Council' (2016), accessed 28 November 2016 at https://fisheries.msc.org/en/fisheries/.

140 Marine Stewardship Council, 'Lakes and Coorong, South Australia' (2015), accessed 28 November 2016 at https://fisheries.msc.org/en/fisheries/.

141 Marine Stewardship Council, 'Australian Western Rock Lobster' (2016), accessed 28 November 2016 at https://fisheries.msc.org/en/fisheries/.

142 Marine Stewardship Council, 'Heard Island and McDonald Islands (HIMI) Toothfish' (2015), accessed 28 November 2016 at https://fisheries.msc.org/en/fisheries/.

143 Marine Stewardship Council, 'Australia Mackerel Icefish' (2015), accessed 28 November 2016 at https://fisheries.msc.org/en/fisheries/.

144 Marine Stewardship Council, 'The MSC in Numbers Marine Stewardship Council' (2015), accessed 28 November 2016 at https://www.msc.org/business-support/key-facts-about-msc.

assessment to gain certification and 8 million for research and management.[145] The government financed the pre-assessment, full assessment and first surveillance audit, and subsequently the costs would burden the relevant fishery.[146] As a result, more than 40 fisheries benefited in their certification efforts.[147]

Cooption within public regulation Australian governments have been reluctant to officially endorse the MSC standard due to potential problems with the WTO rules regarding trade in fisheries products and the fact that the standard is set by a non-government body.[148] However, the MSC has had an important impact on the country's fisheries policies. Specifically, the government has made changes in legislation, policies and management in order to comply with the MSC.[149] Likewise, the MSC principles and criteria have influenced the format of the government's Strategic Assessment for fisheries. In this regard, the Australian fishing industry has noted that the Strategic Assessment process is executed with a higher level of scrutiny by the Australian Government as a result.[150]

Development of domestic standards as counter reaction For a long time, there has been a push from the industry to develop an Australian standard, which has been discouraged by many different parties including the WWF.[151] The perceived lack of direct benefits and the costs of the MSC certification prompted the development of industry driven approaches like the Southern Rock Lobster Clean Green program.[152] However, in contrast to the Alaskan case such efforts did not enjoy similar support neither from the relevant target group nor the state. We explore the reasons why in more detail below.

---

145 Western Australia Department of Fisheries, 'Western Australian Government Fisheries Policy Statement' (2012), accessed 28 November 2016 at http://www.fish.wa.gov.au/Documents/corporate_publications/wa_govt_fisheries_policy_statement.pdf.

146 Interview with Heather Brayford, Western Australia Department of Fisheries (Amsterdam, The Netherlands, 6 June 2014).

147 Interview with Peter Trott, WWF (Amsterdam, The Netherlands, 8 May 2014); Brayford (n 146).

148 Haward (n 59).

149 Trott (n 147); Brayford (n 146).

150 Haward (n 59).

151 Trott (n 147); Brayford (n 146).

152 Haward (n 59).

Explaining responses in Australia

Perceived credibility of the standard All interviewees consider credibility a crucial aspect when choosing to support/endorse a standard. In the words of one interviewee, 'If the standard cannot deliver a credible, scientifically robust, defendable, transparent, rigorous, consistent, measure of fisheries in its portfolio of certified fisheries then it is not worth investing in'.[153] In this context, another source states that the third-party nature of the MSC provides such trust and confidence to the general public that fisheries are under sustainable management.[154] Moreover, other commentators argue that the third-party assessment of the fisheries ensures they are meeting sustainability standards.[155] Testifying to that perception, the Western Australia government has decided to have all its fisheries assessed by the MSC because it makes processes much more explicit and transparent – thus credible – for the community and industry.[156] In addition, and in contrast to the Alaskan case, Australian consumers have resisted industry and public-led standards as they have little trust in business, fishermen or politicians. Instead, they tend to place their trust in other types of organizations like non-profit (MSC) and NGOs (WWF and Greenpeace).[157] In this regard, the MSC is considered to give the public confidence because it makes certification processes much more explicit and transparent.[158]

Complementarity to public regulation In Australia, the Department of Fisheries, established under the Public Sector Management Act 1994, is the department that assists the Minister of Fisheries in the administration of the following fisheries related acts and regulations: Fish Resources Management Act 1994 (FRMA), Fish Resources Management Regulations 1995 (FRMR), Pearling Act 1990, Fisheries Adjustment Schemes Act 1987, Fishing and Related Industries Compensation (Marine Reserves) Act 1997 and Fishing Industry Promotion Training and Management Levy Act 1994.

More specifically, the FRMA's objective is 'to conserve, develop and share the fisheries' resources of the State for the benefit of present

---

[153] Interview with David Carter, Austral Fisheries (Amsterdam, The Netherlands, 28 May 2014).
[154] Trott (n 147).
[155] Brayford (n 146).
[156] ibid.
[157] Carter (n 153).
[158] Brayford (n 146).

and future generations'.[159] Furthermore, the Department of Fisheries has implemented Ecosystem Based Fisheries Management (EBFM). This policy provides the operating basis for the implementation of ecosystem management and sustainable fisheries. It is important to point out that Western Australia fisheries legislation and policy has to conform to the Commonwealth Government fisheries and environmental laws. In this regard, the Department of Sustainability, Environment, Water, Populations and Communities is in charge of the Environment Protection and Biodiversity Conservation Act 1999 (EPBC), which states that the Australian Government, through the Commonwealth Minister, has the legislative responsibility to ensure that all fisheries, from which products are exported, undergo assessment to ensure the fishery is managed in an ecologically sustainable way.[160]

This Act, in particular, was modelled on the MSC standard[161] and thus the assessment is made against indicators similar to the principles and criteria established by the MSC.[162] In this context, and in contrast to the Alaskan case, all interviewees consider that the MSC complements public regulation, observing a reciprocal relationship between the MSC and the public regulation in Australia; they have evolved hand by hand complementing each other.[163] Likewise, another commentator reports that the Western Australia Government, in particular, perceived the MSC an important element of ensuring they are continuingly reviewing and improving their processes.[164]

Importance for international trade and market access All interviewees contend that market access is the main reason for certification. For instance, the Western Australia rock lobster is the most valuable fishery in the country.[165] It is worth AUS$ 200–400 million per year.[166] In 2010, the total contribution to the State from Western Australia's commercial

[159] Rhys Brown, 'Governance of the Western Rock Lobster Fishery and Marine Stewardship Council Principle 3 Effective Management' (Western Australia Department of Fisheries 2011) 9.

[160] Ibid.

[161] Marine Stewardship Council, 'Net Benefits the First Ten Years of MSC Certified Sustainable Fisheries' (2009) <http://www.msc.org/documents/email/Net-Benefits-report.pdf> accessed 9 June 2014.

[162] Haward (n 59).

[163] Trott (n 147).

[164] Brayford (n 146).

[165] Gale and Haward (n 6).

[166] Simon Nageon De Lestang, *Stock Assessment for the West Coast Rock Lobster Fishery* (Fisheries Dept of WA 2012).

fishing, pearling and aquaculture was estimated to be in the order of AUS$ 818 million.[167] Products from this fishery are sold to domestic markets and also to Japan, Taiwan, China, Hong Kong, the United States and Europe.[168] The Australian northern prawn frozen products are mainly exported to Japan and China.[169] The king prawns are sold in Australia, the United States, Singapore and the European Union[170] and the Toothfish is exported to China, Japan, the United States and Eastern Europe.[171]

After the Asian economic crisis in the late 1990s, Australian producers looked towards European markets. The MSC provided a market leverage given the importance food safety and quality have for these markets.[172] The European Union has tariffs for foreign products going to Europe and the MSC was a powerful tool in reducing by half the fee for Australian products.[173] While in the domestic market, the MSC is less visible comparatively to European markets,[174] this could change in the future. Indeed, Patrick Caleo, MSC country manager, states that the 'demand for third-party verified sustainably caught seafood is growing and leading retailers and brands are responding. We have around 250 MSC labelled products on supermarket shelves in Australia.'[175]

In sum, in Australia the MSC was seen more positively in relation to Alaska. Australia, and specifically the Western Australia Government, has supported the MSC and has provided public funds for fisheries certification. This can be explained in particular by the perceived complementarity of the standard to public regulation, the relative skepticism of the public towards public and industry-led standards as well as the

---

167 Western Australia Department of Fisheries (n 145).

168 Marine Stewardship Council, 'Australian Western Rock Lobster Marine Stewardship Council' (2016), accessed 28 November 2016 at https://fisheries.msc.org/en/fisheries/.

169 Marine Stewardship Council, 'Australia Northern Prawn' (2015), accessed 28 November 2016 at https://fisheries.msc.org/en/fisheries/

170 Marine Stewardship Council, 'Spencer Gulf King Prawn' (2016), accessed 28 November 2016 at https://fisheries.msc.org/en/fisheries/

171 Marine Stewardship Council, 'Heard Island and McDonald Islands (HIMI) Toothfish' (2015), accessed 28 November 2016 at https://fisheries.msc.org/en/fisheries/.

172 Haward (n 59).

173 Marine Stewardship Council, 'Net Benefits' (n 73).

174 Haward (n 59).

175 Marine Stewardship Council, 'World's First Mahi Mahi And Australia's First Tuna to Seek the MSC Tick this Sustainable Seafood Day' (2014), accessed 28 November 2016 at https://www.msc.org/newsroom/news/worlds-first-mahi-mahi-and-australias-first-tuna-to-seek-the-msc-tick-this-sustainable-seafood-day.

increasing importance of the European market as an export destination for Australian fisheries products.

3.3 Ecuador

In Ecuador, the dolphinfish, or 'mahi-mahi', is the most important artisanal fishery. It generates several sources of income from exports and employment. It has been seeking MSC certification since April 2008.[176] In 2009, after the MSC pre-assessment was completed, a Fishery Improvement Project (FIP)[177] was developed with the WWF and key stakeholders. In 2010 a FIP National Plan of Action (NPOA) was created describing the necessary activities, responsible parties and timeframes required in order to meet the MSC standard. The NPOA was implemented by the Ecuadorian government in 2011 and it was reviewed and updated in 2013.[178] Several projects are being executed within the framework of the mahi-mahi NPOA. The objective is to increase the knowledge of the stock and to improve the management of the fishery in order to become MSC certified in the future.[179]

State responses in Ecuador

Development of public funds The MSC certification project is integrated into public policy and public funds in Ecuador.[180] An example of this is the mahi-mahi fishery where the government has invested between US$ 350,000 to US$ 400,000 per year for the execution of the NPOA (according to WWF estimates). This may seem like a small amount, but for a

---

[176] Mónica Pérez-Ramírez and Salvador Lluch-Cota, 'Fisheries Certification In Latin America: Recent Issues And Perspectives' (2010) 35 *Interciencia* 855.

[177] Fishery improvement projects are based on an alliance of seafood producers, buyers and suppliers. They work together with the goal of improving a fishery by pressing for better management and policies, while voluntarily changing purchasing and fishing practices to reduce problems e.g. bycatch and illegal fishing. (Sustainable Fisheries Partnership 'Fishery Improvements', accessed 28 November 2016 at https://www.sustainablefish.org/fisheries-improvement.

[178] World Wildlife Fund, 'FIP Handbook. Guidelines for Developing Fishery Improvement Projects' (WWF-US Fisheries Program 2013), accessed 28 November 2016 at http://awsassets.panda.org/downloads/wwf_fip_final_web_version.pdf.

[179] Marine Stewardship Council, 'Net Benefits the First Ten Years of MSC Certified Sustainable Fisheries.' (2009) <http://www.msc.org/documents/email/Net-Benefits-report.pdf> accessed 9 June 2014.

[180] Interview with Xavier Chalen, Ministry of Agriculture, Livestock, Aquaculture and Fisheries (Amsterdam, The Netherlands, 22 May 2014).

small country like Ecuador, with more pressing priorities like poverty, is quite significant. Furthermore, after the implementation of the FIP the number of inspectors in charge of monitoring the Ecuadorian coast (~1,000 km) increased from 5 to 100, amassing to the public budget dedicated to fisheries sustainability.[181]

Co-option within public regulation In Ecuador, the implementation of the FIP Action Plan aims to improve the environmental performance and management of the mahi-mahi fishery in order to obtain MSC certification in the future.[182] The stakeholders involved in the implementation of the FIP are the following: Ecuador's Vice Ministry of Aquaculture and Fisheries (VMAP), Secretary of Fishery Resources (SRP), Whitefish Exporters Association (ASOEXPEBLA), National Federation of Fisheries Cooperatives of Ecuador (FENACOPEC) and Eastern Pacific Fisheries School (EPESPO).[183] According to one of the interviewees, Ecuador has one of those governments that are actively working on certification projects and helping their fisheries receive certification as there is collaboration between government, fisheries and NGOs for meeting the MSC standard. In fact, the government has adopted the National Plan of Action (NPOA), which helps fisheries to meet the MSC criteria.[184]

More specifically, the NPOA establishes the activities the government will implement for the promotion of more sustainable fishing practices.[185] It is implemented through ministerial agreements.[186] The Ministerial Agreement 407 of 2011, in particular, limits the fishing effort for the Ecuadorian longline fleet within the FIP for mahi-mahi. The Ministerial Agreement 070 (2011) bans fishing activities between July and October (each year) to protect mahi-mahi stocks. The Ministerial Agreement 024 (2011) mandates the creation of an observer program to gather data from at least 10 per cent of the trips made by longline fishing vessels of more than 20 meters in length. This last agreement was adopted in order to comply with the IATTC's resolution C-11-08 (2013) requiring the member states to observe the coverage on at least 5 per cent of the fishing effort of longline vessels.[187]

---

[181] Interview with Pablo Guerrero, WWF Latin America and Caribbean (Amsterdam, The Netherlands, 7 May 2014).

[182] World Wildlife Fund (n 178).

[183] Ibid.

[184] Cross (n 83).

[185] World Wildlife Fund (n 178).

[186] Guerrero (n 181).

[187] World Wildlife Fund, 'WWF Position Statement for the 85th Meeting of the Inter-American Tropical Tuna Commission (IATTC)', accessed 28 November

Thus, participation in the MSC program involves the creation or modification of public policy to regulate important aspects of the fishery. The objective is to follow a similar path to Australia, where the government adopted the MSC standards as its measuring bar. This does not imply that all the fisheries in Ecuador will become MSC certified but that the MSC standard can be used as a guideline to improve the management of fisheries in the country.[188]

Development of domestic standards as counter reaction The experts mention that the MSC did not prompt the development of competing domestic standards. In contrast, the Ecuadorian government is committed to improve the management of fisheries like mahi-mahi in order to obtain the MSC certification.[189]

Explaining responses in Ecuador

Perceived credibility of the standard All interviewees agree on credibility being one of the main reasons why the Ecuadorian government supports the MSC. In this regard, interviewees commend MSC's rigorousness, in particular, as a central element of its credibility.[190]

Complementarity to public regulation The main problem regarding the conservation and sustainability of fisheries in Ecuador is that the regulatory framework has been outdated and weak according to our interviews.[191] More recently, however, the government led by Rafael Correa has implemented macro legal frameworks as part of the new constitution which address many fishing, environmental and sustainability issues, mainly in terms of food safety, security and sovereignty.[192] In this regard, it establishes the right of the people to live in a healthy and ecologically balanced environment, which ensures sustainability and good living. It is in the public's interest to ensure environmental preservation, conservation of ecosystems, biodiversity and integrity of the genetic patrimony of the country, prevention of environmental damage and recovery of degraded

---

2016 at http://www.iattc.org/Meetings/Meetings2013/June/pdfs/IATTC-WWF-Position-Statement.pdf.

[188] Guerrero (n 181).

[189] Chalen (n 180); Guerrero (n 181).

[190] Interview with Martin Hall, Inter-American Tropical Tuna Commission (Amsterdam, The Netherlands, 7 May 2014).

[191] Hall (n 190); Chalen (n 180).

[192] Chalen (n 180).

natural areas.[193] Additionally, the State 'guarantees' a sustainable model of development, environmentally balanced and respectful of cultural diversity, preserving biodiversity and the natural regeneration capacity of ecosystems, which ensures satisfaction of the needs of present and future generations.[194]

The government also follows the second cycle of implementation of the National Plan for Good Living (2013–2017) which promotes 'production and productivity sustainably, encouraging inclusion and redistributing production factors and resources in the agricultural, aquaculture and fishing sectors'.[195] Furthermore, Ecuador belongs to the Inter-American Tropical Tuna Commission (IATTC), so the regulations that are implemented by this commission are mandatory for the fleets operating in the country.[196] The government has translated goals on food safety, security and sovereignty into regulation that should be followed by the industry in order to preserve the natural resources for future generations. Accordingly, one of the interviewees stated that the government is implementing this type of measures to increase competitiveness in the sector, to ensure markets, secure livelihoods and food security and to maintain and create jobs.[197]

However, the government has had a reactive instead of a preventive approach with regard to fisheries policies, and governmental regulations have had a patchy character towards emerging problems. This 'regulation by reaction' is carried out through Ministerial Agreements as demonstrated above. Many of these are passed as a way to comply with MSC requirements for certification and not as a spontaneous initiative from the government's side.

Ecuador also suffers from the inability to meet the current legal framework; activities related to monitoring and surveillance are weak and need to be strengthened.[198] This is where the MSC's contribution lies in particular. Moreover, and in contrast to perceptions in Alaska, market-based mechanisms, like the MSC, are considered to reinforce public authority and increase state willingness to use the tools that are now available for management.[199]

---

[193] Constitution of Ecuador, article 14.

[194] Constitution of Ecuador, article 395.1°.

[195] National Secretariat of Planning and Development, National Plan for Good Living (2013–2017) 81.

[196] World Wildlife Fund, 'WWF Position Statement' (n 187).

[197] Guerrero (n 181).

[198] Chalen (n 180); Hall (n 190).

[199] Chalen (n 180).

Importance for international trade and market access The experts consider market access the major reason for certification. Securing international markets is a keystone in Ecuadorian policy because it means maintaining or increasing employment, safeguarding livelihoods and guaranteeing food security.[200]

As consumers in the North are likely to care more about the sustainability of fisheries, Ecuadorian fisheries dedicated to export feel more pressure from the receiving markets regarding sustainability issues than those dedicated to the domestic market.[201] In 2010 half of the catch of mahi-mahi in Ecuador (~12,000 tons) and Peru (~40,000 tons) was exported to the United States.[202] The application of the MSC criteria is expected to allow a better positioning of Ecuador's fisheries products in the world markets in the short or medium term; and expand their market access in the long term.[203]

Despite the great support the MSC has had in Ecuador, there has also been criticism against the standard. Specifically, it is considered elitist as the costs of certification could be an exorbitant amount for developing countries' fisheries. In the particular case of Latin America, there is also a lack of capacity because the MSC only has two representatives to monitor all the fisheries in the entire continent, one in Chile and one in Brazil. Nevertheless, in recent years the MSC has developed new tools for risk-based evaluations, of special importance for data deficient fisheries in developing countries. This is why FIPs are now being promoted heavily among fisheries with low technical management, limited data availability and scarce monitoring.[204]

In sum, the state is fully committed to achieving MSC certification for the mahi-mahi fishery in Ecuador. To do so, it has developed public regulation to enhance the positioning of the fishery against the MSC criteria and it has also provided public funds. There has been a continuous process of improvement of public regulation inspired by the MSC requirements which are considered credible and essential for greater access in global markets.

---

200 Guerrero (n 181); Chalen (n 180); Hall (n 190).
201 Hall (n 190).
202 Pérez-Ramírez and Lluch-Cota (n 176).
203 Guerrero (n 181).
204 Guerrero (n 181).

4. CONCLUSIONS

This chapter aimed to delineate and explain state responses to the Marine Stewardship Council fisheries certification program in Alaska, Australia and Ecuador. The analysis was performed in two parts. We first examined state responses on the basis of three indicators, namely development of public funds, support within public regulation and development of domestic standards as a counter reaction. In this context, we found strikingly different responses in the cases we examined: while in Alaska the state gradually withdrew its support to the MSC standard in favor of a domestic one, in Australia and Ecuador the state embraced the MSC standard both materially with the development of public funds to support certification and in a regulatory manner, by co-opting the MSC criteria within public regulation.

We then explained the variation in state responses on the basis of three hypotheses: (a) states support private transnational according to their perceived credibility; (b) states are more likely to support private transnational standards which complement public regulation; and (c) states support private transnational standards to maintain and/or expand international markets.

We found that in Ecuador and Australia the MSC is perceived as a credible standard. In Alaska, however, the MSC has been widely criticized by many stakeholders for inconsistent fisheries assessments and for not respecting its own principles and criteria.

Regarding the perceived complementarity to public regulation we found again differences among our cases. In Australia, there is a reciprocal relationship between the MSC and public regulation. In fact, the MSC is an element to ensure the continuous improvement of fisheries management in Western Australia. In Ecuador, the situation is different. In contrast to Australia and Alaska, the country did not have sufficient public regulation in place. The goal of achieving the MSC certification for mahi-mahi prompted the development of more stringent regulation inspired by the MSC. In Alaska, there is no agreement among experts as to whether it complements the already stringent public regulation, but MSC certification is considered unnecessary and redundant by the salmon industry.

We found that market access is the main reason for certification (or not) with the MSC. Both Australia and Ecuador strategically use the MSC standard to gain access in high value markets, such as the European one. Alaska, however, does not depend on exports as most of the salmon produced is consumed domestically. This in turn facilitated its decision to drop MSC certification in favor of a domestic program.

In sum, we find sufficient support for our theoretical propositions about state responses to private transnational governance on the basis of the three case studies presented here. While transnational private standards and certification schemes are flourishing they are not supported unequivocally. State support may tilt in favor of domestic alternatives when there is erosion of transnational standards' credibility, they are not considered superior or complementary to public regulation, and their necessity for market access is challenged.

12 Overcoming food safety challenges through regulatory cooperation: Evidence from the UEMOA

Kévine Kindji and Michael Faure

INTRODUCTION

Recent trends in food safety regulation at the international level highlight a fundamental shift from end-product sampling and inspection into preventative risk-based safety and quality systems.[1] Subsequently, addressing food safety risks in a more efficient manner implies an increased cooperation between public and private actors to take into account a broad range of interests, and when necessary reconcile conflicting interests.

This type of regulatory arrangements has been referred to as hybridism. Interactions between public and private sectors might take many forms or involve different state and/or non-state actors. Levi-Faur identifies four major forms of hybrid regulations where responsibility for regulatory design or regulatory enforcement is either shared by the regulator and the regulatees, or relies mainly upon one of them.[2] This chapter intends to draw on that scheme to highlight regulatory mechanisms used within the West-African Economic and Monetary Union (UEMOA) to improve food safety systems both at national and regional levels. This approach is important since most of the reforms that occur in the region are public initiatives which incidentally involve private operators. These private operators are mostly actors in Member States involved in export supply chains, ranging from primary producers to food processing plants, and including professional and consumer associations. In this context, this chapter attempts to ascertain whether the involvement of private stake-

[1] Lahsen Ababouch, G. Gandini and J. Ryder, 'Causes of Detentions and Rejections in International Fish Trade', *FAO Fisheries Technical Paper*. No. 473. Rome, FAO, 2005, 5.

[2] David Levi-Faur, 'Regulation and Regulatory Governance' in D. Levi-Faur (ed.) *Handbook on the Politics of Regulation* (Edward Elgar 2011) 3–21, 10–11.

holders in food safety regulation and enforcement within the UEMOA has contributed to improved food safety governance, or can compensate the insufficiency of public capacities in Member States.

By contrast to the progressive evolution in many developed countries following a proactive pattern, food safety regulation within the UEMOA tends to follow a reactive approach stemming from the need to sustain market access. Food safety governance developed as a part of various strategies to achieve a common market, thereby strengthening the competitiveness of financial and economic activities among Member States to ensure higher goals of regional and international integration and improved levels of development. As a result, a greater involvement in food safety governance amounts to adopting not only a regulatory framework that is conducive to trade and market access, but also to building the institutional capacity that enables an effective implementation and enforcement of food safety requirements. This process resulted in a multi-level governance involving a mix between the regional body (UEMOA Commission) and diverse institutions in Member States, as well as the involvement of export-oriented food supply chains stakeholders that provided support to public actions to the extent necessary to facilitate the implementation of the food safety requirements. These private actors mainly sought ways to increase awareness as regards food safety issues, and used public channels to get adequate training and infrastructure to ensure compliance with more stringent requirements.

After providing some background information on the UEMOA and the former state of food safety within the region (1), this chapter further explains the steps towards regulatory cooperation within the UEMOA (2). The third section gives an insight on the results achieved (3) while the fourth section addresses food safety governance challenges within the UEMOA (4). The last section (5) provides some concluding remarks.

1. BACKGROUND

1.1 Origins of the UEMOA

The UEMOA is considered a model of economic integration in West Africa. Created in 1994 by the Treaty signed in Dakar on 10 January 1994, in the beginning the UEMOA brought together the seven countries of West Africa which shared the use of the CFA franc, namely Benin, Burkina Faso, Ivory Coast, Mali, Niger, Senegal and Togo. The treaty entered into force on 1 August 1994 after ratification by the Member States. The circle was extended three years later, on 2 May 1997, to

Guinea Bissau after its accession to the monetary system of the CFA franc.

The similarities in UEMOA Member States' legal and administrative frameworks were rather conducive to harmonization within the region. The laws of UEMOA countries are derived from the legacy of French or Portuguese colonization. Therefore, the legal system falls in general within the Romano-Germanic system, while food safety programmes are mainly integrated in 'French public law', with some elements of private company law and the progressive inclusion of principles derived from international law.[3] This system places the law and central State administrations at the base of food law, which is primarily defined as a special police activity of State services, encompassing a set of administrative control powers, regulation, prohibition and sanctions whose legitimacy is the protection of public health and economic order.[4] A major feature is that the powers related to inspection or control are scattered and dissolved through many ministries or ministerial departments, raising important accountability issues. This results in overlap and can make the legal structure confusing for the enforcement agents, producers and distributors, resulting in a duplication of efforts and gaps in enforcement.[5]

1.2 Food Safety in the UEMOA

The situation of food safety and conformity assessment was impaired by several shortcomings, which could suggest that a high level of safety protection in the region would be hardly attainable. One could, inter alia, refer to the virtual inexistence of national quality infrastructure in most countries, the lack of national or regional accreditation bodies or the absence of well-defined product or process standards. In this context, existing laws are also very poorly implemented and enforced,[6] and do

---

[3] François Féral and Hélène Coulibaly, Programme Spécial Régional pour la Sécurité Alimentaire des Etats Membres de L'Union Economique et Monétaire Ouest Africaine. Rapport de Synthèse des Rapports des Experts Internationaux concernant le Cadre Juridique et Institutionnel de la Sécurité Sanitaire des Aliments et des Contrôles, les Moyens et l'Organisation Pratique de la Surveillance et des Contrôles, les Moyens d'Analyse en Laboratoire et la Décentralisation et la Société Civile face à la Sécurité Sanitaire des Aliments. (2004) Projet UTF/UEM/001/UEM-Projet TCP/RAF/075, 19.

[4] Idem.

[5] Caroline Smith DeWaal and Nadine Robert, *Global and Local: Food Safety around the World* (Centre for Science in the Public Interest 2005) 27.

[6] Idem.

not sufficiently involve the judicial system to ensure the legitimacy of the actions undertaken.

The inapplicability of laws is explained mainly by the fact that the food safety regulations resulted from the colonial era, or laws were adopted through a process of transplantation that did not fit properly to the local social, economic, scientific, and legal realities of the countries. In fact, most UEMOA countries had no legislation covering standards and conformity assessment issues and, despite the provisions for the mutual recognition of conformity assessment procedures in the UEMOA Treaty, there were no arrangements to ensure the implementation.[7]

Beyond all these deficiencies, it is important to underline the issue of laboratories, because ultimately, and even in a system that emphasizes control at all stages through a farm-to-fork approach, laboratories remain essential tools for the establishment of efficient control systems. Within the UEMOA, there is a general lack of modern laboratory testing equipment. Most laboratories did not work according to the accreditation standard ISO/IEC 17025.[8] Moreover, analytical, testing and calibration laboratories of UEMOA countries have serious difficulties such as the failure to comply with the standards of laboratory installations and Good Laboratory Practices (GLP), the poor knowledge of the ISO 17025 reference standard by all laboratory personnel, the high cost of consumables and the weakness of inter-laboratories comparison.[9]

Within this context, UEMOA Member States were facing similar challenges because the same imperfections seem to materialize in their administrative systems, thus generating similar results with regard to the implementation of laws. Likewise, there was an increasing need to ensure more visibility and meaningful participation in international fora. Combining their strength to overcome their weaknesses seemed the best available option to address the food safety issues in individual countries.

---

7 Steffen Kaeser and Bernard Bau, 'The UEMOA Quality Programme. A Novel Regional Approach at UEMOA for the Implementation of Compliance related Business Environment Reform: Lessons for Future Donor Interventions', Paper delivered at Creating Better Business Environments for Enterprise Development – African and Global Lessons for More Effective Donor Practices, Africa Regional Consultative Conference (UNIDO 2007) 4.

8 Idem.

9 Justin Bayili, 'Programme pour la Mise en Place d'un Système d'Accréditation, de Normalisation et de Promotion de la Qualité au sein de l'UEMOA' (EU/RAF/01/001), Coordination Technique du programme, Synthèse Générale des rapports techniques Sur l'état des lieux détaillé de la situation des pays de l'UEMOA en matière d'accréditation et de certification (ONUDI/UEMOA/UE 2003) 6.

While there was a general failure to meet international standards, countries like Benin, Ivory Coast, Togo, and Senegal were facing compliance issues with regard to their exports to the European Union and were confronted with the urgent need to upgrade their laws and institutions to avoid an EU ban. In fact, this situation was the catalyst for major reforms in these countries and also contributed to shape many reforms at the UEMOA level.

The UEMOA endeavoured to identify priority sectors in Member States so as to provide the assistance that would be more relevant for a given country. While countries like Benin or Togo benefitted from the support of the UEMOA to enhance their food safety systems with regard to fish and fish products, other countries received assistance to improve non-food sectors such as cotton.

2. REGULATORY COOPERATION WITHIN THE UEMOA

As described by Levi-Faur, as far as 'multi-level regulation' is concerned, regulatory authority is allocated to different levels of territorial tiers. This authority can be allocated either:

> on a functional basis (whereby regulatory authority is allocated to different tiers according to their capacity to deal with the problem) or on a hierarchical basis (where supreme authority is defined in one of the regulatory tiers), or simply be a product of incremental, path-trajectory processes (where the regime is the result of the amalgamation of patches, each designed to solve a particular aspect as it occurred on the regulatory agenda).[10]

Within the UEMOA, the allocation of regulatory authority did not follow a clear-cut pattern. For food safety issues, regulatory cooperation occurred as the result of donors' involvement that led the UEMOA Commission to taking regulatory steps to ensure harmonization of Members' food safety frameworks for improved compliance with newer trends in international food safety regulation.

Hybrid food governance in the UEMOA targets originally the lawmaking process to ensure harmonization so as to facilitate intra-regional trade. But, in the face of the compliance issues faced by several Member States, this cooperation was rather heavily focused on ensuring coordination between Members to promote a better implementation and enforcement with more

---

[10] Levi-Faur (n 2) 10–11.

stringent requirements. Most national food safety laws were indeed the result of a transplantation aiming at complying with EU food safety law.

While the food safety policy covers the food sector as a whole, the implementation of the law is more focused on the food sectors that are facing or are likely to face compliance issues. This refers for example to food sectors oriented towards the export of sensitive products, such as fish, to the European Union. In these sectors, efforts at implementation are more noticeable. It thus appears that the allocation of regulatory authority to the UEMOA Commission is rather a product of incremental processes aiming at settling pressing compliance needs.

It is interesting to note that the insufficiency of resources contributed significantly to the strengthening of the cooperation between public authorities and private companies and stakeholders involved in export-oriented supply chains. This cooperation is mainly through support to companies or industries, and other stakeholders involved in the food supply chain to help them comply with safety and quality requirements. Public authorities mainly provide training to relevant private stakeholders and organize awareness raising campaigns. In a few cases, governmental authorities also provided financial support in export-oriented sectors to help food processing companies comply with more stringent requirements. This was the case, for example, in the shrimp export sector in Benin. Likewise, public authorities subsidize consumers' associations in Burkina Faso to contribute to overall awareness raising as regards food safety issues.

In the same way, private laboratories are relied upon to address the shortcomings of public laboratories. In Benin, for example, feasibility studies revealed that some public laboratories were not sufficiently equipped to carry out all the required analyses at their respective levels. Accordingly, it was decided not only to bring together various public laboratories in a central laboratory, but also to involve the private laboratory IRGIB[11] to assist in performing compulsory laboratory analysis. While IRGIB was not accredited, it was at least part of international networks of laboratory inter-comparison.[12]

In the same way, one might also refer to the greater involvement of non-governmental actors such as inter-professional associations in the

---

[11] IRGIB is a private institute for training and applied research that supports agribusiness professionals and provides, through its laboratory, microbiological analysis of locally manufactured or imported food (meat products, vegetables, fish), as well as analyses on pesticides and other agricultural inputs and hydrocarbons.

[12] Sylvie Mialet, 'Appui aux Systèmes d'Information sur les Mesures Sanitaires et Phytosanitaires au Bénin', Projet STDF 127, Rapport de mission, Mission du 2 au 13 août 2010, 25.

implementation process. These stakeholders try to involve primary producers by providing them with training to ensure a better compliance with more stringent safety requirements in export-oriented sectors. These associations also attempt to reach closer public-private cooperation to not only influence the decision-making process, but also to get the support of public authorities for a better compliance of primary producers, middlemen as well as food processing plants with food law requirements.

2.1 Building a Regulatory Food Safety Framework within the UEMOA

The UEMOA adopted an ambitious set of objectives in the field of standardization, certification and quality promotion for its members. Due to the overall insufficiency of resources, the completion of the regional programmes to achieve these objectives was only possible thanks to the funding of external actors, such as the European Union and the Food and Agriculture Organization (FAO). Two major programmes can be acknowledged in their involvement in regulatory and institutional reforms within the UEMOA, namely the Regional Special Program for Food Security (PSRSA), and the UEMOA Quality Program.

On the one hand, the design of the current UEMOA food safety regulation was achieved through the PSRSA. The PSRSA is a cooperation agreement between the FAO and the UEMOA that incorporates a twofold objective. First, it aims at the establishment of a legislative and regulatory framework as well as the institutions for the implementation in the animal health, phytosanitary and food safety sectors. Second, the programme focuses on the strengthening of national food security special programmes.

The implementation of the PSRSA was carried out through extensive surveys of the legislative and institutional framework of Member States, their monitoring, control and analytical capacities. In this process, private stakeholders were also given the opportunity to share their experiences so as to provide inputs for the design of better fitting legislations. These private actors are mostly consumer associations, professional associations, Non-Governmental Organizations (NGOs), trade unions, and private enterprises. Through these surveys, many private companies across the UEMOA were able to express their needs or expectations in the fields of standardization and regulation at both national and international levels. In Benin, for example, shrimp processing plants also had the opportunity to voice their concerns with regard to the Competent Authority of Benin[13] as the certification body for exported fishery products.

---

13 The Competent Authority enforces, monitors and verifies the compliance

Professional and consumers associations could furthermore pinpoint high-risk products and the practices they consider unacceptable or inappropriate, as well as the areas that require greater attention from public authorities for improved food safety systems and enhanced consumer awareness on food safety issues. Moreover, these associations asked for support to better carry out their tasks in promoting consumer participation in activities aiming at improving the safety and quality of goods and services. In Burkina Faso for example, while there are two main consumer associations, only one enjoys a relative recognition from the general public and benefits from state subsidies. While the impact of these consumer associations on the safety of exported food products is not yet important, public authorities expect an increased awareness about food safety issues that could lead to a higher demand for better standards. In this way, there would be a synergy effect that would contribute to an overall improved compliance with food safety requirements.

Generally speaking, private stakeholders called for their greater involvement in the standards development process, a better coordination with the competent authorities and their involvement in outreach and education programs. Likewise, they highlighted a regulatory gap as regards consumer protection, and the necessity for a clearer division of tasks between public authorities and actors involved in export supply chains.

The UEMOA food safety framework is intended to provide a basic framework for all UEMOA countries as regards their national food safety rules so as to ultimately facilitate the harmonization of food legislations at the Community level. The most important legislation is Regulation 07/2007 on the Safety of Plants, Animals and Food in the UEMOA, which is often referred to in Member States' laws. The protection of consumers' health, the prevention of the spread of diseases and the enforcement of food trade procedures are all acknowledged as a 'fundamental necessity' in the preamble to Regulation 07/2007.

While national legislations of UEMOA Member States mainly strive to comply with the food laws of their trading partners, it is noticeable that the UEMOA regulatory framework rather puts more emphasis on the compliance of its texts with WTO international agreements, specifically the Agreement on the Application of Sanitary and Phytosanitary Measures (SPS Agreement). Drawing on the principles in international food safety

---

of food operators with the requirements of the food law, through surveillance and controls systems at all stages of production, processing and distribution of food. The EU requires all third countries exporting to the EU to designate a Competent Authority which must certify food products before they are exported to the EU.

regulation, the food law of the UEMOA is based on principles such as the free movement of goods, equivalence or mutual recognition. The UEMOA encourages its Members to base their food law on risk analysis as an objective and justifiable method for evaluating and managing health risks, and where necessary to apply the precautionary principle. The regulatory process entails a proper communication on food risks throughout the decision-making process.[14]

On the other hand, the execution of the Quality Program is the most important agenda item of the Common Industrial Policy. The UEMOA Quality Program was initiated in 2002 for the establishment of a system of accreditation, standardization and quality promotion in order to increase the volume of regional and international trade. The first component of the programme was executed by the United Nations Industrial Development Organization (UNIDO)[15] with EU funding amounting to 12.5 million euro for a period of three years. The implementation of the Quality Program resulted in the adoption in 2005 of Regulation 01/2005, establishing a scheme for the harmonization of accreditation, certification, standardization, and metrology activities within the UEMOA. Through this scheme, regional structures could be created to coordinate the activities of national standardization bodies in Member States. The second phase of the Quality Program was launched in 2008 and also included the countries of West Africa, which are not members of the UEMOA. The European Union funded this phase with 14 million euro. The UEMOA component aimed to consolidate the achievements of Phase 1 by helping the UEMOA to implement its Community safety legislation and to use the tools previously developed to remove safety-related barriers encountered in the marketing of priority products on Community and export markets.[16]

---

[14] Regulation (UEMOA) 07/2007 on Safety of Plants, Animals and Foods in the UEMOA [2007], article 9.

[15] UNIDO is the specialized agency of the United Nations that promotes industrial development for poverty reduction, inclusive globalization and environmental sustainability in developing countries and economies in transition (see www.unido.org).

[16] UEMOA, Lancement de la Composante UEMOA du Programme Qualité Afrique de l'Ouest, *La Semaine de l'UEMOA/Bulletin Hebdomadaire de l'UEMOA No 200* (2008) 1.

2.2 Governance through Institutions

2.2.1 Designing a regional institutional framework

To make the implementation of the regional legislation effective, the UEMOA also designed an institutional framework that could match the ambitions of the laws. In this regard, the programme of restructuring and upgrading the industries of UEMOA Member States was adopted according to the modalities of the annex to Decision 12/2006.[17] This programme supports the capacity building process within the UEMOA.

This initiative is rooted in the desire to turn the overall insufficient capacities in Member States into an asset that would lead to strengthened collaboration between private and public actors for a more efficient food safety governance. As such, the UEMOA aims at giving support to industrial production within the region, promoting investment and employment so as to foster economic competitiveness both at regional and international levels. One component of this programme is to support selected private companies in Member States.

In any event, for the effective implementation of the safety principles established, Regulation 007/2007 has set an important institutional framework that brings together various regional and national structures. The UEMOA legislation created many Committees that should coordinate the institutions involved in food safety management in Member States.

2.2.2 Regional Committee of Safety of Plants, Animals and Food

The Regional Committee of Safety of Plants, Animals and Food must act as a technical and advisory structure with regard to all health-related matters in the sense of articles 5 to 8 of Regulation 01/2005. This Committee is responsible for assisting the UEMOA Commission in the organization of health cooperation between Member States and contributing to the coherence of a safety policy by providing the appropriate technical advice. The Committee plays a supporting role for both the Commission and Member States in relation to international trade negotiations as regards the SPS Agreement.[18]

To carry out its activities properly, the Regional Committee of Safety of Plants, Animals and Food is subdivided into three subcommittees, each of which is specialized in one aspect of safety namely food, plants or animals.

---

[17] Decision (UEMOA) 12/2006 adopting the program of restructuring and upgrading of the industry of WAEMU Member States [2006], article 1.

[18] Regulation (UEMOA) 07/2007 on Safety of Plants, Animals and Foods in the UEMOA [2007], articles 13–14.

Table 12.1 Overview of networks created in support of the Regional Committee of Safety of Plants, Animals and Food (Article 18 Regulation 07/2007)

Network of experts	The network of experts supports regional safety structures of safety, on their request, by providing scientific advice, particularly during health crises.
Network of laboratories	The regional network of analytical laboratories brings together public and private laboratories in Members that may constitute reference institutions for analyses.
Alert network	The regional alert system is responsible for monitoring and immediate transmission of information on health risks to relevant structures.
Network of national organizations	The regional network of national safety agencies reinforces health cooperation between Members and ensures the circulation of information in the areas of health policy of the Union.
Network of training institutions	The regional network of training institutions contributes to improving training within the UEMOA.

The Committee also relies upon the expertise and cooperation mechanisms based on networks and observatories. In principle, in each area there must be a set of networks including a network of experts, a network of laboratories, an alert network, a network of national organizations, and a network of training institutions.[19] Observatories are responsible for creating and managing databases necessary for health cooperation and establishing an inventory of international safety texts and agreements binding Member States.[20]

Table 12.1 provides an overview of the networks that were created in the execution of article 18 of Regulation 07/2007.

The institutional provisions of Regulation 07/2000 could be schematized as shown in Figure 12.1.

The functioning of these institutions is dependent on the ability of their counterparts in Member States to carry out their missions. For example, national standardizations bodies must be able to gather and monitor all the standards and regularly send them to the relevant Regional Committee.

19 Idem, article 18.
20 Idem, article 19.

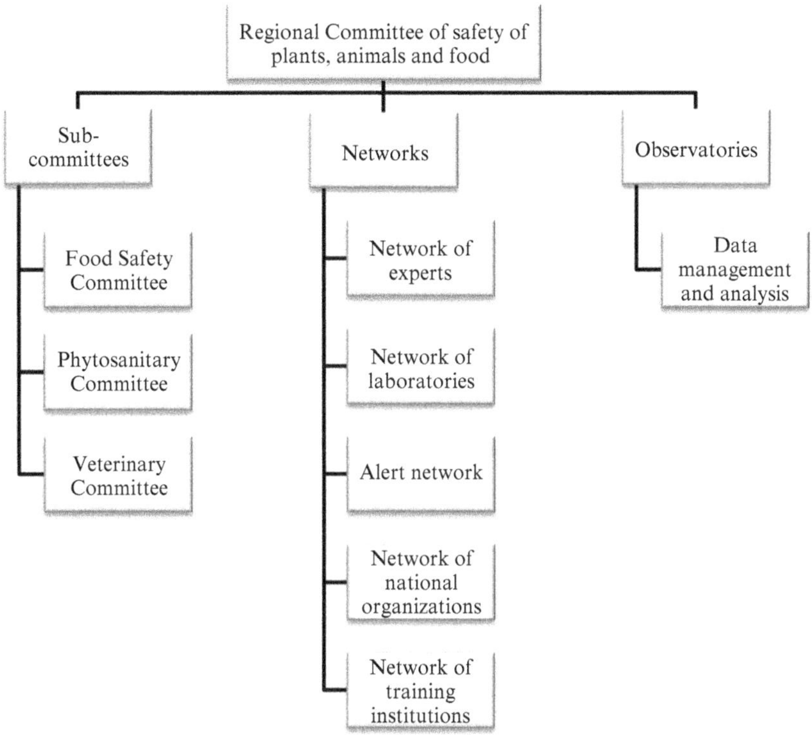

Figure 12.1 Institutional safety framework of the UEMOA

The implementation of the network of training institutions involves the collaboration with private training institutions to supplement public institutions.

It is worth mentioning that while there are many experts and researchers within the region, the latter are not involved in risk assessment, and international experts are often hired to conduct specific tasks on behalf of public authorities within the UEMOA. In this regard, the UEMOA intends through its network of experts to create a platform that would enable to make efficient use of the knowledge available to advise both the UEMOA and Member States in dealing with food safety policies and risks.

3. COOPERATION RESULTS

3.1 Improving Food Quality

If the results in respect of the harmonization of national legislations are somewhat mixed, the efforts at achieving high quality has greatly contributed to raise the capabilities of Member States to effectively implement a food safety policy likely to meet international standards. These achievements stemmed from the systemic and holistic approach of the Quality Program, which is based on three pillars, including the development of a quality policy, the promotion of quality and the completion of the quality infrastructure (standardization, certification, metrology and accreditation). The approach to harmonization is mainly based on the support and strengthening of institutions involved in food safety management throughout the region with the view to achieve their accreditation. Given the significant changes induced, this step had to be regarded as a process revolving around two poles. First, the wide diffusion to the whole industrial network of the 'UEMOA quality culture' was necessary to enable the effective dissemination of standards and certification. Second, the certification of companies had to be promoted to help ensure in the short term, to defend, conquer, and consolidate export positions by the most competitive ones. It should be emphasized that most of the actions to be undertaken are the responsibility of the Member States. The UEMOA Commission only provides a framework for sharing experiences, while creating a UEMOA quality Oscar, intended to serve as incentive. As for Member States, they should start the certification process through the 'quality audit' of companies.

With regard to the quality policy, the Quality Program enabled, inter alia, the strengthening of the technical capacity of UEMOA's regional organizations of standardization, certification, metrology and accreditation. At the national level, a national quality policy or legal framework was adopted in Burkina Faso, Mali, Niger and Togo. The promotion of the quality policy is the component that aimed at developing a closer cooperation between public authorities and private stakeholders such as exporting companies or grassroots actors. In the fishery sector for example, associations were created on the initiative of the actors in the export-oriented supply chain to create awareness about good hygiene practices to fishermen, fishmongers and wholesale merchants through guided training and assistance. Public control officers were often called upon to support these initiatives so as to raise sufficient awareness concerning safety and quality issues and facilitate compliance with relevant requirements. The promotion of quality enabled for example the development of tools such as the awarding of the National/UEMOA Quality Award to deserving companies, or the capacity development of staff of consumer associations. These tools contributed to enhance the willingness of private stakeholders for voluntary compliance with food safety and quality requirements.

Essentially, through this component, training was given to the staff of several companies with regard to quality and quality management systems for food products and to internal quality auditors. Likewise, some companies received a certification to ISO standards, while a few consultants were certified third-party auditors. In general, training sessions were organized to provide targeted companies, laboratories and national and regional organizations with qualified staff, experts and/or auditors trained to international standards such as relevant ISO standards (for example ISO 9001, 22000, 17025). In the same way, the UEMOA supported the upgrading process in Member States by providing equipment for tests and analyses.

As far as the quality infrastructure is concerned, the most notable achievement as regards standardization is the creation of a Regional Secretariat of Standardization, Certification and Quality Promotion called NORMCERQ, which enabled the adoption of regional standards, and contributed to the development and the revitalization of national standardization bodies (NSBs) while ensuring a better convergence at the regional level. Owing to these activities, the national standardization bodies of Côte d'Ivoire, Mali and Senegal have become full members of the International Organization for Standardization (ISO), while the standardization bodies in Benin, Burkina Faso, Niger and Togo have become ISO's corresponding members. The establishment of a regional system of standardization created a ripple effect in the UEMOA region to strengthen national capacities. For example, through the development of a regional framework, NSBs may be established in Niger and Guinea-Bissau, while existing NSBs in other countries could be strengthened.

3.2 Accreditation and Conformity Assessment

With regard to accreditation, the West African System of Accreditation (SOAC) was established as a regional accreditation system for the UEMOA. The Quality Program enabled the development of cooperation agreements between the SOAC and the French and Tunisian accreditation bodies, respectively COFRAC and TUNAC. Moreover, the West African System of Metrology (SOAMET)[21] was established along with a regulation on Metrology within the UEMOA. For the purpose of

[21] The NORMCERQ, the SOAC and the SOAMET are technical structures of quality established by article 6 of Regulation 03/2010 (Regulation (UEMOA)

international integration, the SOAMET is affiliated with the International Organization of Legal Metrology (OIML).

In the field of conformity assessment, the UEMOA contributed mainly to staff training and the upgrading of equipment in many laboratories in Member States to help them obtain international accreditation. The assistance provided to the national laboratories to achieve accreditation is important for the credibility of conformity assessment bodies in the UEMOA. This assistance provided the framework for the networking of laboratories that can facilitate the harmonization of test methods for food products so as to enable laboratory comparisons. It is worth mentioning that article 7 of Regulation 03/2010 also created a Regional Committee for Quality (CREQ) the mission of which is to assist the UEMOA Commission in the implementation of the Community policy as regards quality.

A summary of the regional bodies involved in technical quality control is provided in Table 12.2.

Table 12.2 Technical quality institutions (Articles 6–7 Regulation 03/2010)

West African System of Accreditation (SOAC)	The SOAC is responsible for accreditation activities within the UEMOA and ensures their compliance with requirements of international institutions. The board of SOAC must promote accreditation in the UEMOA and set directions and priorities for accreditation.
Regional Secretariat of Standardization, Certification and Quality Promotion (NORMCERQ)	The NORMCERQ must collect Member States' national standards, receive their annual standardization programmes and ensure their management. It must coordinate the transmission of standards-related information between Member States and the process of mutual recognition. Standards that are the subject of consensus are proposed for Community accreditation.
West African System of Metrology (SOAMET)	The SOAMET must contribute to the definition and implementation of the Community policy on metrology. It must ensure the development of metrology in the UEMOA and the establishment of an infrastructure that meets international standards, through the coordination of metrology's activities.
Regional Committee for Quality (CREQ)	The CREQ must assist the UEMOA Commission in the implementation of the Community policy in terms of quality.

03/2010 laying down the harmonization scheme of activities of accreditation, certification, standardization and metrology in the UEMOA [2010]).

4. FOOD SAFETY GOVERNANCE CHALLENGES WITHIN THE UEMOA

4.1 Insufficient Public-Private Cooperation

Despite intensive surveys carried out prior to the adoption of the food safety framework of the UEMOA, the fact remains that the current legislation places great emphasis on compliance with international standards, but still seems insufficiently considerate of the needs and capacities of the private sector, as well as the realities on domestic markets. Public authorities strove within their limits to provide assistance to some private companies to bridge the gap between the capacity required to effectively implement the law and their actual capacities.

Although public authorities made apparent efforts, both at national level and within the framework of the UEMOA, poor implementation and enforcement of food safety requirements still prevail. In this context, the efforts of interested private operators to help achieve a better public enforcement tend to attain mixed results. The private sector itself is still relatively dependent on the public sector to ensure sufficient compliance with food safety and quality requirements. Needs with regard to adequate training and awareness raising are not yet adequately met. This refers in some cases to the lack of legitimacy of professional associations, because public opinion does not see them as sufficiently representative. In other cases, the lack of resources is overly detrimental to ensure properly organized activities. Moreover, conflicting relationships may also arise between public and private stakeholders and impede sustained activities to attain compliance. In Benin for instance, public authorities released financial resources to help shrimp processing plants in building the necessary infrastructure to comply with the requirements deriving from the food law transplanted to comply with the EU food safety law. A second financial support failed to occur due to a conflict between public and private sectors as regards an unclear use of the previously allocated resources, leading to the loss of confidence of local banks in the shrimp processing industry and their refusal to provide further support, and eventually the collapse of the shrimp export sector.[22]

It is now acknowledged that cooperation between public and private

---

[22] See further on this case of shrimp export Kévine Kindji and Michael Faure, 'Shrimp Export from Benin versus Food Safety in Europe. Reconcilable Interests?' (2014) 5(2) *European Journal of Risk Regulation* 187, 200; Kévine Kindji Gaspard, *Market Access Issues in International Food Trade. Shrimp Exports from Benin to the EU* (Intersentia 2015) 385.

spheres in relation to standard setting does not necessary intend to reconcile conflicting interests. The involvement of private actors in food governance and the development of private standards contributed to enhanced compliance in many developed countries. In fact, 'private standards can be useful tools for implementing public policy'.[23] In this regard, private control mechanisms and private certification could be important to help compensate the gap where public implementation is insufficient or inadequate. This could be especially true within the context of many developing countries to help alleviate the shortcomings deriving from weak public capacity.

The question arises whether this public-private intertwinement could contribute to improved food safety governance within the UEMOA. While market forces can make compliance with private standards mandatory and contribute to enhanced compliance, the impact of private food safety standards in agro-food exports from developing countries is not clearly demarcated.[24] Within the UEMOA, the ability of reliance on private certification to help enhance the implementation of public food laws is rather difficult to ascertain.

First, the incentive to develop standards to regulate intra-regional trade does not exist because this trade is rather limited. Private stakeholders in export value chains get involved in food safety governance only to the extent necessary to safeguard their export interests. For example, Colen and Maertens underlined in their report on the horticultural sector in Senegal that 'the decision on GlobalGAP certification is most often taken by export firms, who are directly confronted with the demands by importers and see advantages in achieving compliance'.[25]

In fact, within the UEMOA, the emphasis on private certification tends to develop as a result of market requirements. These requirements stem mainly from the European Union's sectoral approach to address health concerns related to specific products. When formal EU prior approval

---

[23] Renata Clarke, 'Private Food Safety Standards: Their Role in Food Safety Regulation and their Impact', Paper prepared for presentation and discussion at the 33rd Session of the Codex Alimentarius Commission (FAO 2010) 5.

[24] Spencer Henson and John Humphrey, 'The Impact of Private Food Safety Standards on Food Chain and on Public Standard-Setting Processes' (2009), Paper prepared for FAO/WHO, accessed 29 November 2016 at http://www.fao.org/3/a-i1132e.pdf, 1.

[25] Liesbeth Colen and Miet Maertens, 'Private Standards and Employment Insecurity: GlobalGAP in the Senegalese Horticulture Sector' (2011), Paper prepared for presentation at the EAAE 2011 Congress Change and Uncertainty, Challenges for Agriculture, Food and Natural Resources.

is not needed to access the EU market, export-oriented sectors are more prone to go a step further to avoid the risk of exclusion by their European customers. In this regard, export-oriented horticultural industries have since the late 1990s been striving for compliance with the demands of their overseas clients.[26] However, experiences with national GAP schemes revealed that this was slow to materialize in African countries. It is however interesting to underline the presence of national GlobalGAP Technical Working Groups in two UEMOA countries, namely Senegal and Côte d'Ivoire.[27] This development is explained by the significance of horticulture exports from these countries to the European Union. In 2010, Côte d'Ivoire was one of the fourth major exporters of fruits and vegetables to the European Union, while somewhat significant industries were also available in other countries such as Senegal.[28]

In the same way, individual exporters to the European Union did manage to get GlobalGAP certifications to maintain their export interests. This refers mainly to producers in four UEMOA countries: Burkina Faso (1), Senegal (103), Mali (108) and Cote d'Ivoire (355).[29]

While these figures are rather promising, the exact impact of these activities on food safety regulation and implementation within the UEMOA is not clear. As a general trend, Jaffee et al. reported on schemes supported by institutions such as the Liaison Committee Europe-Africa-Caribbean-Pacific (COLEACP), UNCTAD and FAO to support industries and national task forces to develop a national quality control system.[30] While these initiatives were intended to provide platforms for consensus building between public and private actors, a rapid shift was observed in the approach of the programs, from an emphasis on national institutional capacity building to a focus on individual enterprise compliance.

Second, despite the efforts of many companies to obtain certifications, the majority of the private sector is itself still lacking the capacity to fully comply with public requirements. Many private companies even rely on public service providers to carry out testing on their products.

---

[26] Steven Jaffee, Spencer Henson and Luz Diaz Rios, 'Making the Grade: Smallholder Farmers, Emerging Standards, and Development Assistance Programs in Africa', Research Program Synthesis, Economic and Sector Work Report No. 62324-AFR (World Bank 2011) 52.

[27] GlobalGAP, *Growing a Stronger Brand*, GlobalGAP Annual report 2012 (2013) 25.

[28] Jaffee et al. (n 26) 65.

[29] GlobalGAP, *Growing a Stronger Brand*, (n 27) 39.

[30] Jaffee et al. (n 26).

Third, there is not enough coordination between private operators to establish a market organization strong enough to enable an improved private certification. Diverse professional organizations and NGOs have been trying to create a synergy between actors at various levels of the production chain. These various initiatives have had mixed results.

In fact, seeking private certification might entail substantial investments for individual companies as well as drastic changes in their production process. Colen and Maertens underlined that 'several companies started their own production and reduced the volume of produce source from smallholders significantly or even completely' as part of their strategy to obtain GlobalGAP certification.[31]

It is therefore questionable whether small-scale operators lacking resources to comply with public food safety requirements will voluntarily engage in seeking compliance with private standards. In countries like Kenya, strong market organization was conducive to the promotion of the KenyaGAP, developed by the private Fresh Produce Exporters Association of Kenya (FPEAK), which is fully benchmarked with the GlobalGAP.[32] At the same time, there is evidence that the participation of small farmers in the export vegetable business has declined as a result of European retailers' requirement for export production to meet the GlobalGAP standard.[33]

Within the UEMOA, most food export value chains target the EU market, and the economic burden to ensure compliance and obtain approval from the European Union is already important for sensitive products. For these products, striving for voluntary compliance with private standards is an additional effort that is not readily available for many small-scale stakeholders, especially considering that the approval of the European Union is generally sufficient to gain market access. At this stage, the weak market organization within the UEMOA, combined with the lack of incentive and resources, is not conducive to the emergence of private standards or monitoring and control schemes that could support adequately public implementation and enforcement of food safety requirements.[34] For products such

---

[31] Colen and Maertens (n 25) 5.

[32] Margret Will, 'GlobalGAP Smallholder Group Certification. Challenge and opportunity for smallholder inclusion into global value chains', in Bernd van der Meulen (ed.) *Private Food Law: Governing Food Chains through Contract Law, Self-regulation, Private Standards, Audits and Certification Schemes* (Wageningen Academic Publishers 2011) 203, 227, 206.

[33] Henson and Humphrey, (n 24) 30.

[34] See on the role played by private standards in promoting and upgrading food safety measures and infrastructure in developing countries, inter alia,

as fruits and vegetables, the risk of marginalization by single EU importers is ever present and leads to constant efforts to obtain private certification.

In the same way, serious problems of capacity arise in public laboratories in many developing countries. Private laboratories often take over, but they often lack required accreditation to test and certify compliance against a certain standard.[35] With regard to the obtainment of accreditation, strict (ISO) rules prevail and cannot be bypassed. First, to obtain accreditation, a laboratory must effectively demonstrate competence and have the equipment necessary to conduct the tests required by international standards. Second, the activities of the laboratory must be sufficient to maintain its competences.

4.2 Ineffective Reforms and Lacking Resources

The upgrading process was confronted with several challenges related in particular to the fragmentation of existing resources in several structures, the disorganization of public services, mandates overlaps and the overall insufficient resources. Moreover, most food exporting countries were involved in food safety regulation with the primary incentive of complying with importers' requirements rather than to satisfy a home-grown demand for better regulation of their food sector to ensure the safety of domestic consumers. In Benin and Togo for example, food safety reforms were initiated only because of compliance issues revealed in the fish products export sector by the European Union, and the subsequent threat of a fish exports ban. Likewise, one study has highlighted that the accreditation process in Senegal, like in all UEMOA countries, is carried out under pressure from the demands of donors, European reference regulation, instead of at the instigation of national coordination.[36] However, upgrading to satisfy importers' requirements might at a later stage result in positive spillovers on domestic markets. Furthermore, this approach could also be beneficial at firms' level, because seeking compliance with international standards can generate economies of scale and production efficiencies, reduce

---

Henson and Humphrey (n 24), and Spencer Henson and John Humphrey, 'Understanding the Complexities of Private Standards in Global Agri-food Chains as they Impact Developing Countries' (2009) 46(9) *Journal of Development Studies* 1628–46.

[35] World Trade Organization (WTO), World Trade Report 2012. 'Trade and Public Policies: A Closer Look at Non-tariff Measures in the 21st Century' (WTO 2012), 153.

[36] Bayili (n 9) 11.

transaction costs,[37] improve the quality of food, thereby enabling greater opportunities to trade with high-value markets.

The lack of underlying incentive on domestic markets also holds true for the upgrading of the food safety infrastructure as a whole. This observation is certainly at the heart of the insufficiently coordinated efforts observed in the adoption and implementation of Community food safety legislation. Many texts adopted were never followed by the appropriate decrees of implementation and some institutions established through regulations were never really set up due mainly to the lack of resources and inappropriate coordination between Member States.

4.3 Challenges at the Legislative Level

While the UEMOA promotes the sovereignty of Member States to decide their appropriate level of protection and the subsequent measures, their dependence on external markets tramples on the sovereignty of the Member States because it limits their regulatory autonomy. This is due to the reactive approach to food safety regulation to deal with proven compliance issues in an attempt to secure or regain market access. The trend is then to make a shift from a barely unregulated sector to a sector that must comply with quite stringent requirements. This strategy skips an evolutionary process that could give more policy space to UEMOA Members to develop the circumstances and the institutions necessary to comply with the food safety regulations, thereby increasing the issues of lack of resources and making them more difficult to overcome.

In the same logic, the private sector is suddenly confronted with enormous challenges to meet, within a short period of time, the needs with regard to training, capacity building and adequate expertise necessitated to comply with newly adopted and 'overly' stringent requirements. These discrepancies are major bottlenecks that hinder the ability of the private sector to take an active part in the implementation process to supplement the public sector.

Furthermore, as required by the SPS Agreement, the burden of proof in demonstrating the equivalence between importer and exporter's legislation rests on the exporting country.[38] Transplanting developed countries laws, especially the law of the European Union, is a valuable alternative

---

[37] World Trade Organization (WTO), WTO Agreement Series. 'Technical Barriers to Trade'. Revised in 2014 (WTO 2014), 22.

[38] World Trade Organization, Agreement on the Application of Sanitary and Phytosanitary Measures (SPS Agreement) (1995), opened for signature 15 April 1994, 1867 UNTS 493 (entered into force 1 January 1995), article 4.1.

for countries with weak capacities because it makes it easier for them to reach recognition of their law by their developed trading partners in case the need arises.

Looking for guidance in other countries' law or international law remains a legitimate choice as long as a proper adaptation of the foreign model to local circumstances is targeted. The adoption of the UEMOA food law followed extensive prior research in the different Member States, but it failed to take sufficient account of the pre-existing legal order, the technological gaps and the previous issues of poor implementation and enforcement. It is obvious that only an effective enforcement of the law could contribute to behavioural changes that increase compliance.[39]

One must also not lose sight that food safety governance equally requires both effectiveness and responsiveness. First, the effectiveness of a transplanted law relies heavily on its ability to be meaningful in the domestic context so as to provide an incentive to citizens to use it and to demand that institutions work to enforce and develop the law.[40]

Second, responsiveness entails the maintenance of institutional integrity while taking into account new problems, new forces in the environment, new demands and expectations.[41] The lack of demand for a high-quality food law on domestic markets in UEMOA countries could hinder responsiveness in the region because these countries do not have an underlying internal incentive to sustain an oversight leading to a continuing enactment of optimal laws and subsequent institutions.

It is worth noting that undertaking reforms reactively to overcome non-compliance issues in the food safety and quality system leaves little room for weighing different policy alternatives and making choices that are most suitable for the domestic circumstances. Huge discrepancies between the existing food safety system and newly targeted regulatory objectives might hinder the efforts of countries to implement and enforce new laws effectively.

The symmetrical development of two food safety systems, one system for the domestic market and the other for the export market, is still and will continue to be a major bottleneck for an effective synergy of

---

[39] Michael Faure, Morag Goodwin and Franziska Weber, 'Bucking the Kuznets Curve: Designing Effective Environmental Regulation in Developing Countries' (2010) 51 *Virginia Journal of International Law* 95–156, 100.

[40] Daniel Berkowitz, Katarina Pistor, Jean-Francois Richard, 'Economic Development, Legality, and the Transplant Effect' (2003) 47(1) *European Economic Review* 165–95, 167.

[41] Philip Selznick, *The Moral Commonwealth: Social Theory and the Promise of Community* (The Regents of the University of California 1992) 336.

food safety schemes on the domestic markets. For this reason, national and regional food safety frameworks are dependent upon the commitment of Member States to cooperate for its effective implementation. Member States must therefore be willing to fulfil the core functions that come with State sovereignty. It is the responsibility of Member States to develop analysis and consultation processes to achieve the improvement or restructuring necessary for the effectiveness and efficiency of their control systems.[42] If some countries do not take the necessary measures, it can have the result that they continue to lag behind despite the opportunity provided by the regional framework. In Togo, for example, despite the ongoing development at the UEMOA level and the assistance of the European Union, the food safety level could not be raised sufficiently to gain approval for the export of fishery products to the European Union, except for live lobsters. In this regard, the focus of private actors on the safeguarding of their economic interests could reveal very beneficial to compel public action for designing better strategies to ensure compliance with essential requirements.

It is worth underlining that the absence or underdevelopment of national frameworks for food safety does not automatically predict the failure of the regional framework. Developing institutions such as a regional accredited laboratory or a regional accreditation body could be very helpful in solving some of the problems encountered by Member States to create such infrastructure at the national level. Furthermore these types of initiatives can provide experiences and collaboration schemes upon which Member States can capitalize to develop these institutions at the national level, thereby progressively improving the supporting institutional environment, which will eventually lead to the emergence of actual food safety management systems.

5. CONCLUDING REMARKS

As it currently stands, it is quite difficult to refer to a conclusive hybridization of food governance within the UEMOA. Coordinated actions have existed for many years between the regional body and institutions in Member States, and have enabled the improvement of both the regulatory and institutional frameworks in individual countries. However, the mission assigned to the UEMOA Commission to promote food safety and

---

[42] Banque Mondiale, 'La Problématique Sanitaire et Phytosanitaire au Niger' (La Banque Mondiale, ESSD/Afrique 2006) 84.

quality so as to raise the levels of protection in Member States has had only mixed results.

The fact remains that this context cannot be disregarded if one wants to make realistic analyses on whether or not the private sector does – or can – influence the mechanisms of regulation and control within the UEMOA. Only this comprehensive approach is likely to explain the absence or underdevelopment of private certification schemes in many countries within the UEMOA. But, if the role of the private sector has been rather limited, there is increased awareness among private stakeholders with regard to the importance of instruments such as third-party certification, not only for compliance purposes, but also for enhanced competitiveness on international markets.

In this regard, regional cooperation does offer a platform for private operators in all eight UEMOA countries to share experiences so as to build step-by-step the necessary organization to significantly impact the decision-making process.

From a more general perspective, it appears clear that there is much value in regional cooperation to overcome food safety challenges, especially for UEMOA countries. Weak regulators can become stronger by networking with other weak actors.[43] Through collective actions, regional cooperation could be a valuable tool to improve participation in the activities of international standard-setting organizations.[44] Undeniably, regional cooperation offers avenues for solving certain issues arising solely from the lack of resources at an individual country level. Multi-level regulation should enable to take advantage of the right competences, whether at national or regional level, to best address regulatory challenges. Within the UEMOA, the allocation of regulatory authority did not specifically take into account the ability of the tiers involved in regulatory processes. This certainly is an additional challenge to improve food safety schemes within the region because it does not enable to efficiently build upon the available financial, human and material resources.

The results of regulatory cooperation are ultimately dependent upon the interests at stake for a particular country. When countries are already engaged in an upgrading process at the national level, such as Senegal and Ivory Coast, they are more likely to derive substantial benefits from regional cooperation. By contrast, in the case of countries such as Benin

---

43 Faure, Goodwin and Weber (n 39) 128.

44 Spencer Henson, Rupert Loader, Alan Swinbank, Mauri Bredahl and N. Lux, *Impact of Sanitary and Phytosanitary Measures on Developing Countries* (University of Reading 2000) 73.

and Togo, the impact of the regional cooperation on the food safety level is slower. This suggests that the extent to which countries reap benefits from this regional cooperation is also dependent upon the true motivation that underlies their food safety regulatory steps. If regional cooperation aims at providing support to existing efforts at the national level, the gains are more likely to be meaningful. Conversely, if regional cooperation is perceived as an initiative to solve national food safety issues, it fails to achieve the expected results. It appears that regional cooperation is only beneficial when the conditions are met at the national level to foster an actual development of food safety initiatives.

Moreover, while taking some regulatory and institutional steps to ensure compliance with importers' food safety requirements, whether the focus is on market share or on food safety, would certainly influence the choice of compliance strategies. Only the appropriate choices are likely to lead to efficient food safety governance. Initiatives by private stakeholders to raise awareness about food safety issues, and help public authorities in monitoring and implementing food safety and quality requirements greatly contributed to the capacity building process. In this regard, the obtainment of GlobalGAP certificates by several producers and the progressive development of GlobalGAP National Technical Working Groups could also have a ripple effect in the region.

However, integrating domestic markets in the strategies of compliance developed by public authorities will better reflect the socio-economic and legal realities, and will lead to a greater synergy for the adoption of more realistic standards which would then be easier to apply. It is therefore essential that UEMOA countries see food safety as a public health policy rather than solely a trade expansion tool. In this regard, UEMOA Member States must seek smarter ways of regulation to better accommodate the socio-economic development of their private sectors and domestic markets.

Index